Lecture Notes
in Business Information Processi

T0238621

José Cordeiro
Karl-Heinz Krempels (Eds.)

Web Information Systems and Technologies

8th International Conference, WEBIST 2012
Porto, Portugal, April 18-21, 2012
Revised Selected Papers

 Springer

Volume Editors

José Cordeiro
Institute for Systems and Technologies
of Information, Control and Communication (INSTICC)
and
Instituto Politécnico de Setúbal (IPS)
Setúbal, Portugal
E-mail: jose.cordeiro@estsetubal.ips.pt

Karl-Heinz Krempels
RWTH Aachen University
Aachen, Germany
E-mail: krempels@dbis.rwth-aachen.de

ISSN 1865-1348   e-ISSN 1865-1356
ISBN 978-3-642-36607-9   e-ISBN 978-3-642-36608-6
DOI 10.1007/978-3-642-36608-6
Springer Heidelberg Dordrecht London New York

Library of Congress Control Number: 2013931190

ACM Computing Classification (1998): H.3.5, J.1, K.4.4, H.5, D.2

Typesetting: Camera-ready by author, data conversion by Scientific Publishing Services, Chennai, India

Printed on acid-free paper

Springer is part of Springer Science+Business Media (www.springer.com)

Preface

This book includes extended and revised versions of a set of selected papers from WEBIST 2012 (the 8th International Conference on Web Information Systems and Technologies), held in Porto, Portugal, in 2012, and organized by the Institute for Systems and Technologies of Information, Control and Communication (INSTICC), in cooperation with and ACM SIGMIS.

The purpose of the WEBIST series of conferences is to bring together researchers, engineers, and practitioners interested in technological advances and business applications of Web-based information systems. The conference has five main tracks, covering different aspects of Web Information Systems, including: Internet Technology; Web Interfaces and Applications; Society, e-Business and e-Government; Web Intelligence; and Mobile Information Systems.

WEBIST 2012 received 184 paper submissions from 41 countries on all continents. A double-blind review process was enforced, with the help of 183 experts from the International Program Committee; each of them specialized in one of the main conference topic areas. After reviewing, 25 papers were selected to be published and presented as full papers and 57 additional papers, describing work-in-progress, as short papers. Furthermore, 31 papers were presented as posters. The full-paper acceptance ratio was 14%, and the total oral paper acceptance ratio was 45%.

The papers included in this book were selected from those with the best reviews also taking into account the quality of their presentation at the conference, assessed by Session Chairs. Therefore, we hope that you find these papers interesting, and we trust they may represent a helpful reference for all those who need to address any of the research areas mentioned above.

We wish to thank all those who supported and helped to organize the conference. On behalf of the conference Organizing Committee, we would like to thank the authors, whose work mostly contributed to a very successful conference, and to the members of the Program Committee, whose expertise and diligence were instrumental to ensure the quality of the final contributions. We also wish to thank all the members of the Organizing Committee, whose work and commitment was invaluable. Last but not least, we would like to thank Springer for their collaboration in getting this book to print.

December 2012

José Cordeiro
Karl-Heinz Krempels

Organization

Conference Chair

José Cordeiro   Polytechnic Institute of Setúbal / INSTICC, Portugal

Program Chair

Karl-Heinz Krempels   RWTH Aachen University, Germany

Organizing Committee

Marina Carvalho   INSTICC, Portugal
Helder Coelhas   INSTICC, Portugal
Patrícia Duarte   INSTICC, Portugal
Bruno Encarnação   INSTICC, Portugal
Liliana Medina   INSTICC, Portugal
Carla Mota   INSTICC, Portugal
Raquel Pedrosa   INSTICC, Portugal
Vitor Pedrosa   INSTICC, Portugal
Daniel Pereira   INSTICC, Portugal
Cláudia Pinto   INSTICC, Portugal
Susana Ribeiro   INSTICC, Portugal
João Teixeira   INSTICC, Portugal
José Varela   INSTICC, Portugal
Pedro Varela   INSTICC, Portugal

Program Committee

Michael Adeyeye, South Africa
Esma Aïmeur, Canada
Guglielmo De Angelis, Italy
Margherita Antona, Greece
Giuliano Armano, Italy
Ismailcem Budak Arpinar, USA
Elarbi Badidi, UAE
Panagiotis D. Bamidis, Greece
David Bell, UK
Orlando Belo, Portugal
Shlomo Berkovsky, Australia

Werner Beuschel, Germany
Maria Bielikova, Slovak Republic
Eva Blomqvist, Sweden
Matthias Book, Germany
Paolo Bouquet, Italy
François Bry, Germany
Maria Claudia Buzzi, Italy
Elena Calude, New Zealand
Iván Cantador, Spain
Cinzia Cappiello, Italy
John Carroll, USA

Giovanni Toffetti Carughi, UK
Sergio de Cesare, UK
Li Chen, Hong Kong
Shiping Chen, Australia
Dan Chiorean, Romania
Dickson Chiu, China
Chin-Wan Chung, Korea, Republic of
Christophe Claramunt, France
Mihaela Cocea, UK
Martine De Cock, Belgium
Christine Collet, France
Marco Comuzzi, The Netherlands
Isabelle Comyn-wattiau, France
Emmanuel Coquery, France
Anna Corazza, Italy
Gianluca Correndo, UK
Michel Crampes, France
Daniel Cunliffe, UK
Florian Daniel, Italy
Antonina Dattolo, Italy
Steven Demurjian, USA
Enrico Denti, Italy
Stefan Dessloch, Germany
Oscar Díaz, Spain
Y. Ding, USA
Peter Dolog, Denmark
Schahram Dustdar, Austria
Vadim Ermolayev, Ukraine
Davide Eynard, Italy
Alexander Felfernig, Austria
Miriam Fernandez, UK
Alberto Fernández, Spain
Josep-Lluis Ferrer-Gomila, Spain
Filomena Ferrucci, Italy
Giovanni Fulantelli, Italy
Tim Furche, UK
Ombretta Gaggi, Italy
John Garofalakis, Greece
Irene Garrigos, Spain
Nicola Gatti, Italy
Panagiotis Germanakos, Cyprus
Massimiliano Giacomin, Italy
Henrique Gil, Portugal
Karl Goeschka, Austria

Anna Goy, Italy
Ratvinder Grewal, Canada
William Grosky, USA
Francesco Guerra, Italy
Aaron Gulliver, Canada
Shanmugasundaram Hariharan, India
Hamid Harroud, Morocco
Ioannis Hatzilygeroudis, Greece
Stylianos Hatzipanagos, UK
A. Henten, Denmark
Larisa Ismailova, Russian Federation
Arun Iyengar, USA
Kai Jakobs, Germany
Monique Janneck, Germany
Ivan Jelinek, Czech Republic
Ireneusz Jozwiak, Poland
Carlos Juiz, Spain
KaterinaKabassi, Greece
Georgia Kapitsaki, Cyprus
Sokratis Katsikas, Greece
Cameron Kiddle, Canada
In-Young Ko, Korea, Republic of
Hiroshi Koide, Japan
Agnes Koschmider, Germany
Karl-Heinz Krempels, Germany
Tsvi Kuflik, Israel
Papanikolaou Kyparisia, Greece
Greg Leighton, Canada
Daniel Lemire, Canada
Stefania Leone, Switzerland
Jianxin Li, Australia
Li Li, USA
Weigang Li, Brazil
Xitong Li, USA
Lin Lin, USA
Dongxi Liu, Australia
Xumin Liu, USA
Ying Liu, Singapore
Marti Navarro Llacer, Spain
Pascal Lorenz, France
Cristiano Maciel, Brazil
Michael Mackay, UK
George Magoulas, UK
Kazutaka Maruyama, Japan

Auxiliary Reviewers

Cauê Clasen, France
Michael Derntl, Germany
Sandra Geisler, Germany
Simon Grapenthin, Germany
Andras Horvath, Italy
Mehdi Khouja, Spain
Isaac Lera, Spain

Patricia Graziely Antunes de
  Mendonça, Brazil
Edie Correia Santana, Brazil
Caterina Senette, Italy
Cleyton Slaviero, Brazil
Jannick Kirk Sørensen, Denmark
Theodoros Tzouramanis, Greece

Invited Speakers

Arlindo Dias   IBM, Portugal
David De Roure   University of Oxford, UK
Jeff Z. Pan   University of Aberdeen, UK

Table of Contents

Part I: Internet Technology

Part II: Web Interfaces and Applications

Part III: Society, e-Business and e-Government

Part IV: Web Intelligence

Part V: Mobile Information Systems

Part I
Internet Technology

Efficient Parallel Algorithms for XML Filtering with Structural and Value Constraints

Panagiotis Antonellis, Christos Makris, and Georgios Pispirigos

Department of Computer Engineering and Informatics, Faculty of Engineering,
University of Patras, Patras, Greece
{adonel,makri,pispirig}@ceid.upatras.gr

Abstract. Information seeking applications employ information filtering techniques as a main component of their functioning. The purpose of the present article is to explore techniques to efficiently implement scalable and efficient information filtering techniques, based on the XML representation, when both structural and value constraints are imposed. In the majority of the provided implementations the use of the XML representation appears in single processor systems, and the involved user profiles are represented using the XPath query language and efficient heuristic techniques for constraining the complexity of the filtering mechanism are employed. Here, we propose a parallel filtering algorithm based on the well known YFilter algorithm, which dynamically applies a work-load balancing approach to each thread to achieve the best parallelization. In addition, the proposed filtering algorithm adds support for value-based predicates by embedding three different algorithms for handling value constraints during XML filtering, based on the popularity and the semantic interpretation of the predicate values. Experimental results depict that the proposed system outperforms the previous parallel approaches to the XML filtering problem.

Keywords: XML filtering, Parallel algorithms, Semantic similarity.

1 Introduction

Information retrieval and information filtering are two different modes of information seeking activities. In information retrieval the users actively participate in the seeking for knowledge by posing queries to a collection of a given documents, while in information filtering the user information needs are represented as profiles and the documents are *pushed* to the users. In a general sense the purpose of information filtering is to dynamically generate information and push it to the information consumer. Information filtering appears into three different forms: content based filtering where the incoming information is mainly filtered with content analysis, collaborative filtering where the incoming information is filtered for a user taken into account the usage history of other users with similar profiles, and hybrid filtering that combines both collaborative filtering and content based filtering; in this work we focus on content based filtering. Information filtering systems (also known as publish/subscribe systems) [1] mainly provide two main services: document selection (i.e., determining the subset of incoming documents that match the stored user profiles) and document

J. Cordeiro and K.-H. Krempels (Eds.): WEBIST 2012, LNBIP 140, pp. 3–15, 2013.

routing (i.e., delivering matching documents from the data sources that produce them to the users). In order to implement efficiently these services, information filtering systems rely upon representations of user profiles, that are generated either explicitly by requesting from the users to state their interests, or implicitly by employing mechanisms for tracking the user access patterns and automatically construct his/her profile. Initial attempts to represent user profiles and match them against new data items, typically employed "bag of words" representations and keyword similarity techniques that are closely related to the well known vector space model representation in the Information Retrieval area. These techniques, however, often suffer from limited ability to express user interests, being unable to fully capture the semantics of the user behavior and user interests. As an attempt to face this lack of richness in the representation there have appeared lately [2, 3, 5, 6, 11] a number of systems that use XML representations for both documents and user profiles and that employ various filtering techniques to match the XML representations of user documents with the provided profiles.

The basic mechanism used to describe user profiles in XML format is through the XPath query language [17]. XPath is a query language for addressing parts of an XML document, while also providing basic facilities for manipulation of strings, numbers and booleans. XPath models an XML document as a tree of nodes; there are different types of nodes, including element nodes, attribute nodes and text nodes and XPath defines a way to compute a string-value for each type of node.

The process of filtering XML documents is the reverse of searching XML documents for specific structural and value information. An XML document filtering system stores user profiles along with additional information (e.g. personal information of the user, email address, etc.). A user profile can store either only structural criteria or both structural and value criteria. When an XML document arrives, the system filters it by exploiting representation of the stored profiles in order to identify with which of them the document matches. After finishing the filtering process, the document can be forwarded to users with matched profiles.

The purpose of the present work is to explore techniques to efficiently implement scalable and efficient representation and filtering techniques, based on the XML representation, where both structural and value constraints are imposed.

2   Background

2.1   Related Work

In recent years, many approaches have been proposed for providing efficient filtering of XML data against large sets of user profiles. Depending on the way the user profiles and XML documents are represented and handled, the existing filtering systems can be categorized as follows:

Automata-Based Systems. Systems in this category utilize Finite State Automata (FSA) to quickly match the incoming XML document with the stored user profiles. While parsing the XML document, each node element causes one or more transitions in the underlying FSA, based on the element's name or tag. In XFilter [2], the user profiles are represented as queries using the XPath language and the filtering engine employs a sophisticated index structure and a modified Finite State Machine (FSM) approach to quickly locate and examine relevant profiles. A major drawback of XFilter is its lack of twig pattern support, as it handles only linear path expressions. Based on XFilter, a new system was proposed in [6] termed YFilter that combined all of the path queries into a single Nondeterministic Finite Automaton (NFA) and exploited commonality among user profiles by merging common prefixes of the user profile paths such that they were processed at most once. Unlike XFilter, YFilter handles twig patterns by decomposing them into separate linear paths and then performing post-processing over the intermediate matching results. In [16] a parallel implementation of YFilter for multi-core systems (shared-memory) is proposed by splitting the NFA into smaller parts, with each part assigned to a single thread. A distributed version of YFilter which also supports value-based predicates is presented in [13]. In this approach the NFA is distributed along the nodes of a DHT network to speed-up the filtering process and various pruning techniques are applied based on the defined value predicates on the stored user profiles. Finally in [9] a parallel XML filtering that supports fine-grained filtering of the incoming XML documents is described. A user can submit an hierarchy of filters and ever incoming XML document will be filtered against the stored filter hierarchies. In addition, the algorithm identifies exactly which parts of the incoming XML documents match with the filters of each user and only those parts are actually send to the user.

Sequence-Based Systems. Systems in this category encode both the user profiles and the XML documents as string sequences and then transform the problem of XML filtering into that of subsequence matching between the document and profile sequences. FiST [11] employs a novel holistic matching approach, that instead of splitting the twig patterns into separate linear paths, it transforms (through the use of the Prüfer sequence representation) the matching problem into a subsequence matching problem. In order to provide more efficient filtering, the user profiles sequences are indexed using hash structures. In XFIS [3] it is employed, a holistic matching approach which eliminates the need of extra post-processing of branch nodes by transforming the matching problem into a subsequence matching problem between the string sequence representation of user profiles and XML documents.

Stack-Based Systems. The representative system of this category is AFilter [5]. AFilter utilizes a stack structure while filtering the XML document against user profiles. Its novel filtering mechanism exploits both prefix and suffix commonalities across filter statements, avoids unnecessarily eager result/state enumerations (such as NFA enumerations of active states) and decouples memory management task from result enumeration to ensure correct results even when the memory is tight. XPush [10] translates the collection of filter statements into a single deterministic pushdown automaton using stacks. The XPush machine uses a SAX parser that simulates a bottom up computation and hence doesn't require the main memory representation of the document. XSQ [15] utilizes a hierarchical arrangement of pushdown transducers augmented with buffers. In [14], the author presents a system for evaluating XPath queries in a distributed environment, consisting of a large number of small mobile devices. Although the proposed system is efficient in such environments, it cannot be actually applied in a single multithreading machine.

Although all of the previously described works have been used successfully for representing a set of user profiles and identifying XML documents that structurally match with the user profiles, little work [9], [12], [13] has been done to support value matching, that is evaluation of value-based predicates in the user profiles. This is a very usual problem in real world applications where the user profiles except for just defining some structural predicates, also introduce value-based predicates. A modern XML filtering system should be able to handle both types of predicates and also scale well in case of a large number of stored user profiles.

2.2   Paper Motivation and Contribution

Most of the research work in the area of XML filtering has been in the context of a single processing core. However, given the wide spread of multi-core processors, we believe that a parallel approach can provide significant benefits for a number of real world applications. In addition, most of the existing approaches concentrate only on the structural characteristics of user profiles, although in many real-world applications the value predicates may be more important.

Based on this motivation, we propose a parallel approach to the problem of structural and value-based XML filtering for shared-memory systems, based on the YFilter algorithm. The main contributions of the proposed parallel algorithm are:

- Parallel execution of the NFA constructed by the YFilter, by utilizing all the cores of the processor.
- Dynamic work load balancing based on the currently active states of the NFA.
- The support of value-predicates in user profiles; we propose approaches for handling efficiently value constraints by dynamically pruning the NFA based on the most "popular" states and by exploiting semantic information concerning the values attached to the value constraint predicates.

In our knowledge, this is one of the few works in parallel XML filtering that deal with support of value-based predicates, mainly inspired by [13]. However though inspired by their work we must emphasize that their evaluation of the value predicates is done in a different way from ours, by apriori identifiying those predicates that may result in the most rejections. We extend this by embedding semantically enhanced criteria, while in our popularity based approach, the decision of which value predicates to use is automatically readjusted after filtering each incoming XML document.

Concerning the difference of our approach to [9], in their approach the parallelization is only applied inside the matching of each filter hierarchy, whereas in our approach the parallelization is applied in the global matching algorithm. In addition, the matching of value-predicates is applied at each step of their filtering process, while in our approach the matching is done efficiently only in the NFA states where it is actually needed.

3   YFilter Overview

The YFilter algorithm constructs a single NFA for a large number of queries and utilizes this NFA to filter a continuous stream of incoming XML documents [6].

In Figure 1 we present an example of such a nondeterministic finite automaton (NFA) constructed from eight user profiles. The user profiles have been chosen appropriately to represent the different types of supported structural relationships. Each intermediate NFA state is represented with a circle, while each final NFA state (e.g. a state that leads to accepting a specific user profile) is represented with a double circle. The user profiles associated with each final state are shown with curly braces next to the state. Finally, each edge transition is triggered when a matching element (tag) name is encountered during the parsing of the incoming XML document.

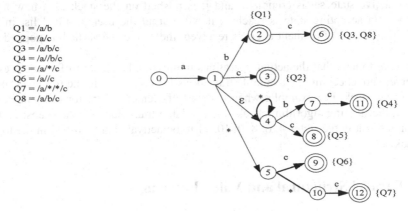

Fig. 1. Example NFA constructed from a set of user profiles

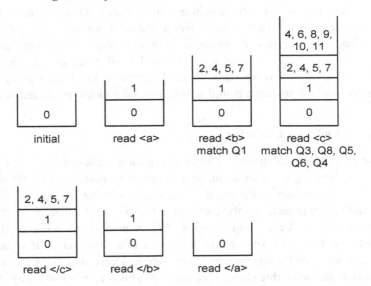

XML document: <a><c></c></a>

Fig. 2. Active states during parsing of an incoming XML document

As we can easily observe, YFilter greatly reduces the number of states by sharing the common prefix paths of the stored user profiles. YFilter uses an event-driven method along with a stack of active states. Each level of the stack represents possible states of the NFA for the XML part of the XML document that has currently already been seen. As shown in Figure 2, once it receives a start-of-element event, the filtering algorithm follows all matching transitions from all currently active states. When checking an available edge transitions, if the incoming element name matches the transition or the transition it is marked by the * symbol, the corresponding state will be added to the new active state set. After all possible transitions have been checked, the new active state set is complete, and it is pushed on the stack as a new level. Whenever an accepting state is reached, it will output the user profiles' list in this state. When an end-of-element event is received, the active states stack is popped one level.

It is vital to note that the actual operations required, when a start-of-element event is received, are checking the available transitions for each state in the top level of the active states stack. For example, when the start-of-element event for element <c> is received, the filtering algorithm checks the available transitions for the states: 2, 4, 5, 7, which result in the states 4, 6, 8, 9, 10, 11 to be activated and pushed in the top of the stack.

4   Parallel Structural and Value Filtering

In this section we describe our new parallelized XML filtering algorithm, based on YFilter. The actual NFA execution is split into the different threads using a dynamic load balancing technique, which always ensures that each thread is assigned with the same work load. The proposed algorithm, in addition to structural filtering, also supports value filtering based on the value-predicates defined in the stored user profiles. In particular our algorithm supports three different ways in supporting value-predicates, all of which are novel contributions, inspired by ideas presented in [13].

4.1   Parallelized NFA Execution

Our goal was to truly parallelize the YFilter algorithm in a balanced way in order for each thread to be assigned with a similar amount of workload during the filtering process. Existing approaches are based on statically splitting the constructed NFA into parts and assigning each specific part at each thread [16]. Similar approaches also exist for distributed NFA execution on top of DHT networks [13]. However, this type of work splitting does not ensure that each thread will actually have the same workload, as the actual state transitions may occur only in a very small part of the whole NFA. In such a case some threads may remain idle, while others are working, thus the NFA execution is not truly parallelized.

For example consider the NFA of Figure 1, split in four parts: {0, 1, 2}, {3, 4, 5}, {6, 7, 8} and {9, 10, 11, 12}, with each part statically assigned to a single thread. When the start-of-element event for element <c> is received, the thread #1 will check one state (state 1), the thread #2 check two states (states 4, 5), the thread #3 will check only one state (state 7) and the thread #4 will remain inactive as none of the currently active states belong to its NFA part. Thus, the actual workload is not equally split to the four available threads.

Based on this notion, the proposed filtering algorithm achieves balanced work splitting, by *dynamically* assigning tasks to each thread during NFA execution. As mentioned before, whenever a start-of-element event is received, the algorithm has to check the transitions of each state included in the top level of the active states stack. Although each active state does not have the same number of candidate transitions with the rest states, we make the assumption that the number of tasks is equal to the number of active states at that time. Based on this assumption, the proposed filtering algorithm creates a task for each active state and pushes them into a queue. Whenever a thread is idle, it is assigned with the next available task (e.g. active state) from the queue. The only drawback of this approach is that in cases that a state has a big number of candidate transitions, the corresponding thread may be late and thus the achieved parallelization will be not the best one.

For example, consider a system with three threads and the NFA of Figure 1, when the start-of-element event for element <c> is received. The currently active states are four (states 2, 4, 5, 7) and thus the thread #1 will be assigned with state 2, the thread #2 will be assigned with state 4 and the thread #3 will be assigned with state 5. Each thread will check the available transitions of its assigned state with the character <c> and in case of a match, it will activate the appropriate new state by pushing it on top of the stack. The first thread that will finish its job will be also assigned with the remaining state 7. From the above example, it is clear that the proposed dynamic parallelization of the NFA execution achieves best results due to actual work balancing based on the currently active states, unlike the existing approaches which are based on statically assigning NFA subsets to each thread.

A slightly different approach can be utilized if the fan-out of the NFA (e.g. number of edges per state) is quite small: in such a case the actual cost of checking all the transitions of each state is quite small, so the overhead of creating a separate task for each active state may overcome the benefits of the actual parallelization. So, it is better to split the set of active states into a list of subsets, based on the number of threads, and assign a subset to each thread.

For example, consider again a system with two threads and the NFA of Figure 1, when the start-of-element event for element <c> is received. Instead of assigning the state 2 to thread #1, the state 4 to thread #2 and waiting for them to finish in order to assign the rest of the states, we can directly assign the states 2, 4 to thread #1 and the states 5,7 to thread #2. That way, we reduce the cost of task initialization for every separate active state, thus achieving a further improvement on the total filtering time.

This variation decreases the overhead introduced of task creation and assignment by creating the least number of tasks. However, if a specific subset of states includes much more transitions than the other subsets, the rest of the threads would have to remain idle for quite a long time, thus increasing the actual filtering time. Based on the above notions, the proposed filtering algorithm uses this approach only if the number of transitions is about the same for every state during NFA construction, based on a predefined threshold of 15%, which was depicted after experimental testing.

4.2   Evaluation of Value-Based Predicates

In the previous section, we described how the structural matching is parallelized by assigning each thread with a subset of the active states to check. In this section, we concentrate on the evaluation of value-based predicates. Consider for example the user profile q:

$$paper[@year=2011]/author[text()="James"],$$

which selects the papers of author "James" during the year 2011. In order to filter an incoming XML document against the user profile q requires to check if the document's structure matches the profile's structure and also whether the value predicates of the user profile q are satisfied by the XML document.

A naïve approach is to integrate the value predicates directly on the constructed NFA, by adding extra transitions for the predicates, thus considering the value predicates as distinct nodes [12]. However, this approach would lead to a huge increase in the number of states and also destroy the sharing of path expressions for which the NFA was selected to begin with, as the value predicates usually form a larger set than the structural constraints of the user profiles. Other approaches, such as bottom-up and top-down [13], have been proposed to address this problem. The common idea behind those approaches is the selection of a small subset of the value predicates for pruning the NFA execution, based on some predefined selectivity criterion. However, in real world applications, the incoming XML documents have been usually generated by different sources and thus vary both in structure and content. In such cases, a selected value predicate may be good for pruning the NFA execution during the filtering of a specific set of XML documents and bad for another set of XML documents. Thus, deciding on which value predicates to utilize during the NFA execution is not straightforward and has a strong impact on the efficiency of the filtering algorithm.

Based on this notion, our proposed filtering algorithm utilizes a novel step-by-step approach for supporting value-based predicates. We propose three new approaches for handling the problem at hand.

Our first approach introduces the idea of "popular" NFA states, that is the NFA states that have been activated a lot during the filtering of the various incoming XML documents. More precisely, we keep a counter for each NFA state that counts the number of activations for that state and we select the top 10% states as the most "popular" states. For example, in Figure 3, the state 4 has been activated two times, while the state 3 has been activated zero times. The value of the threshold can change to balance the pruning of the NFA, but it is initialized to 10% which resulted in better results during the experiments. The idea of utilizing the most "popular" states has the benefit that dynamically defines the set of NFA states that trigger value predicate checking (and thus may stop the NFA execution), only based on the set of previously filtered XML documents and not some user-defined selectivity criterion, like in [13]. Thus there is no need for a-priori knowledge of the semantics of incoming XML documents in order to decide the those states. This approach is based on the idea that a state that has been activated a lot during the filtering of previous XML documents has a greater possibility to be activated during the filtering of subsequent XML documents, and thus an unsatisfied value predicate in that state will stop the NFA execution (prune this execution path).

Our second approach builds on the selectivity estimation formulae of [13] by embedding semantic information in the calculation as it is provided by WordNet [4], and by employing the Wu and Palmer similarity metric. In particular we define as the *semantic selectivity* of a text or attribute predicate [pred =v] the fraction of elements e reachable by any path, whose value *is semantically close* to v. By the term semantically close we call those values whose Wu and Palmer distance between their respective senses is greater than a user defined threshold; in the case of polysemous values we take the average value of the Wu and Palmer similarity metric between all combinations of the senses of the respective values.

We remind the reader that WordNet is a lexical database of English words, organizing English nouns, verbs, adjectives and adverbs into equivalence classes termed *synsets* (synonym sets) that are interlinked into a semantic networks with various relations (semantic and lexical); there are also versions of WordNet for various other languages besides English (see [20]). Moreover the Wu and Palmer semantic similarity metric between two senses s_i and s_j in the semantic network of WordNet is defined as:

$$similarity\ (s_i, s_j) = \frac{2depth\ (LCA\ (s_i, s_j))}{depth\ (s_i) + depth\ (s_j)}$$

where *LCA()* denotes the Least Common Ancestor of the respective nodes, and *depth()* the depth of the involved node in the hierarchy.

Finally our third approach (hybrid) combines the two first approaches by employing a selective criterion that linearly combines the popularity and the semantic similarity criterion, into a unified criterion. Concerning the weight of significance of the involved factors in the linear combination, we have experimented with various choices tending to finally let them be equal.

With regards to the practical aspect of the implementation and for all variants of our value-based predicate selection technique, during the NFA construction, at each state we store a set of the corresponding value-based predicates along with the query id of each predicate. This set of predicates will be used during the filtering in order to decide whether the current execution path will continue or stop. Whenever an incoming XML document arrives, we parse it and create a list of candidate predicates based on the text data of nodes and attributes. This list of candidate predicates will be used during candidate checking at the filtering procedure. Checking a set of predicates assigned to a state against the list of candidate predicates contained in an XML document may be a slow procedure, due to the big number of candidate predicates. Thus, instead of checking the predicates at each active state, the filtering algorithm applies the candidate checking only on the most selective states, where the selectivity criterion will be one of the three described before. During this check, we check if at least one of the state predicates is included in the list of document's candidate predicates. In such a case, the execution path will continue normally on this state. On the other hand, if none of the state predicates is part of the candidate predicates, then there is no need to continue this execution path as none of the corresponding user profiles are satisfied, thus the state is not activated.

The only drawback of this approach is that at the end of filtering process, all the matched user profiles must be checked against the incoming XML document based on their value-based predicates, as the filtering algorithm does not check the value predicates in all the states. However, usually the number of matched user profiles is a small portion of the total number of stored user profiles and thus the cost is very small compared to the cost of checking the value predicates at each NFA state.

5   Experiments

We tested our filtering system against the most relevant to our algorithmic setting parallel approach to XML filtering [16]. In that article the authors propose a method for statically splitting the NFA into subparts and assign each subpart to a separate thread. However, this approach does not support value-based predicates, so for the sets of experiments that compared its performance with our technique we were restricted to use structural-only user profiles. Our filtering system was implemented in Java using the freeware Eclipse IDE. In order to obtain comparable and reliable results, we also implemented the other parallel algorithm in Java as well.

In our experiments we used three different datasets: DBLP dataset [18], Shakespeare's plays dataset [19] and synthetic Treebank data generated by an XML generator provided by IBM [7]. We also generated three user profile sets, one set for each dataset, using the XPath generator available in the YFilter package. The final set of user profiles consisted of the three different user profile sets, each set constructed from the corresponding XML dataset. We used that approach in order to emulate a real-world filtering system where the stored user profiles are usually different from each other and the same also stands for the incoming XML documents. All the experiments were run on a quad-core hyper threading (thus 8 threads) Linux machine running Kubuntu 11.04 with 8 Gb RAM.

In order to calculate the speed-up gained by the proposed parallelization compared to the parallel algorithm presented in [16], we measured the average filtering time of an XML document with size approximately 5500 nodes through 7000 stored user profiles, by varying the number of threads between 1 and 8 (Experiment 1). In addition, we measured the average filtering time as the number of stored user profiles increases between 1000 and 10000, for 4 threads (Experiment 2). As far as the value-predicate filtering, we utilized the synthetic Treebank data and the DBLP dataset to create a mixed set of 100 user profiles with various value-based predicates. We filtered a set of 50 XML documents and calculated the Recall, Precision and F-measure of the filtering results for the 3 proposed techniques and the technique described in [13] (Experiment 3).

Figure 3 shows the results of the first experiment. As it can be easily observed both approaches achieve a speed-up of the total filtering process as the number of utilized threads increases. However, although our approach starts slower (for 1 thread), it turns out that it takes greater advantage of the increasing number of threads and finally achieves better filtering times after the 4 threads. In fact the achieved speed-up in filtering time is 7 (14000ms to 2000ms) for 8 threads, while the other algorithm actually achieving a speed-up of 2.5 (10000ms to 4000ms) for 8 threads. The results can be easily explained, as the overhead for creating a separate task for each active state can slow down the total filtering process if the number of threads is small (in the current experiment: 1- 3 threads), but as the number of threads increases, the proposed dynamic parallelization works efficiently and the total filtering time is greatly reduced. On the other hand, the approach proposed in [16], which is based on splitting the NFA into subsets and assigning each subset into a separate thread, cannot achieve the same speed-ups as the number of threads increases. This can mainly be attributed to the fact, that it doesn't apply a balanced workload splitting into the available threads, as each NFA subset execution may require different work, and thus some threads may remain idle for quite large amount of time.

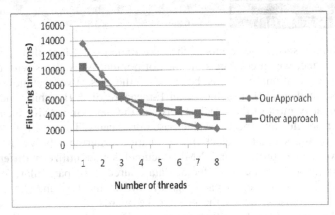

Fig. 3. Filtering time as the number of threads increases (*Other Approach* is the approach described in [16])

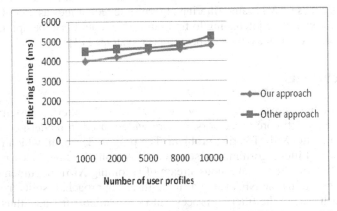

Fig. 4. Filtering time as the number of user profiles increases (*Other Approach* is the approach described in [16])

Figure 4 shows the results obtained from the second experiment. It is clear that the filtering time of both algorithms slightly increases as the number of stored user profiles increases. This is expected, as a greater number of user profiles results to a larger NFA and thus to a bigger number of active states during NFA execution. Thus, the actual workload increases and this is depicted in the total filtering time. However, the filtering time does not increase analogously to the total number of stored user profiles, which means that both approaches scale very well as the number of user profiles increases. Again, as the number of user profiles increases, our proposed parallel approach scales better than the algorithm proposed in [16], achieving an average of 15% better filtering time for 4 threads.

Table 1. Results of the third experiment

Technique	Recall	Precision	F-measure
1st - Popular NFA states	0,84	0,79	0,82
2nd- Semantic Selectivity estimation	0,89	0,90	0,89
3rd - Hybrid	0,92	0,91	0,91
Miliaraki & Koubarakis [13]	0.89	0.85	0,87

Finally, Table 1 shows the results of the third experiment. It is clear that the third proposed technique, which combines the idea of popular NFA states with the semantic selectivity estimation, performs better than the first two techniques and the technique described in [13]. It achieves an F-measure of 0,91, which means that it succeeds to identify most of the matches between the incoming XML documents and the stored user profiles, in aspect of value-based predicates. This result was expected, as the usage of the semantic selectivity estimation criterion, allows us to capture matches between user profiles and XML documents that utilize a different set of tags/keywords (probably due to different data sources). In particular, WordNet is utilized to identify the senses of each tag/keyword in the text and the matching is performed on the senses, not on the original keywords. As a result, this approach achieves to identify more matches than the others. This advantage, combined with the technique of utilizing the most popular NFA states for pruning the NFA execution leads to the best balance between speed-up and precision in value-based filtering.

We consider these XML value filtering algorithmic techniques as a contribution of our paper and it would be interesting to find out if they could also be applied to other parallel architectures such as those of peer to peer systems [13].

6   Conclusions

In this paper we have presented an innovative parallel XML filtering system that takes advantage of the multi-core processors that are widely used in modern computers, in order to speed up the XML filtering problem. The proposed system, which is based on the well-known YFilter algorithm, constructs a NFA from the stored user profiles and utilizes this NFA to filter a continuous stream of incoming XML documents. However, instead of executing the NFA using a single-thread approach, it splits the workload required at each step of the filtering process into the available threads, thus providing a big speed-up to the total filtering time required. The number of threads depends on the number of available cores and can vary, but the proposed filtering algorithm can work with any number of threads. In addition, the proposed filtering system extends the YFilter in order to efficiently support value-based predicates in the user profiles, enabling both structural and value-based filtering of the incoming XML documents. We tested four approaches with our main contributions being a value-based filtering that is applied using a dynamic top-down approach, where the NFA execution is pruned only in the most popular states, which results to small overhead and big speed-up due to early pruning and a semantic similarity extension of the selectivity criteria employed in [13]. The experimental results showed that the proposed system outperforms the previous parallel XML filtering algorithms by fully utilizing the available threads. In addition, the proposed techniques for handling value-based predicates perform very well in the experimental data, with the third one outperforming the rest.

Acknowledgements. This research has been co-financed by the European Union (European Social Fund - ESF) and Greek national funds through the Operational Program "Education and Lifelong Learning" of the National Strategic Reference Framework (NSRF) - Research Funding Program: Thales. Investing in knowledge society through the European Social Fund.

References

1. Aguilera, M.K., Strom, R.E., Stunnan, D.C., Ashey, M., Chandra, T.D.: Matching Events in a Content-based Subscription System. In: Proceedings of the ACM Symposium on Principles of Distributed Computing, PODC 1999, pp. 53–61 (1999)
2. Altinel, M., Franklin, M.L.J.: Efficient Filtering of XML Documents for Selective Dissemination of Information. In: VLDB, pp. 53–64 (2000)
3. Antonellis, P., Makris, C.: XFIS: an XML filtering system based on string representation and matching. International Journal on Web Engineering and Technology, IJWET 4(1), 70–94 (2008)
4. Budanitsky, A., Hirst, G.: Evaluating WordNet-based measures of lexical semantic relatedness. Association for Computational Linguistics 32, 32–47 (2006)
5. Canadan, K., Hsiung, W., Chen, S., Tatemura, J., Agrrawal, D.: AFilter: Adaptable XML Filtering with Prefix-Caching and Suffix-Clustering. In: VLDB, pp. 559–570 (2006)
6. Diao, Y., Altinel, M., Franklin, M.L.J., Zhang, H., Fischer, P.: Path sharing and predicate evaluation for high-performance XML filtering. TODS 28(4), 467–516 (2003)
7. Diaz, A.L., Lovell, D.: XML Generator,
   http://alphaworks.ibm.com/tech/xmlgenerator
8. Fellbaum, C. (ed.): WordNet, an electronic lexical database. MIT Press, Cambridge (1998)
9. Grummt, E.: Fine-grained parallel XML filtering for content-based publish/subscribe systems. In: Proceedings of the 5th ACM International Conference on Distributed Event-Based System, DEBS 2011 (2011)
10. Gupta, A.K., Suciu, D.: Stream processing of XPath queries with predicates. In: SIGMOD, pp. 419–430 (2003)
11. Kwon, J., Rao, P., Moon, B., Lee, S.: FiST: Scalable XML Document Filtering by Sequencing Twig Patterns. In: VLDB, pp. 217–228 (2005)
12. Kwon, J., Rao, P., Moon, B., Lee, S.: Value-based predicate filtering of XML documents. Data and Knowledge Engineering (KDE) 67(1) (2008)
13. Miliaraki, I., Koubarakis, M.: Distributed structural and value XML filtering. In: DEBS, pp. 2–13 (2010)
14. Olteanu, D.: SPEX: Streamed and Progressive Evaluation of XPath. IEEE Trans. on Knowl. and Data Eng. 19(7), 934–949 (2007)
15. Peng, F., Chawathe, S.: XSQ: A streaming XPath Queries. TODS, 577–623 (2005)
16. Zhang, Y., Pan, Y., Chiu, K.: A Parallel XPath Engine Based on Concurrent NFA Execution. In: Proceedings of the IEEE 16th International Conference on Parallel and Distributed Systems, ICPADS 2010, pp. 314–321 (2010)
17. http://www.w3.org/TR/xpath
18. http://kdl.cs.umass.edu/data/dblp/dblp-info.html
19. http://xml.coverpages.org/bosakShakespeare200.html
20. http://www.globalwordnet.org/gwa/wordnet_table.html

Cross-Platform Development Using HTML5, jQuery Mobile, and PhoneGap: Realizing a Smart Meter Application

Alexander Zibula[1] and Tim A. Majchrzak[2]

[1] best practice consulting AG (bpc), Münster, Germany
[2] Department of Information Systems, University of Münster, Münster, Germany
a.zibula@uni-muenster.de, tima@ercis.de

Abstract. With mobile computing devices becoming prevalent, applications for them greatly increased in importance. These apps make devices more versatile. Unfortunately, developing them at the moment means that each plattform has to be addressed separately. Alternatively, Web-based solutions can be used that do not provide a "native" look and feel. To investigate novel methods of multi-platform app development and to review HTML5, we built an app using several up-to-date development frameworks. Our scenario is a smart meter tool, which is an active area of research in itself. We introduce approaches in the field of multi-platform app development and illustrate the technological background. We then give an overview of our development process. Eventually, we evaluate our app and discuss our findings with the aim of providing generalizable results.

Keywords: App, Mobile application, Cross-platform, Multi-platform, Android, iOS, HTML5, PhoneGap, jQuery Mobile, Smart Meter, Apache Cordova.

1 Introduction

Since the advent of the Internet as a universal technology, mobile computing has continuously increased in importance. Beginning with smartphones, in particular the iPhone in 2007 [1], mobile Internet usage has greatly increased. For example, in Germany it rose from 9 % to 16 % from 2009 to 2010 [2]. At the same time, mobile devices—i.e. mobile phones, smartphones, and tablet computers (*pads*)—have been equipped with increasing amounts of memory and computational power. Consequently, there is a demand for software that makes the most of these devices.

Mobile applications already generate significant revenue—USD 5.2 billion in 2010 according to Gartner [3]. These so called *apps* have become commonplace, even though technologically they are "ordinary" computer programs. In the simplest form, a Web site optimized for mobile devices (*Webapp*) is already considered an app. In a more dedicated form, Web-based content is rendered by a mobile device's internal browser but displayed within an app installed on it. This can offer access to device features but might not provide much more than an icon on the device's home screen, changing the users' perception. The third category are native apps that have been written for a specific platform—either a virtual machine or a mobile (device) operating system.

J. Cordeiro and K.-H. Krempels (Eds.): WEBIST 2012, LNBIP 140, pp. 16–33, 2013.

Developing apps is far from hassle-free. Due to rapid progress in hardware development, software development has not kept up the pace (as illustrated in Section 2).[1] To some extent it is unclear whether classical software development methods can be applied to mobile devices. Even worse, there are a number of incompatible platforms. Development of PC programs for multiple platforms is much more convenient than it used to be. A Java program runs on any system that can host an adequate virtual machine. Even programs natively developed for one platform can usually be cross-compiled for other platforms (e.g. in C++ via Gtk+ [5]) if they do not heavily make use of platform-dependent functionality. Traditional development for mobile apps means writing programs for each platform from scratch. Only few approaches existed to circumvent this problem.

To investigate possibilities of cross-platform development, we designed an app using HTML5 [6], PhoneGap [7], and jQuery Mobile [8]. Our aims were to understand how they are used, how development differs from classical applications, and how well the apps perform. To add rigor while working on a highly relevant topic, and to broaden the scope of our research, we selected *smart metering* [9] as our scenario. We thereby developed a new kind of app that is demanding w.r.t. mobile device resource utilization.

Smart grids have been proposed as an energy grid upgrade [10] in order to more efficiently distribute and use energy, particularly in light of regenerative sources [11]. Despite the need for cautions [12] their emergence can be taken for granted. Smart meters are part of smart grids. They measure energy throughput and offer the possibility to better control consumption [13]. For example, energy-pricing throughout a day can be adjusted by demand. An analysis of benefits from smart metering has been described by Gnilka, Meyer-Spasche & Folta [14]. The architecture of smart meters and smart grids is complex because it involves various communication partners, communication channels, and intermediaries.

Our work makes several contributions. Firstly, it presents a novel approach for developing mobile applications against multiple platforms with a single code-base. Secondly, it introduces an innovative smart meter application. Thirdly, it discusses the findings in the light of future development projects. And fourthly, it briefly compares current approaches for cross-platform app development.

This paper is structured as follows. Section 2 outlines related work and alternative approaches. Our work's technological background is sketched in Section 3. Section 4 explains the app development. Evaluation and discussion are given in Section 5. Section 6 draws a conclusion.

2   Related Work and Alternative Approaches

Related work can be discussed from various perspectives. Firstly, other approaches for developing mobile applications for multiple platforms are highlighted. Secondly, papers on HTML5 are assessed. Finally, smart meter apps are reviewed. With regard to approaches for multi-platform development, we leave out Webapps and apps that can be installed natively but only use the internal browser to render HTML 4.01 or XHTML 1.1. Even if Web pages are optimized for mobile devices, they cannot be

---

[1] This surprisingly aligns with what is known as the *software crisis* [4] for stationary computers.

expected to have a "native" look and feel and they are unable to use device-specific functionality.

The following five multi-platform development approaches will likely become important in the near future. Firstly, *HTML5* [6] promises to combine the convenience of developing Web user interfaces (UI) with the ability to use a device's specific functionality. It is introduced in Section 3. Secondly, *hybrid apps* combine the features of HTML with native code that is provided by specialized frameworks [15]. In general, programmers do not require detailed knowledge of the target platform but only of Web technologies. An example is PhoneGap [7]. Thirdly, *interpreted apps* can be used. Instead of writing platform-dependent code, scripting languages that are interpreted on the target platform are used. An example is Appcelerator Titanium [16]. Fourthly, with *cross-compilers* code is written once and compiled to platform-dependent apps. An example is XMLVM [17]. Fifthly, *model-driven software development* (MDSD) can be applied. The idea is to describe an app in an abstract notation (the model) that is transformed and compiled to platform-dependent apps. An example is applause [18], which is based on a domain-specific language (DSL). Neither of the approaches can yet be seen as a definite solution. Nevertheless, good results can be achieved for a number of scenarios if the framework is chosen wisely [19]. Further frameworks exist that fall in between the above sketched categories. Cross-platform app development not only is a topic of academic research but also for practitioners [20]; this underlines its relevance.

Although HTML5 is still considered a "working draft" [6], standardization is at an advanced stage. This is also reflected by the appearance of practitioners' textbooks such as that by PILGRIM [21]. Even Webapp development for Android and iOS using HTML is covered [22,23]. Most scientific articles that have been published in this field do not directly relate to our work. They cover issues such as Web3D [24], accessibility [25], mashups [26], and HTML5 usage in general [27]. We did not identify scientific papers on HTML5 in the context of app development besides a paper by MELAMED & CLAYTON [28]. The authors compare HTML5 to J2ME and native app development in the context of *pervasive media applications*. They find that HTML is a "good solution" for "creating and distributing most pervasive media applications" [28]. Only few non-scientific sources exist that develop proof-of-concept apps [29,30].

It is not feasible to review papers on smart grids or on smart meter devices. A myriad of articles exist but they are beyond the scope of this work since all facets of smart metering are addressed. From the relevant papers, some address distinctive implementation issues (e.g. [31,32]) or software that concerns its embedding into infrastructures (for instance [33]). However, these approaches have little in common with our app.

The work presented by WEISS, MATTERN, GRAML, STAAKE, & FLEISCH [34] is similar to ours. They propose a Web-based API to access smart meters and visualize data on mobile phones. The device used appears to be an iPhone; however, WEISS et al. focus on smart metering aspects rather than on the app itself. Therefore, their work and ours are complementary. WASSERMAN [35] compiled a short article on "software engineering issues" for app development. He thereby predicts some of our findings.

Many smart meter apps can be identified that have not been developed with scientific progress in mind. We expect that several proof-of-concept apps exist that are not publicly described. Two free examples are Google PowerMeter [36] and Vattenfall Smart

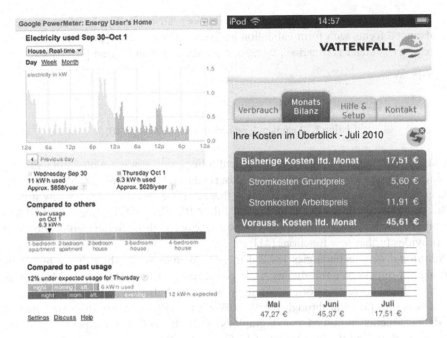

Fig. 1. Google PowerMeter [36] and Vattenfall Smart Meter App [37]

Meter App [37]. They are depicted in Figure 1. Google PowerMeter is a Webapp that allows users to view energy consumption by day, week, or month. It also provides some predictive analysis. The app is based on Web technology. It offers a lot of functionality, is well-documented, and has an open API. Unfortunately, it has been discontinued. The Vattenfall solution is a native app for iOS. Both apps are similar in concept to our work although not using any advanced technology for cross-platform development.

3   Technological Background

HTML5 is expected to change the Web's technological landscape [38]. The term HTML5 is usually understood in a broad sense that covers the core markup specification as well as other Web standards, technologies, and APIs [39]. This definition is also assumed in this paper even though some aspects are actually published in separate specifications.[2]

Differences between HTML4 and HTML5 have been compiled into a concise document [40]. HTML5 features a new short document type definition to trigger standard rendering mode as well as a shorter charset definition as shown in Listing 1. It adds, changes, and removes several elements and attributes, including new semantic sectioning elements such as `<header>`, `<footer>`, `<section>`, `<article>`, `<nav>`,

---

[2] Please note that we name several APIs that HTML5 relies on. We do not cite their specification since there are links in the HTML5 specification [6] and detailed coverage is outside the scope of this work.

and <figure> as well as custom data (data-*) attributes. Furthermore, it speci-fies advanced forms with form validation and several new input types including tel, search, url, email, number, range, color, date and time [40].

```
<!DOCTYPE html>
<html>
    <head>
        <meta charset="utf-8">
```

Listing 1. Document type and charset definition [40]

Classic Web applications lacked persistent, client side storage with sufficient size. Cookies and proprietary solutions like IE UserData or Adobe Flash Local Shared Objects have severe limitations. With HTML5, there are five specifications for new storage APIs: Web Storage, Indexed Database API, File API, Web SQL Database, and Offline Web applications. HTML5 also allows device access e.g. through the Geolocation API and provides further new functions [41].

Additional new technologies [39,21] include WebSockets, which bring high per-forming, bi-directional, full-duplex TCP connections; Cross Document Messaging, which enables secure cross-origin communication; and also asynchronous JavaScript, which becomes possible through the Web Workers API. A highly discussed part of HTML5 concerns multimedia and graphics with the HTML5 elements canvas, video, audio, and the integration of SVG into HTML documents. A series of new CSS3 module specifications define new styling features such as media queries, selec-tors, backgrounds and borders, as well as transformations.

Browser support for HTML5 is becoming more prevalent but is still far from com-plete [42,43]. The recommended way for finding out if a certain HTML5 feature can be used is testing every needed feature instead of general user agent (browser) detection. Details are given by PILGRIM [21]. There is also a JavaScript library called *Modernizr* that is useful for this task [39].

JavaScript is an object-oriented, interpreted, and weakly-typed programming lan-guage [44]. It has become specifically important due to the proliferation of Ajax (Asyn-chronous JavaScript and XML). Framework support greatly improves development. For example, *jQuery* is a concise, open source, cross-browser JavaScript framework that simplifies development [45]. Its current use is predominant: more than 57 % of the 10.000 most visited Web sites [46] employ it. The corresponding mobile-optimized plug-in is *jQuery Mobile* [47,48].

JSON (JavaScript Object Notation) is a simple, text-based, human-readable data-interchange format. It is language independent but based on a subset of JavaScript [44]. JSON is used as a lightweight alternative to XML, e.g. in conjunction with Ajax or RESTful Web services [49,50].

Android is an open operating system and mobile device platform based on a modi-fied Linux kernel. The main development language is Java [51]. Apps can not only be loaded from the *Android Market* but also from others sources.

iOS is Apple's system for its mobile devices. It has a layered system architecture; programming is done in Objective-C [52]. For practical development and testing, there is no alternative to a Mac running Xcode and iOS SDK. Current releases of Android and iOS support HTML5 based on the WebKit [53] layout engine.

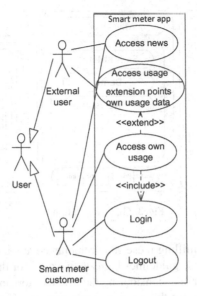

Fig. 2. Use case diagram for our prototype

4   Development of the App

In the following sections, we describe the development of the prototype by sketching the requirements, explaining the specification, and highlighting some implementation details.

4.1   Requirements Analysis

The basic idea for the project originates from an energy provider's request to *best practice consulting AG (bpc)*. However, requirements for our prototype were developed independently. The targeted case is the fictive energy providing company *EnergyXY* that has a substantial smart meter installation base and already runs a customer self-service smart meter Web portal. This portal is integrated with a comprehensive functional backend, such as *SAP for Utilities* (IS-U) [54].

The primary objective of the app is to enable customers to access their utility consumption and thereby provide cost and usage benefits, insights on consumption, environmental protection, and energy efficiency. Further goals concern cross-platform support, usability, and technology evaluation. Platforms that have to be supported are Android and iOS. However, easy extension to other mobile platforms such as Blackberry or Windows Phone should be possible.

In terms of usability, the app has to address specific mobile challenges such as users' attention span, smaller displays of various sizes and resolutions, and distinctive user interfaces (e.g. touchscreens) [55]. One important requirement is to sensibly support device orientation changes. Furthermore, the app should comply with standard UI guidelines for the target platforms such as the "iOS Human Interface Guidelines" [56] and

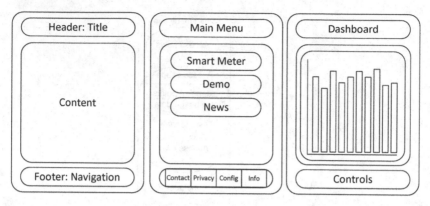

Fig. 3. GUI illustrations

"Android Design" [57]. Fulfilling these requirements covers a majority of mobile usability issues. However, these guidelines focus native apps for the specific platform and
partly contradict each other, e.g. considering the usage of top and bottom bars.

The identified use cases for the app are summarized in Figure 2. The app should
enable access to consumption data and news provided by EnergyXY. It should also
provide a *demo mode* with random (but plausible) data. According to the use cases, a
data model and a first GUI sketch were created. The latter is shown in Figure 3.

4.2 Design

The high-level sketch of the application architecture is shown in Figure 4. There is no
direct connection between the smartphone and the smart meter assumed. Please note
that there actually may be multiple (intermediary) information systems on the right
hand side. The internal architecture of the app follows the hybrid approach, falling in
between a native app and a Webapp. Native apps offer amenities in terms of device
feature access, performance, marketing, and sales advantages through *app stores*. Webapps are beneficial in terms of portability, development costs, asset specificity, and
development cycle and update cycle time [58,15].

Two trends decrease the differences between the two alternatives and make it possible to combine advantages of both. Firstly, new Web technologies such as HTML5
provide features that enable offline applications, increase performance, enable device
access, and provide user interfaces (UI) that come close to those of native apps. Secondly, it is possible to embed a Web application into a native application, thus forming
a hybrid application. These are also known as *embedded apps*, which internally use the
browser to render Web content but provide access to device features [15]. We chose
a hybrid approach as it combines the advantages and balances the features of both alternatives. Such apps can be distributed via online market stores and are portable in
nature.

The development of hybrid applications can be dramatically simplified with the use
of frameworks such as *PhoneGap* [7], *Rhodes* [59], or *Appcelerator Titanium* [16]. All
of these are free and support at least Android and iOS. They require knowledge of

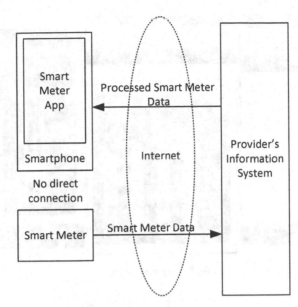

Fig. 4. Simple smart meter architecture

HTML, JavaScript, and CSS (as well as Ruby in case of Rhodes); knowledge of native device programming is not necessary. PhoneGap was chosen due to having greater platform support (including iOS, Android, Blackberry, WebOS, Windows Phone, Symbian, and Bada) [60], an active development community, a comprehensive API of exposed native features, and good documentation (cf. [58,7]). PhoneGap is gaining attention with dedicated books that appeared in late 2011 and early 2012 [61,62,63]. It has recently been contributed as an Apache project under the name *Apache Cordova* [64]. PhoneGap was originally created by Nitobi Software, which recently has been acquired by Adobe [65].

The design of the UI was mainly influenced by choosing a framework that supports interfaces for mobile Webapps *and* hybrid apps. We compared *jQuery Mobile* [8] and *Sencha Touch* [66]. jQuery Mobile is a jQuery plug-in and focuses Web UI programming through semantic markup (HTML) for a wide range of platforms (iOS, Android, Windows Phone, WebOS, Blackberry, Meego, and Symbian [67]). In contrast, UI definition in Sencha Touch is soley done in JavaScript, without a single manually written HTML element within the document body. Platform support is limited to iOS, Android and Blackberry. We chose jQuery Mobile because it is lightweight, allows basic Web frontend programming, and supports more platforms. It offers several UI components that are optimized for touch interaction on a multitude of screens and devices. Examples include toolbars at the top or bottom of a page, various buttons and other form elements, and list views. Moreover, it provides a comprehensive page, dialog, and navigation model as well as various animations.

In Figure 5, screen sketches of the application are depicted. They include the main menu and the dashboard with a yearly and a monthly chart. In the two dashboard views, different options for the selection of the time interval were compared. The second

Fig. 5. Screen sketches

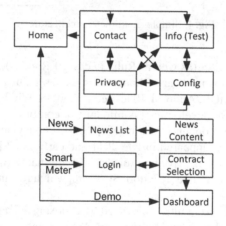

Fig. 6. Click graph for our prototype

solution with the navigation bar at the bottom was favored because of its visual consistency with the main menu. Possible navigation paths are visualized in a click graph (Figure 6).

For the generation of charts, we compared three different JavaScript charting libraries: *jqPlot* [68], *Highcharts* [69], and *gRaphaël* [70]. Highcharts was chosen because is provides highly interactive charts including animation during chart construction, click event handling, zooming, and mouseover events (e.g. for tooltips). It offers various chart types, a comprehensive API, good documentation and easily integrates with jQuery [69].

To improve accessibility, the app uses *progressive enhancement*, which is also employed in jQuery Mobile [71]. This approach starts with a basic version with simple markup that provides a functional experience that is compatible with most browsers, platforms, and devices. Then, layers that enhance the functional experience are progressively added. The advantages of progressive enhancement are universal access, cleaner and more modular code, a single code base, and compatibility [71].

In order to realize loosely coupled, interoperable, and reusable communication between the smart meter app and the backend, Web services are generally suitable. However, rather than SOAP-based services, our app uses REST HTTP services [72,50,49] that limit the available operations to the HTTP protocol. They offer advantages in terms of performance and simplicity. JSON as the data format offers similar advantages over XML. It considerably eases parsing to JavaScript objects and has minimal overhead. Both decisions are well suited to the small scale of the developed app. JSON Schema [73] was used to define the interface. Instead of using an annotation-based approach found in JAX-RS implementations (Java API for RESTful Web Services [74]) and Spring MVC 3 [75], a simple Java backend application using hand-written servlets is sufficient. It provides services for login as well as retrieval of smart meter data and news.

Smart meter data is stored on the device. Out of the five possibilities introduced in Section 3, Web SQL is discontinued [76] and Indexed Database API is not yet supported on iOS and Android. We selected Web storage in the form of local storage, which is a simple key value store in the browser with a typical maximum size of 5 MB (increasable upon request) [21]. It is suitable for JSON formatted data conforming to the defined JSON schema.

4.3   Implementation

For the first prototype Android and iOS were selected as target platforms. Regarding the environment a Mac with Xcode and iOS SDK was used for iOS; for Android, the Android SDK was utilized along with the Android Developer Tools and Eclipse. In Listing 2, loading of the front page of the app is defined. In non-PhoneGap Android applications, the activity would simply inherit from the `Activity` class. In case of a PhoneGap app, it inherits from the PhoneGap provided class `DroidGap`. Invoking `onCreate()` loads the entry page of the Webapp. This is the only native Java Code that needs to be changed for running a PhoneGap application on Android. The remainder of the logic of PhoneGap—in particular the interfaces and implementations for providing device features—is bundled with the Java archive `phonegap.jar` and the JavaScript source `phonegap.0.9.5.js`. Furthermore, some changes will need to be applied to `AndroidManifest.xml`, concerning metadata and permissions. For the iOS application, the only change necessary was the definition of the supported interface orientations.

```java
public class SmartMeterActivity extends DroidGap {
    // Called when the activity is first created.
    @Override
    public void onCreate(Bundle savedInstanceState){
        super.onCreate(savedInstanceState);
        super.loadUrl("file:////www/index.html");
    }
}
```

Listing 2. Loading of the front page of the Android app [77]

The Webapp is independent of the platform; the same code was used for Android and iOS. It uses a single HTML file with multiple internal pages that are part of jQuery Mobile's page model. jQuery Mobile handles dynamic *show* and *hide* of multiple pages via JavaScript and CSS. Pages requested via Ajax are instantly available. The markup for an internal page are nested `<div>` elements with `data-role` attributes `page`, `header`, `content` and `footer`.

The implemented internal pages correspond to the GUI Model and are connected as shown in Figure 6. jQuery Mobile uses various other custom data attributes for defining the user interface, such as dialogs, links, transitions, list views, and navigation bars. The JavaScript code has to wait for PhoneGap to complete loading before making API calls to it. The respective event is called `deviceready`. Afterwards, native features can be accessed via the PhoneGap API [78]. An example of using *vibration* is given in Listing 3. The click event on the button with the identifier `btnVibrate` is caught and the PhoneGap function `navigator.notification.vibrate` is called. The parameter defines the vibration length in milliseconds.

```
$('#btnVibrate').click(function () {
    navigator.notification.vibrate(1000);
});
```

Listing 3. Example for using vibration

jQuery Mobile detects device orientation changes and redraws the page using the `orientationchange` event. The earlier definitions of supported screen sizes for Android and iOS merely enabled the possibility of orientation changes but not the correct adaption of the content.

In order to load and display smart meter data, a `SmartMeterDataService` generates a statistical distribution of smart meter readings, aggregates them to the requested time scale, converts to the requested type and unit (e.g. consumption in kWh or CO_2 pollution in kg) and finally returns a JSON String to the responsible servlet. The mobile application requests this data through the jQuery Ajax function `$.ajax(...)`, stores it via `window.localStorage.setItem(...)`, and parses it to a JavaScript object via `$.parseJSON(...)` so that Highcharts is able to process and draw it.

5   Evaluation and Discussion

To reflect our work, we discuss our findings, their implications, and current limitations.

5.1   Considering the App

The home screen of the app is used as the starting point for navigation (see Figure 6). jQuery Mobile's dialogs were used for notification in case of errors, for example due to a missing network connection during login, contract selection, or loading of new data. All other operations are available offline. The login screen uses an HTML5 email form field for which iOS provides an adapted conveniently usable on-screen keyboard with direct availability of the @ and the *dot* key. On the news screen, current news are displayed in a scrollable list view.

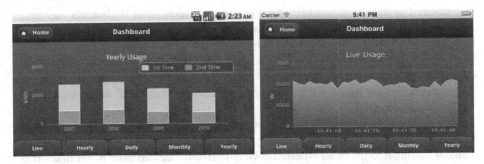

Fig. 7. Comparing the Android and iOS interfaces

Figure 7 shows the dashboard of the app in landscape mode on the Android emulator (left) and the iPhone 4 simulator (right). Android shows data aggregated to years, differentiated between daytime (yellow) and nighttime (blue). Clicking columns yields a detailed time scale. Tooltips appear if a *touch and hold* gesture is performed on a column. The legend allows click events to show or hide a time zone using an animation. The iPhone shows a live view, which updates every two seconds. For a live view in a productive app, direct connection to the meter would be required; we thus used simulated data (cf. Figure 4).

The app satisfies the main aim of giving customers feedback on consumption. It runs cross-platform on Android and iOS. Extension to other platforms is possible due to the compatibility of PhoneGap and jQuery Mobile. Usability requirements were largely met. The app adapts to different screen sizes and resolutions regarding e.g. button sizes, device orientation, and animations. Moreover, it effectively utilizes the touchscreen.

The cross-platform development has highlighted the relevance of continuous testing against all platforms for several reasons: having a single code base for the embedded Webapp, the fact that bugs might be present or reproducible on only one platform, the observation that (framework) patches lead to ambiguous effects, and the low maturity of jQuery Mobile at the beginning of development (versions Alpha 2 to Alpha 4.1). Manual testing was performed on the Android emulator (versions 2.1 to 2.3.3 with various screen resolutions), two physical Android devices (HTC Desire HD running Android 2.2, HTC Legend running Android 2.1), the iOS simulator 4.2, an iPhone 4 running iOS 4.2.1, and various desktop browsers on Windows XP and Mac OS X 10.6. In addition to manual testing, Selenium [79] was used for automated frontend testing. Debugging was done using Android Dalvik Debug Monitor Service (DDMS), Xcode Instruments, Firebug [80], Chrome and Safari built-in developer tools, and the iPhone simulator Web debugging console. These tools were very useful to us; however, an elaborate discussion is outside the scope of this work.

Problems encountered during development concerned stability, performance, and UI differences. A special problem was the fixed positioning of the lower navigation bar, which is a prominent feature for native (looking) apps, especially on iOS. The jQuery Mobile implementation had severe bugs, which were mostly fixed in subsequent versions. The navigation bar was either shown multiple times, displaced, or did not stay at a fixed position while scrolling. Main performance issues were memory usage and processing speed of animations. Extensive memory usage of Highcharts could partly be countered against by manual freeing operations. It seems that Highcharts' resource consumption is designed primarily for PCs. Performance on the Android emulator was unsatisfactory. This did not vary noticeably with the SDK version or assigned main memory size of the emulator. The performance test on the HTC Legend was acceptable; performance on the HTC Desire HD was considerably better. Updates of jQuery Mobile up to version Alpha 4.1 showed noticeable improvements in all configurations (not limited to Android).

On a device running iOS, the device orientation change is shown with a smoother transition than on Android. In fact, the iPhone 4 had a general performance advantage, even comparing it to the faster Android device. Performance was even better in the iOS simulator, which does *not* emulate the iPhone hardware. As expected, best results were seen on desktop browsers. However, these were not a development target and were only tested for the sake of comparison.

5.2 Evaluation of the Design

The decision for a hybrid application was made for reasons including (1) device access, (2) evaluation of new technologies, (3) portability, (4) offline availability, and (5) access to online market stores. During the design phase of the app it turned out that only few device features (1) were actually necessary. Both versions use device orientation change, retrieve device information, and show native notifications. The latter are either audible (beeps), tactile (vibrations), or visual (popup windows). However, they were only used for testing and demonstration. An example is the visual native notification of device information loaded by a call to the PhoneGap API (Figure 8).

Use of new technologies (2) and portability (3) are achievable without PhoneGap, solely by means of HTML5 and jQuery Mobile. Offline availability (4) would also be possible with HTML5 although slightly more complex. The majority of the features of PhoneGap were not used because they were not required by the app. This means that a mobile Webapp using the HTML5 offline cache may have also sufficed.

An important remaining question is to weigh the advantages of the marketing and distribution opportunities of the app stores (5) against the disadvantages of additional development complexity and the time and costs of registration as well as review processes. For a non-free application, the decision is simple: a hybrid app would be preferable because setting up a payment system that is accepted by a considerable number of customers is difficult. At the moment, smart meter applications are usually offered for free (cf. Section 2). They are financed through earnings from the smart metering product. Therefore, currently a Webapp is sufficient. However, an extension of scope to advanced topics such as smart homes, smart grids, e-mobility, or even augmented reality could profit from using additional device features such as cameras or other additional sensors.

One aim of HTML5 and Webapps is to make device features available and reduce the need for native apps. Consequently, frameworks such as PhoneGap are transitional technologies but likely to ultimately become obsolete. To a high extent, HTML5 is already usable. Many functions are stable. Local storage, custom data attributes, new form elements, and canvas (through Highcharts) were used in the implementation. However, due

Fig. 8. Android and iOS native popup windows

to incomplete universal support for many features, it is not seen as a general solution, yet [81].

Native apps will always perform better in comparison to Webapps. However, it is unclear whether these differences will continue to be relevant for the majority of apps. For performance intensive applications such as 3D games, there will likely continue to be certain performance considerations. Most others will be realizable using Webapps. POGUE [82] argues that mobile Webapps are only a bridge technology, i.e. to bridge the gap after the release of the iPhone until the opening of Apple's app store. He predicted that they would vanish again [82]. We do not share this estimation. Strong evidence for the success of standards can be seen in the success of Web applications on non-mobile devices.

5.3 Discussion of Frameworks Decisions

The decisions for PhoneGap and jQuery Mobile proved to be reasonable except for some stability issues due to limited maturity (especially for the latter). By now, Phone-Gap 1.8.1 and jQuery Mobile 1.1.0 are available, offering stability and performance improvements, new features, and expanded platform support.

jQuery was mainly used for event handling and Ajax communication, where it performed well. However, the release of jQuery 1.5 with a rewritten Ajax implementation broke jQuery Mobile's Ajax navigation when combined with PhoneGap. This was rapidly fixed with version 1.5.1. A problem with Highcharts on Android (*SVG* compatibility) could be solved by falling back to an older release (Highcharts 1), which uses HTML5 canvas.

5.4   Limitations

Due to the novelty of our research and the use of many technologies that have not yet been assessed in a scientific context, our work has limitations. The backend did not yet use real data. Connecting with SAP backend systems [54] or a third party meter data system using e.g. Web services is a feasible task, though. More detailed and rigorous evaluation of the usability and the efficiency of the application is required. A comparative implementation with Sencha Touch or new Web application frameworks (e.g. app-UI [83] and kendoUI [84]), or in pure HTML5 without any framework usage would be insightful. Nevertheless, neither of the limitations detracts the significance of our findings and the recommendations made.

6   Conclusions and Future Work

We presented work on an app that was developed for multiple platforms. While many new technologies have emerged and several ways of developing hybrid apps have been proposed, there is no *universal* solution, yet. Consequently, we did not identify a large body of work that was directly related to our scenario, a smart meter app. Development of our prototype using PhoneGap, jQuery Mobile, and HTML5 has been described in detail. We presented notable insights about this way of building hybrid apps. In conclusion, our choice of technology is viable and advisable for similar projects. However, we expect rapid progress and predict that many of the current approaches will be succeeded by standardized technology. At the same time, new frameworks might enable hybrid apps in currently unsupported fields.

The novelty of the used technologies underlines a need for future work. We need to keep track of the development and keep pace with emerging mobile Web technologies. Future questions do not only concern the technical dimension. Usability and value for users also need to be assessed. It needs to be investigated how apps will be used in the future, and how the business plans for app development could look like. Nevertheless, there still will be a variety of technical problems to be solved. It is without question that the future development in this field will be exciting even though (or probably *because*) it is hard to be predicted.

Future work could comprise extension to more platforms, inclusion of additional features, and more detailed evaluations. Eventually, testing should be executed by actual users. Despite being only an example in this work, research on smart metering is a very interesting area, and yet demanding. Our work will include the evaluation of other frameworks and approaches for hybrid development (also cf. [19]). We intend to become able to provide project-specific advice on technology and framework selection.

Acknowledgements. We would like to thank Marc Fischer and Florian Blenkle from best practice consulting AG for inspiring this paper's topic, for professional support, and for helpful discussions. Furthermore, we are grateful for stylistic suggestions made by Tim Kane and Veronika Hassel.

References

1. Macedonia, M.: iPhones Target the Tech Elite. Computer 40, 94–95 (2007)
2. Mobile Internetnutzung über das Handy 2010 stark gestiegen (2012),
   http://www.destatis.de/jetspeed/portal/cms/Sites/destatis/
   Internet/DE/Presse/pm/2011/02/PD11_060_63931/
3. Gartner Says Worldwide Mobile Application Store Revenue Forecast to Surpass $15 Billion
   in 2011 (2012), http://www.gartner.com/it/page.jsp?id=1529214
4. Dijkstra, E.W.: The Humble Programmer. Communications of the ACM 15, 859–866 (1972)
5. Logan, S.: Gtk+ Programming in C. Prentice Hall, Upper Saddle River (2001)
6. HTML5 (2012), http://www.w3.org/TR/html5/
7. PhoneGap (2012), http://www.phonegap.com/
8. jQuery Mobile (2012), http://jquerymobile.com/
9. Popa, M., Ciocarlie, H., Popa, A.S., Racz, M.B.: Smart metering for monitoring domestic
   utilities. In: Proc. INES 2010, pp. 43–48. IEEE Press (2010)
10. Javadi, S., Javadi, S.: Steps to smart grid realization. In: Proc. CEA 2010, pp. 223–228.
    WSEAS, Stevens Point (2010)
11. Knab, S., Strunz, K., Lehmann, H.: Smart grid. TU Berlin (2010)
12. Meehan, E.: The smart grid: the smart choice? In: Proc. InfoSecCD 2010, pp. 173–176.
    ACM, New York (2010)
13. Lee, J., Park, G.L., Kim, S.W., Kim, H.J., Sung, C.O.: Power consumption scheduling for
    peak load reduction in smart grid homes. In: Proc. SAC 2011, pp. 584–588. ACM, New York
    (2011)
14. Gnilka, A., Meyer-Spasche, J., Folta, N.: Smart Metering. LBD-Beratungsgesellschaft
    (2009)
15. Barney, L.S.: Developing Hybrid Applications for the iPhone. Addison-Wesley (2009)
16. Appcelerator (2012), http://www.appcelerator.com/
17. XMLVM (2012), http://www.xmlvm.org/
18. applause (2012), https://github.com/applause/
19. Heitkötter, H., Hanschke, S., Majchrzak, T.A.: Comparing cross-platform development ap-
    proaches for mobile applications. In: Proc. 8th International Conference on Web Information
    Systems and Technologies, WEBIST. SciTePress (2012)
20. Allen, S., Graupera, V., Lundrigan, L.: Pro Smartphone Cross-Platform Development:
    iPhone, Blackberry, Windows Mobile and Android Development and Distribution. Apress
    (2010)
21. Pilgrim, M.: HTML5: Up and Running. O'Reilly (2010)
22. Oehlman, D., Blanc, S.: Pro Android Web Apps: Develop for Android using HTML5, CSS3
    & JavaScript. Apress (2011)
23. Layon, K.: The Web Designer's Guide to iOS Apps. New Riders Pub., Thousand Oaks (2010)
24. Di Cerbo, F., Dodero, G., Papaleo, L.: Integrating a Web3D interface into an e-learning plat-
    form. In: Proc. Web3D 2010, pp. 83–92. ACM, New York (2010)
25. Pfeiffer, S., Parker, C.: Accessibility for the HTML5 <video> element. In: Proc. W4A 2009,
    pp. 98–100. ACM, New York (2009)
26. Aghaee, S., Pautasso, C.: Mashup development with HTML5. In: Proc. Mashups 2009/2010,
    pp. 10:1–10:8. ACM, New York (2010)
27. Harjono, J., Ng, G., Kong, D., Lo, J.: Building smarter web applications with HTML5. In:
    Proc. CASCON 2010, pp. 402–403. ACM, New York (2010)
28. Melamed, T., Clayton, B.: A Comparative Evaluation of HTML5 as a Pervasive Media Plat-
    form. In: Phan, T., Montanari, R., Zerfos, P. (eds.) MobiCASE 2009. LNICST, vol. 35, pp.
    307–325. Springer, Heidelberg (2010)

29. Rogers, R.: Developing portable mobile web applications. Linux J. 2010 (2010)
30. Suhonos, M.J.: Building a Location-aware Mobile Search Application with Z39.50 and HTML5. Code4Lib (2010)
31. Song, K., Seo, D., Park, H., Lee, H., Perrig, A.: OMAP: One-Way Memory Attestation Protocol for Smart Meters. In: Proc. ISPAW 2011, pp. 111–118. IEEE CS, Washington, DC (2011)
32. McLaughlin, S., Podkuiko, D., Delozier, A., Miadzvezhanka, S., McDaniel, P.: Embedded firmware diversity for smart electric meters. In: Proc. HotSec 2010, pp. 1–8. USENIX Association, Berkeley (2010)
33. Capodieci, N., Pagani, G.A., Cabri, G., Aiello, M.: Smart meter aware domestic energy trading agents. In: Proc. IEEMC 2011, pp. 1–10. ACM, New York (2011)
34. Weiss, M., Mattern, F., Graml, T., Staake, T., Fleisch, E.: Handy feedback: connecting smart meters with mobile phones. In: Proc. MUM 2009, pp. 1–4. ACM, New York (2009)
35. Wasserman, A.I.: Software engineering issues for mobile application development. In: Proc. FoSER 2010, pp. 397–400. ACM, New York (2010)
36. Google PowerMeter's first device partner (2012),
    http://googleblog.blogspot.com/2009/10/
    google-powermeters-first-device-partner.html
37. Vattenfall Smart Meter App (2012),
    http://itunes.apple.com/de/app/id381931965/
38. Vaughan-Nichols, S.J.: Will HTML 5 Restandardize the Web? Computer 43, 13–15 (2010)
39. Lubbers, P., Albers, B., Smith, R., Salim, F.: Pro HTML5 Programming. Apress (2010)
40. HTML5 differences from HTML4 (2012), http://www.w3.org/TR/html5-diff/
41. Device APIs Working Group (2012), http://www.w3.org/2009/dap/
42. HTML5 Test Suite Conformance Results (2012),
    http://w3c-test.org/html/tests/reporting/report.html
43. The HTML5 test (2012), http://html5test.com/
44. Crockford, D.: JavaScript: The Good Parts. O'Reilly (2008)
45. Steyer, R.: jQuery. Addison-Wesley (2010)
46. jQuery Usage Trends (2012),
    http://trends.builtwith.com/javascript/JQuery/
47. Reid, J.: jQuery Mobile. O'Reilly (2011)
48. Firtman, M.: jQuery Mobile: Up and Running. O'Reilly (2011)
49. Richardson, L., Ruby, S.: Restful Web Services. O'Reilly (2007)
50. Webber, J., Parastatidis, S., Robinson, I.: REST in Practice. O'Reilly (2010)
51. Ableson, F., Collins, C., Sen, R.: Unlocking Android. Manning, Greenwich (2009)
52. Neuburg, M.: Programming iOS 4. O'Reilly (2011)
53. WebKit (2012), http://www.webkit.org/
54. Frederick, J., Zierau, T.: SAP for Utilities. SAP Press, Bonn (2011)
55. Bieh, M.: Mobiles Webdesign. Galileo Press (2008)
56. iOS Human Interface Guidelines (2012),
    http://developer.apple.com/library/ios/DOCUMENTATION/
    UserExperience/Conceptual/MobileHIG/MobileHIG.pdf
57. Android Design (2012), http://developer.android.com/design/
58. Stark, J.: Building Android Apps with HTML, CSS, and JavaScript. O'Reilly (2010)
59. Rhodes (2012), http://rhomobile.com/products/rhodes/
60. PhoneGap Supported Features (2012), http://phonegap.com/about/features/
61. Ghatol, R., Patel, Y.: Beginning PhoneGap: Mobile Web Framework for JavaScript and HTML5. Apress (2012)
62. Lunny, A.: PhoneGap Beginner's Guide. Packt Pub. (2011)

63. Myer, T.: Beginning PhoneGap. Wrox (2011)
64. Apache Cordova (2012), http://incubator.apache.org/cordova/
65. Adobe: Adobe Announces Agreement to Acquire Nitobi (2011),
    http://www.adobe.com/aboutadobe/pressroom/pressreleases/
    201110/AdobeAcquiresNitobi.html
66. Sencha Touch (2012), http://www.sencha.com/products/touch/
67. Mobile Graded Browser Support (2012), http://jquerymobile.com/gbs/
68. jqPlot (2012), http://www.jqplot.com/
69. Highcharts JS (2012), http://www.highcharts.com/
70. gRaphaël (2012), http://g.raphaeljs.com/
71. Parker, T.: Designing with Progressive Enhancement. New Riders (2010)
72. Fielding, R.T.: Architectural Styles and the Design of Network-based Software Architectures. PhD thesis, University of California, Irvine (2000)
73. JSON Schema (2012), http://json-schema.org/
74. Burke, B.: RESTful Java with JAX-RS. O'Reilly (2010)
75. Walls, C.: Spring in Action. Manning (2011)
76. Web SQL Database (2012), http://dev.w3.org/html5/webdatabase/
77. PhoneGap Get Started Guide (2012),
    http://www.phonegap.com/start/#android
78. PhoneGap API Reference (2012), http://docs.phonegap.com/
79. Selenium (2012), http://seleniumhq.org/
80. Firebug (2012), http://getfirebug.com/
81. Mobile Web Metrics Report H2/2011 (2011),
    http://www.netbiscuits.com/mobile-metrics-report-2011/
82. Pogue, D.: iPhone: the Missing Manual. O'Reilly (2007)
83. app-UI (2012), http://triceam.github.com/app-UI/
84. Kendo UI (2012), http://www.kendoui.com/

A Simulation-Based Method for Eliciting Requirements of Online CIB Systems

Alexandre Parra Carneiro da Silva and Celso Massaki Hirata

Technological Institute of Aeronautics
Department of Electrical Engineering and Computer Science
Praça Marechal Eduardo Gomes, 50, Vila das Acácias, São José dos Campos, Brazil
{parra,hirata}@ita.br

Abstract. Many approaches for requirements elicitation have been proposed to help the design of virtual collaborative systems. The design of virtual collaborative systems with CIB activities presents a challenge due to the needs of users to process, interpret, and share information collaboratively. However, most of the design approaches fail in capturing the users' needs, because they are not designed to capture precisely the main users' activities during the interplay between 'collaboration' and 'information'. This paper describes a requirement elicitation method that captures the interactions of potential users in collaborative environments considering CIB activities. The method is based on the simulation of activities it was employed in the design of a virtual collaborative system - a collaborative puzzle - in order to illustrate its usage.

Keywords: CIB, Collaborative system, Requirements elicitation, Simulation, Virtual Teams.

1   Introduction

Collaboration is an essential aspect of many types of daily activities [1]. One activity that is central to people's personal and professional lives is information seeking [1]. An important factor of Collaborative Information Seeking (CIS) practice is to make sense of the information found, i.e., Collaborative Sensemaking (CS) [2],[3]. CS is the process whereby individuals process information, integrate and interpret it and through social interaction they share their understandings [2]. The objective of process CS is to provide a shared understanding about information, goals, priorities and problems that individuals face in collaborative settings to make decisions and act effectively. Without some shared knowledge base or an effective interaction between team members, severe gaps are likely to occur in the understanding of reality [4].

The research area of Collaborative Information Behavior (CIB) has received increased interest in recent years [1]. The CIB area concerns about the behavior exhibited when people work together with information to gain a better understanding of various activities such as CIS, CS and others that happen at the interplay between 'collaboration' and 'information' [1].

It is hard to define requirements for an ideal collaborative environment, because they depend on the organization, context, problem, participants and other factors [5]. There

J. Cordeiro and K.-H. Krempels (Eds.): WEBIST 2012, LNBIP 140, pp. 34–52, 2013.

are some agreements on the characterization of a collaborative environment. Dargan in [6] proposes seven capabilities that a collaborative environment should have. In turn, Baasch in [5] adds two more capabilities to the Dargan's list. Among the capabilities there are some that are directly related to the interplay of 'information' and 'collaboration', such as: rapidly find the right people with the right expertise; build, find, and exchange information across organizational boundaries; deliver the right information to the right people as soon as it is available, and keep a record of all collaborations for further reference.

A collaborative system is one where multiple users or agents are engaged in a shared activity, usually from remote locations. Comparing with other distributed systems, collaborative systems are distinguished by the fact that the agents are working together towards a common goal and have a critical need to interact closely with each other [7]. To achieve this distinction, collaborative systems should have effective mechanisms for communication, coordination, cooperation and awareness. According to [8], Communication consists of the exchange of information in negotiations among people; Coordination is related to the management of people, their activities and resources; and Cooperation is the production that takes place in the shared workspace. The participants obtain feedback from their actions and feed through from the actions of their companions by means of awareness information related to the interaction among participants.

Räsänen and Nyce [9] argue that many systems have failed because developers have neglected the social context where technology is used. Social context is formed by actors and relationships among them. The correct identification of actors and relationships among them may help developers to better understand how software technology should be inserted in such context [10]. The success of an information system depends on the quality of the definition of requirements [10]. The quality of the requirements is greatly influenced by techniques employed during requirements elicitation [11]. Requirements elicitation techniques are methods used by analysts to determine the needs of customers and users, so that systems can be built with a high probability of satisfying those needs [12]. However, consensus exists that one elicitation technique cannot work for all situations [13],[14],[15],[12]. There are lots of requirements elicitation techniques described in literature [16],[13],[14],[15],[17].

In our survey of the elicitation of requirements, we have not found techniques that take into account the needs of users in collaborative environments considering CIB activities. The understanding of user needs in such contexts is essential to provide mechanisms for effective collaboration. We believe that a technique that focuses on the understanding of the actors during their activities in a collaborative environment in order to fully take advantage of the synergy among stakeholders to achieve common goals is required.

This paper presents a method for requirements elicitation in collaborative environments that is focused on the observation of actors interacting to perform activities that occur in the interplay between collaboration and information. The method allows stakeholders in the design of collaborative systems to achieve a more effective requirements elicitation by capturing the needs of users whose collaborative activities are investigated. The method is based on the simulation of the targeted collaborative system. In the simulation, restrictions and permissions are defined to the participating users in order to provide a close environment of the target system whereby the interactions among them can be monitored.

The remainder of the paper is structured as follows. Section 2 presents definitions, concepts about CIB, the difficulty of requirements elicitation, and the related work. Section 3 describes the proposed method for requirements elicitation. The application of proposed method is showed in section 4, more specifically, we present the experimental environment wherein the experiments were carried out, results of experimentations, and analysis of results. In section 5 we analyze the proposed method. Section 6 concludes the paper and discusses future work.

2 Background

In recent years, researchers from a diverse range of disciplines conducted various studies [18],[19],[4],[1] within organizational and non-organizational settings and have provided many key insights about activities that happen at the interplay between 'collaboration' and 'information' [20]. To integrate the various terminologies associated with Collaborative Information Behavior (CIB) in the studies, Karunakaran et al. in [20] define a working definition of CIB as "totality of behavior exhibited when people work together to identify an information need, retrieve, seek and share information, evaluate, synthesize and make sense of the found information, and then utilize the found information".

Among the activities that comprise the behaviors investigated in CIB, those underlined above, the activity sensemaking is a critical element of collaborative work [4],[1]. Sensemaking is the process through which individuals view and interpret the world and then act accordingly [4]. Sensemaking determines the way in which people respond to certain events and construe their perceptions regarding goals, priorities and problems they face [4]. Convergent evidence shows that Collaborative Sensemaking (CS) cross-cuts the other activities within CIB [1]. CS occurs when multiple actors with possibly different perspectives about the world engage in the process of making sense of 'messy' information [21],[22] to come at shared understandings [4] and then to act accordingly for coming more near their common goal. CS is an important aspect of Collaborative Information Seeking (CIS) [1]. CIS is defined as "the study of systems and practices that enable individuals to collaborate during the seeking, searching, and retrieval of information" [19]. CIS occurs when "a group or team of people undertakes to identify and resolve a shared information need." [18]. Resolving a shared information need often consists of finding, retrieving, sharing, understanding, and using information together [23]. Reddy and colleagues in two investigations in healthcare providers environments identify some reasons that lead to the occurrence of CS, such as [24],[1]: ambiguity of available information, role-based distribution of information, lack of domain expertise, complexity of information need, and lack of immediately accessible information. CS involves tasks whereby individuals: share information and sense, prioritize relevant information, contextualize awareness information with respect to activities, and create and manipulate shared representations [23].

The construction of software system requires a software development process that includes the following phases: requirements elicitation, design, implementation, verification and maintenance. We believe that one of main difficulties in the process is to correctly elicit the requirements due to the needs of individuals in CS.

As Sommerville and Ransom in [25], the goal of the requirements elicitation is to understand the real needs of the users which must be supported by the software to be developed. During the requirement elicitation phase, the stakeholders exchange information about the context and the activities that will be supported by the software under development [26]. Laporti and colleagues also comment that this phase is seldom problem free. Viewpoint, mental model and expectation differences among users and analysts make this task hard and conflicting. Sommerville in [27] points out that problems in this phase are responsible for 55% of computer systems' troubles and that 82% of the effort devoted to correcting mistakes is related to this phase. Some techniques that consider social context are proposed to elicit requirements of collaborative systems as shown in [12],[28],[29],[30]. Machado et al. in [30] propose a method to support requirements elicitation in organizations which combines traditional cognitive and ethnographic methods and focuses on the capture of the actual activities being executed in the context of the workplace. Their approach assumes that there is a difference between information obtained from stakeholders during interviews, and the rich, dynamic and complex reality of workplaces. However, their method does not take into account the collaborative interactions from the information needs and other activities that support the needs. These activities are main triggers of work in collaborative settings [18],[24],[1]. Moreover, they established some premises for using the method such as: field studies at organizations should clearly demand by improvements in existing systems, and ethical or methodological concerns are already addressed - i.e., after initial contacts and objectives clarification with users, they allow and consent the observations about their working activities. In additional, ethnography research is very time intensive and it has high costs [31].

Simulation is a technique, not a technology, to replace or amplify real experiences with guided experiences that evoke or replicate substantial aspects of the real world in a fully interactive manner [32]. A critical point that has often been missed is that the process of using simulators and simulations is a "social practice" [33]. A social practice can be defined as a contextual event in space and time, conducted for one or more purposes, in which people interact in a goal-oriented fashion with each other, with technical artifacts (the simulator), and with the environment (including relevant devices). To regard simulation as a social practice puts an appropriate emphasis on the reasons why people take part in it and how they choose to interpret the various simulation endeavors [34].

The simulation is chosen due the following advantages: conditions can be varied and outcomes investigated; critical situations can be investigated without risk; it is cost effective; simulations can be speeded up so behavior can be studied easily over a long period of time, and they can be slowed down to study behavior more closely. The simulation of the collaborative setting can be used to address types of knowledge, skills, attitudes, or behaviors that people have in specific imposed stimulus, rules or objectives. We believe that these impositions help to show potential problems and deficiencies that users may face in their collaborative environments. Thus, developers can act to solve or mitigate them through computer systems more effective in the environment. In addition, the collaborative environment can be more effective with the participation of users in the simulations because they can recognize difficulties to collaboration in poorly designed organizational processes.

Our proposed approach for requirements elicitation in collaborative settings is focused on the observation of actors interacting to perform activities that occur in the interplay between collaboration and information. The environment wherein the actors interact is simulated. We believe that this approach we provide a more effective elicitation of requirements.

3   Proposed Method

The proposed method consists of a simulation of the activities that make up CIB. We consider the following CIB activities: identify an information need; search, retrieve and share information; evaluate, synthesize and make sense of information found, and use the information found. The identification of information needs is the main factor that drives collaborative activities. In order to design the collaborative environment properly, the proposed method seeks to simulate the virtual setting emphasizing CIB activities. The simulation is made in a co-located environment with restrictions of collaborative systems artificially enforced. The idea is to monitor the users' interactions in a simulated collaborative environment, so that is possible to identify collaborative requirements and build systems. The simulation method consists of following phases whose the principal activities are outlined in Fig. 1:

– **Definition of the System, its Environment, and Restrictions and Permissions of Communication, Coordination, Cooperation, and Awareness (3C+A).** The activities are defined based on their importance for achieving the common objectives pursued in a collaborative environment. Potential users, their roles and business rules are originated from the definition of key collaborative activities (CIB and business activities) and the objectives to be achieved. The collaborative activities to be investigated in the simulation are mainly those which have intrinsically features of the interplay between collaboration and information. The restrictions and permissions of 3C+A are those that the potential users face when interacting with the actual system. The output of this simulation activity is a document describing the aforementioned items, mainly the restrictions and permissions, of the system and its environment.
– **Planning the Simulation.** Define the procedures, techniques and tools that capture and analyze user interactions during collaboration. Data are collected in order to identify both the breaks of restrictions and needs of 3C+A in the interactions. Define roles and responsibilities of researchers' team, e.g. monitors (observers) and their role for monitoring the simulation. The output is a list of procedures, techniques and tools to capture and analyze the data related to the users' interactions. The planning output also includes the definition of procedures to monitor and control the simulations.
– **Execution, Monitoring, and Control.** Execute, monitor and control the simulation, in accordance with the plan. In this activity, the potential users take part in

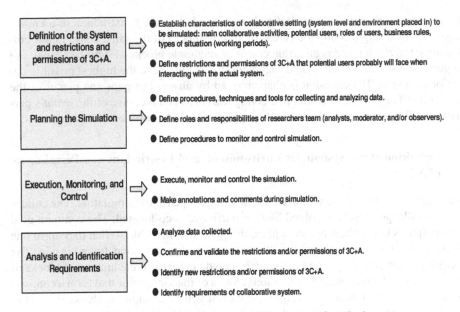

Fig. 1. Activities in the phases of the proposed method

the simulated activities whereby their interactions with the system and with other users are monitored. The outputs are information and data collected and a set of annotations describing changes accomplished during simulations.

- **Analysis and Identification of Requirements.** Analyzes the data collected previously according to the chosen procedures and techniques used and/or defined. The purpose of the analysis is both to validate the proposed restrictions and/or permissions of 3C+A and identify new needs (requisites) also related to restrictions and permissions of 3C+A. The identification of the requisites is a result of the restrictions an/or permissions that were suitably proposed and proposals of new ones according to the confirmation and validation of data collected during simulations.

4   Experiments, Results and Analysis

In order to illustrate the usage and evaluate the proposed method, we conducted experiments in a simulated collaborative workplace. The aim of the method is to find the appropriate requirements of communication, coordination, cooperation and awareness (3C+A) for the system or subsystem to be developed for the targeted collaborative environment. The (actual) collaborative environment is a Web environment whereby participants can work together to solve a puzzle challenge. In a basic puzzle, one is intended to put together pieces in a logical way in order to come up with the desired solution. Puzzles are often contrived as a form of entertainment, but they can also stem from serious mathematical or logistical problems. The type of puzzle that inspired us to create a collaborative environment for study is Tiling Puzzles. Tiling puzzles are two-dimensional packing problems in which a number of flat shapes have to be assembled into a larger given shape without overlaps (and often without gaps) [35]. Unlike tiling puzzles, the collaborative puzzle defined is not guided by the construction of a known image, but by a single contiguous area containing blocks of the same color. In our collaborative puzzle, a piece is an arrangement of rectangle blocks of defined shapes and the goal is to set the pieces in an arragement that should have the highest possible degree of cohesion. The cohesion is characterized by absence of gaps and pieces of the same color. The change of colors in a contiguous area is a measure of the teamt's performance. Below we apply the method proposed to collaborative environment target.

4.1 Definition of the System, Its Environment, and Restrictions and Permissions of 3C+A

As a result of the first phase we have the following scope for the simulation. The collaborative challenge must be resolved by four participants co-located. The common goal of participants in the challenge is to place the pieces on the table so that they form one cohesive contiguous area (puzzle) with a minimum of empty areas (gaps) inside. The pieces have different shapes and each piece is made up of different amount of blocks of the same color. Above fourteen contiguous blocks of the same color that form a contiguous area is enough to score. Therefore, the eleven yellow contiguous blocks showed in Fig. 2 is not considered a contiguous area that scores. The team earns points according to the cohesive contiguous area formed. For achieving the maximum degree of cohesion, it is necessary that the area formed by the pieces covers the available space with all blocks of the same color without any gap.

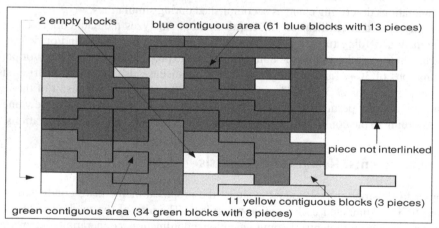

Fig. 2. Sample of single contiguous area formed with three minor contiguous areas

Private pieces are a tentative to represent the individual tacit information whereas public pieces try to represent information that is shared by the group of people. The placeholder is a simulated space that its owner has access (knowledge). The owner is restricted in its ability to show his pieces by time and amount. We discuss some restrictions/rules about actions and behaviors of participants in the challenge based on the descriptions of the main collaborative characteristics, see Table 1, and discussions about collaborative activities, both considered of the simulated collaborative setting.

Table 1. Characteristics of the simulated collaborative setting

Code	Characteristics
C1	Each participant has a number of private pieces initially and they can be presented to other participants when placed on the table.
C2	The amount of private pieces is not necessarily the same for all participants.
C3	Each participant has a placeholder (box) wherein his/her private pieces are.
C4	On a public area (table) some pieces are present from the beginning of the challenge and they are called public pieces, and any participant can access them.
C5	Private pieces presented on the table become public regardless of whether they are placed in the puzzle or not.
C6	All pieces, private or public, are made of colorful blocks.
C7	The pieces have different shapes and sizes and each piece is unicolor.

The activities identified in the collaborative environment are described in Table 2. The activities A1 - A5 were identified by the characteristics of collaborative environment of the challenge and by the common goal that has to be achieved. The activities A6 - A10 come from the probable interactions of participants in the challenge as actions or operations that support the activities A1 - A5. As described, we consider the private pieces like information and knowledge to each participant in the challenge. The pieces already presented on the table are information known to (shared by) the group of participants. Each one can simply present his/her information on the table (activity A1), without giving meaning to them. On the other hand, a participant may connect his/her information with others (activity A2) or just connect the information that is already on the table (activity A3), thus giving the information a particular meaning in the context. The various possibilities for links of information are due to different interpretations of them. The interpretations may be the products of both activities, make sense (activity A10) and evaluate information (activity A7), both executed collectively. The interpretations may also occur during the activity disconnect pieces (activity A4). Sharing information (activity A8) on the table by each participant is encouraged due to information needs that arise as the resolution of the challenge goes on. Identifying these needs (activity A9) depends on the interpretation and evaluation of information available to all participants, for example, the information from the computation of group performance (activity A5).

Possible actions/behaviors of the participants on some activities identified and characteristics have been defined. Group members must meet the following rules (R):

– (R1) Only one group member at a time has access to the puzzle to carry out his/her activities.
– (R2) The next member to access the table to play is chosen by the group members themselves.
– (R3) Each member to perform activities A1 - A4 must justify the reason for his/her act.

Each group member, during his/her participation, can act as follows:

   • (R4) Execute the activity A1 or A2 at most once.
   • (R5) If the results of activities A2 - A5 performed by a member, are not considered by the group, it is the responsibility of the member to undo the work.

Table 2. Activities of the simulated collaborative setting

Code	Description of Activities
A1	Present one private piece on the table.
A2	Present one private piece and place together it with other pieces on the table.
A3	Arrange public piece(s) that are on the table.
A4	Disconnect piece(s) of puzzle.
A5	Compute the performance of the group according to the pieces placed together.
A6	Come to the consensus.
A7	Evaluate information collectively.
A8	Share Information.
A9	Identify information need.
A10	Make sense collaboratively.

- (R6) The pieces that are placed on the table must remain on it regardless they are interlinked or not to the other pieces in the puzzle.
- (R7) The solution presented by the group members as the final solution is just one single strongly connected area, i.e., there exists a path from each block to every other block.

Group members have the following permissions (P):

- (P1) Perform activities A3 and A4 as many times as necessary in each participation and the member can be assisted by other group members during these activities.
- (P2) The group can measure their performance, activity A5, during the challenge at any time.

Participants are not limited to actions/behaviors defined. In other words, they may take other actions/behaviors, but without violating the aforementioned restrictions.

4.2   Planning the Simulation

We decide to divide the planning into three stages: pre-experiment, experiment and post-experiment. In the pre-experiment stage, four participants are informed of the details of the challenge, such as the characteristics, rules and how the group is evaluated. The form of evaluation of the group, in particular, is thoroughly explained with the help of illustrations of possible solutions. Doubts of participants should be answered before proceeding to the next stage. Only after the participants understand the challenge, the challenge can be initiated.

During the challenge the participants can ask questions to the monitors of the simulations. However, the participants are aware that the time spent with questions is considered as play time. The end of the challenge occurs when the group presents its final solution or when the challenge reaches its limit of 30 minutes. The second stage begins at the signal of the monitor. The monitor, turn on the video camera to record the behaviors and actions of group members. In other words, the stage comprises the running of simulation to collect data from users' interactions of interest. Before going to the last stage, the solution presented by the group is evaluated by the monitors and the result announced to the group. After all members know their performance in group, each member receives a questionnaire to answer it. It is the final stage.

We analyze the data of questionnaires using the method content analysis [36]. Our objective is to capture the perceptions of each member about the rules imposed and collaborative activities that they perform. With their answers, we can know what rules, permissions and collaborative activities (i.e., CIB and business activities) are most problematic, difficult, awkward, and challenging. With this information, we can look for reasons for these problems. This can be achieved through the analysis of the recorded videos of the challenges made. The use of videos is suitable to analyze the interactions of the actors when they perform their activities. According to Ruhleder and Jordan [37], there are several advantages of using video for interaction analysis, and the main reason is that video is permanent information that can be recurrently analysed. It provides the opportunity to several researchers to perform their own interpretations and a collaborative multidisciplinary analysis can create an unbiased view of the events. Video-based Interaction Analysis (VbIA) also avoids the say/do problem, i.e., what people say they do and what they really do may not necessarily be the same. VbIA exposes mechanisms and antecedents due to the fact that the video provides process data rather than snapshot data. Since video records the phenomenon of interest in context, it is possible to ask about antecedents, varieties of solutions produced on different occasions, and questions of what led up to any particular state. The third source of information is the notes of the monitors. These notes highlight the perceptions they had of episodes that attracted their attention during the simulations.

Twelve persons are invited to participate in the challenge. They are chosen among the students enrolled in the undergraduate course of engineering at the Technological Institute of Aeronautics (ITA). Students are both informed about the objectives of the experiment and asked to participate. The twelve students faced the same challenge but in three groups of four. The three groups are established according to the students' choice. Two monitors monitor and control the three simulations to be performed. The degree of their participation is restricted to answer questions of participants (as shown in Fig. 3a), take notes of the simulation (as illustrated in Fig. 3b), check the capture of images by the camera and apply the questionnaire to participants.

Four sets of private pieces were chosen and offered to members of each group. The pieces in these sets were chosen randomly by the monitors, meeting the characteristics C1 and C2. For each group, the pieces are placed in four boxes of different colors. Before starting each experiment, the boxes are chosen by members. Thus, each member does not know its contents in advance and also uses the boxes during the challenge as a placeholder. Each member is unaware of the contents of the boxes of the other members during the challenge, respecting the characteristics C3 and C5. Before each experiment, nine public pieces are already available on the table, satisfying C4. These pieces and the quantity were also chosen randomly. Before starting each challenge, a camera is adjusted and turned on to capture the actions and behaviors of the group members. The camera is placed on the table inside the room where the simulations takes place, as can be seen on the table that is at the bottom of the two pictures in Fig. 3.

(a) Questions are answered by monitor

(b) Monitor, the right in the photo, observes the group and take notes of events that call her attention

Fig. 3. Group members collaborating in a puzzle observed by monitors

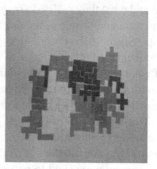

(a) Contiguous area of group G1   (b) Contiguous area of group G2   (c) Contiguous area of group G3

Fig. 4. Final results presented by three groups: G1, G2 and G3

4.3   Executing Simulation

The simulation of three collaborative challenges generated the following data: video recordings of the simulations, notes of the interactions that called attention, the performance of groups that was calculated according to the final solution presented to the monitors, and the solutions that were photographed, the latter shown in Fig. 4.

All groups took the period of 30 minutes to build their solutions. The performances of the groups were then calculated. The first, second and third group achieved the degree of cohesion of 83.4%, 65% and 56% respectively. We stress that the same pieces were used in three simulations, both public and private ones.

4.4   Analysis and Identification Requirements

As the last phase of the method we analyze the collected data to identify requirements for building the collaborative challenge on the Web. The analysis and identification of requirements were conducted as planned in the second phase, i.e., following the steps as

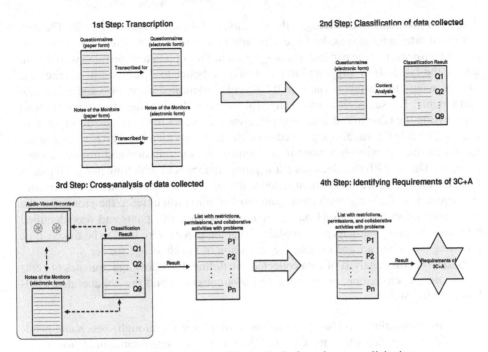

Fig. 5. Steps of the last phase of the method of requirements elicitation

outlined in Fig. 5. First, data collected in questionnaires responded by participants were copied into electronic form before being analyzed. Stretches of audio-visual recorded also were copied into electronic form. In the second step, we classify the data collected from the open questions of the questionnaires in the following units of content: *(Q1) How do you evaluate the rule R1 as to the group's performance? Justify your evaluation. (Q2) How do you evaluate the rule R2 as to the group's performance? Justify your evaluation. (Q3) How do you evaluate the rule R3 as to the group's performance? Justify your evaluation. (Q4) How do you evaluate the rule R4 and permission P1 as to the group's performance? Justify your evaluation. (Q5) How do you evaluate the rule R5 as to the group's performance? Justify your evaluation. (Q6) How do you evaluate the rule R6 as to the group's performance? Justify your evaluation. (Q7) During the evaluation of pieces connected and disconnected the participants had any problem? If so, describe them. (Q8) Making sense in a group, i.e., participants with different perspectives and goals engage in making sense together of how to arrange the pieces available and interpret them, and understand what information (pieces) are needed and where. Did you have any problems during this activity? If so, describe them. (Q9) There were problems to arrive at consensus on actions taken by the participants? If so, describe them.*

After sorting the data collected from questionnaires we analyze the data collected. This activity is the third step as illustrated in Fig. 5. The analysis consisted of the comparisons of the participants' perceptions with the monitors' perceptions, i.e., notes and analysis of the videos. In other words, it is characterized by the cross-analysis performed with different types of data. By cross-analyzing the data collected we realize that some problems arose during to the resolution of the collaborative puzzle. The definition of who must access the table was based on consensus by the group members, rule R2. However, some participants suggested another option to determine who should access the table. They suggested that it would be better to determine in advance the turn of access to the table. The rule R4 was also identified as an obstacle by several participants. The suggestion is to change R4 for the following: the group member who is accessing the table may display and place various pieces in the puzzle during his/her access. The rule R5 was also suggested to be changed: any member who is accessing the table, can undo previously actions if the member asks permission and justifies his/her changes. The rule R6 that does not allow group members to withdraw non used pieces from the table (that are not interconnected to the puzzle) brought problems. This restriction overloaded the group with pieces and resulted into difficulties to the group to make sense and decisions. The overload was reported by the participants and was identified by monitors. Many participants complained that the pieces were hard to be linked, thus polluting the public are and making the resolution of the challenge harder.

Based on cross-analysis of data collected, we define the following requisites of communication, coordination, cooperation and awareness to build the collaborative challenge for the Web:

- **Communication.** (a) Use synchronous communication through speech and handwriting. The characteristics C1 and C3 oblige a restricted communication as the video, e.g., use a tool as video-conference. Thus, to support coordination, cooperation and awareness among group members they must have a similar tool to chat, but without the video conferencing feature. (b) Communication must be flexible, i.e., unicast and broadcast. This requirement is due to the need for each group member having to report and seek information with others in a particular and broadcast way. For example, when you want to know who has pieces of a similar format and specific color, or request to a specific member to rearrange pieces.
- **Coordination.** (a) Allow access to the virtual table of only one group member at a time. (b) The next group member to access the virtual table is determined by vote and the decision will be by consensus (to be established through the synchronous communication as occurred in the simulations). Another option is to define the order of access of all members in advance. The group can change the form of selection of the next member. The first option is defined because three participants reported that they lost time with the rule R2 and that it should be possible to determine the order of their moves earlier. (c) The access to the table will have a maximum time pre-determined by the group members. The member who is supposed to access the table can yield the access to the next member. If the maximum time is reached the member loses his/her access and the table will be available for the next group member. The time spent in accessing the table in the simulations by the group members varied widely. So to avoid that a member locks the access to the table each member will have a time limit of access.
- **Cooperation.** (a) Allow that more than one private piece be presented in the table by a group member at a time. Several participants complained and we also observe in the videos that the rule R4 was not helpful for the group performance. Because of

this the group members decided to simply "circumvent" this rule. As they could not place more than one piece or arrange pieces on the table, the members asked several consecutive accesses to the table to perform the activities. (b) Pieces that the group believes that are not useful, should not remain on the table and should be returned to the members who presented the pieces. Thus, the computation of the degree of cohesion of the solution becomes simpler. (c) The calculation of the degree of cohesion of contiguous areas can be made automatically if a member requests. Although we believe that the calculation is not difficult, in the simulations we found that two groups have not coordinated their activities. (d) Undo interconnections and disconnections reverting to the previous play can be executed by any group member, but it should only be performed by one group member. In practice the participants will not recognize the rule R5.

– **Awareness.** (a) Allow group members to chain messages exchanged based on a specific event and its sequences. This requirement aims to bring understanding to group members on decisions and their consequences. (b) Each piece on the table must indicate to whom it belonged. Public pieces do not have this identification. Thus, a piece at a specific time can be removed from table by member who placed it. (c) The following information must be visible to all members of the group: who is accessing the table at a given time and how long he/she is taking. This information can help coordination and cooperation of the group. (d) Each member must be notified when the table is available to him.

Moreover, by cross-analysis of data collected (mainly analyzing notes and videos), we also perceive that the group that has the best performance was the one with better co-ordination, cooperation and awareness. G1 began to address the challenge by defining a strategy. The strategy was based mainly on two steps: understanding (in group) what degree of cohesion of a contiguous area is, and how to obtain the area with the highest possible degree of cohesion. All members of the group at the beginning of the challenge sought to make sense of all information presented to them. The result of this search yielded a unique understanding of the problem leading to better group performance. This was not seen in the activities of the other two groups. We note the difficulties of G2 and G3 to coordinate their activities because the different perceptions of members of these groups on how to achieve the goal of the collaborative challenge. The cooperation of members of these groups was not productive due to the lack of a shared understanding among them. Shared understanding was reached by G1 only after making sense of the information together. G2 and G3 did not explicitly define a suitable strategy as G1, but by analyzing the video and other data sources we realize that they had strategies, but divergent. At the start of their challenge, each member of groups G2 and G3 seemed to be worried for creating large contiguous sub-areas of a specific color by themselves. At some point of the challenge, a member wanted to join his area to build a single contiguous area, satisfying the rule R7. Of course, there were some conflicts and time wasting. As result of the strategy, G2 handed in a puzzle with 40 pieces and G3 a puzzle with 49 pieces. As previously reported, the degrees of cohesion of their solutions were, respectively 65% and 56%. G1 needed only 24 pieces for reaching 83.4%.

5 Analysis of the Proposed Method

The proposed method is based on simulation of collaborative activities that are important to achieve the objectives of stakeholders. The method allowed us to find unexpected behaviors. The simulation study was defined it according to the objective, constraints, and permissions for the users. The restrictions were validated by performing experiments with potential users of the collaborative environment. The result was the identification of requirements for communication, coordination, cooperation and awareness (3C+A) for the development of the collaborative puzzle on Web.

The effort spent in the simulation of the collaborative puzzle can be considered low when we compare with other existing methods, for instance, ethnographic investigations. This is due to the fact that the collaborative environment simulated is less complex, i.e., has a small number of actors involved and the resources employed in the simulation are of low cost. However, we consider the puzzle a collaborative challenge which allows analyzing the behaviors and interactions in a collaborative environment based on the concepts of CIB, in particular the concept of collaborative sensemaking. We believe that the simulation method can be employed for more complex collaborative environments where there are several roles and artifacts. In these environments the method can be used in the key scenarios of environments that need research due to a poor knowledge of the interactions of the actors.

In this method, the perspective of monitors and developers are captured through notes during the simulations, and the perspective of users by means of questionnaires. The two perspectives aim to identify common findings and discrepancies. The discrepancies can be further investigated with the help of the video-based analysis.

If the elicitation of requirements for 3C+A is not made in a satisfactory manner, the collaborative environment simulation can be performed again on specific scenarios that presented problems.

We are aware that there are various techniques for gathering and analyzing information, but the utilization of the questionnaire, notes of observations and video, and content analysis and video-based interactive analysis showed to be adequate in the collaborative puzzle simulation. The techniques were chosen because of the following characteristics of the collaborative challenge: number of users collaborating is low, number of activities performed by users is not high, and the common goal is not complex to understand. The choice of collection and analysis techniques of information to be used must consider the characteristics of the environment to be studied - for example the context and situation - as pointed out in [12],[28],[38].

Some problems reported by participants such as: the difficulty to physically place the pieces in the collaborative puzzle and the complexity of computing the performance of collaborative groups can be readily removed when the challenge occurs in the Web. The virtual environment to be developed can place the pieces with a drag of mouse and make the computation of the team's performance automatically on each piece insertion or removal.

The method, however, is unable to capture some requirements, for instance, those related to log and presentation of the history of usage by the participants. The history might be useful to roll back (undo moves) to past configurations.

Another restriction is physical limitation of the usage of the co-located simulation. For the collaborative puzzle, the simulation is not adequate if the number of users is high. If the number of users is high, coordination requirements should be investigated deeply and elicited.

Other limitation has to do with the synchronism of the collaboration. Our proposed method was effectively employed for a synchronous collaborative puzzle. We envision that the method can be employed to other synchronous collaborative applications; however, it may not result in the same success if it is applied to asynchronous collaborative environments.

In summary, our proposed method presents the following advantages: it allows the identification of requirements of 3C+A in an efficient manner in terms of time and resources; it is suitable to be used in synchronous collaborative environments, and it allows capturing perceptions of major actors involved in the development of the collaborative system. On the other hand, the method has the following disadvantages: it does not capture/save the history of the interactions of the users involved in collaborative activities; and it may not allow investigating satisfactorily collaborative environment that has many actors, roles and resources involved - i.e. it is physically limited to be employed.

6   Conclusions

In this research work, we propose a method of requirements elicitation in collaborative environments considering activities CIB, especially the collaborative sensemaking activity. The method utilizes the simulation of the target environment to capture requirements of the following aspects of collaboration: communication, coordination, cooperation and awareness (3C+A). The simulation environment is defined by restrictions and permissions of the collaborative aspects. The method was illustrated on an environment of collaborative puzzle. It allowed finding requirements for all collaborative aspects considered in simulation through verifications and inconsistency identifications of the restrictions and permissions assigned to the environment under study.

Some difficulties encountered in the co-located simulations of collaborative environments can be mitigated simply because these environments come to be supported by computer systems. For instance, in the collaborative puzzle two difficulties arose: handle pieces of the puzzle and calculate the group performance during the challenge. The difficulties can be solved easily in a virtual version of the challenge on the Web, as described in the previous session. On the other hand, the support of computer systems can bring new problems that are not necessarily perceived during the simulation of collaborative environments, for instance the feedback from actors can be inefficient because the computer system may have restrictions on capturing and presenting interaction information - e.g. gestures, expressions, tone of voice, etc, and the actors may not have confidence or may not have the knowledge to effectively use the system interfaces, especially in critical collaborative environments, as in air traffic control [39].

The results of experiments also showed that members of the group G1 presented crisp characteristics of management of its collaborative activities. The other two groups did not present management behaviors and activities. However, the group G1 had a significantly better performance than the other groups, although they had the same resources and challenge.

As the next steps this research work, we are developing the virtual collaborative puzzle and soon after its development we will perform experiments on it to evaluate the gains and the difficulties. If the evaluation of virtual collaborative puzzle also presents problems of management, we intend to extend the investigation about effectiveness of virtual teams considering well-built collaborative systems based on CIB activities but with management processes well structured. In addition, we are planning to expand the use of the method in other collaborative environments, for example in health care settings.

Acknowledgements. Alexandre Parra was partially sponsored by a grant No. 140345/ 2009-4 from Conselho Nacional de Desenvolvimento Científico e Tecnológico (CNPq - Brazil). Thanks also to the researcher Juliana de Melo Bezerra by help in the design and participation in the experiments.

References

1. Paul, S.A., Reddy, M.C.: Understanding Together: Sensemaking in Collaborative Information Seeking. In: The 2010 ACM Conference on Computer Supported Cooperative Work, pp. 321–330. ACM, New York (2010)
2. Feldman, M.S., Rafaeli, A.: Organizational routines as sources of connections and understandings. Journal of Management Studies 39(3), 309–331 (2002)
3. Weick, K.E.: Sensemaking in Organizations. Sage Publications, California (1995)
4. Ravid, S., Rafaeli, A., Shtub, A.: Facilitating Collaborative Sensemaking in Distributed Project Teams Using Computer Supported Cooperative Work (CSCW) Tools. In: The 2008 ACM Conf. on Human Factors in Computing Systems, pp. 1–5. ACM, Florence (2008)
5. Baasch, W.K.: Group Collaboration in Organizations: Architectures, Methodologies and Tools. Storming Media, Virginia (2002)
6. Dargan, P.A.: The Ideal Collaborative Environment. Journal of Defense Software Engineering - Web-Based Applications 14(4), 11–15 (2001)
7. Ivan, I., Ciurea, C., Visoiu, A.: Properties of the Collaborative Systems Metrics. Journal of Information Systems & Operations Management 2, 20–29 (2008)
8. Fuks, H., Raposo, A., Gerosa, M.A., Pimentel, M., Filippo, D., Lucena, C.J.P.: Inter and Intra-relationships between Communication, Coordination and Cooperation in the Scope of the 3C Collaboration Model. In: 12th International Conference on Computer Supported Cooperative Work in Design, pp. 148–153. IEEE Press, Beijing (2008)
9. Räsänen, M., Nyce, J.M.: A New Role for Anthropology? - Rewriting 'Context' and 'Analysis'. In: Proceedings of Nordic Conference on Human-Computer Interaction, pp. 175–184. ACM, New York (2006)
10. Martins, L.E.G.: Activity Theory as a feasible model for requirements elicitation processes. Journal Scientia: Interdisciplinary Studies in Computer Science 18, 33–40 (2007)
11. Hickey, A., Davis, A.: The Role of Requirements Elicitation Techniques in Achieving Software Quality. In: The 8th International Workshop on Requirements Engineering: Foundations for Software Quality, pp. 165–171. Elsevier Science, Essen (2002)
12. Hickey, A., Davis, A.: Elicitation Technique Selection: How Do Experts Do It? In: The 11th IEEE International Conference on Requirements Engineering, pp. 169–178. IEEE Press, Washington (2003)

13. Macaulay, L.A.: Requirements Engineering. Springer, London (1996)
14. Kotonya, G., Sommerville, I.: Requirements Engineering: Processes and Techniques. John Wiley & Sons, New York (1998)
15. Glass, R.L.: Searching for the holy grail of software engineering. Communications of the ACM 45(5), 15–16 (2002)
16. Byrd, T.A., Cossick, K.L., Zmud, R.W.: A Synthesis of Research on Requirements Analysis and Knowledge Acquisition Techniques. MIS Quarterly 16, 117–138 (1992)
17. Lauesen, S.: Software Requirements: Styles and Techniques. Addison-Wesley (2002)
18. Poltrock, S., Grudin, J., Dumais, S., Fidel, R., Bruce, H., Pejtersen, A.M.: Information seeking and sharing in design teams. In: The 2003 International ACM SIGGROUP Conference on Supporting Group Work, pp. 239–247. ACM, New York (2003)
19. Foster, J.: Collaborative Information Seeking and Retrieval. Annual Review of Information Science and Technology 8, 329–356 (2006)
20. Karunakaran, A., Spence, P.R., Reddy, M.C.: Towards a Model of Collaborative Information Behavior. In: 2nd International Workshop on Collaborative Information Seeking - ACM Conference on Computer Supported Cooperative Work. ACM (2010)
21. Ntuen, C.A., Munya, P., Trevino, M.: An approach to collaborative sensemaking process. In: 11th International Command and Control Research and Technology Symposium (2006)
22. Paul, S.A., Morris, M.R.: CoSense: enhancing sensemaking for collaborative web search. In: 27th International Conference on Human Factors in Computing Systems, pp. 1771–1780. ACM, New York (2009)
23. Paul, S.A., Reddy, M.C.: A Framework for Sensemaking in Collaborative Information Seeking. In: 2nd Workshop on Collaborative Information Retrieval (2010)
24. Reddy, M.C., Jansen, B.J.: A model for Understanding Collaborative Information Behavior in Context: A Study of two Healthcare Teams. Information Processing and Management 44, 256–273 (2008)
25. Sommerville, I., Ransom, J.: An Empirical Study of Industrial Requirements Engineering Process Assessment and Improvement. ACM Transaction on Software Engineering and Methodology 14, 25–117 (2005)
26. Laporti, V., Borges, M.R.S., Braganholo, V.: Athena: A collaborative approach to requirements elicitation. Journal of Computers in Industry 60, 367–380 (2009)
27. Sommerville, I.: Software Engineering. Addison-Wesley, Boston (2006)
28. Zoowghi, D., Coulin, C.: Engineering and Managing Software Requirements. Springer, New York (2005)
29. Broll, G., Hussmann, H., Rukzio, E., Wimmer, R.: Using Video Clips to Support Requirements Elicitation in Focus Groups - An Experience Report. In: 2nd International Workshop on Multimedia Requirements Engineering, pp. 1–6. IEEE (2007)
30. Machado, R.G., Borges, M.R.S., Gomes, J.O.: Supporting the System Requirements Elicitation through Collaborative Observations. In: Briggs, R.O., Antunes, P., de Vreede, G.-J., Read, A.S. (eds.) CRIWG 2008. LNCS, vol. 5411, pp. 364–379. Springer, Heidelberg (2008)
31. Myers, M.D.: Investigation Information Systems with Ethnographic Research. Communications of the Association for Information Systems 2(4), 1–20 (1999)
32. Gaba, D.M.: The future vision of simulation in health care. The Journal of the Society for Simulation in Healthcare 13, 126–135 (2007)
33. Laucken, U.: Theoretical Psychology. Bibliotheks-und Informations system der Universität, Oldenburg, Germany (2003)
34. Dieckmann, P., Gaba, D., Rall, M.: Deepening the theoretical foundations of patient simulation as social practice. Journal of the Society for Simulation in Healthcare 2(3), 183–193 (2007)
35. Tiling Puzzle. Wikipedia: The Free Encyclopedia, http://en.wikipedia.org/wiki/Tiling_puzzle

36. Stemler, S.: An overview of content analysis. Practical Assessment, Research & Evaluation 7(17) (2001), http://pareonline.net/getvn.asp?v=7&n=17
37. Ruhleder, K., Jordan, B.: Capturing, complex, distributed activities: video-based interaction analysis as a component of workplace ethnography. In: The IFIP TC8 WG 8.2 International Conference on Information Systems and Qualitative Research, pp. 246–275. Chapman & Hall, London (1997)
38. Davis, A., Dieste, O., Hickey, A., Juristo, N., Moreno, A.M.: Effectiveness of Requirements Elicitation Techniques: Empirical Results Derived from a Systematic Review. In: 14th IEEE International Requirements Engineering Conference, pp. 176–185. IEEE, Washington (2006)
39. Merlin, B., Hirata, C.: Collaborative System Experience in a Critical Activity Context: Air Traffic Control. In: Brazilian Symposium on Collaborative Systems, pp. 17–24. IEEE (2010)

Reducing Latency and Network Load
Using Location-Aware Memcache Architectures

Paul G. Talaga and Steve J. Chapin

Syracuse University, Syracuse, NY, U.S.A.
{pgtalaga,chapin}@syr.edu

Abstract. This work explores how data-locality in a web datacenter can impact the performance of the Memcache caching system. Memcache is a distributed key/value datastore used to cache frequently accessed data such as database requests, HTML page snippets, or any text string. Any client can store, manipulate, or retrieve data quickly by locating the data in the Memcache system using a hashing strategy based on the key. To speed Memcache, we explore alternate storage strategies where data is stored closer to the writer. Two novel Memcache architectures are proposed, based on multi-cpu caching strategies. A model is developed to predict Memcache performance given a web application's usage profile, network variables, and a memcache architecture. Five architecture variants are analyzed and further evaluated in a miniature web farm using the MediaWiki open-source web application. Our results verified our model and we observed a 66% reduction in core network traffic and a 23% reduction in Memcache response time under certain network conditions.

Keywords: Memcache, Latency, Network Utilization, Caching, Web-farm.

1 Introduction

Originally developed at Danga Interactive for LiveJournal, the Memcache system is designed to reduce database load and speed page construction in a web serving environment by providing a scalable key/value caching layer available to all web servers. The system consists of Memcache servers (memcached instances) for data storage, manipulated by client libraries which provide a storage API to the web application over a network or local file socket connection. No data durability guarantees are made, thus Memcache is best used to cache regenerable content. Data is stored and retrieved via keys, that uniquely determines the storage location of the data via a hash function over the server list. High scalability and speed are achieved with this scheme as a key's location (data location) can easily be computed locally. Complex hashing functions allow addition and removal of Memcache servers without severely affecting the location of the already stored data.

As web farms and cloud services grow and use faster processors, the relative delay from network access will increase as signal propagation is physically limited. Developing methods for measuring and addressing network latencies is necessary to continue to provide rich web experiences with fast, low latency interactions.

As an example, consider a webserver and a Memcache server on opposite ends of a datacenter the size of a football field. The speed of light limits the fastest round-trip time

J. Cordeiro and K.-H. Krempels (Eds.): WEBIST 2012, LNBIP 140, pp. 53–69, 2013.

in fiber to about $1\mu s$. Current network hardware claim a round-trip time (RTT) for this situation between $22\mu s$ and 3.7ms[1], more than an order of magnitude slower than the physical minimum. Assuming Memcache uses optimal network transport, 100 Memcache requests would take between 2.2ms and 370ms, ignoring all processing time. Compare this to the 200ms recommended page response time for web content and Memcache latency becomes significant in some situations. This is backed by multiple measurements of latencies in both Google App Engine and Amazon EC2 showing between $300\mu s$ and 2ms RTT between two instances[2,3].

Related to latency is network load. More network utilization will translate into more latency, leading to costly network hardware to keep utilization low[1]. Reducing network load, especially the highly utilized central links, will keep latency low.

This work explores how data locality can be exploited to benefit Memcache to reduce latency and core network utilization. While modern LAN networks in a datacenter environment allow easy and fast transmission, locating the data close to where it is used can lower latency and distribute network usage resulting in better system performance[4]. When looking at inter-datacenter communication, latency becomes even more pronounced.

We present five architecture variants, two novel to this area based on prior multiprocessor caching schemes, two natural extensions, and the last the typical Memcache architecture. In addition to showing performance for a single application and hardware configuration, we develop a network and usage model able to predict the performance of all variants under different configurations. This allows mathematical derivation of best and worst case situations, as well as the ability to predict performance.

Our contributions are outlined below:

1. A model for predicting Memcache performance
2. A tool for gathering detailed Memcache usage statistics
3. Two novel Memcache architectures based on multi-CPU caching methods
4. Mathematical comparison between five Memcache architectures
5. Experimental comparison of five Memcache architectures using MediaWiki

The rest of the paper consists of: Sect. 2 reviews background Memcache material. Section 3 describes the model and its features. Next, Sect. 4 describes our developed tool for logging and analyzing Memcache's performance which is used to build an application's usage profile. Sect. 5 describes the five Memcache architectures along with estimation formula for network usage and storage efficiency. Section 6 mathematically analyzes the five architectures with respect to latency. Our experimental results are shown in Sect. 7. A discussion of relevant issues is given in Sect. 8, followed by related work in Sect. 9, and our conclusion in Sect. 10.

2   Memcache Background

As previously mentioned, Memcache is built using a client-server architecture. Clients, in the form of an instance of a web application, store or request data from a Memcache server. A Memcache server consists of a daemon listening on a network interface for

TCP client connections, UDP messages, or alternatively through a file socket. Daemons do not communicate with each other, but rather perform the requested Memcache commands from a client. An expiration time can be set to remove stale data. If the allocated memory is consumed, data is generally evicted in a least-recently-used manner. Data is only stored in memory (RAM) rather than permanent media for speed.

The location of a Memcache daemon can vary. Small deployments may use a single daemon on the webserver itself. Larger multi-webserver deployments generally use dedicated machines to run multiple Memcache daemons configured for optimal performance (large RAM, slow processor, small disk). This facilitates management and allows webservers to use as much memory as possible for web processing.

The Memcache daemon recognizes 16 commands as of version 1.4.13 (2/2/2012), categorized into storage, retrieval, and status commands. Various APIs written in many languages communicate with a Memcache daemon via these commands, but not all support every command.

Below is an example of a PHP snippet which uses two of the most popular commands, set and get, to quickly return the number of users and retrieve the last login time.

```
function get_num_users(){
    $num = memcached_get('num_users');
    if($num === FALSE){
        $num = get_num_users_from_database();
        memcached_set("num_users", $num, 60);
    }
    return $num;
}
function last_login($user_id){
    $date = memcached_get('last_login' . $user_id);
    if($date === FALSE){
        $date = get_last_login($user_id);
        memcached_set('last_login' . $user_id, $date, 0);
    }
    return $date;
}
```

Rather than query the database on every function call, these functions cache data in Memcache. In get_num_users, a cache timeout is set for 60 seconds which causes the cached value to be invalidated 60 seconds after the set, triggering a subsequent database query when the function is called next. Thus, at most once a minute the database will be queried, with the function returning a value at most a minute stale. To cache session information, the last_login function stores the time of last login by including the $user_id in the key. This will store separate data per user/session. Periodically, or on logout, another function clears the cached data. During an active session the last_login function will only access the current session's data with no other user needing the data. Thus, if sticky load balancing (requests from the same session are routed to the same web server or rack) is used the data could be stored locally to speed access and reduce central network load. Alternatively, as in get_num_users, some data may be used by all clients. It may make sense for a local copy to be stored, rather than each webserver requesting commonly used data over the network. Caching data locally, when possible, is the basis for the proposed architectures.

3 Memcache Performance Prediction Model

When evaluating different Memcache architectures it is useful to predict performance of the desired system. Using the constants and formula developed here allows a rough estimation of latency and network utilization for a memcache system.

To simplify our model we assume the following traits:

1. **Linear Network Latency.** Network latency is linearly related to network device traversal count [1].
2. **Sticky Sessions.** A web request in the same session can be routed to a specific rack or webserver.

3.1 Assumed Network Topology

Network topology influences the performance of any large interconnected system. A physical hierarchical star network topology is assumed consisting of multiple web, database, and Memcache servers.

Web servers, running application code, are grouped into racks. Instances within the same rack can communicate quickly over at most two network segments. Communication is faster intra-rack than inter-rack.

Racks are connected through a backbone link. Thus, for one webserver in a rack to communicate to another in a different rack at least 4 network segments connected with 3 switches must be traversed.

3.2 Model Constants and Calculation

To generalize the different possible network configurations, we assume network latency is linearly related to the switch count a signal must travel through, or any other device connecting network segments. In our rack topology, the estimated RTT from one rack to another is l_3 because three switches are traversed, where $l_3 = 3 * 2 * switch + base$ for some $switch$ and $base$ delay times described later.

Similarly, l_2 represents a request traversing 2 switches, such as from a rack to a node on the backbone and back. l_1 represents traversing a single switch and l_{local} is used to represent this closest possible network distance. This metric differs from hop count as every device a packet must pass through is counted, rather than only routers.

Fig. 1 depicts the data-flow through the model to calculate a final latency estimate.

Each block represents a set of variables or formula in the model. Table 1 describes variables in the Network Performance block.

The Web Application Profile contains variables inherent to the web application, such as the size of objects, key distribution throughout the web application, percent of memcache commands which are reads, memcache commands used, and command distribution. The command distribution dictates the Command Weights, used later. Table 2 describes these variables in detail.

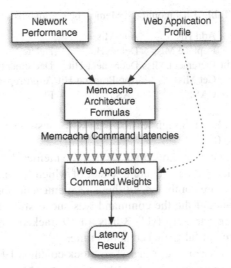

Fig. 1. Latency Estimation Calculation

Table 1. Network Performance Variables

$l_{localhost}$ or l_0 Average RTT (ms) to localhost for the smallest
size packet possible
l_{local} or l_1 Average RTT (ms) to a nearby node through one network device
l_n Average RTT (ms) traversing n devices
r Number of racks used in system
k Data replication value, when available
$size_{note}$ Average size of data location note (bytes)
$switch$ Delay time (ms) per switch or network device traversed
$base$ Constant OS, network delay, and Memcache overhead (ms)
bw Minimum network bandwidth in system (Mbps)

Table 2. Web Application Profile Variables

ps Proportion of memcache commands used on the average page that
are only referenced by a single HTTP session [0-1]
rw_{cmd} Percent of memcache commands which are reads [0-1]
rw_{net} Percent of network traffic based on data transfer which are reads [0-1]
$size_{object}$ Average size of typical on-wire object (bytes)
$usage_m$ For a specific application usage scenario, proportion of each memcache
command used plus duplicates for command failures (Table 3) [0-1]
where $m = 0$ to 19 and $\sum_{m=0}^{19} usage_m = 1$

The ps value is central to our approaches. It gives a measure of how many session specific Memcache requests are used per web page. If an application only stores session information in Memcache $ps = 1$. If half the memcache requests on a page are session specific and half used by other users/sessions, then $ps = 0.5$. For example, if an application used the above get_num_users() and last_login($id) in Sect. 2 once per page then for 100 user sessions Memcache would store 101 data items, of which

Table 3. 19 monitored Memcache commands

Set	Add Hit	Add Miss	
Replace Hit	Replace Miss	Delete Hit	Delete Miss
Increment Hit	Increment Miss	Decrement Hit	Decrement Miss
Get Hit	Get Miss	App/Prepend Hit	App/Prepend Miss
CAS1[1]	CAS2[1]	CAS3[1]	Flush

100 are session specific. Even though session data will consume 99% of all stored data, our ps value will still be 0.5.

The $usage_m$ variable captures how often each of the memcache commands are used. Only commands that manipulate data are tracked, of which there are 13. The `append` and `prepend` commands are combined. Of these 13 memcache commands, 7 have different latency performance if the the command was successful or not, thus we break these into a `Hit` or `Miss` variants. Table 3 lists all 19 tracked memcache commands. Note `CAS` commands are not fully tracked at this time.

The `Memcache Architecture Formulas` block contains 19 formula, each using the `Network Performance` and `Web Application Profile` variables to estimate the latency for a specific memcache command. These formula are specific to the memcache architecture being used. Sect. 5 discusses standard and proposed architectures, with a mathematical comparison using this model in Sect. 6. All formula are available at http://fuzzpault.com/memcache.

The final `Latency Result` value is calculated by obtaining latency values for each of the `Memcache Architecture Formulas` and weighting each using $usage_m$ `Command Weights` and summing.

4 MemcacheTach

Predicting Memcache usage is not easy. User demand, network usage, and network design all can influence the performance of a Memcache system. Instrumentation of a running system is therefore needed. The Memcache server itself is capable of returning the keys stored, number of total hits, misses, and their sizes. Unfortunately, this is not enough information to answer important questions: What keys are used the most/least? How many clients use the same keys? How many Memcache requests belong to a single HTTP request? How much time is spent waiting for a Memcache request?

To answer these and other questions we developed MemcacheTach, a Memcache client wrapper which intercepts and logs all requests, available at http://fuzzpault.com/memcache. While currently analyzed after-the-fact, the log data could be streamed and analyzed live to give insight into Memcache's performance and allow live tuning. Analysis provides values for the `Network Performance` and `Web Application Profile` model variables above, plus the ratio of the 19 Memcache request types, and other useful information. Table 4 shows the measured values for MediaWiki from a

---

[1] CAS - Compare-and-Swap

CAS1 = Key exists, correct CAS value.

CAS2 = Key exists, wrong CAS value.

CAS3 = Key does not exist.

Table 4. MediaWiki usage values (full caching)

switch (ms) : 0.21 (ms)		ps : 0.56	Avg. data size (Kbytes): 3.3
base (ms) : 3.0 (ms)		rw_{cmd} : 0.51	Mem. requests per page: 16.7
Avg. net size (bytes): 869			
Set hit: 24%	Replace hit : 0%		Inc hit : 0%
Set miss : 0%	Replace miss : 0%		Inc miss : 21%
Add hit : 0%	Delete hit : 2%		Dec hit : 0%
Add miss : 0%	Delete miss : 0%		Dec miss : 0%
Get hit : 44%	CAS1 : 0%		App/Prepend hit : 0%
Get miss : 7%	CAS2 : 0%		App/Prepend miss : 0%
Flush : 0%	CAS3 : 0%		

Table 5. MemcacheTach Overhead

State	Avg page generation time (ms)	std.dev	samples (pages)
Off	1067	926	13,800
Logging	1103	876	13,800

single run in our mini-datacenter with full caching enabled for 100 users requesting 96 pages each.

The average page used 16.7 Memcache requests, waited 46ms for Memcache requests, and took 1067ms to render a complete page.

56% of keys used per page were used by a single webserver, showing good use of session storage, and thus a good candidate for location aware caching.

As implemented, MemcacheTech is written in PHP, not compiled as a module, and writes uncompressed log data. Thus, performance could improve with further development. Two performance values are given in Table 5. `Off` did not use MemcacheTech, while `Logging` saved data on each Memcache call. On average MemcacheTech had a statistical significant overhead of 36ms. MemcacheTach is available at http://fuzzpault.com/ memcache.

5   Memcache Architectures

Here we describe and compare Memcache architectures currently in use, two natural extensions, and our two proposed versions. All configurations are implemented on the client via wrappers around existing Memcache clients, thus requiring no change to the Memcache server.

Estimation formula for network usage of the central switch and space efficiency are given using the variables defined in Sect. 3.2. An in-depth discussion of latency is given in Sect. 6.

5.1   Standard Deployment Central - SDC

The typical deployment consists of a dedicated set of memcached servers existing on the backbone (l_2). Thus, all Memcache requests must traverse to the Memcache server(s) typically over multiple network devices. Data is stored in one location, not replicated.

This forms the standard for network usage as all information passes through the central switch:

Network Usage: 100%

All available Memcache space is used for object storage:

Space Efficiency: 100%

5.2   Standard Deployment Spread - SDS

This deployment places Memcache servers in each webserver rack. Thus, some portion of data $(1/r)$ exists close to each webserver (l_1), while the rest is farther away (l_3). Remember that the key dictates the storage location, which could be in any rack, not the local. This architecture requires no code changes compared to SDC, but rather a change in Memcache server placement.

With some portion of the data local, the central switch will experience less traffic:

Network Usage: $\frac{r-1}{r}\%$

All available space is used for object storage:

Space Efficiency: 100%

5.3   Standard Deployment Replicated - SDR

To add durability to data, we store k copies of the data on different Memcache daemons, preferably on a different machine or rack. While solutions do exist to duplicate the server (repcached[5]), we duplicate on the client and use locality to read from the closest resource possible. This can be implemented either through multiple storage pools or, in our case, modifying the key in a known way to choose a different server or rack. A write must be applied to all replicas, but a read contacts the closest replica first, reducing latency and core network load.

Reading locally can lower central switch usage over pure duplication:

Network Usage: $rw_{net} \times (1 - \frac{k}{r}) + (1 - rw_{net}) \times (k - \frac{k}{r})\%$

The replication value lowers space efficiency:

Space Efficiency: $1/k\%$

5.4   Snooping Inspired - Snoop

Based on multi-CPU cache snooping ideas, this architecture places Memcache server(s) in each rack allowing fast local reads[6,7]. Writes are local as well, but a data location note is sent to all other racks under the same key. Thus, all racks contain all keys, but data is stored only in the rack where it was written last. This scheme is analogous to a local-write protocol using forwarding pointers[8]. An update overwrites all notes and data with the same key. To avoid race conditions deleting data, notes are stored first in parallel, followed by the actual data. Thus, in the worst case multiple copies could exist, rather than none. A retrieval request first tries the local server, either finding the data, a note, or nothing. If a note is found the remote rack is queried and the data returned. If nothing is found the data does not exist.

The broadcast nature of a set could be more efficient if UDP was used with network broadcast or multicast. Shared memory systems have investigated using a broadcast medium, though none in the web arena[9].

Based on the metric ps, the proportion of keys used during one HTTP request which are session specific, and the message size $size_{message}$, we have the following estimation for central switch traffic:

Network Usage: $rw_{net} \times (1 - ps) + \frac{(1-rw_{net}) \times size_{message} \times r}{size_{object}} \%$

Storage efficiency depends on the size of the messages compared to the average object size:

Space Efficiency: $\frac{size_{object}}{size_{message} \times (r-1) + size_{object}} \%$

5.5 Directory Inspired - Dir

An alternate multi-CPU caching system uses a central directory to store location information [6,7]. In our case, a central Memcache cluster is used to store location information. Each rack has its own Memcache server(s) allowing local writes, but reads may require retrieval from a distant rack. A retrieval request will try the local server first, and on failure query the directory and subsequent retrieval from the remote rack. A storage request first checks the directory for information, clears the remote data if found, writes locally, and finally sends a note to the directory.

Rather than many notes being sent per write as with Snoop, Dir is able to operate with two distant requests, one to retrieve the current note, and the second to *set* the new one, no matter how many racks are used. This allows Dir to stress the central switch the least.

Network Usage: $rw_{net} \times (1 - ps) \times \frac{size_{message} + size_{object}}{size_{object}} + \frac{(1-rw_{net}) \times size_{message} \times 2}{size_{object}} \%$

Likewise with Snoop, message size dictates storage efficiency:

Space Efficiency: $rw_{net} \times (1 - ps) \times \frac{size_{message} + size_{object}}{size_{object}} + \frac{(1-rw_{net}) \times size_{message} \times 3}{size_{object}} \%$

6 Latency Estimation

The above architecture options are evaluated by estimating latency using the model described in Sect. 3. The Memcache Architecture Formulas were derived for each architecture variant.

In general, each formula estimates the latency for a specific memcache command using the following components:

- **Bandwidth.** Time the average sized object will require to traverse the network given the provided bandwidth, if data is transferred.
- **Switching.** Time needed to traverse the network given a specific network distance.
- **Architecture.** Time for additional communication due to the architecture.
- **Read/Write.** Time weighting for the proportion of reads to writes.
- **Location.** Additional time if data is not stored locally.

As an example, the set hit command would have a latency (ms) of $l_2 + \frac{size_{object}}{bw \times conv}$, where $conv = 1024 * 1024/8/1000$, under SDC factoring in distance and bandwidth. SDS would have $\frac{1}{r} \times l_{local} + \frac{r-1}{r} \times l_3 + \frac{size_{object}}{bw \times conv}$ for a set hit because some portion

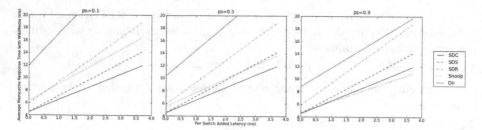

Fig. 2. MediaWiki profile under different switch speeds and ps values

of the keys would be local ($\frac{1}{r}$), and thus faster, while the rest ($\frac{r-1}{r}$) would need to travel farther. The same bandwidth calculation applies. SDR would take $l_3 + \frac{size_{object}}{bw \times conv}$ because multiple sets can be issued simultaneously. Snoop would need $l_{local} + l_3 + \frac{size_{object} + size_{message}}{bw \times conv}$ with data being sent to the local rack and messages sent to all others in parallel.

Using a specific Web Application Profile and Network Performance statistics, here from a run of MediaWiki[10], we can vary individual parameters to gain an understanding of the performance space under different environments. A bandwidth (bw) value of 100 Mbps was used for all.

We first look at how network switch speed can effect performance. Remember we assumed the number of devices linearly relates to network latency, so we vary the single device speed between $12.7\mu s$ and $1.85ms$, with an additional $4.4ms$ OS delay, in the Fig. 2 plots. Latency measures round trip time, so our X axis varies from 0.025ms to 3.7ms. Three plots are shown with ps values of 10%, 50%, and 90% with weightings derived from our MediaWiki profile.

As seen in Fig. 2, as ps increases the latency for the location-aware schemes improve. When ps=0.9 and a switch latency of $0.3ms$, SDS and Snoop are equivalent, with Snoop preforming better as switch latency increases further.

Next we take a closer look at how ps changes response time in Fig. 3 using a fixed switch latency of $1.0ms$ and our MediaWiki usage profile.

Predictably all 3 location-averse schemes (SDC, SDS, and SDR) exhibit no change in performance as ps increases. As ps increases Snoop and Dir improve with Snoop eventually overtaking SDC when ps=0.86.

So far we've analyzed performance using MediaWiki's usage profile. Now we look at the more general case where we split the 19 possible commands into two types: read and write, where read consists of a get request hit or miss, and a write is any command which changes data. MediaWiki had 51% reads when fully caching, or about one read per write. Fig. 4 varies the read/write ratio while looking at three ps values.

With high read/write ratios Snoop is able to outperform SDC, here when switch=1.0ms at $rw = 0.75$.

These plots show when ps is near one and slow switches are used, Snoop is able to outperform all other configurations. In some situations, like session storage ($ps = 1$) across a large or heavily loaded datacenter, Snoop may make larger gains. From an estimated latency standpoint Dir does not preform well, though as we'll see next, its low network usage is beneficial.

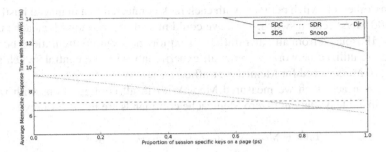

Fig. 3. MediaWiki profile under different *ps* values

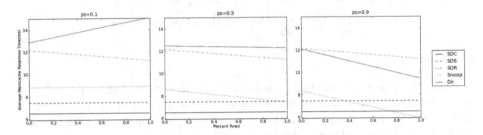

Fig. 4. Varying read/write ratio and *ps* values

7   Experimental Results

To validate our model and performance estimation formula, we implemented our alternate Memcache schemes and ran a real-world web application, MediaWiki[10], with real hardware and simulated user traffic. Three MediaWiki configurations were used:

1. Full - All caching options were enabled and set to use Memcache.
2. Limited - Message and Parser caches were disabled, with all other caches using Memcache.
3. Session - Only session data was stored in Memcache.

The simulated traffic consisted of 100 users registering for an account, creating 20 pages each with text and links to other pages, browsing 20 random pages on the site, and finally logging out. Traffic was generated with jMeter 2.5 generating 9600 pages per run. The page request rate was tuned to keep all webservers busy, resulting in less-than optimal average page generation times. A run consisted of a specific MediaWiki configuration with a Memcache configuration.

The mock datacenter serving the content consisted of 23 Dell Poweredge 350 servers running CentOS 5.3, Apache 2.2.3 with PHP 5.3, APC 3.1, PECL Memcache 3.0, 800MHz processors, 1GB RAM, partitioned into 4 racks of 5 servers each. The remaining 3 servers were used for running the HAProxy load balancer, acting as a central Memcache server, and a MySQL server respectively. Four servers in each rack produced web pages, with the remaining acting as the rack's Memcache server.

To measure Memcache network traffic accurately the secondary network card in each server was placed in separate subnet for Memcache traffic only. This subnet was joined by one FastEthernet switch per rack, with each rack connected to a managed FastEthernet (10/100 Mb/s) central switch. Thus, we could measure intra-rack Memcache traffic using SNMP isolated from all other traffic. To explore how our configurations behaved under a more utilized network we reran all experiments with the central switch set to Ethernet (10 Mb/s) speed for Memcache traffic.

Using MemcacheTach we measured MediaWiki in all configurations with results presented in Table 6. Only non-zero Memcache commands are listed for brevity.

Table 6. MediaWiki usage for each configuration

Parameter	Full	Limited	Session	Parameter	Full	Limited	Session
Set	24%	23%	50%	ps	.56	.59	1
Delete hit	2%	3%	0%	rw_{cmd}	.51	.49	.5
Inc miss	22%	24%	0%	rw_{net}	.61	.78	.54
Get hit	44%	42%	50%	Avg. net size (bytes)	870	973	301
Get miss	8%	8%	0%				

7.1 Latency

To predict latency we require two measurements of network performance, *switch* & *base*. These were found using an SDS run and calculating the relative time difference between Memcache commands in-rack (l_{local}) and a neighboring rack (l_3) and subtracting the delay from limited bandwidth. For the 100Mbps network, $switch = 0.21$ms and $base = 3.0$ms. The 10Mbps network had, $switch = 0.22$ms and $base = 4.0$ms.

The resulting predicted and observed per Memcache command latences are given in Table 7.

Table 7. Expected and Measured Memcache Latency

| | Predicted Latency (ms) | | | Observed Latency | | | Predicted Latency | | | Observed Latency | | |
Scheme	Full	Limited	Session	Full	Limited	Session	Full	Limited	Session	Full	Limited	Session
	100Mb/s Central Switch						10Mb/s Central Switch					
SDC	3.5	3.5	3.4	3.5	3.9	3.2	5.2	5.2	4.7	12.1	13.9	3.5
SDS	4.2	3.6	3.6	3.8	4.1	3.6	5.3	5.4	4.8	20.1	20.6	4.6
SDR	5.7	5.0	3.5	5.1	5.4	5.3	7.0	7.4	4.8	35.6	29.5	9.2
Snoop	5.9	5.2	5.1	6.1	6.6	7.3	6.3	7.0	6.9	15.6	17.0	10.9
Dir	8.4	7.5	8.5	5.5	5.8	5.8	9.2	9.5	11.6	9.3	9.9	6.3

In the case of fast switching, SDC was the best predicted and observed performer. The location-aware schemes, Dir and Snoop, both don't fit the expected values as close as the others. This is likely due to the interpreted nature of the architecture logic in PHP. Future work will explore native C implementations.

When the central switch was slowed to 10Mb/s utilization increased and latency also increased. Here we see that Dir was able to outperform SDC in the Full and Limited caching cases due to the lower central switch utilization, as we'll see in the next section. Snoop still performed worse than expected, though still beating SDS and SDR in the Full caching case.

7.2 Network Load

Using the formula developed in Sect. 5 combined with the MediaWiki usage data we can compute the expected load on the central switch and compare it to our measured

Table 8. Expected and Measured Network Load

Scheme	Predicted Usage (%) Full	Limited	Session	Observed Usage Full	Limited	Session	Predicted Usage Full	Limited	Session	Observed Usage Full	Limited	Session
	100Mb/s Central Switch						10Mb/s Central Switch					
SDC	100	100	100	100	100	100	100	100	100	100	100	100
SDS	80	80	80	80	81	73	80	80	80	83	82	81
SDR	99	81	105	101	87	106	99	81	105	106	89	110
Snoop	49	43	76	45	48	116	49	43	76	47	50	118
Dir	38	39	30	35	34	69	38	39	30	37	35	71

values. We used a $size_{message}$ value of 100 bytes, higher than the actual message to include IP and TCP overhead. The comparison is given in Table 8.

Notice SDR's low network usage even though data is duplicated. This is a result of a location-aware strategy that writes to different racks and reads from the local rack if a duplicate is stored there. The low rack count, 5 in our configuration, assures that almost half the time data is local.

The actual central switch usage measurements match well with the predicted values. Note the location-aware rows. These show the largest skew due to the small message size and therefore the higher relative overhead of TCP/IP. This was validated by a packet dump during SDC/Full and the SDC/Session runs in which absolute bytes and Memcache bytes were measured. For SDC/Full, with an average network object size of 870 bytes, 86MB was transfered on the wire containing 61MB of Memcache communication, roughly a 30% overhead. SDC/Session transferred 9.8MB with 301 byte network objects, yet it contained 5.7MB of Memcache communication giving an overhead of 41%. Additional traces showed that for small messages, like the notes transferred for Dir and Snoop, 70% of the network bytes were TCP/IP overhead. This is shown by the higher than expected Session column when location-aware was used due to the smaller average object size. This shows that Memcache using TCP is not network efficient for small objects, with our location-aware schemes an excellent example. Future work measuring network utilization for Memcache using UDP would be a good next step, as has been investigated by Facebook[11,12].

If $size_{message}$ was 50 bytes, which may be possible using UDP, we should see Dir and Snoop use only 24% and 33% respectively as much as SDC on the central switch. Using the binary protocol may reduce message size further, showing less network usage.

7.3   Review

These results show that the model, application profile, and performance estimation formula do provide a good estimate for latency and network usage. While the actual Memcache latency values did not show an improvement over the typical configuration on our full speed hardware, they did support our model. In some cases, as shown by our slower network hardware configuration as well as described in Sect. 6, we'd expect locality-aware schemes to perform better than the typical. High rack densities and modern web-servers, even with modern network hardware, may increase network utilization to a point similar to our Ethernet speed runs and show increased latency under high load. Location-aware configurations lower core network utilization allowing more web and Memcache servers to run on the existing network. Network usage proved difficult to predict due to additional TCP/IP overhead, but nonetheless the experimental data backed up the model with all architectures reducing core traffic, and the best reducing it to 34% of the typical SDC case.

8 Discussion

8.1 Latency, Utilization, and Distributed Load

Through this work we assumed network latency and utilization are independent, but as we saw in the last section they are closely related. A heavily utilized shared-medium will experience higher latencies than an underutilized one. Thus, SDC, SDS, and SDR's latency when used on the slow network were much higher than predicted due to congestion. Unfortunately predicting the saturation point would require dozens of parameters such as link speeds, specific network devices, server throughput, as well as an estimation of other traffic on the network. At some point simulation and estimation outweigh actual implementation and testing.

8.2 Multi-datacenter Case

Thus far we have assumed a Memcache installation within the same datacenter with appropriate estimates on latency. In general, running a standard Memcache cluster spanning datacenters is not recommended due to high (relative) latencies and expensive bandwidth. The location-agnostic architectures, SDC, SDS, and partly SDR would not be good choices for this reason. We can apply our same analysis to the multi-datacenter situation by viewing the datacenter as a rack, with a high l_3 value for intra-datacenter latency. SDC is no longer possible with its l_2 latency, with SDS taking its place as the typical off-the-shelf architecture. Assume a l_3 value of 40ms, a best case CA to NY latency, with $l_1 = 5$ms inside the datacenter. For Dir's directory we assume it spans both datacenters like SDS. See Fig. 5 for the plotted comparison.

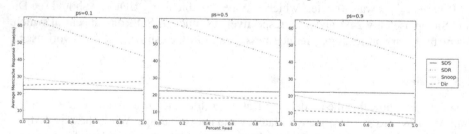

Fig. 5. Varying read/write ratio and ps values with an East and West coast DC

Here the difference between locality aware and averse is more pronounced. Snoop and Dir are able to outperform SDS when ps is above 0.5, especially for high read/write ratios. SDR preforms poorly due to consistency checks and multiple writes. Interestingly as more datacenters are added SDS becomes worse due to a higher proportion of data being farther away while the location aware architectures can keep it close when ps is high.

8.3 Selective Replication

Replication of a relational database can increase performance by distributing reads. Unfortunately entire tables must be replicated, possibly including seldom used data. In a key/value system such as Memcache, replication can offer speed benefits as we saw in SDR. We looked at the static case where all data is replicated, but selectively replicating frequently used data could save space while increasing speed. Snoop and Dir could be easily augmented to probabilistically copy data locally. Thus, frequently used but infrequently changed data would be replicated allowing fast local reads. Unused Memcache memory is a waste, so by changing the probability of replication on the fly memory could be used more optimally. We intend to investigate this in further work.

8.4 Object Expiration

In Memcache, if the allocated memory is consumed objects are generally removed in a least-recently-used manner. In a standard deployment this works well, but in our case where meta information is separate from data a possibility exists where meta expiration may cause orphaned data. The new Memcache command *touch*, which renews an object's expiration time, can be used to update the expiration of meta information reducing the chance of orphaned data, though the possibility does still exist. In a best-effort system such as Memcache such errors are allowed and should be handled by the client.

8.5 Overflow

The location-agnostic configurations (SDC, SDS, and SDR) all fill the available memory evenly over all servers due to the hashing of keys. Location aware configurations will not fill evenly, as is the case when some racks set more than others. Data will be stored close to the sets, possibly overflowing the local Memcache server while others remain empty. Thus, it is important to evenly load all racks, or employ some Memcache balancing system.

8.6 System Management

Managing a Memcache cluster requires providing all clients a list of possible Memcache servers. Central to our location-aware strategies is some method for each Memcache client to prioritize Memcache servers based on the number of network devices traversed. This can be easily computed automatically in some cases. In our configuration, IP addresses were assigned systematically per rack. Thus, a client can calculate which Memcache servers were within the same rack and which were farther away based on its own IP address. Using this or similar method would minimize the added management necessary to implement a location-aware caching scheme.

9 Related Work

Memcache is part of a larger key/value NoSQL data movement which provides enhanced performance over relational databases by relaxing ACID guarantees. Scalability is achieved by using a hashing system based on the key to uniquely locate an object's storage location. To achieve locale-aware caching we must modify the typical key/location mapping system. Here we discuss similar systems to Memcache and concentrate on those which have some locality component.

The Hadoop Distributed File System[13] is designed to manage distributed applications over extremely large data sets while using commodity hardware. They employ a rack-aware placement policy able to place data replicas to improve data reliability, availability, and network bandwidth utilization over random placement. Reads can read from a close copy rather than a remote one. Additionally, they identify bandwidth limitations between racks, with intra-rack faster, supporting our architectures. Their mantra of "Moving Computation is Cheaper than Moving Data" works for large data sets, but in our web case where data is small this mantra does not hold. File meta-data is stored and managed in a central location similar to our Dir architecture.

Cassandra can use a rack and datacenter-aware replication strategy for better reliability and to read locally[14]. This is convenient when multiple datacenters are used so a read will never query a remote datacenter. Voldemort uses a similar system for replicas using zones[15][4]. While the above three systems use some locality aware policy for replicas they all use a hashing strategy for primary storage, thus possibly writing the data far from where it will be used.

Microsoft's AppFabric provides very similar services to Memcache with object storage across many computers using key/value lookup and storage [16] in RAM. No mention of key hashing is given to locate data, though they do mention a routing table to locate data similar in practice to our Snoop architecture. No mention of how this table is updated. Their routing table entries reference a specific cache instance, whereas our Snoop note refers to a hash space, or rack, possibly containing thousands of Memcache instances, thereby giving more storage space and flexibility. Durability can be added by configuring backup nodes to replicate data, though unlike our architectures all reads go to a single node until it fails, unlike ours where any copy can be read.

EHCACHE Terracotta is a cache system for Java, containing a BigMemory module permitting serializable objects to be stored in memory over many servers. Java's garbage collection (GC) can become a bottleneck for large in-application caching, thus a non-garbage collected self-managed cache system is useful while ignoring typical Java GC issues. Essentially BigMemory implements a key/value store using key hashing for Java objects similar to Memcache. Additional configurations are possible. For example it allows a read and write through mode, backed by a durable key/value storage system, thereby removing all cache decisions from the application code. Replication is done by default (2 copies) and configurable[17].

The HOC system is designed as a distributed object caching system for Apache, specifically to enable separate Apache processes to access others' caches[18]. Of note is their use of local caches to speed subsequent requests and a broadcast-like remove function, similar to our SDS with duplication.

10   Conclusions

We've seen that when a web application has a high ps value, many reads per write, or slow a network, a location-aware Memcache architecture can lower latency and network usage without significantly reducing available space. The developed model showed where gains could be made in latency or network usage for each Memcache configuration under specific usage scenarios. Our tool, MemcacheTach, can be used to measure a web application's detailed Memcache usage to estimate performance with other architectures. Our example web application, MediaWiki, showed that the implemented Memcache architectures could reduce network traffic in our configuration by as much as 66%, and latency by 23%. Our proposed reformulation of multi-CPU cache systems for Memcache show better performance can be gained within the web datacenter under certain circumstances, with further gains found for more geographically distributed datacenters over current techniques.

References

1. RuggedCom: Latency on a switched ethernet network (2011)
2. Newman, S.: Three latency anomalies (2011)
3. Cloudkick: Visual evidence of amazon ec2 network issues (2011)
4. Voldemort, P.: Project voldemort (2011)
5. KLab: repcached - add data replication feature to memcached (2011)
6. Hennessy, J.L., Patterson, D.A.: Computer Architecture: A Quantitative Approach, 4th edn. Morgan Kaufmann Publishers Inc., San Francisco (2006)
7. Li, K., Hudak, P.: Memory coherence in shared virtual memory systems. ACM Trans. Comput. Syst. 7, 321–359 (1989)
8. Tanenbaum, A.S., Steen, M.V.: Distributed Systems: Principles and Paradigms, 1st edn. Prentice Hall PTR, Upper Saddle River (2001)
9. Tanenbaum, A.S., Kaashoek, M.F., Bal, H.E.: Using broadcasting to implement distributed shared memory efficiently. In: Readings in Distributed Computing Systems, pp. 387–408. IEEE Computer Society Press (1994)
10. mediawiki: Mediawiki (2011)
11. Saab, P.: Scaling memcached at facebook (2008)
12. Thusoo, A., Shao, Z., Anthony, S., Borthakur, D., Jain, N., Sen Sarma, J., Murthy, R., Liu, H.: Data warehousing and analytics infrastructure at facebook. In: Proceedings of the 2010 ACM SIGMOD International Conference on Management of data, SIGMOD 2010, pp. 1013–1020. ACM, New York (2010)
13. Borthakur, D.: Hdfs architecture guide (2011)
14. Bailey, N.: Frontpage - cassandra wiki (2011)
15. rsumbaly: Voldemort topology awareness capability (2011)
16. Sampathkumar, N., Krishnaprasad, M., Nori, A.: Introduction to caching with windows server appfabric (2009)
17. Terracotta: Ehcache documentation cache-topologies (2011)
18. Aldinucci, M., Torquati, M.: Accelerating Apache Farms Through Ad-HOC Distributed Scalable Object Repository. In: Danelutto, M., Vanneschi, M., Laforenza, D. (eds.) Euro-Par 2004. LNCS, vol. 3149, pp. 596–605. Springer, Heidelberg (2004)

Modelling Capabilities as Attribute-Featured Entities

Sami Bhiri, Wassim Derguech, and Maciej Zaremba

Digital Enterprise Research Institute, National University of Ireland, Galway, Ireland
firstname.lastname@deri.org
www.deri.org

Abstract. The concept of capability is a fundamental element not only for Service Oriented Architecture but also for Enterprise Information Systems. This concepts denotes what an action (i.e., a service, a program, a business process, etc.) can do from a functional perspective. Despite its importance, current approaches do not model it properly: either they confuse it with an annotated invocation interface or do not go beyond the classical IOPE paradigm which, from an end user perspective, does not have an intuitive description of what is the capability being modeled. In this paper, we present a conceptual model as an RDF-schema for describing capabilities as attribute-featured entities which is more user friendly. Actually, we consider a capability as an action verb and a set of domain specific attributes that relates to an exact business meaning. This way, we are able to represent capabilities at several levels of abstraction from the most abstract one with just an action verb to the most concrete one that corresponds to the exact need of an end user which is not possible with current capability modelling approaches. We are also able to interlink capabilities for creating a hierarchical structure that allows for improving the discovery process. Our meta model is based on RDF and makes use of Linked Data to define capability attributes as well as their values.

Keywords: Capability modelling, Web services, Business process, RDF.

1 Introduction

From IT perspective, the concept of service has evolved from the notion of remote invocation interface (such as WSDL) to a more comprehensive entity. In this paper, we share the same vision of OASIS Reference Model[1] and consider a service as an access mechanism to a capability. Within this vision the invocation interface is only one aspect of the whole service description. Another core aspect of a service, in which we are interested in this paper, is the notion of capability which describes what a service can do.

The notion of capability is a fundamental concept not only for SOA (Service Oriented Architecture) but also for enterprise information systems. The ARIS architecture [12] recognizes the importance of the functional perspective in enterprise information systems and considers it as one of its views.

A capability can be modeled at several levels of abstractions such that it can be as abstract as a category and denotes a class of actions, as it can be very concrete and

---

[1] OASIS Reference Model for Service Oriented Architecture 1.0,
http://www.oasis-open.org/committees/download.php/19679/soa-rm-cs.pdf

J. Cordeiro and K.-H. Krempels (Eds.): WEBIST 2012, LNBIP 140, pp. 70–85, 2013.
© Springer-Verlag Berlin Heidelberg 2013

corresponds to a specific consumer request. For instance the category "Shipping" that denotes all functions for shipping is a capability. "Shipping a package of 10 Kg from Ireland to Singapore on the 15th of January 2012 for the price of 200 Dollars" is also a capability but less abstract than the previous one.

In real world settings it is quite often very hard, even impossible, to model statically concrete capabilities due to the following reasons:

– Combinatory explosion: at concrete level, one needs to take care of all possible combinations which may lead to a explosion of capabilities (services). For example, a shipping service serves only certain routes (combination of the *source* and *destination* attributes). Defining statically the corresponding concrete capabilities means defining a capability for each route.

– Dynamicity: an aspect of a given capability (the value of an attribute) may depend on a dynamic variable. For instance, the price of a concrete shipping capability may depend on the exchange rate or on the company workload.

– Sensitivity: for business reasons, providers do not want to reveal the values of certain sensitive attributes as part of the static service description. They rather require to engage in a certain interaction before revealing the concrete value of a sensitive attribute.

In this paper, we propose a solution to the above mentioned problems. We propose a conceptual model, as an RDF-Schema, for describing capabilities. Unlike current approaches that describe capabilities via Input, Output, Preconditions and Effects [11,8], our meta model defines capabilities as an action verb and a set of domain-specific attributes. It is also able to describe capabilities at different levels of abstractions/-concreteness and establish links between them. Most importantly, our model enables describing concrete capabilities which are directly consumable by and delivered to consumers contrary to current meta models which describe the abstractions of these descriptions. Our model enables taking into account attributes dynamicity, sensitivity and interdependency. Our model is based on RDF and makes use of Linked Data to define capabilities attributes as well as their values.

Throughout the paper, we will consider the shipping domain for illustrating several parts of our conceptual model. In such domain, from the service consumer perspective, it is much more valuable to operate on concrete, consumable shipping offers such *"Shipping using FedEx Europe First, price 100 EUR, from Germany to Ireland, delivery within 1 day"* rather than to operate on abstract service descriptions such *"FedEx shipping company ships packages up to 68 Kg, between various source and target destinations"*. Current service descriptions require manual work in order to move to the service offer level. Our conceptual model aims at making this step automated.

The remainder of the paper is organized as follows. Section 2 presents our conceptual model for describing capabilities, introduces our attribute-featured principle and details the different types of attributes we consider. It shows also how abstract capabilities can be defined while respecting the attribute-featured principle and serving as declarative specifications for generating concrete capabilities. Section 3 shows how we distinguish different levels of abstractions and shows the relation that may exist between abstract and concrete capabilities and presents semantic links that may exist between them. Section 4 illustrates the relation between the customer request and the capability categories and offers by sketching a matching scenario between the customer request and the capability categories. Section 5 discusses some related work and Section 6 concludes our paper.

2 Capability Meta Model

In this Section, we introduce the concept of capability, then we explain our attribute-featured principle that we consider for modelling the capability attributes and we present the possible attribute types covered by our meta-model.

Definition 1 introduces the concept of capability in our meta-model.

Definition 1 (Capability). A tuple *Cap = (ActionVerb,Attributes)* is a capability, where:

- *ActionVerb*: This concept has been previously introduced by [10] in order to define, in a natural language, what is the action being described. Different to [10], we consider the action verb as a concept from a domain related ontology that comes form a shared aggreeement on its semantics.
- *Attributes*: Represents a set of pairs *(Attribute, AttributeValue)* that corresponds to the set of characteristics of the capability. An *Attribute* corresponds to a particular property and *AttributeValue* corresponds either to the value or the possible values that this *Attribute* can have.

Figure 1 shows a detailed UML class diagram of the capability metal model. It depicts the concepts previously introduced (i.e., Capability, ActionVerb, Attribute and AttributeValue) as well as other ones that will be introduced in the rest of this section.

Additionally, in our work, we distinguish between several abstraction levels of capabilities. As shown in Figure 1, we consider the relations *"specify"* and *"extend"* to express the relations between capabilities. These relations will be detailed later in this paper.

In the rest of this section, we will discuss our attribute-featured principle in Section 2.1 as well as the possible AttributeValue types in Section 2.2. Section 3, will define the capability abstraction relations.

2.1 Attribute-Featured Principle

We have, recently, noticed a wide adoption of the Linked Data [2,13] principles, and a growing amount of data sets specified in RDF. It is clear that Linked Data provides the best practices for publishing structured data on the Web. Linked Data is published using RDF where URIs are the means for referring various entities on the Web giving the possibility to interlink them. Currently, organizations are highly interested in publishing their data in RDF [6] as well as various public vocabularies (ontologies) are being released. Consequently, we have decided to define our meta model based on RDF and make use of Linked Data principles in order to define capability attributes as well as their values. Listing 1.1 shows a fragment of the capability Ontology in RDF using a human readable N3 notation.

In Listing 1.1, we define the concept *cap:Capability* as an *rdfs:Class*. We define the concept *cap:ActionVerb* as a sub class of *skos:Concept*. *"The skos:Concept class allows to assert that a resource is a conceptual resource. That is, the resource is itself a concept.*"[2]. And we define the concept *cap:AttributeValue* as an equivalent class to *owl:Thing* because we need it to be the most general class to allow for the reuse of existing vocabularies for possible attribute values for example using *vcard* open vocabulary for defining addresses.

The property *cap:do* allows linking a *cap:Capability* to its corresponding *cap:ActionVerb*. We created the property *cap:attribute* even though we are going to redefine it for each created attribute its corresponding range. This will have the advantage to create properties where the domain is always set to a *cap:Capability*. In other words, all attributes that will be created as an *rdfs:subProperty* of *cap:attribute* will be interpreted as a property of a capability.

Listing 1.1. Capability Ontology Snippet

```
1   @prefix rdf:    <http://www.w3.org/1999/02/22−rdf−syntax−ns#>.
2   @prefix owl:    <http://www.w3.org/2002/07/owl#>.
3   @prefix rdfs:   <http://www.w3.org/2000/01/rdf−schema#>.
4   @prefix skos:   <http://www.w3.org/2004/02/skos/core#>.
5   @prefix cap:    <http://.../ontology/capability#>.
6
7   cap:Capability a rdfs:Class.
8
9   cap:ActionVerb rdfs:subClassOf skos:Concept.
10
11  cap:AttributeValue owl:equivalentClass owl:Thing.
12
13  cap:do a rdf:Property;    rdfs:domain cap:Capability;
14                            rdfs:range cap:ActionVerb.
15
16  cap:attribute a rdf:Property;   rdfs:domain cap:Capability;
17                                  rdfs:range cap:AttributeValue.
```

We can define a domain related ontology in order to define a particular capability (i.e., its action verb and attributes). Taking as example the shipping domain, Listing 1.2 shows a snippet of such ontology. In order to define the action verb, we use *skos:prefLabel* (Line 5). The rest of the listing illustrates how two attributes *cap:from* and *cap:pickUpDate* are defined in our shipping ontology. Both attributes are *rdfs:subProperty* of *cap:attribute* (Line 7 and 9).

Listing 1.2. Shipping Domain Ontology Snippet

```
1   @prefix vcard:  <http://www.w3.org/2006/vcard/ns#>.
2   @prefix cap:    <http://.../ontology/capability#>.
3   @prefix ship:   <http://.../ontology/ship_domain#>.
4
5   :shipment a cap:ActionVerb; skos:prefLabel ''Ship''.
6
7   ship:from rdfs:subProperty cap:attribute;  rdfs:range vcard:VCard.
8
9   ship:pickUpDate a rdfs:subProperty cap:attribute; rdfs:range ship:date.
```

---
[2] SKOS Core Guide, W3C Working Draft 2 November 2005,
http://www.w3.org/TR/2005/WD-swbp-skos-core-guide-20051102/

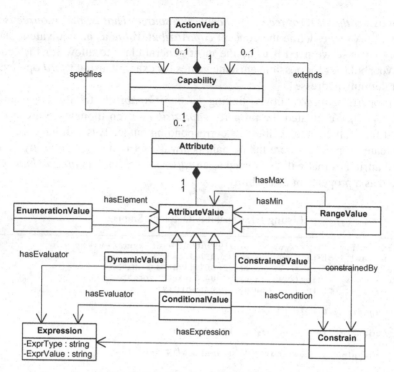

Fig. 1. Capability UML class diagram

The range of the attribute *cap:from* is *vcard:VCard* to refer to an address. The range of the attribute *cap:pickUpDate* is a concept defined in the same shipping ontology. Other attributes in subsequent listings are defined similarly.

2.2   Attribute Value Types

This section details how the set of attributes of a certain capability can be defined from a service provider perspective. As depicted in Fig. 1, we consider five classes used for describing the values of a capability attributes.

Using these classes separately or in combination, a capability can specify (i) the possible values attributes can have, (ii) and how to compute their values. We use a capability, called *BlueCap*, as an example to illustrate the use of these classes. Before detailing these classes, we need to introduce the concepts of *Constraint* and *Expression* which some attribute values may refer to.

Constraint and Expression.   A constraint enables to specify the possible values an attribute can have. The class *Constraint* represents all constraints. The class *Expression* enables to specify expressions among them the value of a given constraint. The class *Expression* has two attributes/properties, *ExprType* which specifies the type of the expression and *ExprValue* which defines the expression itself. The type of the expression, *ExprType*, indicates how to build the corresponding queries during a matching process. Currently, the only type of expression our meta model supports is SPARQL (queries).

Listing 1.3 shows an example for expressing a constraint on the weight of the package. The constraint *PackgConstraint* is defined in line 1. This constraint has an expression of type SPARQL. The value of the constraint expression (line 5) indicates that the weight of the package has to be lower than or equal to 50 Kg.

Listing 1.3. Example of a Constraint

```
1   : PckgConstraint  a  cap: Constraint;  cap: hasExpression  : PckConstraintExpr .
2
3
4   : PckgConstraintExpr   a   cap: Expression;   cap: exprType  "SPARQL";
5                   cap: exprValue  "? weight =< 50? && ? weightUnit = dbpedia :KG".
```

Constrained Value. The class *ConstrainedValue* enables defining the possible values an attribute can have by specifying a set of constraints on its value. As depicted in Fig. 1, a *ConstrainedValue* is constrained by a set of constraints. Listing 1.4 shows how *BlueCap* can specify that it can ship packages of weight under 50 Kg. The value X, of the attribute *Item*, is a *ConstrainedValue* (lines 1 and 3). X is constrained by the constraint *PckgConstraint* (line 5) which is detailed in Listing 1.3.

Listing 1.4. Example of a Constrained Value

```
1   : BlueCap   ship: Item   :X.
2
3   :X   a   ship: Package , cap: ConstrainedValue ;
4            ship: hasWeight [ ship: hasValue ?weight ; ship: hasUnit ?weightUnit ];
5            cap: constrainedBy   : PackgConstraint .
```

Dynamic Value. A *DynamicValue* defines how to compute the value of an attribute which value depends on (i) consumer provided attributes, (ii) dynamic values, or (iii) hidden variables. As shown in Fig. 1 a *DynamicValue* refers to an expression that defines how to compute it.

Listing 1.5. Example of a Dynamic Value

```
1   : BlueCap   ship: price   :Y.
2
3   :Y   a   ship: ShippingPrice , cap: DynamicValue ;   ship: hasValue   ?price ;
4            ship: hasUnit   dbpedia :USD;   cap: hasEvaluator  : PriceExpression .
5
6   : PriceExpression  a  cap: Expression ;   cap: hasType   "SPARQL";
7                   cap: exprValue   "? price := fn: ceiling (? weight )*5.5+41".
```

Listing 1.5 shows an example of how to compute the shipping price. The value Y, of the attribute *price*, is a *DynamicValue*. It has as evaluator the expression *PriceExpression* (lines 4) which is a SPARQL expression (line 6). Line 7 specifies the formula for computing the price based on the weight of the package.

Conditional Value. A *ConditionalValue* assigns an Attribute Value to the corresponding attribute if a certain condition holds. As shown in Fig. 1, a *ConditionalValue* has a condition expressed as a constraint and an element which corresponds to the corresponding attribute value.

Listing 1.6. Example of a Conditional Value

```
1   : BlueCap   ship : price   : Y.
2
3   : Y   a   ship : ShippingPrice , cap : ConditionalValue; ship : hasValue ?price;
4          cap : hasCondition   : PriceCondition; cap : hasElement   : EuropeanPrice.
5
6
7   : PriceCondition a cap : Constraint;
8          cap : hasExpression [ cap : hasType "SPARQL"; cap : hasValue "?trgCountry
9                               skos : subject dbpedia-cat : European_countries "].
10
11  : EuropeanPrice a cap : DynamicValue; cap : hasEvaluator   : PriceExpression.
```

Listing 1.6 gives an example showing how to specify a shipping price when the target country is a European country. The value Y, of the attribute *price*, is a *ConditionalValue* (lines 3). It assigns the Attribute Value, *EuropeanPrice*, when the *PriceCondition* holds (line 4). *PriceCondition* is a *Constraint* which requires that the target country is in Europe (Lines 7-9). *EuropeanPrice* is a *DynamicValue* (line 11) and has as evaluation expression *PriceExpression* which is detailed in Listing 1.5.

3   Different Levels of Abstractions

As mentioned above, capabilities can be defined at several abstraction levels. A capability that is proposed to an end user is actually the least abstract (i.e., a concrete) capability that we call *Capability Offer*. In contrast, each abstract capability is called *Capability Category*. Navigation between different abstraction levels is made through semantic links between the various capabilities.

In this paper, we present three special relations: `variantOf`, `specifies` and `extends`, which enable defining a hierarchy of capabilities in a given domain, from the most general and abstract one to the most concrete ones. Definitions 2, 3 and 4 define respectively the relations `variantOf`, `specify` and `extend`.

Please note:

- For abbreviation purposes and by misnomer we say that a certain capability *cap* has an attribute *at*.
- We refer to the attribute *at* of *cap* by *cap.at*.
- We refer to the set of attributes of *cap* by *cap.attributes*.
- We say that two capabilities C_1 and C_2 (or more) share the same attribute *at* if both of them have the attribute *at* (but possibly with a different value).

Definition 2 (variantOf). This relation holds between two resources (A capability is itself a resource.). It unifies, in fact, the two properties *rdf:type* and *rdfs:subClassOf*[3].

---

[3] We consider instantiation a special kind of sub classing where the instance is in fact no more than a sub class (subset) with only one element.

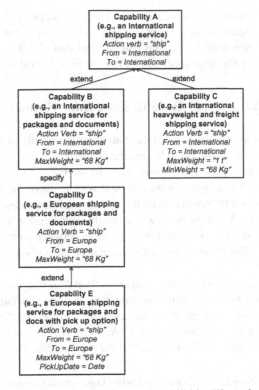

Fig. 2. Example of Shipping Capabilitics Hierarchy

A resource r_1 `variantOf` a resource r_2 if r_1 is an instance (*rdf:type*) or a subclass (*rdfs:subClassOf*) of r_2.

Definition 3 (specifies). Given two capabilities C_1 and C_2, C_1 `specifies` C_2 if (i) all the attributes of C_2 are also attributes of C_1 (In other terms C_1 inherits all the attributes defined in C_2), (ii) for every shared attribute *at*, the value of $C_1.at$ is either equal to or `variantOf` the value of $C_2.at$, and (iii) there exists at least one shared attribute *at'* such that the value of $C_1.at'$ `variantOf` $C_2.at'$.

Definition 4 (extends). Given two capabilitites C_1 and C_2, C_1 extends C_2 if (i) C_1 has all the attributes of C_2 and has additional attributes, and (ii) for every shared attribute *at*, the value of $C_1.at$ is equal to the value of $C_2.at$.

The relations `specifies` and `extends` enable defining a hierarchy of capabilities. In Fig. 2, we show an example of a hierarchy of capability descriptions. As a root of this hierarchy, we define *Capability A*. It represents an abstract capability description for shipping goods from any source and destination at an international scale. This capability can be extended either to *Capability B* or *Capability C*. Both extend the initial capability by 1 or 2 attributes. As an example of specification relation between capabilities, we refer to the link between *Capability D* and *Capability B*. *Capability D* specifies *Capability B* as it becomes a European shipping capability instead of International. It is also clear that *Capability E* extends *Capability D*.

Similar to domain ontologies which define shared concepts and shared attributes/ properties, top level capability in a given domain can also be defined as an ontology where an agreement about their meaning is reached and shared. Like any other ontology concepts, this capability top level layer can be reused to define other ones.

4   Capability Category, Offer and Customer Request

An important concept, complementary to the concept of capability in many scenarios, is the concept of *Consumer Request* which specifies what the client wants to achieve. This concept deserves a conceptual model for its own. In the following, we need to refer to some parts of the customer request, in an informal way, to show the interplay between it and capabilities. But we do not elaborate beyond that informal description.

In order to illustrate the relation between capability category, offer and customer request, we give an overview of the matching process between a customer request and a capability category. The purpose is not to cover in detail the matching or discovery phase.

Let's consider for our case a shipping company called *Blue* that has a special shipping offer called *BlueOffer*. Listing 1.7 illustrates how we can define the capability *BlueOffer* according to our capability model. *BlueOffer* consists of offering: "*a shipping service from Ireland to Singapore of a package of 10 Kilograms. The shipping will cost 200 USD and the package will be delivered the earliest on the 12th of December 2011.*"

Listing 1.7. BlueOffer Capability Description Snippet

```
1    : blueOffer  a    cap : Capability ;
2
3               cap : do  [a  cap : ActionVerb ;
4                      skos : prefLabel  ''Ship ''];
5
6               ship : from  [a  ship : SourceAddress ;
7                      vcard : address  dbpedia : Ireland ];
8
9               ship : to  [a  ship : TargetAddress ;
10                      vcard : address  dbpedia : Singapore ];
11
12              ship : item  [a  ship : Package ;
13                      ship : hasWeight  [ ship : hasValue  10;
14                      ship : hasUnit  dbpedia : Kilogram ]];
15
16              ship : price  [a  ship : ShippingPrice ;
17                      ship : hasValue  200;
18                      ship : hasUnit  dbpedia :USD];
19
20        ship : deliveryDate  [a  ship : ShippingDeliveryDate ;
21                      ship : earliest  ''2011 − 12 − 13''
22                      ^^ xsd : date ].
```

The description of concrete capabilities such as *BlueOffer* (See Listing 1.7) depends on the corresponding customer request. More specifically the values of certain attributes are in fact defined in the customer request. For instance the values of the attributes *ship:from* and *ship:to* of the capability *BlueOffer* (described in Listing 1.7) are specified in the given customer request.

Before going into detail about the matching phase (See Section 4.3), we need to introduce the attribute types based on who is providing the value of that attribute in Section 4.1 and the property assignments that allow to provide concrete values of some capability attributes in Section 4.2.

4.1   Attribute Types

We distinguish three types of attributes depending on the source of their values. In general, three sources are involved in a scenario of capability consumption. These sources are the *consumer* who has a request and is looking for a (concrete) capability to achieve, (ii) the *provider* who provides capabilities for achieving consumer requests and (iii) the *interaction context*.

The values of a concrete capability attributes are provided/computed by one of these players. According to who provides the value of an attribute, we distinguish three sub-classes of attributes namely *Co*, *Pro* and *Co&Pro* attributes. It is important to emphasize that this classification is *based on which role provides the value of the corresponding attribute*:

- *Consumer or Context* (**Co**) attributes are attributes which values are specified by the consumer or provided by the interaction context. For instance the attributes *ship:to* and *ship:from* in the *BlueOffer* capability are **Co** attributes.
- *Provider* (**Pro**) attributes are attributes which values are specified or computed by the capability provider. For instance the attribute *ship:Price* in the *BlueOffer* capability is a **Pro** attribute.
- *Consumer then Provider* (**Co&Pro**) attributes are attributes which values are firstly specified by the consumer but may be changed by the provider. For instance, the attribute *ship:DeliveryDate* is a **Co&Pro** attribute; the consumer can select his preferred delivery date and the provider can change it if some of his working constraints do not fit the exact proposed date.

4.2   Property Assignments

Property assignments define dependencies between *Co*, *Co&Pro* and *Pro* attributes. Property assignments are utilised during the matchmaking process to provide concrete values for *Co&Pro* and *Pro* attributes. Dependencies between properties that do not change frequently can be formalised in property assignments. Each property assignment defines constraints (SPARQL FILTER) and assignment statements (SPARQL BIND).

Listing 1.8 in lines 2–8 shows an example of property assignment. It creates a value of the *ShippingDelivery Pro* property if source and destination constraints are satisfied (i.e., European countries).

In many cases not all dependencies between *Co*, *Co&Pro* and *Pro* attributes can be explicitly specified using *property assignments*. It can be due to the dynamicity of attributes, complexity of dependencies between attributes, or their business sensitivity. In such cases, values of *Co&Pro* and *Pro* attributes must be obtained on-the-fly from service provider's back-end system that is accessed via a referred endpoint. In such cases we propose using data-fetching interfaces. A data-fetching interface is a public service interface that is used during the discovery process to dynamically fetch *Co&Pro* and *Pro* properties. The data-fetching interface represents a request-response interaction with the service endpoint.

Listing 1.8 in lines 11–18 shows an example of the data-fetching interface. This data fetching interface is executed only if the source country is in Europe and the destination country is in Asia (lines 14–15). Instances of *ShippingPrice* and *ShippingDelivery* concepts will be obtained by invoking the service safe endpoint (line 16). Lowering in line 17 refers to the mapping from RDF to XML, while lifting in line 18 refers to the mapping from XML to RDF.

Listing 1.8. Property assignments, Data-fetching interfaces and Hard constraints

```
1   /*Property assignment — delivery for addresses in EU*/
2   :deliveryEU a cap:PropertyAssignment;
3     cap:hasCoAttribute    ship:SourceAddress, ship:TargetAddress, ship:Package;
4     cap:hasProAttribute   ship:ShippingPrice, ship:ShippingDelivery;
5     cap:hasValue  "?srcCountry skos:subject d:European_countries.
6                    ?trgCountry skos:subject d:European_countries.
7                    BIND(3, ?delivery). BIND(d:Business_day, ?deliveryUnit)."
8                    ^^cap:SPARQL.
9
10  /*Data—fetching (dynamic price) — shipping between Europe and Asia*/
11  :priceDeliveryEurope a ser:DataFetching;
12    cap:hasCoAttribute    ship:SourceAddress, ship:TargetAddress, ship:Package;
13    cap:hasProAttribute   ship:ShippingPrice, ship:ShippingDelivery;
14    cap:hasConstraint  "?srcCountry skos:subject d:European_countries.
15                    ?trgCountry skos:subject d:Asian_countries."^^cap:SPARQL;
16    cap:hasEndpoint   "http://.../FedEx/endpoint";
17    cap:hasLowering   "http://.../Lowering.rq";
18    cap:hasLifting    "http://.../Lifting.rq".
19
20  /* Service hard constraints — max. package size */
21  :supportedMaxPckgSize a cap:HardConstraint; )
22    cap:hasCoAttribute    ship:Package;
23    cap:hasValue        "FILTER (?length + ?width + ?height < 105
24                    && ?lUnit=d:Centimetre && ...)"^^cap:SPARQL.
```

In addition to defining property assignments and data-fetching interfaces, capability providers can also define some hard constraints on a capability usage. Capability hard constraints can be specified on: (1) *Co* attributes (e.g., $length + girth < 108cm$), (2) *Co&Pro* and *Pro* attributes (e.g., $deliveryTime < 8$), and (3) a combination of *Co*, *Co&Pro* and *Pro* attributes (e.g., $price/weight < 10$). Listing 1.8 in lines 21–24 shows an example of a hard constraint imposed on the package size.

4.3   Matching Scenario

By analogy to Object Oriented Programming, a capability category can be seen as a class and capability offers as objects. Similar to objects, which are instantiated from classes, capability offers are generated from capability categories. Certain capability categories are, declarative specifications for generating capability offers for particular consumer requests. If possible, a capability offer is dynamically generated from a capability category for a particular consumer request. We say that a particular capability offer is variant of the capability category it derives from.

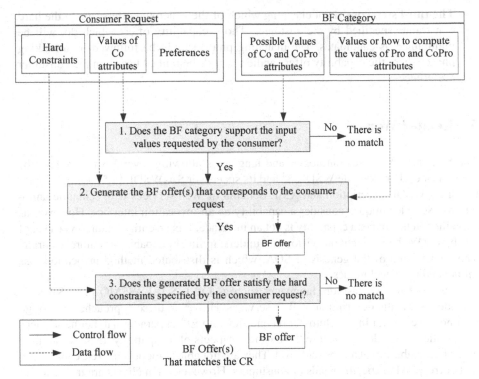

Fig. 3. Overview of the matching process of a customer request and a capability

Fig. 3 gives an overview of the matching process and shows which artifact is used in each step. The matching phase has as input the customer request and a capability category and as output the customer offers variant that matches the request.

As shown in Fig. 3, a consumer request specifies (i) the values of Co attributes, (ii) hard constraints on some Pro and Co&Pro attributes, and (iii) preferences on Co, Pro and Co&Pro attributes. A capability category specifies (i) the possible values Co and Co&Pro attributes can have while considering their interdependencies, and (ii) the values or how to compute the values of Pro and Co&Pro attributes.

The matching process consists of:

- **The first step** checks whether the capability category supports the values of the Co and Co&Pro attributes specified in the customer request. If the answer is negative then there is no capability offer variant of the given category that matches the customer request. If the answer is positive, the process moves to the following step.
- **The second step** consists of generating the capability offers that correspond to the customer request. A capability category and its offers have the same attributes but with different values for some of them. The generated capability offers will be constructed as follows. The value of Co attributes will be those specified by the customer request. The value of the Pro and Co&Pro attributes will be specified or computed as described in the capability category.

- **The third step** consists of checking which of the generated offers satisfy the hard constraints specified by the customer. Those capability offers which do, will be maintained as candidates. The matching phase should be followed by a ranking phase where the capability offer candidates will be ranked based on the consumer preferences.

5   Related Work

The Semantic Web uses ontologies and languages allowing several ways to describe web services. For example WSDL-S[4] and its successor SA-WSDL [4,5] use ontologies to enrich WSDL description and XML Schema of Web services with semantic annotations. Such techniques consider a capability as an invocation interface. However, as explained in this paper a capability is not an interface. It is an entity featured via a set of attributes. We believe that our vision and understanding of capability is more accurate. The background of the genesis of SOA, which is distributed method invocation, has influenced these techniques.

In a more refined fashion, languages such as OWL-S [8], WSMO [11], SWSO[5], provide a semantic description of Web services. However, these approaches do not go beyond the classical Input, Output, Precondition and Effect paradigm to define services capabilities. They do not feature the business aspects of a capability. In addition, they describe capabilities at an abstract level. They are not able to model concrete capabilities that correspond to specific needs of consumers. However, what clients are interested in are concrete capabilities. The matching of consumer requests has to be against concrete capabilities.

Oaks et al., [10] propose a model for describing service capabilities going one step beyinf the IOPE paradigm by distinguishing in particular the corresponding action verb and informational attributes (called roles in the paper [10]). However, the semantics of capabilities remain defined via the IOPE paraddigm and therefore has the same problems of the previously described approaches.

The notion of (service) offer is currently not addressed in service description languages such as Universal Service Description Language(USDL[6]). Service descriptions have a varying level of concreteness depending on the stage of a matchmaking and configuration. This notion is currently missing from the USDL. Introducing different levels of concreteness in USDL Functional Module should make USDL applicable for describing highly configurable services.

Other related works worth mentioning are [3,15,17]. These works have identified the gap between current modeling techniques and real world requirements and initiated the discussions about abstract services and concrete offers descriptions. Similar to all related work, the concept of capability was not tackled as first-class entity. The focus was rather on the service model. In addition, [15] and [17] rely on and extend the Input, Output, Precondition and Effect paradigm without making explicit and clear the

---

[4] http://www.w3.org/Submission/WSDL-S.
[5] http://www.w3.org/Submission/SWSF-SWSO
[6] www.internet-of-services.de

business features of services functionalities. They also do not explicitly distinguish be
tween abstract services and service offer, nor do they define the links between them.

Different from IOPE paradigm, EASY [9] and SoffD [16] propose to describe
services via a set or attributes. Using such presentation, services are organised respectively as a directed acyclic graph or a tree. This allows for improved matchmaking techniques that relies on exploring the organizing structure. However, in these approaches,
attributes used are not intrinsic business features as they contain even non-functional
properties which do not describe the capability from a business perspective. Unlike
these contributions, we represent a capability as an action verb and a set of domain specific properties (i.e., attributes). The action verb as well as these attributes are defined
in a domain ontology that, to some extend, provides the possibles values each attribute
can have.

6   Conclusions and Future Work

In this paper, we presented an original meta model for describing Capabilities which
presents several advantages.

First, contrary to the Input, Output, Precondition and Effect paradigm it features the
business and functional characteristics which consumers are mostly interested in and
which are specified in their requests.

Second, our meta model can deal with capabilities at different abstraction levels in
a uniform way. In addition, it establishes relations between Capabilities at different
abstraction levels. In particular, it provides the required declarative specification to dynamically generate concrete Capabilities from abstract ones.

Furthermore, our meta model defines semantic links between Capabilities. By using
these relations Capability owners can rapidly and easily define new Capabilities by
reusing previous definitions. In addition, these relations define a cloud of Capabilities
where navigation techniques can be developed as an alternative to goal based discovery
techniques.

A cloud of capabilities description can be easily queried using SPARQL. Actually, we use RDF as a lightweight language for describing and linking capabilities descriptions whereas we can use SPARQL for advanced querying including the usage of
SPARQL as a rule language [1].

Finally, since our meta model is RDF based it can be easily extended, while pre-
serving the attribute-featured principle, by considering other types of attributes (such as
optional and mandatory attributes) and other types of attribute values.

However, we provide with our model a coarse-grained semantics of the capability
effect or changes on the state of the world. While this coarse-grain semantics is adequate for conducting discovery, it is insufficient when automated chaining is required
such as in composition and planning scenarios. By coarse grain semantics we mean
defining shared agreement on coarse grain entities such as capability in our case. Automated chaining requires finer-grained semantics. For that purpose, we consider a domain related ontology that define a detailed (i.e., fine grained) semantics of the abstract
capabilities. This domain related ontology taken together with some relations between
attributes can help to determine the fine grained semantics of a capability description.

This particular idea of generating fine-grained semantics from a detailed domain ontology is part of our future work.

We did not give much attention in this paper to the concept of Action Verb. We do not want to tight the use of this concept to a simple literal or a verb. This concept is not the actual label that a capability can have, it is a concept from a domain ontology that might be accompanied by a label which is an expression describing the actual service action in a natural language. It is also possible to enrich this label by other related terms such as synonyms. Natural Language Processing [14] can be applied together with Word-Net verb synsets for generating possible synonyms to generate a particular label for the action verb concept of the capability description. It is possible to use concepts from a domain related ontology/taxonomy or a categorization schema like NAICS[7] or UN-SPSC[8] for this label in order to be more compliant to the domain vocabulary. Otherwise, as it has been stated by [10], we can use the MIT Process Handbook [7] for determining the label of a service capability. A capability can be matched to a particular process in the process handbook. We can also use the meronymy and the hyponymy relations described in that process handbook for creating the hierarchy of capabilities.

As part of our future work, we plan to:

- investigate other relations that might be useful for creating the capabilities hierachy/cloud. The possible other relations under definition are: *share*, *shareSame*, *shareDifferent*, *differMore* and *differLess*. Some of these relations do not bring much information on themselves. They are used in fact to compute other relations.
- explore what we call extended relations in contrast to basic relations that we are currently considerering. Basic relations are coarse-grain relations/links while extended relations are more fine-grained. An extended relation specifies which attribute the basic relation, it derives from.
- provide an automation support for maintaining the capabilities hierarchy. We aim to provide an automation support to add or remove any capability from the hierarchy/cloud.
- provided a domain ontology, we plan to define some guidelines for end users in order to create new capabilities.
- define a methodology that allows to generate fine grained semantics of the actions of capabilities using a detailed domain ontology.

Acknowledgements. This work is funded by the Lion II project supported by Science Foundation Ireland under grant number 08/CE/I1380.

References

1. Polleres, A.: From SPARQL to rules (and back). In: WWW 2007, Banff, Alberta, Canada. ACM (2007)
2. Bizer, C., Heath, T., Berners-Lee, T.: Linked Data - The Story So Far. IJSWIS 5(3) (2009)

---

[7] North American Industry Classification System,
http://www.census.gov/eos/www/naics/
[8] United Nations Standard Products and Services Code, http://www.unspsc.org/

3. Kopecký, J., Simperl, E.P.B., Fensel, D.: Semantic Web Service Offer Discovery. In: SMRR. CEUR Workshop Proceedings, vol. 243 (2007)
4. Kopecký, J., Vitvar, T., Bournez, C., Farrell, J.: SAWSDL: Semantic annotations for WSDL and XML schema. IEEE Internet Computing 11(6) (2007)
5. Lathem, J., Gomadam, K., Sheth, A.P.: Sa-rest and (s)mashups: Adding semantics to restful services. In: ICSC. IEEE Computer Society (2007)
6. Lebo, T., Williams, G.T.: Converting governmental datasets into linked data. In: I-SEMANTICS. ACM (2010)
7. Malone, T.W., Crowston, K., Herman, G.A. (eds.): Organizing Business Knowledge: The MIT Process Handbook, 1st edn. The MIT Press (September 2003)
8. Martin, D., Paolucci, M., Wagner, M.: Bringing Semantic Annotations to Web Services: OWL-S from the SAWSDL Perspective. In: Aberer, K., Choi, K.-S., Noy, N., Allemang, D., Lee, K.-I., Nixon, L.J.B., Golbeck, J., Mika, P., Maynard, D., Mizoguchi, R., Schreiber, G., Cudré-Mauroux, P. (eds.) ISWC/ASWC 2007. LNCS, vol. 4825, pp. 340–352. Springer, Heidelberg (2007)
9. Mokhtar, S.B., Preuveneers, D., Georgantas, N., Issarny, V., Berbers, Y.: Easy: Efficient semantic service discovery in pervasive computing environments with qos and context support. Journal of Systems and Software 81(5), 785–808 (2008)
10. Oaks, P., ter Hofstede, A.H.M., Edmond, D.: Capabilities: Describing What Services Can Do. In: Orlowska, M.E., Weerawarana, S., Papazoglou, M.P., Yang, J. (eds.) ICSOC 2003. LNCS, vol. 2910, pp. 1–16. Springer, Heidelberg (2003)
11. Roman, D., de Bruijn, J., Mocan, A., Lausen, H., Domingue, J., Bussler, C., Fensel, D.: WWW: WSMO, WSML, and WSMX in a Nutshell. In: Mizoguchi, R., Shi, Z.-Z., Giunchiglia, F. (eds.) ASWC 2006. LNCS, vol. 4185, pp. 516–522. Springer, Heidelberg (2006)
12. Scheer, A.W., Schneider, K.: ARIS Architecture of Integrated Information Systems. Bernus Peter Mertins Kai Schmidt Gunter (2006)
13. Sheridan, J., Tennison, J.: Linking UK Government Data. In: LDOW 2010 (2010)
14. Sugumaran, V., Storey, V.C.: A semantic-based Approach to Component Retrieval. SIGMIS Database 34 (August 2003)
15. Vitvar, T., Zaremba, M., Moran, M.: Dynamic Service Discovery Through Meta-interactions with Service Providers. In: Franconi, E., Kifer, M., May, W. (eds.) ESWC 2007. LNCS, vol. 4519, pp. 84–98. Springer, Heidelberg (2007)
16. Zaremba, M., Vitvar, T., Bhiri, S., Derguech, W., Gao, F.: Service Offer Descriptions and Expressive Search Requests – Key Enablers of Late Service Binding. In: Huemer, C., Lops, P. (eds.) EC-Web 2012. LNBIP, vol. 123, pp. 50–62. Springer, Heidelberg (2012)
17. Zaremba, M., Vitvar, T., Moran, M., Haselwanter, T.: WSMX Discovery for the SWS Challenge. In: ISWC, Athens, Georgia, USA (November 2006)

Governance Policies for Verification and Validation of Service Choreographies*

Antonia Bertolino[1], Guglielmo De Angelis[1], and Andrea Polini[2]

[1] CNR– ISTI, Via Moruzzi 1, 56124 Pisa, Italy
[2] Computer Science Division, School of Science and Technologies, University of Camerino,
62032 Camerino, Italy
{antonia.bertolino,guglielmo.deangelis}@isti.cnr.it,
andrea.polini@unicam.it

Abstract. The Future Internet (FI) sustains the emerging vision of a software
ecosystem in which pieces of software, developed, owned and run by different
organizations, can be dynamically discovered and bound to each other so to readily start to interact. Nevertheless, without suitable mechanisms, paradigms and
tools, this ecosystem is at risk of tending towards chaos. Indeed the take off of
FI passes through the introduction of paradigms and tools permitting to establish
some discipline. Choreography specifications and Governance are two different
proposals which can contribute to such a vision, by permitting to define rules and
functioning agreements both at the technical level and at the social (among organizations) level. In this paper we discuss such aspects and introduce a policy
framework so to support a FI ecosystem in which V&V activities are controlled
and perpetually run so to contribute to the quality and trustworthiness perceived
by all the involved stakeholders.

Keywords: Service choreography, SOA governance, V&V Policies, On-line
testing, Ranking, Reputation, Service oriented architecture.

1 Introduction

Services are pervasive in modern society and enable the Future Internet (FI) architecture [1]. Many research projects are undertaken from all over the world to re-design the
FI architecture so to address the various emerging needs, including trustworthiness, security, mobility, scale, flexibility, content distribution, adaptation. As highlighted in [1],
the FI cannot be achieved by "assembling different clean-slate solutions targeting different aspects", instead a coordinated comprehensive approach addressing new design
principles is required.

One shared fundamental principle is that, due to the inherent inter-organization nature of the FI, *social* aspects become preponderant over merely *technical* [2] ones.
Indeed, to permit the effective integration and definition of independently developed
services, methodologies and approaches must be conceived that support their smooth
integration towards providing users with composite services, fulfilling their changing
requests.

* This paper is supported by the European Project FP7 IP 257178: CHOReOS, and partially by
the European Project FP7 NoE 256980: NESSoS.

J. Cordeiro and K.-H. Krempels (Eds.): WEBIST 2012, LNBIP 140, pp. 86–102, 2013.
© Springer-Verlag Berlin Heidelberg 2013

In this line two main proposals can be identified. The first one concerns the introduction of application-level global protocols that service providers can take as a reference in the development of their own services. These specifications, typically defined and managed by third party organizations, are generally referred to as **Choreographies**. Specifically a service choreography is a description of the *peer-to-peer* externally observable interactions that cooperating services should put in place [3]. Such multi-party collaboration model focuses on message exchange, and does not rely on a central coordination of the described activities. Therefore, service choreographies can be one of the right instruments to solve "technical and social" issues posed by FI, as they model a higher level of abstraction with respect to those of services.

The second proposal is the introduction of a clear and explicit SOA governance [4]. Generally speaking, governance is the act of governing or administrating, and refers to all measures, rules, decision-making, information, and enforcement that ensure the proper functioning and control of the governed system. SOA governance addresses specific aspects of SOA life-cycle [4]. Specifically, SOA governance approaches include: SOA policy management and enforcement; registry and meta-data management; data collection for statistical and Key Performance Indicators; monitoring and management; application and service life cycle management.

Choreographies and SOA governance are also needed in order to support the progressive moving of traditional Software Engineering activities from the only pre-runtime phases towards "also at run-time" [5], i.e., during normal operating of deployed services. Specifically, during the last years, various research works [6–8] argued in favor of extending testing activities from the laboratory to the field, i.e., towards run-time.

SOA on-line testing foresees the proactive launching of selected test cases that evaluate the real system within the services' real execution environment, according to the established SOA test governance process.

In this paper, we continue the investigation on such topic proposing a V&V policy framework aiming at sustaining the governance of on-line V&V.

In this paper the focus is mainly on V&V policies on which governance of choreography is based, specifically to support V&V on-line activities. Of course, these policies cover only part of the complex task of choreography governance, and other policies are needed to support overall choreography management. The rest of the paper is organized as follows: Section 2 introduces a classification for policies enabling V&V activities. In the following sections 3, 4 and 5 we respectively illustrate policies for activation, rating and ranking both of services and choreographies. In Section 6 we introduce some policies related to Choreography enactment and in Section 7 policies for test case selection are discussed. Then the paper closes with Section 8 in which policies are illustrated with real examples and Section 9 in which we draw some conclusions and opportunities for future work.

2 Governance Policies Enabling V&V Activities

SOA governance is meant as a set of best practices and policies for ensuring interoperability, adequacy, and reuse of services over several different platforms [4] and among different organizations.

Policies are at the heart of governance: they define the rules according to which systems and their owners should behave to ensure the mutual understanding, interaction and cooperation. More specifically, the concept of a policy has been introduced as representing some constraint or condition on describing, deploying, and using some service [9]. Indeed, SOA governance asks for the definition of policies and supporting tools to take into account the social and runtime aspect of FI above highlighted.

In the next sections we propose and discuss a set of policies and rules that could be adopted and implemented within a given V&V governance framework. For clarity of exposition we organize such policies according to the following classification:

1. **V&V Activation Policies** that describe rules for regulating the activation of the on-line testing sessions. As described in the following, such activation could be either periodical, driven from the events about the lifecycle of a service, or linked to some kind of quality indicator;
2. **V&V Rating Policies** that prescribe which aspects have to be considered for rating the quality of both choreographies, and services.
3. **V&V Ranking Policies** defining the rules and the metrics for computing the quality parameters expressed into the V&V Rating Policies;
4. **Choreography Enactment Policies** that prescribe rules for deciding when a service choreography could be enacted;
5. **Test Cases Selection Policies** regulating the testing strategies that can be applied at run-time.

The rest of the paper describes such policies in detail by considering a given choreography C.

3   V&V Activation Policies

The idea of V&V governance was originally proposed in [10] to support an on-line testing session when a service asks for registration within a registry. In this vision, only services passing the testing phase are logged in the registry. As a result, the registry is expected to include only "high-quality" services that passed the validation steps foreseen by a more general governance framework. In addition to the registration of a new service, the on-line validation process could be also extended to other events. For example, during the life-cycle of a choreography C, a service that was originally registered to play a given role in C could be modified or become deprecated. This event might impact on the regular progress of some of the activities described in C. Thus, the V&V governance should support rules that verify if the registry still points at one or more active services that could play all the roles subscribed by the removed service in C.

Besides, the service provider might omit to notify the deprecation of a service to the service registry. For these cases, the monitoring system infrastructure of the V&V governance architecture could cooperate with the Service Registry in order to verify and notify if any registered service is not reachable anymore.

Within a choreography a service may play one or more roles. Also, the same service may be involved in several choreographies. Service provider may decide to change the roles that their services are playing in the choreographies in order to fulfill new needs, new business requirements, or the evolution of the technical solutions offered by the service.

In all these scenarios, one of the V&V governance rules we propose is that any modification (i.e. activation, modification, cancellation) to the role of a service in C should activate a new testing session. Specifically:

activation : when a new role A is added to a service S in C, execute the integration test suite for A in C and run it through S. Evaluate the impact of the result of such on-line testing session on the testing scores of the choreography C (as detailed in Section 4).

cancellation : when a role A is deleted from the roles that a service S in could play in C, verify that the service registry still points to at least one active service that could play A in C.

modification : this step could be processed as a sequence of a cancellation and an activation of a role for a service in C.

V&V activation policies could also regulate on-line testing sessions by referring to rating management architectures (e.g. based either on trust, or reputation models). As an example, they can specify the admissible ranking rates that each service participating in a choreography must yield, and then trigger on-line testing sessions whenever the rank of a service decreases below such thresholds. We introduce ranking policies in Section 5.

Finally, in addition to the event-driven activation of the on-line testing sessions (e.g. service registration, etc), V&V policies can also regulate the "perpetual" testing of software services either periodically, or when a specified deadline is met.

4   V&V Rating Policies

This section describes the V&V governance policies rating both a single service that is bound to a choreography C, and also C as a whole. We partition these policies in two main categories: rating policies based on objective testing scores; and rating policies based on subjective evaluation (i.e. feedbacks).

Concerning the first category, we refer to a scenario implementing some perpetual validation techniques, e.g. [11, 7]. The results of the testing sessions somehow allow us to quantify the service trustworthiness values according to the testing goals. Thus, we can use such results to determine what service is trustable according to an objective estimation (i.e. test passed VS. test failed). Several trust models could be associated to V&V governance aspects; in Section 5.2 we detail a metric based on testing results.

Similarly to the rating of trustworthiness for single services the V&V governance framework could refer to some objective trust models in order to estimate the potential trustworthiness score for the whole choreography. In particular, for each role A defined in C, the trust model could consider the trustworthiness based on testing score of all the services on the registry that can play as A. The trustworthiness of the whole

C is a function of the testing scores computed for all the roles, and it could be interpreted as the resulting and objective potential quality state (e.g. a benchmark) of the whole choreography. A concrete metric that instantiates this trust model is described in Section 5.1.

Concerning the subjective category, we refer to service reputation. As argued in [12], in this context we consider service reputation as a metric of how a service is generally perceived by its users. Thus, differently from the testing-based trust systems described above, that are based on objective measures, here reputation systems are based on subjective judgments.

We consider reputation as an interesting indicator to be referred within governance policies for V&V activities. The basic idea of a reputation system is to let parties rate each other, for example after the completion of an interaction, and use the aggregated ratings about a given party to derive a reputation score, which can assist other parties in deciding whether or not to interact with that party in the future [12]. Currently, reputation systems represent an interesting and significant trend in decision support, service provision, and service selection (e.g. the Google's +1 button, the eBay's feedback forum, the Facebook's Thumbs Up button, the LinkedIn's Recommendations). Several and configurable reputation models could be associated to this V&V governance aspect; in particular Section 5.3 describes a model implementing this kind of reputation rule.

Finally, V&V governance policies could refer to some compositional model of the user's feedbacks in order to estimate a potential reputation score for the whole choreography. In particular, for each role A defined in C, the trust model could consider the reputation score (i.e. positive feedbacks VS. negative feedbacks) of all the services on the registry that can play as A. The reputation score of C (as a whole) is a function of the feedback scores computed for all the roles. Thus here, the reputation score of C is interpreted as a benchmark of subjective judgments for the choreography.

5   Ranking Rules for V&V Rating Policies

Rating policies rely on some metrics to evaluate the choreography as well as its participating services. In this section we propose some possible ranking rules for this purpose. In particular, Section 5.1 describes a rule for ranking a service choreography according to both the topology of the choreography itself and the ranking of the available/known services that can play a role specified by the choreography. Then, according to the V&V Rating Policies described in Section 4, we provide two possible strategies for calculating the service ranking function. Specifically, Section 5.2 describes an objective ranking strategy that is based on the results of the testing sessions, while Section 5.3 describes a subjective ranking strategy that is based on a reputation model.

Other different criteria for service ranking could be considered in future extensions, for example an interesting way to complement our proposed numerical rankings could be to also take into account ontological matching, as proposed in [13].

5.1   Choreography Rank

The ranking metric for a service choreography described in the following is based on the well-known PageRank algorithm [14] used by Google.

Differently from the other web search engines that have been used until year 2000, Google dominated the market due to the superior search results that its innovative PageRank algorithm delivered. As described in [12], the PageRank algorithm can be considered as a reputation mechanism because it ranks the web pages according to the number of other pages pointing at it. In other words, the algorithm interprets the collection of hyperlinks to a given page as public information that can be combined to derive an objective reputation score.

In the original definition [14] [15], the PageRank algorithm considers a collection of web pages as a graph where each node is a web page, and the hyperlinks of the pages where modeled as outgoing edges of the graph. In this sense, the strategy proposed by PageRank algorithm can be applied to any problem that can be formulated in terms of a graph.

Our interpretation of the PageRank algorithm considers both the services involved in a choreography, and the graph that the choreography subsumes. Specifically, let us denote S as a set of services. We define :

$$\mathcal{A}_C = \{A | A \text{ is a role in C}\} \tag{1}$$

as the set of all the roles defined in C, and:

$$\Omega_C(A) = \{\omega \in S | A \in \mathcal{A}_C, \omega \text{ plays } A \text{ in C}\} \tag{2}$$

as the set of all the services in S that can play the role A in C. Also, given a relation of dependency among the roles in a choreography, for each role A in C we denote both the set of roles in C on which A depends (i.e. $N_C^+(A)$), and the set of roles in C that depend on A (i.e. $N_C^-(A)$). Specifically:

$$N_C^+(A) = \{B | A \in \mathcal{A}_C, B \in \mathcal{A}_C, \exists \text{ dep. from } A \text{ to } B \text{ in C}\} \tag{3}$$

$$N_C^-(A) = \{B | A \in \mathcal{A}_C, B \in \mathcal{A}_C, \exists \text{ dep. from } B \text{ to } A \text{ in C}\} \tag{4}$$

Note that the definitions above are given in terms of an abstract notion of dependency that can occour among the roles belonging to a choreography. Section 8.1 will present an example by using a specific dependency relation.

Let us denote R as a ranking function for a given service (see either Section 5.2, or Section 5.3), thus Equation 5 defines the ranking function of a role A in a choreography C.

$$\mathcal{R}(A, t, C) = \frac{\displaystyle\sum_{\omega \in \Omega_C(A)} R(\omega, t)}{|\Omega_C(A)|} \tag{5}$$

Specifically, Equation 5 gives rank values based on the ranking of all the services that are implementing A in C: the more the services that can play A in C rank well, the better A will perform in the choreography. The effect of such impact is normalized according to the number of services playing the role A. On the other hand, the equation computes a poor ranking for A if there exist only few and poorly ranked services that can play A in C. In other words, this means that A could be considered critical for the enactment of C.

Nevertheless, the role ranking in Equation 5 does not take into account the context where the role is used. Equation 6 introduces a correction factor of the ranking $\mathcal{R}$ taking into account the role dependencies implied by a choreography specification.

$$\delta(A,t,\mathsf{C}) = \begin{cases} \lambda\mathcal{R}(A,t,\mathsf{C}) + (1-\lambda) \sum_{B\in N_{\mathsf{C}}^+(A)} \dfrac{\mathcal{R}(B,t-1,\mathsf{C})}{\left|N_{\mathsf{C}}^-(B)\right|} & \text{for } t\geq 1 \\[2em] \varphi & \text{otherwise} \end{cases} \tag{6}$$

Given a role A in choreography C, the case $t = 0$ in Equation 6 defines the initial condition for δ, while the recursive definition for the case $t \geq 1$ is an interpretation of the PageRank algorithm [14] [15]. Specifically, such definition is composed by two terms: using the terminology adopted within the PageRank algorithm, the first term of Equation 6 is the *source-of-rank* which is a parameter influencing the final rank. In our case the *source-of-rank* is $\mathcal{R}$, giving rank values based on the evaluation of all the services that are implementing A in C.

The second term in Equation 6 gives rank values as a function of the other roles in C on which A depends. In other words, we consider that if the behaviour foreseen for A in C relies on the actions performed by another role B (e.g. B is the initiator of a task with A), then the rank values scored by B should impact the ranking of A within the whole C. This metric is generally helpful, however we consider it particularly significant when B is badly ranked, for example because most of the services playing B are not reliable. Note that, as the metric in Equation 6 does not take into account the enactment status of the choreography C, the effect of how much B impacts on A is proportionally calculated by considering the number of all the roles that depend from B.

The parameter λ can be used to tune the contribution of each term in the computation of the role's ranking function; in the literature on the PageRank algorithm, typically its most cited value is 0.85 [15].

Finally, we denote the ranking function for the whole choreography C as:

$$\mathbb{R}(\mathsf{C},t) = \sum_{A\in\mathcal{A}_{\mathsf{C}}} \delta(A,t,\mathsf{C})\mathcal{R}(A,t,\mathsf{C}) \tag{7}$$

5.2   Testing-Based Service Rank

As described in Section 4, in those scenarios including perpetual V&V activities, the analysis of the results of each testing session can be used for building a trust model for services.

The very general idea of this assumption is that data from testing results (i.e. both test passed, and test failed) represents quantitative facts that permit to determine how much a service playing a given role is trustable according to an objective estimation. For example, if the testing sessions that are executed focus on integration issues, the

testing-based service rank explains how a service is behaving with respect to the sce
nario foreseen by a choreography.

Furthermore, as service behaviour may continuously evolve (e.g. change in the implementation, dynamic binding with other services), a trust model should consider that
the closer in time a service has been tested the more reliable are the results obtained
from the testing session. Thus the definition of a testing-based ranking for services
should decrease over time.

The logistic function is a well-studied mathematical function that was originally proposed in [16], and is often used in ecology for modeling population growth. Specifically,
in one of its most common formulation, the logistic function offers a non linear evolution of the population function P over the parameter t (e.g. the time) depending on the
two parameters: the carrying capacity K, and the growth rate r.

The testing-based ranking we propose defines a function of trust basing on the logistic function, where K is interpreted as the highest admissible level of trust, while for
each service w, r is the number of the tests passed over the total number of test executed
(see Equation 8).

$$r_\omega = \frac{\#\text{passedTest}_\omega}{\#\text{runTest}_\omega} \tag{8}$$

For a given service $\omega \in \Omega_C(A)$ that can play the role A in C, Equation 9 defines a
test-based trust model based on the logistic function.

$$\mathcal{T}(t,\omega) = \frac{K v_{\text{Fade}} e^{(-r_\omega(t-h_{\text{Offset}}))}}{K + v_{\text{Fade}}(e^{(-r_\omega(t-h_{\text{Offset}}))} - 1)} \tag{9}$$

Specifically, in Equation 9, the h_{Offset}, and the v_{Fade} are configurable parameters useful
for translating, and fading the values returned by the trust model. In addition, as the
trust model $\mathcal{T}$ is actually an instantiation of the logistic function, the setting of the
parameters for $\mathcal{T}$ must keep satisfying the stability criteria foreseen by logistic function
(e.g. $K > 1$).

Finally, Equation 10 defines a testing-based ranking function for a given service ω
playing a given role A in C (i.e. $\omega \in \Omega_C(A)$). As introduced in Section 5.1, such
service-level ranking function can be exploited in order to compute the testing-based
rank of the role A (see Equation 5), and consequently the testing-rank of the whole
choreography C (see Equation 7).

$$R(t,\omega) = \begin{cases} \mathcal{T}(t,\omega) & \text{if } t < h_{\text{Offset}} \\ 0 & \text{else} \end{cases} \tag{10}$$

According to the definition in Equation 10, the configurable parameter h_{Offset} is interpreted as the maximum observation period (e.g time, hours, days, week, etc.) after
which the testing-based service rank is considered not sufficiently reliable, and then
a new testing session for the service is recommended.

As an example, Figure 1 depicts the evolution of the function $R(t,\omega)$ with respect to
t (i.e. time), and by considering different values of r_ω. Specifically the figure shows the
case all the test cases passed (i.e. $r_\omega = 1$), the case some of the test cases passed (i.e.
$r_\omega = 0.75$), the case half of the test cases passed (i.e. $r_\omega = 0.50$), and the case most of
the test cases failed (i.e. $r_\omega = 0.25$).

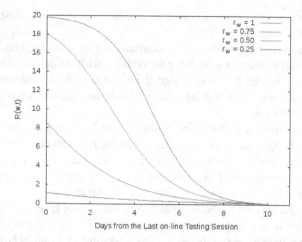

Fig. 1. Examples of the Evolution of the Testing-based Service Rank Function

5.3   Reputation-Based Service Rank

Reputation systems provide a widely adopted solution in order to share subjective evaluation of a service based on feedbacks after the direct experience of its users.

Several ranking models have been proposed in order to combine user's feedbacks and derive reputation ratings [12]. In this section we will refer to a reputation model based on the Beta Density function (β), and originally proposed in [17]. Specifically, the authors in [17] argue how reputation systems based on the β function are both flexible, and relatively simple to implement in practical applications. Furthermore, such systems have good foundation on the theory of statistics.

Let us consider a service ω playing a given role A in C (i.e. $\omega \in \Omega_C(A)$). Than, we denote $f_\omega^+, f_\omega^- \geq 0$ as the number of positive and negative feedbacks collected by the service ω, respectively.

According with the formulation given in [17], the β function can be written as reported in Equation 11, where Γ is the well-studied Gamma function.

$$\beta(p, f_\omega^+, f_\omega^-) = \frac{\Gamma(f_\omega^+ + f_\omega^- + 2)}{\Gamma(f_\omega^+ + 1) * \Gamma(f_\omega^- + 1)} * p^{f_\omega^+} * (1 - p)^{f_\omega^-} \tag{11}$$

The interesting consideration about the β function is that its mathematical expectation is trivial to compute; it is given by the Equation 12.

$$E(\beta(p, f_\omega^+, f_\omega^-)) = \frac{f_\omega^+ + 1}{f_\omega^+ + f_\omega^- + 2} \tag{12}$$

In other words, the feedbacks that the users reported during past interactions with a service ω are interpreted by Equation 12 as the probability of collecting a positive feedback with ω on average in the future interactions. For example, if E for the service ω is 0.8 means that is still uncertain if ω will collect a positive feedback in the future (i.e. due to a positive interaction), but it is likely that this would happen.

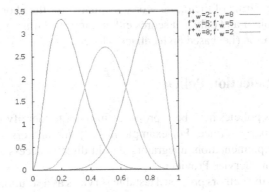

Fig. 2. Examples of the β Function

Figure 2 depicts three instantiation of the β function: the case most of the feedback are negatives (i.e. $f_\omega^+ = 2, f_\omega^- = 8$), the case half of the feedback are positives (i.e. $f_\omega^+ = 5, f_\omega^- = 5$), and the case most of the feedback are positives (i.e. $f_\omega^+ = 8, f_\omega^- = 2$).

Finally, Equation 13 defines a reputation ranking function based on user's feedbacks for a given service ω playing a given role A in C (i.e. $\omega \in \Omega_C(A)$).

$$R(t, \omega) = E(\beta(p, f_\omega^+, f_\omega^-)) \tag{13}$$

As introduced in Section 5.1, also such service-level ranking function can be exploited in order to compute the reputation-based rank of the role A (see Equation 5), and consequently the reputation-rank of the whole choreography C (see Equation 7).

6   Choreography Enactment Policies

When the design of a choreography is completed, it could be made available by registering its specification on a dedicated Choreography Registry. In addition to the canonical registry functionalities based on service choreographies (i.e. store and retrieve choreography specifications), a Choreography Registry should also store meta-information; for example about the status of a choreography, i.e., if a given choreography C is enactable or not.

Thus, from the registration of a choreography specification on a Choreography Registry, the lifecycle at run-time of the choreography could be regulated by means of a set of V&V governance policies; among the others, some concerning the rules under which a choreography could be considered enactable.

Many kind of strategies could be applied in order to classify a choreography as enactable. For example, a policy defines a choreography C enactable if for any role A in C, it is possible to point to a set of services (i.e. one or more services) that can play A in C.

In addition, Section 4 describes some V&V governance policies based on rating mechanisms for both services and choreographies. Thus, enactment policies for C could be also regulated in terms of the rating scores evaluated for the choreography. For example, C is enactable if and only if it scores either a minimal trust (i.e. based on tests), or a minimal reputation (i.e. based on feedbacks) level.

7 Test Cases Selection Policies

In literature various policies have been proposed in order to identify a proper test suite for testing a third party service. For example in [18], the authors suggested that for testing a service implementation, integrators should directly access and use test cases provided by the same Service Provider.

In [19] and [20], the authors proposed testable services as a solution to provide third-party testers with structural coverage information after a test session, yet without revealing their internal details.

The main drawback of such approaches is that both integrators, and service testers, do not have enough information to improve their test set when they get a low coverage measure because they do not know which test requirements have not been covered. In [21] the authors propose an approach in which testable services are provided along with test meta-data that will help their testers to get a higher coverage.

Nevertheless, all these ideas could fit well with the specification of both governance policies, and rules enabling V&V activities. Specifically, policies could require such meta-data as complementary documentation that service providers should supply for making their service testable.

All the policies described above select test cases from the test suite provided by the Service Provider. In some cases, such approaches could not provide completely objective test suites focusing on integration aspects.

An alternative approach is the definition of test cases selection policies that enable the derivation of test cases from models provided by the Service Provider, for example during the registration of the service. Specifically, similarly to [22], it could be equally useful to derive test cases from the service choreography. In fact, a choreography specification defines both the coordination scenarios in which a service under registration plays a role, and the abstract behaviour expected by each role.

8 Examples

Most of the policies proposed in the previous sections are quite intuitive and we have given simple examples while introducing them. For lack of space we provide in the following more detailed examples of implementations only for ranking policies (Section 8.1) and selection policies (Section 8.2).

8.1 A Simple Example about Rankings

Section 5.1 defines the ranking function of a role in terms of an abstract notion of dependency that can occour among the roles belonging to a choreography. Specifically, for each role A in a choreography C, such dependency is referred in order to compute

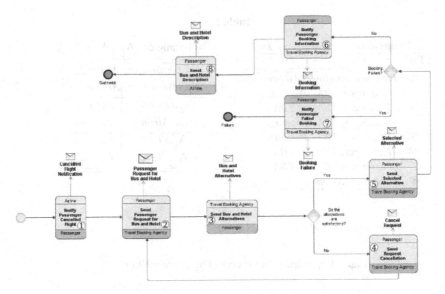

Fig. 3. Example from the Passenger-Friendly-Airport Choreography

both the sets $N_C^+(A)$, and $N_C^-(A)$. In the following we describe a dependency relation that will be implemented within the V&V governance framework.

Let us consider a choreography C, and let us denote the set of tasks defined within C:

$$T^C = \{\tau | \tau \text{ is a task defined in C}\} \tag{14}$$

the set of roles participating in a given task of C:

$$Part(\tau, C) = \{A | A \in \mathcal{A}_C, \tau \in T^C, A \text{ is involved in } \tau\} \tag{15}$$

and, for each task τ in C, $Init(\tau)$ is the role that initiates a task τ.

Thus, given A, B roles in C, the dependency definition we propose relates A with B if and only if B is the initiator of a task were also A is involved. In other words, in order to accomplish a given task in C, A requires some action from B. More formally, we denote this dependency relation on C as $\leadsto^C \subseteq \mathcal{A}_C \times \mathcal{A}_C$, so that:

$$
\begin{aligned}
A1 \leadsto^C A2 &\Leftrightarrow \exists \tau \in T^C, \text{ and} \\
&A1 \neq A2, \text{ and} \\
&A1, A2 \in Part(t, C), \text{ and} \\
&A2 = Init(\tau)
\end{aligned}
\tag{16}
$$

For example, Figure 3 depicts a simple service choreography modelled with the BPMN Choreography Diagram notation. With respect to this example, the sets described above are instantiated as it follows:

- $\mathcal{A}_C = \{ Passenger, Airline, TBA \}$
- $T^C = \{①, ②, ③, ④, ⑤, ⑥, ⑦, ⑧, \}$

Table 1.

a) Instantiation of $Part$, and $Init$

Task	$Part$	$Init$
①	Passenger, Airline	Airline
②	Passenger, TBA	Passenger
③	Passenger, TBA	TBA
④	Passenger, TBA	Passenger
⑤	Passenger, TBA	Passenger
⑥	Passenger, TBA	TBA
⑦	Passenger, TBA	TBA
⑧	Passenger, Airline	Passenger

b) Examples : $N_C^+(A)$, $N_C^-(A)$

$N_C^+(Passenger)$	Airline, TBA
$N_C^-(Passenger)$	Airline, TBA
$N_C^+(Airline)$	Passenger
$N_C^-(Airline)$	Passenger
$N_C^+(TBA)$	Passenger
$N_C^-(TBA)$	Passenger

Fig. 4. Dependency Graph according to the relation $\leadsto^C$

In addition, for each task $\tau \in T^C$, Table 1.a reports both the set $Part(\tau, C)$, and $Init(\tau)$; while Figure 4 depicts the dependency graph resulting from the instantiation of the relation $\leadsto^C$ on this simple example. Finally, according to the definitions given in both Equation 3, and Equation 4, Table 1.b reports the sets $N_C^+(A)$, and $N_C^-(A)$ resulting form the specific instantiation of the dependency relation here adopted.

In the following, the example will only focus on the testing-based service rank described in Section 5.2; however similar results, and considerations can be achieved by using the reputation-based service rank presented in Section 5.3.

Thus let us assume several services can implement each role in C. Specifically, this example considers : 2 services acting as *Passenger*, 4 services acting as *Airline*, and 5 services acting as *TBA*. In this scenario, the example foresees that each of these services is associated with a specific test suite, whose periodical execution provides the index r_ω presented in Section 5.2.

Clearly, for each service, the experiment can refer to a specific timeout simulating the execution of a new testing session, and thus the definition of new values for the indexes r_ω. Also, for each of service, the experiment can also use the parameter h_{Offset} introduced in Equation 9 in order to control the decaying process of the results from the latest testing session simulated.

Nevertheless, in order to keep the presentation of the results simple, the simulation we run over this example considered for all the services involved both the same h_{Offset}, and the same timeout for launching the new testing sessions.

Figure 5 depicts the results of the simulation we executed. In particular, the up-most diagram of the figure depicts the rank for the whole choreography computed according to Equation 7; while the other diagrams show the computed rank for the three roles (i.e. *Passenger, Airline, TBA*). In each diagram, the vertical green bars denote when the execution of a new testing session occurred. After each testing session, the ranks of each role can either grow or decrease depending on the results collected from the testing of

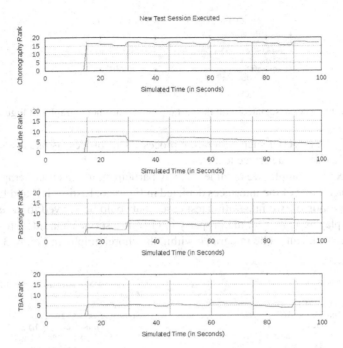

Fig. 5. Results of the Ranking Simulation on the Passenger-Friendly-Airport Choreography

the services playing it. Between two testing sessions, each role fall-off in ranking as prescribed by Equation 10.

8.2 A Simple Example about Test Cases Selection

This section describes how a V&V Manager could define V&V policies concerning the derivation test cases from the service choreography.

For example, the V&V Manager can define the test case selection process by means of the formulation of test purposes in form of reachability properties, similarly to [22]. According to the choreography specification introduced in Figure 3, a simple property defined as a test cases selection policy, could be:

> *"The test cases must include task ②, followed (in a future) by task ⑤, and then either by task ⑥, or ⑦"*
> (17)

As detailed in [22], such a policy can be expressed in a temporal logic formula (such as in LTL, CTL, Hennessy-Milner Logic) so that it could be automatically processed by a test cases generation framework.

Nevertheless, as more participants are involved in a choreography task, from the same property the policy can select different test suites; usually one for each service participating in the choreography. Thus, in addition to the property in (17) driving the generation of test cases over the service choreography, a test cases selection policy also

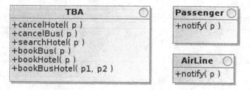

Fig. 6. Interfaces associated with the participants to the choreography in Figure 3

has to specify the target of such generation process. This process is usually referred as projection of a trace on a service test case.

In this specific example, we assume that any participant to the choreography in Figure 3 implements one of the interfaces depicted in Figure 6. Listing 1.1, and Listing 1.2 show the projection of two integration test cases that could be derived for a service that is willing to play as *TBA* from the property in (17). If a service candidate to *TBA* fails one of such tests, it cannot be integrated within the choreography in Figure 3.

```
1    b = searchBus(p1);
2    if (! isValid(b) )
3        return TestFailed;
4    h = searchHotel(p2);
5    if (! isValid(h) )
6        return TestFailed;
7    r = bookBusHotel(b,h);
8    if (r.isAKindOf(BookingInformation)
         || r.isAKindOf(
         BookingFailure))
9        return TestPassed;
10   else
11       return TestFailed;
```

```
1    s = searchBusHotel(p1,p2);
2    if ((!isValid(s.b)) || (!isValid(s
         .h)))
3        return TestFailed;
4    r = bookBusHotel(b,h);
5    if (r.isAKindOf(BookingInformation
         ) || r.isAKindOf(
         BookingFailure))
6        return TestPassed;
7    else
8        return TestFailed;
```

Listing 1.1. Example of Integration Test Case derived for *TBA*

Listing 1.2. Another Integration Test Case derived for *TBA*

9   Conclusions and Future Work

Choreography and SOA governance are important instruments to enable the dynamic and flexible interoperability among independent services which is at the basis of the FI. Our work concerns the on-line V&V of services and choreographies, which relies on a disciplined policy-based governance approach. Implementation of such a framework is a huge undertaking, facing theoretical and technical challenges. We have identified in this paper a set of policies, including activation, rating, ranking, enactment and test case selection policies. We have discussed how such policies can support V&V and provided some preliminary examples. The policies illustrated here are undergoing implementation in the context of the European project CHOReOS[1].

Future work will include the implementation of a governance registry for the management of such policies, and their instantiation within the CHOReOS demonstration scenarios.

Furthermore, another important motivation for V&V policies is to enable the scaling up of on-line testing as the dimensions of the tackled choreographies increases.

---

[1] http://www.choreos.eu/

Indeed, within the FI any software will be by nature characterized as an Ultra-Large-Scale (ULS) software system, where a ULS system *"is ultra-large in size on any imaginable dimension"* [23], like in the resulting number of lines of codes, in the number of people employing the system for different purposes, in the amount of data stored, accessed, manipulated, and refined, in the number of hardware elements (i.e. heterogeneity), and finally in the number of possibly cooperating organizations. Therefore, future work will also include the identification of further policies to help mitigate ULS effects in V&V of FI choreographies.

References

1. Pan, J., Paul, S., Jain, R.: A survey of the research on future internet architectures. IEEE Communications Magazine 49, 26–36 (2011)
2. Fiedler, M., Gavras, A., Papanikolaou, N., Schaffers, H., Wainwright, N.: FIA Research Roadmap - Towards Framework 8: Research Priorities for the Future Internet. Technical report, The Future Internet Assembly Working Group (2011)
3. Barker, A., Walton, C.D., Robertson, D.: Choreographing web services. IEEE T. Services Computing 2, 152–166 (2009)
4. Woolf, B.: Introduction to soa governance (2007) (accessed on June 15, 2011)
5. Trossen, D., Briscoe, B., Mahonen, P., Sollins, K., Zhang, L., Mendes, P., Hailes, S., Jerman-Blaciz, B., Papadimitrou, D.: Starting the Discussions: A white paper from the EIFFEL Think-Tank. Technical report, Eiffel TT (2009)
6. Greiler, M., Gross, H., van Deursen, A.: Evaluation of online testing for services: a case study. In: Proc. of PESOS, pp. 36–42. ACM (2010)
7. Bertolino, A., De Angelis, G., Kellomäki, S., Polini, A.: Enhancing service federation trust-worthiness through online testing. IEEE Computer 45, 66–72 (2012)
8. Ghezzi, C.: The fading boundary between development time and run time. Keynote at ECOWS, p. 11. IEEE (2011)
9. MacKenzie, C., Laskey, K., McCabe, F., Brown, P., Metz, R.: Reference model for service-oriented architecture. Technical report, OASIS (2006)
10. Bertolino, A., Polini, A.: Soa test governance: Enabling service integration testing across organization and technology borders. In: Proc. of ICSTW, pp. 277–286 (2009)
11. Bertolino, A., Frantzen, L., Polini, A., Tretmans, J.: Audition of Web Services for Testing Conformance to Open Specified Protocols. In: Reussner, R., Stafford, J.A., Ren, X.-M. (eds.) Architecting Systems. LNCS, vol. 3938, pp. 1–25. Springer, Heidelberg (2006)
12. Jøsang, A., Ismail, R., Boyd, C.: A survey of trust and reputation systems for online service provision. Decision Support Systems 43, 618–644 (2007)
13. Arroyo, S., Sicilia, M.Á.: Sophie: Use case and evaluation. Information & Software Technology 50, 1266–1280 (2008)
14. Page, L., Brin, S., Motwani, R., Winograd, T.: The pagerank citation ranking: Bringing order to the web. Technical report, Stanford University (1999)
15. Kamvar, S.D., Haveliwala, T.H., Manning, C.D., Golub, G.H.: Exploiting the block structure of the web for computing pagerank. Technical report, Stanford University (2003)
16. Verhulst, P.F.: Notice sur la loi que la population poursuit dans son accroissement. Correspondance Mathématique et Physique 10 (1838)
17. Jøsang, A., Ismail, R.: The Beta Reputation System. In: Proc. of the Bled Electronic Commerce Conference (2002)
18. Tsai, W.T., et al.: Scenario-based web service testing with distributed agents. IEICE Transaction on Information and System E86-D (2003)

19. Eler, M., Delamaro, M., Maldonado, J., Masiero, P.: Built-in structural testing of web services. In: Proc. of Brazilian Symp. on Soft. Engineering, pp. 70–79 (2010)
20. Bartolini, C., Bertolino, A., Elbaum, S.G., Marchetti, E.: Bringing white-box testing to service oriented architectures through a service oriented approach. Journal of Systems and Software 84, 655–668 (2011)
21. Eler, M.M., Bertolino, A., Masiero, P.: More testable service compositions by test metadata. In: Proc. of SOSE. IEEE CS (2011)
22. De Angelis, F., De Angelis, G., Polini, A.: A counter-example testing approach for orchestrated services. In: Proc. of ICST 2010, pp. 373–382. IEEE CS (2010)
23. Pollak, B. (ed.): Ultra-Large-Scale Systems - The Software Challenge of the Future. Software Engineering Institute - Carnegie Mellon (2006)

Part II
Web Interfaces and Applications

Real-Text Dictionary for Topic-Specific Web Searching

Ari Pirkola

University of Tampere, School of Information Sciences, Tampere, Finland
`ari.pirkola@uta.fi`

Abstract. We present a new type of dictionary that is intended as a search assistance in topic-specific Web searching. The method to construct the dictionary is
a general method that can be applied to any reasonable topic. The first implementation deals with climate change. The dictionary contains real-text phrases
(e.g. *rising sea levels*) in addition to the standard dictionary forms (*sea-level
rise*). The phrases were extracted automatically from the pages dealing with climate change, and are thus known to appear in the pages discussing climate
change issues when used as search terms. Different variant forms of the same
phrase, such as *sea-level rise*, *sea level rising*, and *rising sea level*, are grouped
together into the same synonym set using approximate string matching. Each
phrase is assigned a frequency-based importance score (IS), which reflects the
significance of the phrase in the context of climate change research. We investigate how effective the IS is for indicating the best phrase among synonymous
phrases and for indicating effective phrases in general from the viewpoint of
search results. The assumptions are that the best phrases have higher ISs than the
other phrases of a synonym set, and that the higher the IS is the better the search
results are. The experimental results confirmed these assumptions. This paper also describes the crawler used to fetch the source data for the climate change dictionary and discusses the benefits of using the dictionary in Web searching.

Keywords: Dictionaries, Focused crawling, Query performance prediction,
Searching, Vertical search engines, Web search engines.

1 Introduction

In a current research project, we developed a vertical search engine (a topic-specific
search engine) [1] and a topic-specific dictionary of real-text phrases, that is, a dictionary of phrases that are extracted from the Web pages discussing the topic in question. Both are dedicated to climate change and their focus is on scientific pages, but
the methods to implement the search engine and the dictionary are general methods
that can be applied to other topics. The search engine and the dictionary are at:
www.searchclimatechange.com.

The proposed real-text dictionary, in short RT-dictionary, has new features compared to the standard dictionaries and thesauri. We present here the existing climate
change RT-dictionary. A similar dictionary can be constructed for any reasonable
topic using the method presented in this paper. The dictionary contains some 5 500
unique real-text phrases related to climate change (keyphrases). They were extracted
from scientific Web pages discussing climate change. Each phrase is assigned a

J. Cordeiro and K.-H. Krempels (Eds.): WEBIST 2012, LNBIP 140, pp. 105–119, 2013.
© Springer-Verlag Berlin Heidelberg 2013

frequency-based importance score, which reflects the significance of the phrase in the context of climate change research. Different variant forms of the same phrase, such as *sea-level rise*, *sea level rising*, and *rising sea level*, are grouped together into the same entry (synonym set) using approximate string matching. The dictionary was developed for use as a search assistance in our search system to support query formulation, but it can be used as well together with the general Web search engines. The phrases represent different aspects of the climate change research. When used in searching the user can browse through the dictionary to clarify his or her information need, or select more directly appropriate search phrases.

The purpose of the importance score (IS) is to provide the user with information on important and less important phrases. Within a synonym set all phrases are not equal from the viewpoint of the search results, but some yield better results than others. It may be that one is significantly better than the other phrases. In the experimental part of this paper we investigate, first, how effective the IS to indicate the best phrase within a synonym set. We expect the phrase with the highest IS to yield the best search results. Our second research question is: Does high IS mean high retrieval performance in general (i.e., when synonymy is not considered). The expectation is that the higher the IS, the better the search results. The results of this study guide our further work: depending on the results we may elaborate the calculation of the IS. The results may also suggest a sensible lower limit of the IS to be applied in the dictionary. The results also guide more generally our work in the further development of the RT-dictionary.

In summary, this paper has two contributions. First, we describe how the RT-dictionary of climate change was constructed (Section 4). The presented methods and tools can be used to a construct a similar RT-dictionary for any reasonable topic. Second, in the experimental part of this paper we investigate how effective the proposed importance score is to indicate the best phrase among synonymous phrases and to indicate effective phrases in general from the viewpoint of the search results (Sections 5 and 6). We also review related research (Section 2) and describe the crawler used to fetch the source data for the climate change RT-dictionary (Section 3). Section 7 presents the discussion, and Section 8 concludes this paper.

2   Related Work

This study is related to research on query performance prediction, which is an important research problem in the field of information retrieval research. A retrieval system that can predict the difficulty of a query can adapt its parameters to the query, or it can give feedback to the user to reformulate the query. Query performance prediction has been the focus of many studies. He and Ounis studied six methods to predict query performance, e.g. average inverse collection term frequency and the standard deviation of inverse document frequency [2]. Cronen-Townsend et al. proposed computing divergence of the query model from the collection model to predict the difficulty of queries [3]. Perez-Iglesias and Araujo proposed the use of the maximum standard deviation in the ranked-list as a retrieval predictor [4]. Different from these studies the IS ranks phrases with respect to each other rather than tries to predict retrieval performance as such.

This work is also related to research on keyphrase extraction. Conventionally, keyphrase extraction refers to a process where phrases that describe the contents of a document are extracted and are assigned to the same document to facilitate e.g. information retrieval. Our approach differs from the conventional approach in that we do not handle individual documents but a set of documents discussing a particular topic. Most conventional approaches are based on machine learning techniques. KEA [5], GenEx [6], and KP-Miner [7] are three keyphrase extraction systems presented in the literature. In these systems, keyphrases are identified and scored based on their length and their positions in documents, and using the TF-IDF weight.

Muresan and Harper also developed a terminological support for searchers' query construction in Web searching [8]. However, unlike our study they did not focus on keyphrases but proposed an interaction model based on system-based mediation through structured specialized collections. The system assists the user in investigating the terminology and the structure of the topic of interest by allowing the user to explore a specialized source collection representing the problem domain. The user may indicate relevant documents and clusters on the basis of which the system automatically constructs a query representing the user's information need. The starting point of the approach is the ASK (Anomalous State of Knowledge) model where the user has a problem to solve but does not know what information is needed [9]. In [10] Lee showed that the mediated system proposed by Muresan and Harper [8] was better than a direct retrieval system not including a source collection in terms of effectiveness, efficiency and usability. The more search tasks the users conducted, the better were the results of the mediated system.

The source data for the climate change RT-dictionary were crawled from the Web sites of universities and other research organizations investigating climate change by the focused crawler described in Section 3. Focused crawlers are programs that fetch Web documents (pages) that are relevant to a pre-defined domain or topic. Only documents assessed to be relevant by the system are downloaded and made accessible to the users e.g. through a digital library or a vertical search engine. During crawling link URLs are extracted from the pages and are added into a URL queue. The queue is ordered based on the probability of URLs (i.e., pages pointed to by the URLs) being relevant to the topic in question. Pages are assigned probability scores e.g. using a topic-specific terminology, and high-score pages are downloaded first.

Focused crawling research has focused on improving crawling techniques and crawling effectiveness [11-14]. Below we consider these papers. We are not aware of any study investigating the use of focused crawling for keyphrase extraction. Perhaps the closest work to our research is that of Talvensaari et al. who also constructed word lists using focused crawling [15]. However, they used focused crawling as a means to acquire German-English and Spanish-English comparable corpora in biology for statistical translation in cross-language information retrieval.

Bergmark et al. use the term tunneling to refer to the fact that sometimes relevant pages can be fetched only by traversing through irrelevant pages [11]. A focused crawling process using the tunneling technique does not end immediately after an irrelevant page is encountered, but the process continues until a relevant page is encountered or the number of visited irrelevant pages reaches a pre-set limit. It was shown that a focused crawler using tunneling is able to fetch more relevant pages than a focused crawler that only counts relevant pages. However, efficiency is lowered due to the downloaded irrelevant pages.

Chakrabarti et al. utilized the Document Object Model (DOM) of Web pages in focused crawling [12]. The DOM is a convention for representing and interacting with objects in HTML, XHTML and XML documents (http://en.wikipedia.org/wiki/Document_Object_Model). A DOM tree represents the hierarchical structure of a page: the root of the tree is usually the HTML element which typically has two children, the HEAD and BODY elements, which further are divided into sub-elements. The leaf nodes of the DOM tree are typically text paragraphs, link anchor texts, or images. In addition to the usual bag-of-words representation of Web pages, the approach proposed by Chakrabarti et al. represented a hyper-link as a set of features <t, d> where t is a word appearing near the link, and d its distance from the link. The distance is measured as the number of DOM tree nodes that separates t from the link node. These features were used to train a classifier to recognize links leading to relevant pages. The links with low distance to relevant text are considered to be more important than links that are far from the relevant text.

In the Context Graph approach by Diligenti et al. a graph of several layers depth is constructed for each page and the distance of the page to the target pages is computed [13]. In the beginning of crawling a set of seed URLs is entered in the focused crawler. Pages that point to the seed URLs, i.e., parent pages, and their parent pages (etc.) form a context graph. The context graphs are used to train a classifier with features of the paths that lead to relevant pages.

Tang et al. built a focused crawler for mental health and depression [14]. The aim was to identify high-quality information on these topics. They found that link anchor text was a good indicator of the page's relevance but not of quality. They were able to predict the quality of links using a relevance feedback technique.

3   Crawler

We developed a focused crawler that is used to fetch pages both for the climate change search system and for use as source data for the RT-dictionary of climate change. The crawler can be easily tuned to fetch pages on other topics. In this section we describe the crawler.

The crawler determines the relevance of the pages during crawling by matching a topic-defining query against the retrieved pages using a search engine. It uses the Lemur search engine (http://www.lemurproject.org/) for this purpose. The pages on climate change were fetched using the following search terms in the topic-defining query: *climate change, global warming, climatic change, research*. We used the core journals in the field to find relevant start URLs. When pages on some other topic are fetched only the search terms and the start URL set need to be changed. So, applying the crawler to a new topic is easy.

To ensure that the crawler fetches mainly scholarly documents its crawling scope is limited, so that it is only allowed to visit the pages on the start URL sites and their subdomains (for example, *research.university.edu* is a subdomain of *www.university.edu*), as well as sites that are one link apart from the start domain. If needed, this restriction can be relaxed so that the crawling scope is not limited to these sites.

A focused crawler does not follow all links on a page but it will assess which links to follow to find relevant pages. We conducted a crawling experiment as an aim to find an effective crawling method. The challenge is how to determine effectively document relevance during crawling. Here the effectiveness means that the higher the proportion of relevant documents among the fetched documents the more effective the crawler is. In other words, among different methods the one that yields most relevant documents is the best when the same number of documents have been downloaded. The four methods below (A, B, C1, and C2) were compared in the experiment. The notational conventions are as follows:

- $Pr(T|u)$, the probability of relevance of the seen page u to the topic T
- $Pr(T|v)$, the probability of relevance of the unseen page v to the topic T
- $rel(u)$, the relevance of the seen page u, calculated by the Lemur search engine
- $rel(<u,v>)$, the relevance of the link between the seen page u and the unseen page v calculated by the Lemur
- N_u, the number of links on page u
- α, a weighting parameter ($0 < \alpha < 1$)

The four methods were as follows (to our knowledge the method C is novel while A and B are known methods):

A. $Pr(T|v) = rel(u)$, i.e., link $<u,v>$ is assigned the same relevance as page u, i.e., $rel(u)$. All links on page u are assigned the same probability score. This method is often used in focused crawling.

B. $Pr(T|v) = rel(<u,v>)$. Link is assigned a relevance score based on its context (*context* is defined below). However, if the link relevance is less than the page relevance ($rel(<u,v>) < rel(u)$), then $Pr(T|v) = rel(u)$. In this way it is ensured that each unseen page is assigned a minimum relevance of the linking page.

C1. $Pr(T|v) = (\alpha * rel(u) * (1/\log(N_u))) + ((1 - \alpha) * rel(<u,v>))$; $\alpha = 0.3$

C2. $Pr(T|v) = (\alpha * rel(u) * (1/\log(N_u))) + ((1 - \alpha) * rel(<u,v>))$; $\alpha = 0.7$

In methods C1 and C2, $Pr(T|v)$ is a sum that consists of two terms: one that depends on the relevance of the page, and one that depends on the relevance of the link. The relative importance of the two terms is determined by the weight α (as shown above, methods C1 and C2 only differ from each other in the value of α). Also, the number of links on page u inversely influences the probability. If $rel(u)$ is high, we can think that the page "recommends" page v. However, if the page also recommends lots of other pages (i.e., N_u is high), we can rely less on the recommendation.

In methods B, C1 and C2 the probability of relevance is determined, in addition to using the relevance of page u, by matching the context of the link against the topic query. The context is the anchor text, and the text immediately surrounding the anchor. The context is defined with the help of the Document Object Model (DOM): All text that is within five DOM tree nodes of the link node is considered belonging to the context.

In the experiment, the number of crawled pages was 500 000 in each four case. The results of the experiment are reported in Table 1, which shows the number of obtained documents above two relevance score thresholds: rel.=0.1 and rel.=0.2. Our observations suggest that the majority of documents with rel. > 0.1 are relevant. It should be noted that we are interested in the relative effectiveness of the four methods, not the exact percentage of relevant documents among the documents with rel. > 0.1 and rel. > 0.2.

Table 1. The effectiveness of the tested methods

Method	# Docs R=0.1	# Docs R=0.2
Method A	1670	361
Method B	1903	313
Method C1	2186	723
Method C2	1969	376

As can be seen in Table 1, crawling based on the method C1 outperforms the other three methods. In the case of rel.=0.1, the method C1 gave 2186 documents while the second best method, C2, yielded 1969 documents. Also in the case of rel.=0.2 method C1 is the best and method C2 the second best. Based on this experiment we selected the method C1 for crawling the source data for the RT-dictionary.

4   Real-Text Dictionary of Climate Change

Constructing the real-text dictionary of climate change involved two main stages: (1) extraction of keyphrases and the calculation of importance scores and (2) identification of synonyms. Section 4.1. describes the first stage and Section 4.2 the second one. Section 4.2 also describes the synonym types contained in the dictionary.

4.1   Keyphrase Extraction

Here *keyphrase* of the topic means a phrase that is often used in texts dealing with the topic and which refers to one of its aspects. Keyphrases typically represent different research areas of the topic (i.e., climate change in this study), some are more technical in nature. The keyphrase extraction method and a climate change keyphrase list, a predecessor of the climate change dictionary. are described in [16]. Here we describe the main features of the extraction method, and present the importance score.

The source data for the dictionary, i.e., pages related to climate change, were crawled from the Web sites of universities and other research organizations investigating climate change by the crawler described in Section 3. When the crawled data were processed the first challenge was to determine which sequences of words are phrases. Here we applied the phrase identification method by Jaene and Seelbach [17]. The main point of the technique is that a sequence of two or more consecutive words constitutes a phrase if it is surrounded by small words (such as *the, on, if*) but do not include a small word (except for *of*). The phrases were extracted from the pages assigned a high relevance score by the crawler.

When constructing RT-dictionary the importance score is needed to prune out out-of-topic phrases from the dictionary. The most obvious out-of-topic phrases receive a low score and are not accepted in the dictionary. The remaining phrases are regarded as keyphrases and are included in the dictionary. This is the first application of the IS. The second one, which is investigated in this paper, is to use the IS as an indicator of the effectiveness of different keyphrases in searching.

The IS is calculated on the basis of the frequencies of the phrases in the corpora of various densities of relevant text, and in a non-relevant corpus. We determined the IS using four different corpora. The relevant corpora are built on the basis of the occurrences of the topic title phrase (i.e., climate change) and a few known keyphrases related to climate change in the original corpus crawled from the Web. Assumedly, a phrase which has a high frequency in the relevant corpora and a low frequency in the non-relevant corpus deserves a high score. Therefore, the importance score is calculated as follows:

$$IS(P_i) = \ln(F_{DC(1)}(P_i) * F_{DC(2)}(P_i) * F_{DC(3)}(P_i) / F_{DC(4)}(P_i)); (F_{DC} > 0) \tag{1}$$

$F_{DC(1)}(P_i)... F_{DC(4)}(P_i)$ = the frequencies of the phrase P_i in the four corpora.
$DC(1)$ = Highly dense corpus
$DC(2)$ = Very dense corpus
$DC(3)$ = Dense corpus
$DC(4)$ = Non-relevant corpus

This method allows us to indicate the importance of the phrase in the Web texts discussing climate change (or any topic for which RT-dictionary is constructed), and separate between keyphrases and out-of-topic phrases based on the fact that the relative frequencies of the keyphrases decrease as the density decreases.

Table 2. Highest ranked keyphrases in the climate change RT-dictionary

Keyphrases	IS
climate change	35.8
climate change research	28.4
global warming	26.7
impacts of climate change	26.3
sea level	26.2
global climate	25.7
greenhouse gas	25.3
sea level rise	25.2
climate change impacts	25.0
sustainable communities	25.0
environmental policy	24.9
environmental change	24.7
global climate change	24.5
sustainable energy	24.5
climate impacts	24.3
integrated assessment	24.2
water resources	24.1
gas emissions	23.9
greenhouse gases	23.9
climate changes	23.8

In the dictionary, the importance scores range from 4.7-35.8. The choice of the lower limit of 4.7 has no experimental basis. As mentioned, one purpose of this study is to consider this issue.

Table 2 shows the 20 highest ranked phrases in the dictionary and their importance scores. Many of the phrases are well-known in the context of climate change research. The dictionary also contains short form phrases, i.e., phrases where one component is omitted. Authors often use such forms. For example, after introducing the full phrase *climate change impacts* the author may refer to it by the phrase *change impacts*. In searching such short forms may strengthen the query and affect document ranking positively when used together with their full forms. However, the short forms are often ambiguous, and often it does not make sense to use a short form without at the same time using its full phrase.

4.2   Synonyms

Synonyms were identified using the digram approximate matching technique. Phrases were first decomposed into digrams, i.e., substrings of two adjacent characters in the phrase (for n-gram matching, see [18]). The digrams of the phrase were matched against the digrams of the other phrases in the phrase list generated in the keyphrase extraction phase (Section 4.1). Similarity between phrases was computed using the Dice formula, and the phrase pairs that had the similarity value higher than the threshold (SIM=0.75) were regarded as synonyms. The output of the digram matching process contained some 10% of wrong matches which were removed manually. In the majority of cases the identification of the wrong matches was a trivial task and it does not require any specific expertise. Currently, we are working to develop a more effective synonym identification method where only a minimal manual intervention is needed. We are testing several approximate string matching methods in combination with stemming and as such, as well as the use of the textual contexts of the phrases.

Table 3. Three example entries in the climate change RT-dictionary

Head phrase	IS	Synonyms	IS
hydrologic cycle	11.3	hydrological cycle	15.1
ice melt	11.5	ice melting	5.7
		melting ice	11.8
		melting of ice	10.3
sea level rising	5.5	rising sea level	13.0
		rising sea levels	18.1
		sea level	26.2
		sea level rise	25.2
		sea level rises	10.8

The dictionary contains the following types of synonyms:

A. Spelling Variants. Phrases that contain the same component pairs but are written slightly differently, e.g. *climate change prediction - climate change predictions.* These kinds of variants are mostly morphological variants.

B. Syntactic Variants. Phrases that contain the same component pairs, but the order of the components is different, e.g. *predicted climate change - climate change predictions.* These kinds of variants may also include type A variation, as in the example above.

C. Short Form Variants. A phrase that is a subphrase of a longer phrase, e.g. *change impacts - climate change impacts.*

The dictionary contains 5 507 unique phrases. Of these, 4 769 phrases have at least one synonym. Table 3 presents three example entries. The dictionary is organized alphabetically, and each phrase acts as a head phrase in its turn.

5   Experiments

In the experiments, we selected test phrases, formulated test queries based on the selected phrases, and run the queries in two search systems. This section describes these tasks. Section 6 presents the evaluation measures and reports the findings.

We investigated spelling and syntactic variants. As discussed above, short forms variants are often ambiguous expressions, and often it does not make sense to use them alone in queries. For this reason, they were not considered in these experiments. We may investigate them in the further research. They may be useful in document ranking, which is one possible application area of the RT-dictionary.

When the test phrases were selected from the dictionary it was ordered in the decreasing order of the ISs, so that high IS phrases were in the beginning and low IS phrases at the end of the dictionary. For both variant types, 25 entries were selected from the beginning and 25 from the middle of the dictionary. An entry contains a head phrase and its synonym(s) (Table 3). In the selection, a candidate entry was discarded if it did not have synonyms, then the next one was tried until there were 50 entries both for spelling and syntactic variants. The synonyms of the selected head phrases varied from high IS to low IS phrases. In the spelling variant test set, 38 head phrases had one synonym, 10 had two, one had three, and one had four synonyms. In the syntactic variant set, these numbers were: 36 head phrases had one synonym, 10 had two synonyms, and four had three synonyms.

Basically, we formulated 50 test topics both for spelling and syntactic variants. The test topics were of the type *climate change AND C*, where *C* is the concept represented by the entry selected for the experiment. Unlike in traditional information retrieval experiments (see http://trec.nist.gov), the relevance of the documents was not assessed by human assessors. Instead, we performed (1) high precision queries, that is, title queries, and high recall queries, that is, full text queries. In (1) the query phrase is required to appear in the title of the document and in (2) the query phrase may appear anywhere in the document. These two types represent a broad spectrum of search results regarding the precision and recall of the results. It should be noted that we are not interested in the precision and recall as such, but the effectiveness of the IS to indicate good query phrases in different situations.

If the phrase occurs in the title of the document, we can be highly confident that the document deals with the issue represented by the phrase. The title queries do not retrieve all documents that are relevant to a particular test topic. However, they retrieve highly relevant documents which usually are the most important for the user. The title queries are important also in that they return a focused set of relevant documents. Common experience suggests that Web searchers usually only look at the top search results. This has also been verified experimentally [19]. Thus, a relatively small set of relevant documents is more important than high recall. The full text queries return highly relevant, marginally relevant and irrelevant documents. They thus yield higher recall but lower precision than title queries.

We run the queries in our climate change search system and in the Google search engine. Google is the biggest search engine on the Web, covering billions of pages, and it is characterized by the heterogeneous information. Google's advanced search mode supports title queries. The climate change search system has indexed 95 819 (public version 73 194) Web pages related to climate change. The pages crawled for the system were indexed using the Apache Lucene programming library (http://lucene.apache.org/). The system supports several types of queries based on Lucene's query language, e.g. queries targeted at the title of documents, and it reports the number of retrieved pages.

In the experiments, each test phrase was run as a query in the climate change search system (in short CCSS in tables) and in Google. All documents indexed by our search system deal with climate change and it was not explicitly expressed in queries, whereas Google queries included the phrase climate change in addition to the test phrases. Google reports the number of retrieved pages which, however, may vary in that the same query returns different number of pages even during a short period of time. However, generally the retrieval results are consistent and meet the expectations.

Below we present some example title queries:

Climate change system - the highest IS phrase
title: "biodiversity loss" [IS=12.6]

Climate change system - other phrase
title: "loss of biodiversity" [IS=11.2]

Google - the highest IS phrase
allintitle: "biodiversity loss" "climate change"

Google - other phrase
allintitle: "loss of biodiversity " "climate change"

6   Findings

In the first experiment, we compared the number of documents retrieved by the highest IS phrases to that retrieved by the other phrases. If the IS is a good indicator of query performance we expect the highest IS phrases to retrieve much larger sets of documents than the other phrases. Tables 4 and 5 report the total number of documents retrieved by the highest IS phrases and the other phrases across the synonym sets for title queries (Table 4) and for full text queries (Table 5). As can be seen, in both cases the highest IS phrases perform far better. The statistical significance was analyzed by the paired t-test. By conventional criteria, the results are statistically significant except for Google / syntactic / title. In Tables 4-5 the significance levels are indicated as follows: *** $p < 0.001$; ** $p < 0.005$; * $p < 0.05$.

Table 4. Number of retrieved documents by the highest IS phrases and other phrases. Title queries.

Variant type Search system	Highest IS # docs	Other # docs
Spelling, CCSS	3545 ***	793
Syntactic. CCSS	1163 ***	295
Spelling, Google	686 854 *	331 556
Syntactic. Google	1 374 087	748 841

Table 5. Number of retrieved documents by the highest IS phrases and other phrases. Full text queries.

Variant type Search system	Highest IS # docs	Other # docs
Spelling, CCSS	53 839 ***	16 403
Syntactic. CCSS	49 146 ***	14 205
Spelling, Google	408 524 000 ***	133 057 300
Syntactic. Google	223 705 000 **	94 023 730

Table 6. Average number of retrieved documents in the six IS categories. Title queries.

Variant type. Average IS for the category	CCSS # documents	Google # documents
Spelling		
IS=24.3	134.3	22 453.5
IS= 20.1	76.9	26 923.3
IS= 15.1	6.7	3 325.8
IS=13.4	2.8	523.5
IS=11.9	6.8	296.2
IS=7.8	0.8	78.2
Syntactic		
IS=21.8	48.4	42 925.8
IS=17.6	17.2	28 877.6
IS=14.4	3.4	31 409.5
IS=12.8	4.7	2 419.1
IS=9.9	0.2	594.1
IS=6.9	0.2	1563.3

The second experiment considered effective phrases in general. The test phrases were put in six categories of equal size, i.e., the same number of phrases, based on their ISs. For spelling variants, each category contained 19 phrases, and for syntactic variants 20 phrases. Tables 6 (title queries) and 7 (full text queries) report the average number of retrieved documents in each category, and the average IS for the categories. As can be seen, the trends are not strictly linear but exhibit downward curvatures in a few cases. However, the trends are still clear: The higher the IS, the more documents are retrieved. Linear regression analysis yielded the correlation coefficients from 0.87 (Google / spelling / title, $p < 0.05$) to 0.92 (CCSS / spelling / title, $p < 0.01$). These indicate a strong relationship between the IS and the search results.

Table 7. Average number of retrieved documents in the six IS categories. Full text queries.

Variant type. Average IS for the category	CCSS # documents	Google # documents
Spelling		
IS=24.3	1317,8	12 071 526.3
IS= 20.1	1612,1	11 427 842.1
IS= 15.1	452,5	1 460 737.8
IS=13.4	121,5	1 482 000.0
IS=11.9	128,6	1 457 136.8
IS=7.8	64,5	605 036.8
Syntactic		
IS=21.8	1983,4	7 620 500.0
IS=17.6	472,4	3 057 610.5
IS=14.4	347,4	1 434 650.0
IS=12.8	291,3	1 372 726.3
IS=9.9	73,4	1 265 878.9
IS=6.9	38,3	362 090.6

In summary, the results of the experiments showed that the importance score is an effective indicator of the effectiveness of the phrases in searching. The trends are clear:

- In a synonym set, the phrase with the highest IS retrieves significantly more documents than the other phrases.
- The higher the IS is, the more documents are retrieved.
- The IS is effective in many search situations.

7   Discussion

Web search engines are query-based search systems. Querying is an effective method when the information need can be expressed using a relatively simple query and the search term is clear, e.g. when the searcher looks for information on the disease whose name he or she knows. However, it is common that the searchers do not know or remember the appropriate search terms. Complex information needs are also difficult to formulate as a query. In situations such as complex work tasks the information need itself may be vague and ill defined [20]. Obviously, a terminology tool containing the most important phrases related to a particular topic would be a helpful tool for searchers searching for information related to that topic, helping to clarify the information need and find good query terms. We developed such a tool: a new type of dictionary that is intended as a search assistance in topic-specific Web searching. The dictionary has the following new features compared to standard dictionaries and the-sauri: It contains real-text phrases and synonym groups, and each phrase is assigned an importance score.

Real-text phrases. The phrases included in the real-text dictionary of climate change were extracted from the pages dealing with climate change, and are thus known to appear in the pages discussing climate change issues when used as search terms. Hence, the proposed approach implicitly involves the idea of reciprocity: the phrases are extracted from relevant Web pages (i.e., pages related to some aspect of climate change), and they in turn can be used in queries to find relevant pages.

Synonymy. It seems that Web searchers are not aware of the effects of synonymy on the search results, because not many search systems provide the searchers with termi-nology tools that support query formulation. The proposed RT-dictionary is such a tool that groups synonymous phrases together. The main limitation of our approach is that it does not find synonyms that are written completely differently. We intend to address this issue in the ongoing project. Wei et al. applied co-click analysis for syn-onym discovery for Web queries [21]. The idea is to identify synonymous query terms from queries that share similar document click distribution. We cannot use the co-click analysis because we do not have sufficient amount of click data, but we can try a similar kind of idea: analyzing documents that share similar in- and out-link distribution.

Importance score. The importance score was devised to be a measure that indicates how important the phrase is from the viewpoint of the search results. The results showed that it works as it was intended to work. It indicates effectively the best phrase among synonymous phrases and effective phrases in general. The IS is effec-tive even in the Google search engine that has indexed billions of pages. Thus, the RT-dictionary provides the user with information on which of the alternative phrases is likely to yield the best search results. In cases where two (or more) query terms have high IS, the results of this study suggest that the user should use both (all) of them (provided that the search system supports disjunction (OR-operator) type que-ries).

RT-dictionary was developed for use as a search assistance to support query for-mulation in Web searching, but it could be used in document indexing as well to im-prove the ranking of documents. In Web search engines, pages are scored with respect to the input query and ranked on the basis of the assigned scores. Ranking schemes typically include a term frequency (tf) component, where term frequency refers to the number of occurrences of the query term in a document. The rationale behind the use of tf is that the more occurrences the query term has in a given document the more likely it is that the document is relevant to the input query. If synonymy is taken into account by summing up the term frequencies of synonyms in a document, more accu-rate relevance scores are achieved in comparison to a conventional approach where synonymy is not taken into account. This can be illustrated using a simple example. Consider a page containing the following phrases with each having one occurrence on the page: *sea level rise*, *rising sea level*, and *rising sea levels*. In the conventional situation where the user only uses base form query term (i.e., *sea level rise*) and the term frequencies of synonyms are not summed up tf=1, whereas when the term frequencies are summed up tf=3, which is more realistic because the concept denoted by the three phrases indeed appears three times on the page. Authors (of Web pages) tend to use alternative phrases and do not only use base form terms but also different syntactic and morphological forms. This means that many important documents are ranked lower than they actually deserve if synonymy is not taken into account.

To be able to systematically explore a given scientific topic, a necessary requirement is to have a terminology assistance (e.g., ontology, dictionary, thesaurus) that is used to divide the topic into meaningful subtopics or concepts. Therefore, RT-dictionary could be applied in any system or method that involves an exploration of a topic. For example, in [22] we applied the dictionary in a Web browsing system focused on scholarly pages related to climate change. In the system, the target pages of the links are grouped under index terms (keyphrases), such as *melting glaciers*, *climate models*, and *sea level rise* based on the occurrences of the keyphrases on the pages. The source of the index terms is the climate change RT-dictionary.

8   Conclusions

We described a method to construct a topic-specific dictionary of real-text phrases to support query formulation in Web searching, and presented the existing climate change RT-dictionary. The proposed method is a general method and can be applied to any reasonable topic. We argued that there is need for such search assistances due to the difficulty to formulate queries in particular for complex information needs. In the experimental part of this paper we showed that the proposed importance score is a good indicator of search success.

The further development of RT-dictionary was discussed in the previous sections. Our plan is also to construct RT-dictionaries for new topics and to add multilingual features to the RT-dictionary.

Acknowledgements. This study was funded by the Academy of Finland (research projects 130760, 218289).

References

1. Pirkola, A.: A Web search system focused on climate change. In: Digital Proceedings, Earth Observation of Global Changes, EOGC, Munich, Germany, April 13-15 (2011)
2. He, B., Ounis, I.: Query performance prediction. Information Systems 31(7), 585–594 (2006)
3. Cronen-Townsend, S., Zhou, Y., Croft, B.: Predicting query performance. In: Proc. of the 28th ACM SIGIR Conference on Research and Development in Information Retrieval, Tampere, Finland, August 11-15, pp. 299–306 (2002)
4. Pérez-Iglesias, J., Araujo, L.: Standard Deviation as a Query Hardness Estimator. In: Chavez, E., Lonardi, S. (eds.) SPIRE 2010. LNCS, vol. 6393, pp. 207–212. Springer, Heidelberg (2010)

5. Witten, I.H., Paynter, G.W., Frank, E., Gutwin, C., Nevill-Manning, C.G.: KEA: Practical automatic keyphrase extraction. In: Proc. of the 4th ACM Conference on Digital Libraries, Berkeley, California, pp. 254–255 (1999)

6. Turney, P.D.: Coherent keyphrase extraction via Web mining. In: Proc. of the Eighteenth International Joint Conference on Artificial Intelligence, IJCAI 2003, Acapulco, Mexico, pp. 434–439 (2003)

7. El-Beltagy, S., Rafea, A.: KP-Miner: A keyphrase extraction system for English and Arabic documents. Information Systems 34(1), 132–144 (2003)

8. Muresan, G., Harper, D.J.: Topic modeling for mediated access to very large document collections. Journal of the American Society for Information Science and Technology 55(10), 892–910 (2004)

9. Belkin, N.J., Oddy, R.N., Brooks, H.M.: ASK for information retrieval: Part I. Background and history. Journal of Documentation 38(2), 61–71 (1982)

10. Lee, H.J.: Mediated information retrieval in Web searching. Proc. of the American Society for Information Science and Technology 45(1), 1–10 (2008)

11. Bergmark, D., Lagoze, C., Sbityakov, A.: Focused Crawls, Tunneling, and Digital Libraries. In: Agosti, M., Thanos, C. (eds.) ECDL 2002. LNCS, vol. 2458, pp. 91–106. Springer, Heidelberg (2002)

12. Chakrabarti, S., van den Berg, M., Dom, B.: Focused crawling: a new approach to topic-specific Web resource discovery. In: Proc. of the Eighth International World Wide Web Conference, Toronto, Canada, May 11-14, pp. 1623–1640 (1999)

13. Diligenti, M., Coetzee, F.M., Lawrence, S., Giles, C.L., Gori, M.: Focused crawling using context graphs. In: Proc. of the 26th International Conference on Very Large Databases, VLDB, Cairo, Egypt, September 10-14, pp. 527–534 (2000)

14. Tang, T., Hawking, D., Craswell, N., Griffiths, K.: Focused crawling for both topical relevance and quality of medical information. In: Proc. of the 14th ACM International Conference on Information and Knowledge Management, CIKM 2005, Bremen, Germany, October 31-November 5, pp. 147–154 (2005)

15. Talvensaari, T., Pirkola, A., Järvelin, K., Juhola, M., Laurikkala, J.: Focused Web crawling in the acquisition of comparable corpora. Information Retrieval 11(5), 427–445 (2008)

16. Pirkola, A.: Constructing topic-specific search keyphrase suggestion tools for Web information retrieval. In: Proc. of the 12th International Symposium on Information Science, ISI 2011, Hildesheim, Germany, March 9-11, pp. 172–183 (2011)

17. Jaene, H., Seelbach, D.: Maschinelle Extraktion von zusammengesetzten Ausdrücken aus englischen Fachtexten. Report ZMD-A-29. Beuth Verlag, Berlin (1975)

18. Robertson, A.M., Willett, P.: Applications of n-grams in textual information systems. Journal of Documentation 54(1), 48–69 (1998)

19. Jansen, B.J., Spink, A., Saracevic, T.: Real life, real users, and real needs: A study and analysis of user queries on the Web. Information Processing & Management 36(2), 207–227 (2000)

20. Ingwersen, P., Järvelin, K.: The Turn: Integration of Information Seeking and Retrieval in Context. Springer, Heidelberg (2005)

21. Wei, X., Peng, F., Tseng, H., Lu, Y., Dumoulin, B.: Context sensitive synonym discovery for web search queries. In: Proc. of the 18th ACM Conference on Information and Knowledge Management, CIKM 2009, Hong Kong, pp. 1585–1588 (2009)

22. Pirkola, A.: A Web browsing system for retrieving scholarly pages. In: Proc. of the Seventh International Conference on Internet and Web Applications and Services, ICIW 2012, Stuttgart, Germany, May 27-June 1 (2012)

Evaluating Cross-Platform Development Approaches for Mobile Applications

Henning Heitkötter, Sebastian Hanschke, and Tim A. Majchrzak

Department of Information Systems, University of Münster, Münster, Germany
{heitkoetter,tima}@ercis.de, sebastianhanschke@gmx.de

Abstract. The fragmented smartphone market with at least five important mobile platforms makes native development of mobile applications (apps) a challenging and costly endeavour. Cross-platform development might alleviate this situation. Several cross-platform approaches have emerged, which we classify in a first step. In order to compare concrete cross-platform solutions, we compiled a set of criteria to assess cross-platform development approaches. Based on these criteria, we evaluated Web apps, apps developed with PhoneGap or Titanium Mobile, and – for comparison – natively developed apps. We present our findings as reference tables and generalize our results. Our criteria have proven to be viable for follow-up evaluations. With regard to the approaches, we found PhoneGap viable if very close resemblance to a native look & feel can be neglected.

Keywords: App, Mobile application, Cross-platform, Multi-platform.

1 Introduction

Smartphones, i.e. mobile phones combining a range of different functions such as media player, camera, and GPS with advanced computing abilities and touchscreens, are enjoying ever-increasing popularity. They enable innovative mobile information systems, often referred to as *apps*. However, the market of mobile operating systems for smartphones is fragmented and rapidly changing. According to Gartner [1], Google's Android, Nokia's Symbian, Apple's iOS, and RIM's Blackberry all have at least a 9 % market share, with Microsoft's Windows Phone expected to increase in popularity as well. The platform distribution among all devices still in use today is even less concentrated. As all platforms differ significantly from each other, software developers that want to reach a large audience of users would be required to develop their apps for each platform separately.

Cross-platform development approaches emerged to address this challenge by allowing developers to implement their apps in one step for a range of platforms, avoiding repetition and increasing productivity. On the one hand, these approaches need to offer suitable generality in order to allow provision of apps for several platforms. On the other hand, they still have to enable developers to capitalize on the specific advantages and possibilities of smartphones.

Our paper first classifies general approaches to cross-platform development of mobile applications. We then analyse and compare existing cross-platform solutions based on Web technologies like HTML, CSS, and JavaScript. As these differ in their general

J. Cordeiro and K.-H. Krempels (Eds.): WEBIST 2012, LNBIP 140, pp. 120–138, 2013.

architecture and their capabilities, it is not obvious which to prefer. We will outline criteria that are important when making a decision as well as evaluate the popular approaches *mobile Web apps*, *PhoneGap* and *Titanium Mobile* according to these criteria.

Our work makes several contributions. Firstly, it gives a comprehensive overview of current approaches for cross-platform app development. Secondly, it proposes a framework of criteria for evaluation. They are not only applicable in this paper but can be used for future assessments. Thirdly, we present a detailed analysis of the considered approaches. Fourthly, we discuss and generalize our findings in order to provide decision advice.

This paper is structured as follows. Related work is studied in Section 2. Section 3 classifies general cross-platform development approaches. Concrete cross-platform frameworks to be evaluated are presented in section 4. We then introduce our catalogue of criteria in Section 5. The evaluation follows in Section 6. In Section 7 we discuss our findings. Eventually, we draw a conclusion in Section 8.

2 Related Work

Much related work can usually be identified for an article that compares various technologies. However, if it deals with cutting-edge technology, the number of similar papers shrinks dramatically. General papers on the technologies dealt with in this paper are cited in the appropriate sections, particularly in Section 4. Thus, this section assesses existing work that compares two or more approaches for cross-platform app development.

Until recently, papers only discussed mobile platforms – or rather operating systems – for mobile devices. An example is the paper by Cho and Jeon [2]. Comparison papers such as by Lin and Ye [3] only marginally help developing multi-platform apps. The same applies to very specialized papers. They usually rather concern the business perspective than deal with technology. An example is a study of mobile service platforms [4]. But even technically-driven papers that address multiple platforms do not necessarily help to develop cross-platform apps. For instance, a study of smartphone malware [5] only roughly hints to platform particularities.

Anvaari and Jansen [6] have compared the predominant mobile platforms with regard to the *openness* of their architectures. Their approach takes a very close look at one aspect and thus can be seen as complementary with our work. Charland and Leroux [7] compare the development of native apps and Web apps. In contrast to our approach, they do not take a cross-platform perspective.

A comparison of iPhone and Android development is presented by Goadrich and Rogers [8]. Despite the topic, which is similar to our work, their aim is different. In fact, they try to answer which platform should be used for the education of students. Another study deals with mobile cloud apps [9]. While the authors deal with cross-platform development, they focus on native thin clients that access cloud services.

A number of publications address more than one platform [10–12]. While these publications foster a better understanding of the platforms, they do not really compare the different approaches. Rather, they explain how to use a technology on a multitude of platforms or devices. Due to the high relevance for practitioners, the topic is also recognized in technology weblogs [13, 14]. Although such articles give valuable advice, they cannot be compared to our structured approach. In an industry study, VisionMobile compared a large number of cross-platform tools based on a developer survey and vendor interviews. This complements our in-depth review, which is based on a set of criteria.

3   Classification of Approaches

When developing *native applications*, developers implement an application for one specific target platform using its software development kit (SDK) and frameworks. The app is tied to that specific environment. For example, applications for Android are typically programmed in Java, access the platform functionality through Android's frameworks, and render its user interface by employing platform-provided elements. In contrast, applications for iOS use the programming language Objective-C and Apple's frameworks. In case multiple platforms are to be supported by native applications, they have to be developed separately for each platform. This approach is the opposite of the cross-platform idea and will serve as a point of reference in this paper. Users will install native apps from the platform's app store or other platform-provided installation means. They receive an app that, by its very nature, has the look and feel of the platform.

In contrast to separate native development, cross-platform approaches allow developers to implement an app as a single code base that can be executed on more than one platform. We distinguish between approaches that employ a runtime environment and those that generate platform-specific apps from a common code base at compile time. The latter, generator-based category includes model-driven solutions and cross-compiling. Up to now, there are no production-ready solutions of this category. Hence, we concentrate on cross-platform solutions that combine the source code of an app with a runtime environment. This environment interprets the app's code at runtime and thereby executes the app. The runtime environment has to be specific for each mobile platform, while the app's source code is platform-independent. Three different kinds of environment can be identified: the Web browser, a hybrid of Web and native components, and self-contained environments.

Mobile Web applications (*Web apps*) implemented with HTML, CSS, and JavaScript use the browser as their runtime environment and thereby capitalize on the good browser support of mobile platforms. When using this approach, developers implement their application as *one* Web site optimized for mobile devices, which the Web browser then interprets. The optimization has to account for the different screen size and usage philosophy of mobile devices. Due to the standardized technologies, the Web site can be accessed in a similar way by mobile browsers on all platforms. However, mobile Web apps cannot use device-specific hardware features such as camera or GPS sensor. They usually cannot be installed on the mobile device but are retrieved via an URL. The upcoming version of HTML, HTML5, will provide some means in both areas, but not a comprehensive solution. Typically, Web apps will at least partially look and behave like common Web pages, differing in appearance and behavior from the native UI elements provided by the platform.

To resolve the lack of access to hardware functionality while still satisfying the desire to employ common Web technologies, *hybrid approaches* emerged as a combination of Web technologies and native functionality. Their runtime environment largely consists of a Web rendering engine, wrapped in a native engine. The source code of hybrid apps uses similar technology like Web apps but additionally has access to an API for platform-specific features. At runtime, the platform's Web view—essentially a browser without user controls—interprets the source code to display Web pages. All calls to hardware APIs are relegated to the native wrapper. Hybrid apps are packaged natively and thus can be (and have to be) installed on the device, unlike Web apps. While their look & feel mostly resembles that of Web apps, they have access to platform-specific features.

Self-contained runtime environments do not reuse any (Web) environment already present on mobile platforms, but use their own, separate runtime environment. Since such an engine is built from scratch and not based on any previous engine, building a self-contained environment needs more work, but also offers more freedom. Self-contained frameworks are not constrained by existing environments and can be designed according to the needs of apps. Hence, they can enable an intuitive and easy development process. Apps are typically packaged with the framework's engine and deployed as native packages.

4 Overview of Frameworks

Based on the classification from above, we chose three concrete cross-platform solutions, i.e. frameworks, and evaluated them, one from each kind of runtime environment: mobile Web apps, PhoneGap as a hybrid framework, and Titanium Mobile as a self-contained approach. On the one hand, their evaluation is useful on its own, because these are popular frameworks among developers[1]. On the other hand, each also stands as an example of their category, so that their evaluation offers additional insight into the general suitability of each category. Together, they make up the largest part of the decision space relevant when thinking about cross-platform development for mobile devices. Native apps will serve as a point of comparison. The following briefly introduces each framework.

Simple Web apps may rely on the browser itself and do not necessarily need to be supported by a concrete framework. However, several frameworks support the optimization for mobile use, e.g. jQuery Mobile [17] or Sencha Touch [18]. Our evaluation mainly applies to Web apps in general, although our tests have used jQuery Mobile as a concrete framework.

The most prominent exponent of the hybrid approach is *PhoneGap* [19]. PhoneGap was originally created by Nitobi Software, which has been acquired by Adobe [15]. The development now takes place in the Apache Cordova project of the Apache Foundation [20], of which PhoneGap is a distribution [21]. There, it is developed as open source under Nitobi's leadership by a diverse community, including developers from major

---

[1] PhoneGap counts more than half a million downloads and thousands of applications built with the framework [15]. Numbers from Appcelerator indicate 30,000 applications using Titanium [16].

software firms like IBM or Microsoft [22]. Using PhoneGap, developers still implement their application with HTML, CSS, and JavaScript. In addition to the Web view, PhoneGap's runtime environment provides a JavaScript API combined with a native bridge to access hardware features. We did our initial review with PhoneGap 1.2, using jQuery Mobile 1.0 for mobile optimization. Where necessary, we have since updated our evaluation to version 1.8.0 of PhoneGap and jQuery Mobile 1.1.0.

As a self-contained runtime environment, Appcelerator *Titanium Mobile* [23] follows a different approach. It does not use HTML and CSS to create the user interface. Instead, the UI is implemented completely programmatically. Developers use JavaScript to build the interface and to implement logic and data, extensively using the Titanium API. The code is then packaged with Titanium's engine. At runtime, this engine interprets the JavaScript code and creates the user interface. Similar to PhoneGap, apps can then be distributed via app stores. However, their look-and-feel resembles the typical platform appearance more closely; the UI is made up of native elements. Titanium Mobile is a product of Appcelerator, which leads development of the basic platform provided as open source [24] and sells additional features and support. We did our initial tests with Titanium Mobile 1.7.2 and have since updated our review to version 2.0.2.

Other frameworks not covered here are, for example, Rhodes [25], a hybrid approach similar to PhoneGap, and model-driven approaches. The latter category has not been included because existing model-driven solutions like iPhonical [26] or applause [27] are still in early stages or not relevant in general practice. The same applies to cross-compiling tools like XMLVM [28].

5 Criteria

In the following, we will elaborate on a list of criteria for evaluating cross-platform development approaches. In Section 6, this set of criteria will be used to compare and review the solutions outlined in the previous section. The selection of these criteria is based on and has been influenced by various sources. An initial set of criteria emerged from discussions with practitioners and domain experts from small- to medium-sized software firms. They outlined their requirements for mobile development approaches. These have been augmented through literature research [29–31] and a compilation of typical problems apparent in online developer communities. Furthermore, important experiences regarding necessary features have been gained from developing prototypical apps.

For a better overview, the consolidated list of 14 criteria has been structured into *infrastructure* and *development* perspective. The infrastructure perspective sums up criteria relating to the life-cycle of an app, its usage, operation and functionality/functional range (see Table 1). The development perspective covers all criteria that are directly related to the development process of the app, e.g. topics like testing, debugging and development tools (see Table 2).

Table 1. Criteria of the infrastructure perspective

I1 License and Costs
This criterion examines whether the framework in question is distributed as free software or even open source, the license under which it is published, if a developer is free to create commercial software, and whether costs for support inquiries occur.
I2 Supported Platforms
Considers the number and importance of supported mobile platforms, with a special focus on whether the solution supports the platforms equally well.
I3 Access to platform-specific features
Includes access to device hardware like camera or GPS and to platform functionality like contacts or notifications. Compared according to application programming interface (API) and Web site.
I4 Long-term feasibility
Especially for smaller companies the decision for a framework might be strategic due to the significant initial investment. Indicators for long-term feasibility are short update cycles, regular bug-fixes, support of newest versions of mobile operating systems, an active community with many developers, and several commercial supporters steadily contributing to the framework's development.
I5 Look and feel
While the general appearance of an app can be influenced during development, it does matter whether a framework inherently supports a native look & feel or whether its user interface looks and behaves like a Web site. Most users seek apps that resemble native apps. Furthermore, this criterion tries to ascertain how far a framework supports the special usage philosophy and life-cycle inherent to an app. Apps are frequently used for a short amount of time, have to be "instant on", and are likely to be interrupted, e.g. by a call. When returning to the app, a user does not want to repeat her input but wants to continue where she left the app.
I6 Application Speed
Tries to compare the application's speed at start-up and runtime, i.e. its responsiveness on user-interaction. For evaluation, instead of measuring the performance, we assess the subjective user-experience.
I7 Distribution
Evaluates how easy it is to distribute apps created with the respective framework to consumers. One part is the possibility to use the app stores of mobile platforms, since users often want to use this distribution channel. However, solely relying on app stores also has disadvantages; a framework offering additional channels also has merits. Furthermore, this criterion assesses whether updates are possible.

6 Evaluation

We have evaluated the four solutions described in Section 4 according to the criteria of Section 5. The evaluation draws on an analysis of the solutions informed by own research and experiences as well as opinions from experienced developers. The experience was mainly gathered by developing a prototypical task management app employing all four solutions. Typical problems arising when using these solutions were compiled from observing the respective developer communities and completed the background information for the evaluation. In addition to a textual evaluation, we assessed a solution's fulfillment of each criterion on a scale from 1 to 6, with 1 meaning "very

Table 2. Criteria of the development perspective

D1 **Development environment**
Evaluates maturity and features of the development environment typically associated with the framework, particularly the tool support (IDE, debugger, emulator) and functionalities like auto-completion or automated testing. The term "ease of installation" summarizes the effort for setting up a fully usable development environment for a framework and a desired platform.
D2 **GUI Design**
This criterion covers the process of creating the graphical user interface (GUI), especially its software-support. A separate WYSIWYG editor and the possibility to develop and test the user interface without having to constantly "deploy" it to a device or an emulator are seen as beneficial.
D3 **Ease of development**
This criterion sums up the quality of documentation and the learning-curve. Therefore, the quality of the API and documentation is evaluated. This part of the criterion is well-fulfilled if code examples, links to similar problems, user-comments, etc. are available. The learning curve describes the subjective progress of a developer during his first examination of a framework. Intuitive concepts bearing resemblance to already known paradigms allow for fast success. This can have a significant impact on how fast new colleagues can be trained and how much additional, framework-specific knowledge a developer needs to acquire.
D4 **Maintainability**
The lines of code (LOC) indicator is employed to evaluate maintainability [32, p. 53f.]. The choice of this indicator is based on the assumption that an application is easier to support when it has less LOC, because e.g. training of new developers will be shorter, source code is easier to read etc. While more sophisticated approaches could also be justified as relevant indicators, these are hard to apply, especially in case of complex frameworks and for apps composed of different programming and markup languages.
D5 **Scalability**
Scalability is based on how well larger developer teams and projects can be conducted using the respective framework. Modularization of framework and app are highly important as this allows increasing the number of concurrent developers and the scope of the app's functionality.
D6 **Opportunities for further development**
Determines the reusability of source code across approaches and thereby assesses the risk of lock-in, which would be increased if a project started with one framework could not later be transferred to another approach.
D7 **Speed and Cost of Development**
Evaluates the speed of the development process and factors that hinder a fast and straightforward development. Costs are not explicitly estimated because they are taken as being dependent on the speed of development, assuming that one can abstract from differences in salary of a JavaScript or Java developer.

good" and 6 "very poor". This allows for a quick overview. Due to space restrictions we present the results in tabular form, with two tables per solution, one for the infrastructure and one for the development criteria, and summarize the main findings for each solution in the following subsections. Section 7 draws a comparison between the solutions and provides decision support.

6.1   Web App

Table 3 and Table 4 present the evaluation of mobile Web apps as a cross-platform development approach. Web apps can be accessed from all smartphones via the platform's browser. They are based on open and mature standards and enable easy and fast development. The disadvantage of this approach is its lack of hardware access and that the look and feel resembles Web sites. While Web apps can easily be accessed via their URL, it is not possible to use the distribution and marketing facilities of app stores. This limits their feasibility for commercial applications.

6.2   PhoneGap

Table 5 and Table 6 present the evaluation of PhoneGap as a hybrid cross-platform development approach. PhoneGap offers generic access to platform-specific features on all major mobile platforms. Because it is based on Web technology, development is only slightly more complicated compared to Web apps. However, as a consequence, the visual appearance and, to a lesser extent, the behavior do not reflect a native look and feel but rather that of a Web site.

6.3   Titanium Mobile

Table 7 and Table 8 present the evaluation of Titanium Mobile as a cross-platform approach based on a self-contained runtime environment. As its main advantage, apps built with Titanium Mobile inherently have the look and feel of native apps, although performance limitations might impair the user experience in certain situations. Titanium only supports iOS and Android; the entire ecosystem is less *open*. Advanced features often require a subscription. Developing apps with Titanium requires a high amount of Titanium-specific knowledge, which, together with the programmatic GUI creation, slows down development.

6.4   Native App Development

Table 9 and Table 10 present the evaluation of native development for Android and iOS. Apps developed specifically for each platform using their APIs and following their conventions inherently results in a native look and feel. However, this has to be done separately for each platform and thus does not represent a cross-platform development approach. Abstracting the results from the concrete platforms it can be said that native development benefits from the best support but requires very specific knowledge.

7   Discussion

This section offers a synthesis of the evaluation and provides general advice for choosing a suitable cross-platform approach. Although native apps benefit from an optimal integration into the respective mobile operating system and good developer support, the analysis showed that cross-platform approaches are a viable alternative. As soon as mobile apps have to be developed for multiple platforms under tight budgets, with small

Table 3. Evaluation of mobile Web applications – Infrastructure perspective

I1 License and Costs	3

Fees may apply for using specific JavaScript frameworks. Although most of these are open-source [17, 18], there are some examples that require commercial licenses [33]. Most communities are very active and usually answer questions in community boards, which might be seen as *free* support. Nevertheless, selling support packages is a typical business model for open-source software. Moreover, costs may occur from hosting (storage and traffic) a Web site.

I2 Supported Platforms	1

All smartphone platforms have their own native browser. Additionally, there are several alternatives, e.g. Mozilla Firefox or Opera Mini. Hence, support of the different platforms only differs in browser quality. Most native browsers use the WebKit library, but there are minor variations in displaying the user interface [34].

I3 Access to platform-specific features	5

JavaScript does not permit any hardware access on smartphones. HTML5 offers "WebStorage" to locally store application data. This concept, however, is in most browsers limited to 5 MB [35]. Playback of video and audio files and the use of multi-touch gestures are no longer a problem.

I4 Long-term feasibility	1

HTML, CSS, and JavaScript are well established techniques undergoing steady improvement. The decision for a specific JavaScript framework can however turn out to be problematic because changing it later on is in most cases expensive. Nevertheless, there are some popular and widespread frameworks that can be assumed future-proof due to a very active development, regular bug-fixes, and a large community.

I5 Look and feel	4

The usage of native UI elements from within the browser is not possible; design and layout of apps depend on CSS. There are several projects trying to imitate the design of a specific platform, e.g. *CSS Theme for iPhone* [36]. jQuery Mobile does not follow this approach and manual work is necessary. CSS3 facilitates simple and fast development of user interfaces. There are major differences in the usage philosophy of a Web site and an app. The browser can be closed at any time and does not have to notify the Web site of this event. Whenever the users returns to a Web app, the app should have memorized settings and input, which, thanks to HTML5, has become possible. By using a manifest file [37], a Web site can request to keep an offline copy, concepts like WebStorage allow Web sites to save data in the local storage.

I6 Application Speed	3

Due to the fact that a Web app has to be loaded via the Internet, launching the app may be slow. WebStorage and the manifest file (as described in I5) limit this phenomenon to the first start of an app. This is comparable to the installation of a native app from an app store. At runtime, Web apps profit from the fact that today's smartphone browsers are highly performance-optimized. Still, the authors' experiments with this approach have shown that especially with a high number of animations and large amounts of content an app can easily reach the limit of a smartphone's CPU.

I7 Distribution	3

Distributing a Web app is simple. Users only need to know its URL and they will automatically get the most recent version. Using app stores is generally not possible. One could package the Web app via PhoneGap or Titanium; however, this is not permitted in Apple's app store as there is no additional benefit of doing so [38].

Table 4. Evaluation of mobile Web applications – Development perspective

D1 **Development environment**	2

There are several development environments for developing with HTML, CSS and JavaScript. They provide almost all desired functionality such as auto-completion. Installing the software development kit (SDK) of the desired platform is mandatory for the use of an emulator, although, for a first impression, a desktop-browser might be enough. In summary, the maturity of development tools is high. Software support for debugging and testing is excellent; in most cases tools like *Firebug* [39] can be employed in addition to a regular browser.

D2 **GUI Design**	1

Most tools for Web UI design offer WYSIWYG editors. These need to have special settings for e.g. display size and resolution to be helpful when developing smartphone apps. As the Web app can rapidly be reloaded on the target device without having to recompile it, GUI design is comparably fast.

D3 **Ease of development**	2

As the quality of documentation (again depending on the framework used) is very high and as concepts used in HTML, CSS and JavaScript are intuitive, the ease of development is higher than with any of the other frameworks. Besides having to know the underlying programming and markup languages (HTML, CSS, and JavaScript), a programmer does hardly need any further knowledge. He has to be aware of characteristics and limitations of a smartphone (display size, Web storage, limited CPU and GPU speed [40]) and can then start developing.

D4 **Maintainability**	1

A *good* JavaScript framework enables short and elegant code. Functionality like sorting of data can sometimes be inserted by using a single keyword. The underlying framework will then supply all necessary methods. The LOC indicator for the prototype application was lowest for the mobile Web application.

D5 **Scalability**	2

Web apps in general can easily be split into a large number of small files that fit into the overall design. This might again depend on the framework employed. Projects using jQuery, for example, tend to become confusing from a certain size [41] while others support modularization very well.

D6 **Opportunities for further development**	1

A project started as a Web app can easily be ported to PhoneGap if access to the native API should become necessary. It might also be packaged with a WebView control in Titanium Mobile or as a native application, although both would contradict the "native" character of these apps and not provide all of the advantages of these approaches. Altogether, opportunities for further development are excellent.

D7 **Speed and Cost of Development**	1

In comparison to all other frameworks, developing the prototype as a Web app has taken the shortest amount of time. Development tools are technically mature, debugging and testing and the design of the user interface can therefore be carried out fast and cost-efficient.

developer teams, and in a short time frame, a cross-platform approach is necessary. However, these approaches are more than a second-best alternative. Developers might prefer using a cross-platform solution even in the absence of these constraints.

Mobile Web apps constitute an ideal starting point for cross-platform, because they do not require advanced knowledge and enable developers to start implementing the app right away. Web apps are a simple approach benefiting from good support by

Table 5. Evaluation of PhoneGap – Infrastructure perspective

I1 License and Costs	2

Both PhoneGap and jQuery Mobile are open source software (distributed under Apache License 2.0 [42], respectively GPL/MIT license [43]). Commercial software can be created free of charge. Nitobi sells support packages from USD 25 to $\geq$ USD 2000 per month, including bug fixes and private telephone support [44].

I2 Supported Platforms	2

PhoneGap supports seven mobile platforms (iOS, Android, BlackBerry OS, Windows Phone, HP WebOS, Symbian, Bada); this is only beaten by Web apps. The amount of supported features differs slightly, even among different versions of the same operating system. As PhoneGap uses a platform's Web view, JavaScript frameworks that are intended to be used in addition to PhoneGap need to support each targeted platform. jQuery Mobile supports all platforms for which PhoneGap is available [45].

I3 Access to platform-specific features	2

PhoneGap gives easy access to most platform-specific features [46]. More sophisticated functionality, e.g. scanning of barcodes, can be added via plugins.

I4 Long-term feasibility	2

As both PhoneGap and jQuery Mobile are comparatively young projects, with their first version released in August 2008 respectively October 2010, long-term feasibility is hard to estimate. Adobe acquiring Nitobi [15], support from IBM [22], becoming an Apache project [20], and regular bug fixes and updates all are in favor of PhoneGap. The same can be said about the active community, which developed numerous plugins and offers support on community boards. This also applies to jQuery Mobile.

I5 Look and feel	3

In contrast to apps developed natively, PhoneGap does not use native user interface elements. Using CSS to imitate the native appearance of a platform requires a high amount of manual work. jQuery Mobile's standard stylesheet tries to imitate the iOS look and feel, but differences remain noticeable. The life-cycle of an app is far better implemented in PhoneGap than it is in Web apps. PhoneGap offers events that are triggered for all relevant changes in an app's status, e.g. pause or resume.

I6 Application Speed	1

Launching a PhoneGap app is fast and user interaction is smooth. Even many tasks did not influence the prototype's performance, which is comparable to a native app.

I7 Distribution	2

Although Apple reserves its right to decline apps that are primarily Web apps, this does not apply to apps developed with PhoneGap, insofar its API is used to access hardware or platform-specific features [47]. Hence, PhoneGap apps and updates can in general be distributed via app stores.

mobile browsers on all platforms. Furthermore, they can be easily ported to other cross-platform approaches.

As soon as platform-specific functionality not available from within browsers has to be accessed or if distribution via app stores is deemed important, other approaches are necessary. Both PhoneGap and Titanium Mobile fulfill these requirements. Their main difference lies with the look & feel of apps developed with these approaches. If it is a strict requirement that an app's user interface should appear like a native app, Titanium is to be preferred. However, Web apps or apps built with PhoneGap merely tend to look slightly different from native apps and more like Web sites, which might

Table 6. Evaluation of PhoneGap – Development perspective

D1 Development environment	2
As is the case with Web apps, the developer is not limited in his choice of a development environment when using PhoneGap. However, not all IDEs offer auto-completion for PhoneGap's API. *PhoneGap Build* is a service that compiles an app for different platforms in the cloud, so that developers do not have to install the platform SDKs [48]. After providing the source of a PhoneGap app, apps are compiled and signed for all chosen platforms and can easily be downloaded.	
D2 GUI Design	1
As for Web apps, designing the graphical user interface can largely be done using a standard browser and WYSIWYG editors like Adobe Dreamweaver.	
D3 Ease of development	2
PhoneGap's documentation is clearly structured and comprehensive [49]. It provides numerous examples – in most cases one quick and one full example – and in some cases mentions problems with specific methods on a certain platform. The documentation of jQuery Mobile is equally good [50]. Almost no further knowledge is required in addition to these APIs. The last releases of PhoneGap had some stability problems, which have, however, been fixed by now [51].	
D4 Maintainability	1
Except for additional code that accesses the hardware, hybrid apps do not require more lines of code than comparable Web apps. Implementing our prototype with PhoneGap, we got the impression that the source code is short and clearly structured, largely due to the use of jQuery Mobile.	
D5 Scalability	2
The evaluation of Web apps with respect to this criterion applies without modification.	
D6 Opportunities for further development	2
A project using PhoneGap can, as long as no platform-specific features are used, also be run as a mobile Web site. This enables a company to reach even those customers that do not own a smartphone with an operating system supported by PhoneGap or that do not want to download and install an app.	
D7 Speed and Cost of Development	1
This is more or less equal to those of a Web app, with only little additional time required for implementing access to hardware functionality.	

even be desirable. This should be kept in mind before postulating native look & feel as a must-have, especially as the look & feel criterion (I5) is the only one where Titanium performs better than PhoneGap. The main disadvantages of Titanium are that it supports only two platforms – albeit the most important ones –, its less open business model, and a more complicated development process. Thus, if there are no hard requirements regarding look & feel or if these might be loosened, the evaluation showed PhoneGap to be the preferable option for cross-platform development.

However, these are only general guidelines that have to be adapted and interpreted for each project individually. The results of our evaluation can be used to support such decisions, for example in semi-formal multi-criteria decision methods like the weighted sum model [64]. Basic decision support can be obtained by weighing the criteria according to the requirements of a given project and calculating a weighted grade. Carefully interpreted and analysed for sensitivity, the result might yield first insights on which solution best matches the requirements at hand.

Table 7. Evaluation of Titanium – Infrastructure perspective

I1 License and Costs	5

While Appcelerator provides a community edition of Titanium Mobile free of charge and as open source, this edition is limited in functionality. Additional functionality is available in proprietary, closed-source modules, which are only available with a subscription [52]. Subscription packages include support, while basic documentation is available in Appcelerator's *developer center*. In general, the Titanium ecosystem is less open than the other solutions.

I2 Supported Platforms	4

As of June 2012, Titanium supports iOS and Android, with Android being slightly less well supported. Consequently, a large number of API methods are "iOS only". While this enables developers to use the latest iOS API, it harms cross-platform compatibility, as platform-specific code might be necessary in certain circumstances. Version 2.0.1 of Titanium introduced the possibility to also generate mobile Web apps. Since this "Mobile Web platform" is still in development and will not support platform-specific APIs [53], we do not consider it further.

I3 Access to platform-specific features	2

Titanium's spectrum of functionality can be compared to that of PhoneGap [54].

I4 Long-term feasibility	3

Appcelerator's Web site explicitly mentions its large community with numerous developers and projects. Nevertheless, the community seems to be less active than PhoneGap's. Some posts in Appcelerator's bulletin board remain unanswered for weeks. This might be explained by the comparatively less open nature of Appcelerator. Appcelerator tries to embed current trends into their framework, e.g. using latest functionality of the operating systems. Updates and bug-fixes occur continuously. However, as Titanium Mobile is driven by a single company, the long-term outlook depends largely on their corporate strategy.

I5 Look and feel	2

Instead of using HTML5 and CSS3, Titanium interprets an app's JavaScript code by creating native UI elements for the app's user interface [55]. At first sight this approach seems to be less intuitive. Even drawing a label or a button requires relatively much knowledge about Titanium's JavaScript API. Ultimately, creating a user interface that resembles a native app requires far less time and effort than with Web apps or PhoneGap. The usage lifecycle of an app can easily be implemented.

I6 Application Speed	5

At start-up, the Titanium prototype did not differ from those created with other frameworks. At runtime, it started to noticeable stutter as soon as many objects and thus a large amount of view elements had to be handled. As the prototype is rather simple, programming errors can quite certainly be ruled out. It is more likely that this stems from the interaction of operating system and Titanium's JavaScript interpreter.

I7 Distribution	2

Titanium apps can be distributed via the different app stores without difficulty.

8   Conclusion and Future Work

In this paper, we presented a comprehensive set of criteria for evaluating cross-platform development approaches for mobile applications. Results have been compiled in tables, which can be used as references. The ensuing analysis of several cross-platform solutions according to these requirements has shown that PhoneGap is to be preferred, unless the interface necessarily has to resemble native apps as closely as possible.

Table 8. Evaluation of Titanium – Development perspective

D1 Development environment	3
Titanium Mobile is tightly integrated into Appcelerator's IDE Titanium Studio [56], which is based on Eclipse. As the IDE is especially tailored to Titanium, it offers auto-completion for the whole Titanium API. Furthermore, it supports deployment to emulators or devices as well as distribution to app stores. Setting up the development environment for Titanium is straightforward but the platform SDKs still have to be installed separately.	
D2 GUI Design	4
GUI design is rather cumbersome and time-consuming, as the user interface is created programmatically via Titanium's JavaScript API. This requires a lot of verbose and repetitive code. Titanium Studio does not offer a WYSIWYG editor to create the interface.	
D3 Ease of development	3
The quality of Titanium's documentation is good. There are numerous, although minimalistic code examples [57]. Nevertheless, initial progress and accustomization to the framework is relatively slow, as a high degree of framework-specific knowledge has to be acquired.	
D4 Maintainability	3
The prototype developed with Titanium has comparatively many lines of code. Anyhow, the app still remains maintainable as Titanium apps can easily be modularized.	
D5 Scalability	2
The aforementioned ability to easily modularize a Titanium app also enables better scalability. Separate files can be included using *Ti.include()* [58] and it is possible to have different windows run in completely separate JavaScript contexts, even though passing data or objects between windows is quite slow.	
D6 Opportunities for further development	5
Source code of apps written for Titanium, at most with the exception of an application's inner logic, can in general not be used with other approaches due to the fact that a large amount of Titanium-specific functions is used. This creates dependencies on the future development of Titanium (compare I4).	
D7 Speed and Cost of Development	5
Developing with Titanium requires a lot of framework-specific knowledge, and does therefore demand a lot of experience. Designing the user-interface is only possible within an emulator or on a device, which slows down development.	

Mobile Web apps offer a quick and simple entrance into cross-platform development. In summary, the maturity of cross-platform approaches reveals that native development is not necessary when implementing mobile applications. Even if only a single platform is to be supported, a cross-platform approach may prove as the most efficient method due to its low entry barriers.

These low barriers are mainly owed to usage of Web technologies. HTML, CSS, and JavaScript in alignment with Web paradigms are highly suitable for developing cross-platform apps because they are standardized, popular, reasonably simple but powerful and well-supported. Combined with additional measures to utilize the special capabilities of mobile devices, they fulfill the requirements of most mobile scenarios. However, particularly for user interfaces, future research will have to scrutinize the current possibilities. Interfaces of games are an exemplary field where available approaches might fall short.

Table 9. Evaluation of native apps for Android and iOS – Infrastructure perspective

I1 License and Costs	3

Android is distributed as open source by the Open Handset Alliance led by Google under a combination of the Apache License 2.0 and GPL [59]. In contrast, iOS is only available in combination with Apple's own hardware and is published under a proprietary end user software license agreement, with some components distributed under GNU GPL and Apple Public Source License. A membership in Apple's developer program for at least USD 99 per year is necessary to be able to deploy apps to end devices or upload them to the app store [60, 61]. Both frameworks can be used to create commercial software.

I2 Supported Platforms	6

Developing apps natively requires to do so separately for each platform, because programming language and APIs differ. Hence, this approach does not support cross-platform development.

I3 Access to platform-specific features	1

Direct access to all features.

I4 Long-term feasibility	1

Studies on the future of the smartphone market forecast that both operating systems will continue to be popular. Developers can rely on large communities, regular bug-fixes and updates.

I5 Look and feel	1

Full support of the platforms usage philosophy and the employment of native UI elements are self-evident. By definition, everything that can be done with cross-platform approaches is possible natively as well.

I6 Application Speed	1

The native prototypes are as fast as the prototype developed with PhoneGap. It might be surprising that they are not faster, but this is likely due to heavily optimized implementations of the WebKit library allowing efficient display of Web pages.

I7 Distribution	2

Native apps can be distributed within the platform-specific app stores, taking into account the provider's – especially Apple's – policies concerning *appropriate* apps.

The list of criteria and the subsequent evaluation was based on input from domain experts. This guarantees a high practical relevance of our work. Furthermore, it hints at promising future improvements in cross-platform development approaches for mobile applications. Future research topics include

- keeping track with progress in mobile development frameworks and reassessing existing technologies as the platforms evolve,
- checking whether Web technology can similarly be used for application to different media,
- verifying our results empirically,
- observing how important platform-specific functions might become available through standardized APIs,
- extending and proposing our framework for evaluations in similar contexts, and
- preparing to provide decision advice based on companies' requirements for app developers.

Our future work will specifically address the refinement and evaluation of our approach in close contact with app developers.

Table 10. Evaluation of native apps for Android and iOS – Development perspective

D1 Development environment	2

Android apps can be developed with any Java-enabled IDE. Most developers will probably use Eclipse with the corresponding Android plugins [62]. iOS developers require Mac OS and Xcode [63]. Both development environments are mature, although the "ease of installation" is slightly higher when targeting iOS provided there is access to Apple hardware, as no separate installation of an SDK or plugin is required.

D2 GUI Design	1

Both Android and iOS come with a WYSIWYG editor, enabling user interface design without repeatedly having to deploy to an emulator or smartphone. Especially the iOS editor is very mature, concepts like storyboards offer the possibility to visualize and create large parts of the application without having to write a singe line of code.

D3 Ease of development	2

As expected, the documentation of both operating systems is very comprehensive and of high quality. Both provide numerous examples. Getting-started guidelines support beginners, Google regularly publishes blog posts and developers can additionally resort to the very active community. Programmers that already know the underlying programming language can progress rapidly although they need to acquire additional knowledge about the mobile operating system.

D4 Maintainability	3

In terms of LOC, both native prototypes are the most comprehensive. This is due to the very detailed and object-oriented implementation with Java and ObjectiveC in contrast to the concise JavaScript code. As they use object-oriented constructs and separate the code into classes, native apps are (in comparison) easy to maintain, although they might appear to be more heavyweight than their pendants developed in scripting languages.

D5 Scalability	1

In both Android and iOS, program logic and GUI can easily be separated from each other. Furthermore, each view of an app can be developed on its own. This and the object-oriented concept of classes enable development teams to scale even better than with the other frameworks.

D6 Opportunities for further development	6

Code written for one native platform can in general not be ported to another platform due to different programming languages and APIs.

D7 Speed and Cost of Development	5

Developing natively requires the highest degree of specific knowledge and experience. Particularly as an application has to be repeatedly developed for every platform, costs of development are much higher than with cross-platform approaches.

Acknowledgements. This paper has been written in cooperation with viadee Unternehmensberatung GmbH, Germany. We would like to thank them for continuous support and fruitful exchange regarding the development of mobile applications.

References

1. Gartner: Market share: Mobile communication devices (2012),
   http://www.gartner.com/it/page.jsp?id=1924314
2. Cho, Y.C., Jeon, J.W.: Current software platforms on mobile phone. In: Proc. ICCAS 2007, pp. 1862–1867 (2007)

3. Lin, F., Ye, W.: Operating system battle in the ecosystem of smartphone industry. In: Proc. of the 2009 Int. Symp. on Information Engineering and Electronic Commerce, pp. 617–621. IEEE CS (2009)
4. Tuunainen, V.K., Tuunanen, T., Piispanen, J.: Mobile service platforms: Comparing Nokia OVI and Apple App Store with the IISIn model. In: Proc. ICMB 2011, pp. 74–83. IEEE CS (2011)
5. Felt, A.P., Finifter, M., Chin, E., Hanna, S., Wagner, D.: A survey of mobile malware in the wild. In: Proc. SPSM 2011, pp. 3–14. ACM (2011)
6. Anvaari, M., Jansen, S.: Evaluating architectural openness in mobile software platforms. In: Proc. ECSA 2010, pp. 85–92. ACM (2010)
7. Charland, A., Leroux, B.: Mobile application development: web vs. native. Commun. ACM 54, 49–53 (2011)
8. Goadrich, M.H., Rogers, M.P.: Smart smartphone development: iOS versus Android. In: Proc. SIGCSE 2011, pp. 607–612. ACM, New York (2011)
9. Lakshman, T.K., Thuijs, X.: Enhancing enterprise field productivity via cross platform mobile cloud apps. In: Proc. MCS 2011, pp. 27–32. ACM, New York (2011)
10. David, M.: Flash Mobile: Developing Android and iOS Applications. Focal Press (2011)
11. Anderson, R.S., Gestwicki, P.: Hello, worlds: an introduction to mobile application development for iOS and Android. J. Comput. Sci. Coll. 27, 32–33 (2011)
12. Firtman, M.: Programming the mobile web. O'Reilly (2010)
13. Newman, B.: Are cross-platform mobile app frameworks right for your business? (2011), http://mashable.com/2011/03/21/cross-platform-mobile-frameworks/
14. Behrens, H.: Cross-Platform App Development for iPhone, Android & Co. (2010), http://heikobehrens.net/2010/10/11/cross-platform-app-development-for-iphone-android-co-%E2%80%94-a-comparison-i-presented-at-mobiletechcon-2010/
15. Adobe: Adobe Announces Agreement to Acquire Nitobi (2011), http://www.adobe.com/aboutadobe/pressroom/pressreleases/201110/AdobeAcquiresNitobi.html
16. Appcelerator: Appcelerator press release November 1, 2011 (2011), http://www.appcelerator.com/2011/11/appcelerator-raises-15-million-in-funding/
17. jQuery Mobile (2011), http://jquerymobile.com/
18. Sencha Touch (2011), http://www.sencha.com/products/touch/
19. PhoneGap (2011), http://www.phonegap.com/
20. Apache Cordova (2012), http://incubator.apache.org/cordova/
21. PhoneGap, Cordova, and what's in a name? (2012), http://phonegap.com/2012/03/19/phonegap-cordova-and-what%E2%80%99s-in-a-name/
22. About PhoneGap (2011), http://phonegap.com/about
23. Appcelerator Titanium Platform (2012), http://www.appcelerator.com/platform
24. Titanium Mobile open source project (2012), https://github.com/appcelerator/titanium_mobile
25. Rhodes (2012), http://www.motorola.com/Business/US-EN/RhoMobile+Suite/Rhodes
26. iPhonical (2010), http://code.google.com/p/iphonical/
27. applause (2012), https://github.com/applause/
28. XMLVM (2012), http://www.xmlvm.org/android/

29. 15 most important considerations when choosing a web development framework (2009), http://net.tutsplus.com/tutorials/other/15-/

30. Pfeiffer, D.: Which cross-platform framework is right for me? (2011), http://floatlearning.com/2011/07/which-cross-platform-framework-is-right-for-me/

31. Lukasavage, T.: Adobe & PhoneGap: Makes sense, mostly (2011), http://savagelook.com/blog/portfolio/adobe-phonegap-makes-sense-mostly

32. Kassinen, O., Harjula, E., Koskela, T., Ylianttila, M.: Guidelines for the implementation of cross-platform mobile middleware. International Journal of Software Engineering and Its Applications 4 (2010)

33. Sencha ext JS (2012), http://www.sencha.com/store/extjs/

34. Koch, P.P.: There is no WebKit on mobile (2009), http://quirksmode.org/blog/archives/2009/10/there_is_no_web.html

35. Pilgrim, M.: Dive into HTML5: Local storage (2011), http://diveintohtml5.info/storage.html

36. CSS theme for iPhone (2011), http://www.predic8.com/iphone-css-layout-theme.html

37. W3C: HTML5: offline web applications (2012), http://www.w3.org/TR/html5/offline.html

38. Apple: App Store review guidelines (2012), https://developer.apple.com/appstore/guidelines.html

39. Firebug (2012), http://getfirebug.com/

40. Dornbierer, C., Ong, J., Boon, P.: Cross-platform mobile application development (2011), http://www.adnovum.ch/pdf/slides/adnovum_jazoon2011_mobile_engineering.pdf

41. Murphey, R.: On jQuery & large applications (2010), http://rmurphey.com/blog/2010/08/09/on-jquery-large-applications/

42. PhoneGap license (2012), http://phonegap.com/about/license/

43. jQuery project license (2012), http://jquery.org/license/

44. PhoneGap support (2012), http://phonegap.com/support#support-packages

45. jQuery Mobile graded browser support (2012), http://jquerymobile.com/gbs/

46. PhoneGap: Supported features (2012), http://phonegap.com/about/features/

47. PhoneGap: FAQ (2012), http://phonegap.com/faq

48. PhoneGap: Build (2012), https://build.phonegap.com

49. PhoneGap: API reference (2012), http://docs.phonegap.com/en/1.8.0/index.html

50. jQuery Mobile documentation (2012), http://jquerymobile.com/demos/1.1.0/

51. Rolling releases: How Apache Cordova becomes PhoneGap and why (2012), http://phonegap.com/2012/04/12/rolling-releases-how-apache-cordova-becomes-phonegap-and-why/

52. Titanium: Plans & pricing (2012), http://www.appcelerator.com/plans-pricing

53. Titanium Mobile 2.0.1.GA release notes (2012), http://docs.appcelerator.com/titanium/release-notes/?version=2.0.1.GA

54. Titanium API (2012),
    http://docs.appcelerator.com/titanium/2.0/index.html#!/api
55. Whinnery, K.: Comparing Titanium and PhoneGap (2012),
    http://developer.appcelerator.com/blog/2012/05/
    comparing-titanium-and-phonegap.html
56. Titanium Studio (2012),
    http://www.appcelerator.com/platform/titanium-studio
57. Titanium documentation (2012),
    http://docs.appcelerator.com/titanium/2.0/index.html
58. Titanium include API (2012),
    http://docs.appcelerator.com/titanium/
    2.0/index.html#!/api/Titanium
59. Google: Android open source project (2012), http://source.android.com/
60. Apple: iOS developer program (2012),
    http://developer.apple.com/programs/ios/
61. Chudnov, D.: A mobile strategy web developers will love. Computers in Libraries 30, 24–26
    (2010)
62. Android Development Tools plugin for Eclipse (2012),
    http://developer.android.com/sdk/eclipse-adt.html
63. Xcode 4 (2012), https://developer.apple.com/xcode/index.php
64. Fishburn, P.C.: Additive utilities with incomplete product sets: Application to priorities and
    assignments. Operations Research 15, 537–542 (1967)

Information Gathering Tasks on the Web: Attempting to Identify the User Search Behaviour

Anwar Alhenshiri, Carolyn Watters, Michael Shepherd, and Jack Duffy

Faculty of Computer Science, Dalhousie University,
6050 University Ave., B3H1W5, Halifax, NS, Canada
{anwar,shepherd}@cs.dal.ca, {cwatters,jduffy}@dal.ca

Abstract. This paper presents a part of a larger research study that concerned investigating the task of information gathering on the Web. The study took several subtasks of the information gathering task for investigations in order to develop recommendations for improving the design of tools intended for this type of task. Since information gathering is a highly search-reliant task, it was important to investigate the kind of search behavior users follow during the task. The research discussed in this paper attempts to identify the user search behaviour during information gathering on the Web. The results of the user study indicate that the user search behaviour during Web information gathering tasks has characteristics of both orienteering and teleporting behaviours.

Keywords: Web, gathering, Information, User, Task, Search, Re-finding, Study.

1   Introduction

To categorize user activities on the Web, researchers often apply models of information seeking [6], [9], [5]. However, because Web users and Web technologies evolve rapidly, those models may be obsolete. The content of the Web—as well as its users—change over time due to the emergence of new genres, topics, and communities on the Web [11]. Existing information seeking models have attempted to categorize user activities. More recent models have emerged to focus on the narrower behaviour of users with particular tasks.

There have been different studies in which the types of activities users perform on the Web were identified and categorized into higher level tasks. Examples of models concerning user tasks on the Web include Broder's taxonomy [4], Rose and Levinson's classification [10], Sellen's model [12], and Kellar's categorization of information seeking tasks [7]. The results of those studies indicate that each task can be further studied for understanding the subtasks involved in the overall task.

Alhenshiri et al. [2] presented a model in which the task of Web information gathering was divided into subtasks each of which involves activities of similar nature that users perform on the Web during the task. The process of information gathering on the Web has been shown to heavily rely on search and organization of information for the task [1]. The search part of the process includes activities users perform to locate pieces of information required in the task which may involve locating

J. Cordeiro and K.-H. Krempels (Eds.): WEBIST 2012, LNBIP 140, pp. 139–152, 2013.

information from different sources, locating related information to the already located pieces, and re-finding information in multi-session tasks [2].

When searching for information on the Web, users orienteer, teleport, or do both [13]. In the former, users start at a certain page (or site) and continue searching for information by following the hierarchy of hyperlinks to find relevant information. In the latter, users rely heavily on frequent submissions of search queries to search engines (or through search features provided on Web pages) to find relevant information. These two types of behaviour have been studied by Teevan et al. [13] who showed that 61% of user search activities did not involve keyword search, denoting orienteering behaviour. Only in 39% of the search activities, teleporting behaviour was involved.

This paper re-examines the findings of Teevan et al. [13] in the case of searching for information during information gathering tasks on the Web. This paper builds on the findings in Alhenshiri et al. [2] and investigates the characteristics of user search behaviour during Web information gathering tasks. The study described in this paper was also intended for investigating other aspects of information gathering on the Web that are reported in Alhenshiri et al. [1]. The research in this paper attempts to answer the following questions: (i) Do users gathering Web information follow a specific kind of search behaviour (orienteering or teleporting)? And how can identifying the user search behaviour benefit the design of future information gathering tools intended for the Web? The paper is organized as follows. Section 2 explores the research rationale. Section 3 illustrates the research study. Section 4 discusses the study results and findings. The paper is concluded in Section 5.

2   Related Work

Information seeking models have focused on identifying activities users perform while they attempt to locate information of interest. The Web has been treated as a special case in some of the older models such as Ellis's [6]. Ellis [6] concluded that there are several main activities applicable to hypertext environments of which the Web is one. Those activities represent user actions during seeking information that is not previously known to the user and which is aimed to increase the user's knowledge. Marchionini [9] stated that the process of information seeking consists of several activities (sub-processes) that start with the recognition and acceptance of the problem and continues until the problem is either resolved or abandoned. Wilson and Walsh's [14] model of information behaviour differs from many of the prior models since it suggests high-level information seeking search processes: passive attention, passive search, active search, and on-going search. Although these models provide accurate characterizations of users' information seeking activities, several activities that users perform on the Web usually are not included in the model. The variations of those models and the continuous modifications make it difficult to choose an appropriate characterization.

Several other frameworks have been suggested to understand and model the different activities users perform specifically on the Web while seeking information. Rose and Levinson [10] attempted to identify a framework for user search goals using ontologies in order to understand how users interact with the Web. Their findings indicated that users' goals can be informational, navigational, or transactional. Similarly, Sellen et al. [12] found that user activities can be categorized into finding, information gathering, browsing, performing a transaction, communicating, and housekeeping. Moreover, Broder [4] studied different user interactions during Web search and identified three types of tasks based on the queries submitted by users. Those types are: navigational, informational, and transactional. In addition, Kellar et al. [7] investigated user activities on the Web to develop a task framework. The results of their study indicated that the four types of Web tasks are: fact finding, information gathering, browsing, and transactions.

Based on the different classifications of Web tasks, research showed that information gathering tasks represent a great deal of the overall tasks on the Web (61.5% according to Rose and Levinson, 2004). Therefore, Alhenshiri et al. [2] developed a model in which the subtasks underlying the overall task of information gathering were identified. Their research indicated that information gathering is heavily search-reliant. Prior to this model, Amin [3] identified different characteristics in Web information gathering tasks. Information gathering was shown to be a more complex task than keyword search tasks. The terms 'information gathering' imply different kinds of search including comparison, relationship, exploratory, and topic searches as well as combinations of more than one type of search (Amin, 2009). Information gathering tasks are characterized, in part, by having high-level goals and requiring the use of multiple information resources [1].

Teevan et al. [13] identified two types of search behaviour (viz. teleporting and orienteering) in e-mails, personal documents, and the Web. In the former, a searcher is most likely to use keywords while seeking information. In the latter, a sequence of steps and strategies is adopted to reach the intended information, i.e. usually by starting search at a particular URL and continuing on the Web hierarchy by following links on Web pages. In this paper, the two types of behaviour are further considered in the case of gathering information from the Web. The goal of this consideration is to decide on the significance of which type of behaviour for the information gathering tasks and to eventually recommend design properties for tools intended for Web-based information gathering tasks.

3   Research Study

Information gathering tasks have been shown to be heavily search-reliant [3]; [1] and very popular on the Web as discussed above. Therefore, the user study discussed in this section was conducted. The study was meant to conclude on the kind of behaviour users follow when performing Web information gathering tasks which would lead to developing support for the design of tools intended for this type of task. To identify the kind of search behaviour users followed during the task of information gathering, the analysis in the study considered: (i) the number of URLs users typed-in to start searching for information; (ii) the number of keyword queries they submitted; (iii) the number of links they followed on the Web hierarchy to locate information for the task; and (iv) correlations among those factors.

3.1   Study Design and Population

The design of the study was complete factorial and counter-balanced with random assignment of tasks to participants. There were 20 participants in the study, equally split between graduate and undergraduate students in Computer Science at Dalhousie University. The study used a special version of the Mozilla Firefox browser (http://www.mozilla.com) called *DeerParkLogger,* which was designed at Dalhousie University. This browser has the ability to log all user interactions during the task.

3.2   Study Tasks

The study used four information gathering tasks that were similar in terms of the complexity of the task and different with regard to the task topic. Each task was created following the guidelines described by Kules and Capra [8] and summarized in the following:

- The task description should indicate uncertainty, ambiguity in information need, or need for discovery.
- The task should suggest knowledge acquisition, comparison, or discovery.
- It should provide a low level of specificity about the information required in the task and how to find such information.
- It should provide enough imaginative contexts for the study participants to be able to relate and apply the situation.

To ensure the equality of the tasks with regard to the complexity level, a focus group met twice to analyze the tasks and make the necessary modifications based on: the time needed to complete the task, the amount of information required to be gathered, the clarity of the task description, and the possible difficulties that the user may encounter during gathering. An example of the tasks used in the study is shown below.

Task.Part1. You heard your friends complaining about bank account service charges in Canada. You are not sure why they are complaining. You want to do research on the Web to find out more about bank account service charges in Canada. State your opinion about the charges and your friends' complaints. Keep a copy of the information you found to support your argument. Provide at most five links to pages where you found the information. Keep the information for possible re-use in a subsequent task.

Task.Part2. After you found out about the bank service charges in Canada, you want to compare account service charges of Canadian banks to those applied by American banks. Search the Web to find information about banks in the US. Find information from at most five pages on the Web. Provide a comparison of service charges in both countries. Use the information you kept in the previous task about the Canadian banks. You should keep a copy of all relevant information you found for both tasks.

3.3   Study Methodology

Every participant was randomly assigned two tasks each of which was divided into two parts as shown in the example above. The reason for splitting each task was to encourage participants to re-find information for the second subtask that was preserved (kept) during the first subtask. The issue of re-finding is beyond the scope of this paper. Other aspects including re-finding information are reported in Alhenshiri et al. [1]. The study had two questionnaires, a pre-study and two post-task questionnaires. All user activities were logged during the study for further analysis.

3.4   Study Results

The user behaviour and its correlation with the kind of activities users perform during the task of information gathering were expected to yield certain findings that would help with the design of future gathering tools. The results reported in this paper concern attempts to identify the user search behaviour during Web information gathering tasks. Users in the study followed either or both of two types of search behaviour that were discussed in the work of Teevan et al. [13]. Those types are orienteering and teleporting. In the former, a user starts the search at a specific URL, and continues by following links on Web pages to find and gather information. Users of this type of behaviour are usually expected to follow more links on the Web and submit fewer search queries to search engines. In the latter, the user tends to rely on the submission of search queries more often to locate information. The user in this case relies less on following hyperlink connectivity on the Web.

To decide on the type of behaviour users followed during the tasks, the analysis of the data considered the number of URLs typed-in, the number of search queries submitted, the number of links followed during the task (click behaviour), and correlations among those factors.

Using Typed in URLs. The analysis of the data took the number of URLs participants typed in to start searching for the task requirements as a distinguishing factor between orienteering and teleporting behaviour users. Based on the average URLs typed in, 70% of the study participants (14 users) were identified to have followed teleporting behaviour to accomplish the tasks. Only 30% (six users) were identified to have followed orienteering behaviour. The difference between the two proportions of participants was significant according to the z-test results ($z=1.96$, $p<0.03$). The actual data regarding the typed-in URLs from the study are shown in Table 1. Six users who typed-in more URLs (above average) were considered teleporting behaviour users while the remaining users were considered orienteering behaviour users. Due the fact that the average URLs typed in did not draw a clear line between two completely different kinds of behaviour based on the data in the study, the analysis went to a different criterion and the number of queries submitted was tried as a distinguishing factor between the two kinds of search behaviour.

Using Submitted Queries. The second factor used to determine which proportion of participants followed which kind of search behaviour during the study was the number of queries submitted for accomplishing the tasks. As shown in Table 2, by taking the average number of queries submitted during the study as a distinguishing factor, half of the participants were considered as orienteering behaviour users while the other half as teleporting behaviour users. As a result, the two groups resulting from using the number of queries submitted as a distinguishing factor did not agree with the two groups that resulted from using the number of typed-in URLs. The analysis used the average number of queries to distinguish users with the two types of search behaviour which was not a reliable choice due to the closeness of the numbers of queries in each group to the average.

Table 1. URLs typed in by users

Type of behaviour	Participant	Number of URLs typed in
participants identified as orienteering behaviour users	P2	17
	P10	13
	P11	8
	P1	6
	P20	6
	P3	5
participants identified as teleporting behaviour users	P14	4
	P8	3
	P12	3
	P13	3
	P15	3
	P6	2
	P17	2
	P8	2
	P7	1
	P9	1
	P19	1
	P4	0
	P5	0
	P16	0
$\bar{x}$		*4*
s		*4.3*

Since the analysis yielded different categorization in the case of using search queries as an alternative to URLs typed in by the user, the number of links followed by users in the latter case was considered for analysis. The reason why the number of links followed on the Web hierarchy was considered in the case of using search queries only and not in the case of URLs typed in is the number of participants that would result from the classification. In the case of using URLs typed in, the number of orienteering behaviour users turned out to be too small (only six participants). The use of such small group may yield insignificant findings when taking a step further in the analysis by involving the links followed on the Web hierarchy during the study. However, the use of queries submitted as a distinguishing factor between orienteering and teleporting behaviour users created two similar groups (10 participants in each). Therefore, it was selected with the analysis of linked followed.

Number of Links Followed. Furthermore, by looking at the number of links each group (orienteering or teleporting) followed on the Web during the study, there was almost no difference between the two groups of participants distinguished by query submissions (ANOVA, $F(1,18)=1.81$, $p=0.19$) as shown in Table 3.

Table 2. Queries submitted during the study

Type of behaviour	Participant	Number of queries submitted
participants identified as teleporting behaviour users	P4	23
	P7	19
	P10	15
	P11	15
	P6	13
	P20	9
	P5	8
	P8	8
	P9	8
	P17	8
participants identified as orienteering behaviour users	P18	7
	P19	6
	P13	5
	P15	5
	P12	4
	P16	4
	P3	3
	P1	1
	P2	0
	P14	0

This finding indicates that: either users' behaviour had characteristics of both orienteering and teleporting search; or the average number of search queries did not suffice for distinguishing the 'expected' two groups of users. Theoretically, orienteering behaviour users submit fewer queries than teleporting behaviour users. The difference was between the number of queries submitted by the two groups was significant according to a single-factor ANOVA $(F(1,18)=23.82$, $p<0.0002)$. Nonetheless, the difference with regard to the number of links followed was not significant.

Table 3. Links followed by users: the case of using search queries

Above average queries (Teleporting)		Below average queries Orienteering)	
Participant	links followed	Participant	links followed
P4	84	P18	61
P7	46	P19	60
P10	28	P13	73
P11	77	P15	22
P6	41	P12	2
P20	25	P16	22
P5	90	P3	53
P8	34	P1	11
P9	76	P2	42
P17	49	P14	57
$\bar{x}$	55	$\bar{x}$	40.3
s	24.4	s	24.3
ANOVA, $f=1.81, p=0.19$			

Measuring Correlations. To further ensure that the user search behaviour was hard to identify in the case of Web information gathering tasks in the study, the analysis of the data involved measuring the correlation between the number of typed-in URLs and the number of queries submitted by the study participants. We used the *Pearson Product Moment* correlation test. We considered measuring the correlation between queries submitted and URLs typed in for all users at first and then we followed by measuring the correlations for each group of users identified as either orienteering or teleporting users using the number of typed-in URLs and then using the number of queries submitted.

The results concerning the correlation between typed-in URLs and queries submitted during the study for the entire group of users showed that there was a very strong positive correlation between the two groups of data ($r=0.95$, $p<0.00001$). Please refer to Tables 1 and 2 for data. This relationship contradicts the expected since a strong positive correlation means that the more queries users submitted, the more URLs they typed in while gathering the information. This can be related to the nature of the user and their activities during the study. However, it is hard to distinguish one kind of behaviour or the other as a result of this relationship.

For further assurance, we tackled the issue from a different perspective by considering that there actually exist two groups of users with two different types of behaviour. Those two groups are first distinguished by the number of URLs typed in, and second by the number of queries submitted.

The results of the Pearson test shown in Table 4 indicate that there was a moderate relationship between the number of URLs typed in and the number of queries submitted with inverse association between the two variables. The participants shown in Table 4 are those initially identified as teleporting behaviour users using the number of typed-in URLs. For orienteering behaviour users, the results of the Pearson test are shown in Table 5. Those results indicate that almost no correlation exists between the queries submitted and the URLs typed-in.

Table 4. Pearson (*r*) correlation test results in the case of using typed-in URLs (teleporting)

Teleporting Participants	Queries submitted	URLs typed-in
P14	0	4
P8	3	3
P12	1	3
P13	2	3
P15	2	3
P6	6	2
P17	3	2
P18	3	2
P7	13	1
P9	3	1
P19	2	1
P4	17	0
P5	4	0
P16	1	0
Pearson Product Moment ($r = -0.5$, $p<0.07$)		

Table 5. Pearson (r) correlation test results in the case of using typed-in URLs (orienteering)

Orienteering Participants	Queries submitted	URLs typed-in
P2	0	17
P10	8	13
P11	6	8
P1	0	6
P20	5	6
P3	1	5
Pearson Product Moment (*r* = 0.04, *p<0.94*)		

The analysis went to the use of the number of queries to decide on the two groups of users expected to follow one kind of behaviour or the other. The data is shown in Tables 6 and 7. There was almost a zero correlation between the submitted queries and the typed-in URLs in the case of participants identified as teleporting behaviour users using the number of queries submitted as a distinguishing factor (Table 6). In the case of orienteering behaviour users identified also using the number of queries submitted, the correlation was strong indicating that an inverse relationship existed (Table 7). However, this was only for half the number of participants since in the case of the rest of participants the correlation was close to zero.

Table 6. Pearson (r) correlation test results in the case of using submitted queries (teleporting)

Teleporting participants	Queries submitted	URLs typed in
P4	23	0
P7	19	1
P10	15	13
P11	15	8
P6	13	2
P20	9	6
P5	8	0
P8	8	3
P9	8	1
P17	8	2
Pearson Product Moment (*r=0.04, p<0.91*)		

Table 7. Pearson (r) correlation test results in the case of using submitted queries (orienteering)

Orienteering participants	Queries submitted	URLs typed in
P18	7	2
P19	6	1
P13	5	3
P15	5	3
P12	4	3
P16	4	0
P3	3	5
P1	1	6
P2	0	17
P14	0	4
Pearson Product Moment (*r= -0.67, p<0.04*)		

The use of the correlation tests was a different investigation step to ensure that the search behaviour of the users in the study—while performing the given information gathering tasks—was hard to identify as either orienteering or teleporting. To this point, the findings indicate that users' search behaviour may have had characteristics of both orienteering and teleporting behaviours. However, the use of averages (URLs typed in or queries submitted) may not be sufficient. For example, it might have not been invalid to put a user who submitted seven queries (too close to the average of eight queries) in the section of orienteering behaviour users only because of a one-query difference. Therefore, we selected another portion of users in the study that is not centred around the mean (i.e. outliers) even though we expected not to have enough participants in groups categorized as outliers.

Using Outliers with Correlations. Even though the use of correlations between queries submitted and URLs typed-in by users during the study further demonstrated that it was hard to draw a line between orienteering and teleporting behaviour users in the study, we took the investigation a step further. In this step, the outliers in both cases: the typed-in URLs and the queries submitted during the study were considered.

In the case of using typed-in URLs, the outliers were taken apart from the rest of the data by considering numbers of URLs greater than 1.5 the upper quartile (from Tables 1) and numbers of URLs less than 1.5 the lower quartile. The results of this selection are shown in Table 8. This table contains the outliers with respect to the number of URLs typed-in on both sides (shaded for clarification). The table also contains the number of queries submitted by each participant and the number of links followed on the Web hierarchy.

Table 8. Outliers data (typed-in URLs)

Participant	Typed-in URLs	Submitted Queries	Links Followed
P16	0	4	22
P5	0	8	90
P4	0	23	84
P19	1	6	60
P9	1	8	76
P7	1	19	46
P11	8	15	77
P10	13	15	28
P2	17	0	42

To ensure whether one type of behaviour or the other (orienteering/teleporting) was followed, three correlations were computed using Pearson Product Moment. The correlation between the number of typed-in URLs and the number of submitted queries turned out to be *weak and negative* ($r = -0.25$, $p=0.51$). The correlation between the number of typed-in URLs and followed links was also *weak* ($r=0.39$, $p=0.29$). The correlation between the submitted queries and the followed links was *weak* ($r=0.29$ and $p=0.44$).

The results show that there was no indication of any specific type of behaviour by any group of users. The *weak* correlations demonstrate that no relationship can be explained by any of the factors involved in the correlations except for the relationship between queries submitted and links followed which turned out to be *weak*. Users who follow teleporting behaviour by relying on query submissions usually tend to follow fewer links on the hierarchies of websites than users who start searching by typing in URLs. However, users who relied on typing in URLs were not shown to have made a significant use of the strategy of following link hierarchies on the Web as shown by the test results.

Furthermore, the analysis considered the outliers in the case of using the number of queries submitted by users during the study. The results are shown in Table 9. The table contains the number of queries (for outliers only) submitted by participants associated with the URLs typed-in and links followed for each participant. The correlations between each two of the three factors were computed using Pearson Product Moment. The results showed that the correlation between the number of submitted queries and typed-in URLs was *weak* ($r=0.41$, $p=0.31$). The correlation between the submitted queries and the followed links was *moderate* and positive ($r=0.57$, $p=0.14$). The correlation between the typed-in URLs and the followed links was *weak* and negative ($r=-0.25$, $p=0.55$).

Table 9. Outliers data (Submitted queries)

Participant	Submitted Queries	Typed-in URLs	Followed Links
P4	23	0	84
P7	19	1	46
P10	15	13	28
P11	15	8	77
P3	3	5	5
P1	1	6	6
P2	0	17	42
P14	0	4	57

Orienteering behaviour users rely usually on typing URLs for starting search for information on the Web. They also follow links on Web pages to locate information of the interest. The weak and negative correlation between URLs typed in and links followed contradicts the definition of orienteering behaviour. Actually, a stronger relationship can be seen in the correlation between submitted queries and followed links, which is contradictory to the teleporting search behaviour definition. The only correlation that agrees with the definitions of search behaviours (orienteering vs. teleporting) is the correlation between queries submitted and URLs typed in. Nonetheless, it was a weak relationship.

4   Discussion

The main research study was an attempt to investigate the activities users perform during information gathering tasks on the Web. The subtasks of finding information and information sources, re-finding information, and managing and organizing information were considered in the investigation. A part of this research was concerned with identifying the search behaviour users follow during the task of information gathering while attempting to accomplish the subtask of finding information and information sources. The analysis of the user search behaviour was performed because of the heavy reliance of users on searching activities to satisfy the task requirements.

The study used the number of typed-in URLs, the number of search queries submitted, and the number of links followed on the Web hierarchy during the tasks in order to identify the type of behaviour users followed while performing information gathering tasks during the study. The results showed that neither factor was sufficient to make a clear distinction between the two groups of users with respect to the search behaviour during the tasks. To further ensure that no clear signs of either behaviour could be identified among participants in the study, the correlation between the typed-in URLs and the search queries submitted during the study was measured for the entire group of users, the two groups distinguished by the number of URLs typed in, and the two groups distinguished by the number of queries submitted.

According to the results of the correlation tests, it was hard to identify which group of participants followed which type of search behaviour while performing the information gathering tasks given during the study. The initial idea behind orienteering and teleporting behaviours is that one is different from the other. Users who follow orienteering behaviour are those who type-in URLs more often and follow hyperlink connectivity on the Web to search for information. Users who follow teleporting behaviour usually rely on the submission of search queries in order to find information. This type of users hardly starts searching at a certain URL and barely follows links on Web pages using a series of clicks to locate information.

Every time the analysis of the study data considered one criterion to make a distinction between the two kinds of behaviour amongst the study participants, it was hard to conclude on which group followed which kind of search behaviour. The results of the analysis indicate that activities users perform during this kind of task belong to both kinds of behaviour. Therefore, the type of search behaviour had no effect on the task and was not affected by the nature of the Web information gathering tasks.

Even with the selection of a subset of users that represented only the outliers in the cases of typed-in URLs and submitted queries, the correlations computed among submitted queries, typed-in URLs, and followed links did not demonstrate that one kind of search behaviour was dominant in the case of any group of participants. Interestingly, the relationship between query submission and following links on the Web was moderate showing that the same users had two features from two different kinds of search behaviour (Table 8).

As a result of the study, any support for information gathering tasks in terms of building tools for the task should consider both characteristics of the two kinds of behaviour. The design should take into account that users gathering information on the Web using the current available tools may adopt varied strategies and use several techniques and features to accomplish the goal of the task. Users submit queries at different levels of frequency, open browser tabs and windows, compare information, collect information from both actively open Web pages in the browser and search hits' summaries, and use different tools to accomplish the task. They use search engines and type in URLs to start searching on the Web hierarchy by following links on Web pages and sites.

In future designs of Web tools intended for information gathering, support should be provided for allowing users to open multiple URLs in a way that eases the information comparison process with which users usually have difficulties when using browser tabs and windows. Support should also be provided to users submitting several queries simultaneously to compare result hit summaries. Those users used browser tabs and windows and lost track of information on several occasions in the study. Moreover, the design should support multiple activities on the same display for users typing-in URLs and trying to follow links on Web pages as they continue to gather information. Finally, the design of Web information gathering tools should consider both searching by following the hierarchy of the Web graph and by submitting search queries in an efficient manner so that the number of times users have to switch among applications and tools is minimized. The significance of the Web information gathering task necessitates that further work is needed since current applications including the Web browser suffer from several pitfalls that degrade the user's ability to effectively perform information gathering tasks on the Web.

5 Conclusions

The paper discussed the results of a part of a user study that was intended to identify and distinguish the kinds of search behaviour Web users follow while gathering Web information. The study results showed that the search approach for gathering the information required in the tasks had several characteristics of both kinds of behaviour. This conclusion reflects two important points. First, this kind of task is complex and requires much effort with several kinds of activities involved in the task. Second, support is needed for several activities in the task of Web information gathering including searching by both following link hierarchies and submitting search queries. The support is also required for comparing information and decision making during the task.

References

1. Alhenshiri, A., Watters, C., Shepherd, M.: Building support for web information gathering tasks. In: Proceedings of the Hawaii International Conference on System Sciences, HICSS45, Grand Wailea, Maui, Hawaii, USA, January 04-07, pp. 1687–1696 (2012)
2. Alhenshiri, A., Watters, C., Shepherd, M.: Improving web search for information gathering: visualization in effect. In: Proceedings of the 4th Workshop on Human-Computer Interaction and Information Retrieval, HCIR 2010, New Brunswick, NJ, USA, pp. 1–6 (2010)
3. Amin, A.: Establishing requirements for information gathering tasks. TCDL Bulletin of IEEE Technical Committee on Digital Libraries 5(2) (2009) ISSN 1937-7266
4. Broder, A.: A Taxonomy of web search. ACM SIGIR Forum 36(2), 2–10 (2002)
5. Choo, C., Detlor, B., Turnbull, D.: A behavioral model of information seeking on the Web–preliminary results of a study of how managers and IT specialists use the Web. In: Proceedings of the Annual Meeting of the American Society for Information Science, Pittsburgh, PA, USA, pp. 25–29 (1998)
6. Ellis, D., Cox, D., Hall, K.: A Comparison of the information seeking patterns of researchers in the physical and social sciences. J. Documentation 49(4), 356–369 (1993)
7. Kellar, M., Watters, C., Shepherd, M.: A field study characterizing web-based information-seeking tasks. J. The American Society for Information Science and Technology 58(7), 999–1018 (2007)

8. Kules, B., Capra, R., Sierra, T.: What do exploratory searchers look at in a faceted search interface? In: Proceedings of the 9th ACM/IEEE-CS Joint Conference on Digital Libraries, Austin, TX, USA, pp. 313–322 (2009)
9. Marchionini, G.: Information seeking in electronic environments. Cambridge University Press, New York (1997)
10. Rose, D., Levinson, D.: Understanding user goals in web search. In: Proceedings of the 13th International Conference on World Wide Web, New York, NY, USA, pp. 13–19 (2004)
11. Santini, M.: Interpreting genre evolution on the Web. In: Proceedings of the EACL 2006 Workshop, Trento, pp. 32–40 (2006)
12. Sellen, A., Murphy, R., Shaw, K.: How knowledge workers use the Web. In: Proceedings of the SIGCHI Conference on Human Factors in Computing Systems, Minneapolis, Minnesota, USA, pp. 227–234 (2002)
13. Teevan, J., Alvarado, C., Ackerman, M., Karger, D.: The perfect search engine is not enough: a study of orienteering behaviour in directed search. In: Proceedings of the 2004 Conference on Human Factors in Computing Systems, Vienna, Austria, pp. 415–422 (2004)
14. Wilson, T., Walsh, C.: Information behaviour: an interdisciplinary perspective. British Library Research and Innovation Report 10, University of Sheffield, Department of Information Studies, Sheffield, UK (1996)

Web-Based Exploration of Photos with Time and Geospace

Dinh Quyen Nguyen and Heidrun Schumann

Institute of Computer Science, University of Rostock, Germany
{nguyen,schumann}@informatik.uni-rostock.de

Abstract. The world of community integrated photo data on the Web challenges us to develop tools and techniques for the visual exploration of photos in terms of not only the imagery contents, but also the other information associated with the photos. In this paper, we investigate solutions for the visual exploration of photos in time and geospace. The three aspects of spatiotemporal photo data (which are: *what* - photo contents, *where* - geo-references, and *when* - time-references) are visually combined at various granularity levels to make an integrated visualization approach. In this way, we support tasks of interactively navigating and browsing through photo collections.

Keywords: Spatiotemporal photos, Photo exploration, Navigating and browsing.

1 Introduction

Today, photos are created, stored, and shared widely on smart devices, computers, and on the Internet. An interesting issue about those photos is that many of them are connected with spatial and temporal frames of references. Time and geospace are therefore interesting aspects for the analysis and exploration of photos. Nevertheless, geospace and time have not been adequately considered in existing photo tools. The common way in exploring photo data is browsing through collections in forms of slide-shows or grid-based views. This is a convenient way, but it is not always suitable for the examination of photos through their various aspects. For example, in the case that users want to see how their photos are geographically distributed, it is much more intuitive if the photos are presented on geographical maps (as seen e.g. on Google Panoramio - www.panoramio.com). Generally speaking, by visually combining photos with their various aspects, we could better navigate and comprehend photos and photo collections.

In [1], Peuquet indicates that when examining spatiotemporal data, one can get not only thematic contents of the data, but also insights with patterns, information, and knowledge from their interrelated data aspects. She shows that with the triplet of *what* (data contents), *where* (geo-references), and *when* (time-references), one can come up with three general combinatory situations: (1) *what* + *when* → *where*, (2) *what* + *where* → *when*, and (3) *when* + *where* → *what*. In the area of visualization, those situations are reviewed by Andrienko, Andrienko, and Gatalsky for numerical spatiotemporal data [2]. In this work, we further concentrate on the visual exploration of spatiotemporal photos. In that regard, we would have the following contextual situations:

J. Cordeiro and K.-H. Krempels (Eds.): WEBIST 2012, LNBIP 140, pp. 153–166, 2013.
© Springer-Verlag Berlin Heidelberg 2013

S1: *What + when → where*: Suppose that users browse specific photos (*what*) with specific timestamps (*when*), and want to know *where* on the earth those photos exist. It would be useful if there are visual hints to show photos with patterns in time so that users can conveniently browse for photos of interest over geospace. This can be considered as an extension compared to the well-known Google Panoramio (because time-referenced searching is not provided in that tool).

S2: *What + where → when*: Another situation, suppose that users are interested in photos with specific contents (*what*) on a geographical map (*where*). In other saying, the photos exist and the places are given. Because those photos were taken and distributed over time, exploring their history (*when*) is another interesting task.

S3: *When + where → what*: And, suppose that users are interested in some selected time points or patterns (*when*) in association with geospace (*where*), and they want to examine related photos of interest (*what*). This would also be helpful to provide means to highlight those photos to users.

Though the three above situations are somewhat interrelated, developers can come up with very specific designs for specific purposes (see Section 2). However, most of existing techniques do not explicitly support a comprehensive exploration of photos with regard to all three aspects: *time*, *space*, and *data contents* of photos. And thus, our basis design consists of a combination of views that simultaneously addresses the three aspects: (i) *what* - photos explored through different levels of granularity: photo, photo thumbnail, tag, and numerical patterns, (ii) *where* - geographical maps, and (iii) *when* - time plots and temporal visual patterns.

The three data aspects are visually combined as follows: (1) *what + when → where*: photo data are represented in terms of time referenced tags by a parallel coordinates' view, each coordinate displays a time-referenced tag set (situation S1 is supported by connecting the tags with geographical maps), (2) *what + where → when*: tags represented in combination with thumbnails on zoom-and-pan maps to show temporal distributions of photos (to support situation S2), and (3) *when + where → what*: time glyphs that show temporal visual patterns on geographical maps are explored to show full-size photos (to support situation S3). By doing so, instead of showing photos, geographical maps, and tag clouds separately as in other tools such as Google Panoramio, our visualization design provides the interlinking of views, and thus supports users to explore photos in terms of Peuquet's questions.

This paper is organized as follows. In Section 2, related work concerning the visualization of photos with a focus on techniques dealing with time and geospace is given. Section 3 presents a general view on our visualization design. Section 4 specifically describes how photo tags are visualized in the temporal frame of references. Section 5 presents how photos, thumbnails, and time-oriented photo data are visualized in the geospatial frame of references. And then, Section 6 integrates all of them into a complete view of the tool PhotoTima for the visual exploration of spatiotemporal Flickr photos. Finally, Section 7 concludes the paper.

2   Related Work

This section presents related work about photo visualization techniques with regard to the exploration of the *what*, the *when*, and the *where* aspects of photos.

2.1 Imagery Photo Exploration

Showing photos (and images, in general) has been considered from the first days of GUI designs. Accordingly, there are now many tools and techniques in presenting photos on screens. Basically, photo visualization techniques are developed in terms of supporting tasks of browsing or searching. Browsing means that users navigate with visual hints to interplay and enjoy the photos. Searching means that users provide visual queries and the systems respond with the data. In both cases, goal of a photo visualization technique is to support users to get information from the photos. In this context, information can be specified by the *what*, the *where*, and the *when* aspects of photos.

A very popular photo visualization technique is showing photos for browsing in forms of slide-shows or grid-based views, where users are assisted to easily find photos in collections. Windows Photo Viewer and Google Picasa (`picasa.google.com`) are examples of this approach. Users scroll a view or navigate forth and back a photo list to examine each photo. The main goal of those applications is to show imagery photos (the *what*), while their geo-references (the *where*) and time-references (the *when*) are just specifically supplemented if needed. One can get that information from the descriptive title (if existing) or the detailed properties of each photo. In general, they only support the *what* aspect (i.e., *what* [+ slightly *where*/ *when*] → *what* or *what* → *what* [+ slightly *where*/ *when*]).

There are other specific designs. Porta in [3] developed some particular forms to arrange photos as "cylinder", "rotor", "tornado", or other views. Bederson created a hierarchical visualization structure that highlights the relations of photos in collections [4]. In PhotoLand [5], Ryu, Chung, and Cho suggested another way to arrange photos on screen: the photos similar to each other (with pre-defined content criteria) are placed close together to form spatial clusters, and the clusters are in turn forming a land-based presentation. By doing so, they showed that users can more flexibly find photos of interest compared to traditional grid-based views.

To interact with those visualizations, users can select an area of interest, change a zooming level (typically for a set of photos), and navigate through the photoset (i.e., interactive browsing). A photo can be shown in a separated view, highlighted with visual attributes (e.g., size, border color), magnified to be distinguishable with other photos (e.g., through a fisheye presentation [6]), or linked with other descriptive data (e.g., in [7], a tag cloud is used where each tag in the cloud can be connected with a slide-show collection of photos).

So far, we have seen techniques for the visual exploration of photos in form of *what* → *what*. In the next subsection, we will see how time and geospace are combined for other situations, which are *when* → *what*, *where* → *what*, and vice versa.

2.2 Photo Visualization with Time and Geospace

We first consider the *time* aspect. Yahoo! Taglines [8] is an example for the visual exploration of Flickr photos, where users are supported to select linear time points in a timeline slide-bar, and then relevant photos are presented on screen. Huynh et al., in another way, used not only the timeline but also a set of graphical charts to connect photo thumbnails with time [9]. Photohelix [10], with spiral-based time visualization, is another example for visualizing photos linking with time. Those are techniques that present a general kind of *when* → *what* (or *what* → *when*) representation.

To present photos with regard to their *geo*-references, geographical maps are usually used. Commercial tools currently provided on the Internet such as Flickr Map (www.flickr.com/map), iMapFlickr (imapflickr.com), or Google Panoramio are typical applications for the exploration of photos based on geographical maps. Those applications support showing photos as thumbnails (Google Panoramio, iMapFlickr) or placemarks (Flickr Map) on the maps. A list of photos is optionally connected with the map on a separated view for referencing. Those tools support the task of browsing photos over geospace, while temporal references of photos are neglected. In other words, those tools express only the situations of *what* → *where* and *where* → *what*.

WWMX [11] can be seen as one of the first known applications that support well the visual exploration of photos connecting with both geospace and time. It is a multiple-views design, with a view representing the geographical map, a view supporting time selection (dots with weights on a timeline presentation), and a view that shows an explored photo linking with a list of thumbnails. Users can select a dot which represents a set of photos on geographical map, and the list of thumbnails, each linked with a timeline view, is updated. However, visual patterns or analytical information from spatiotemporal photos are not considered. To deal with it, recent research in exploratory visual analysis of spatiotemporal photos, such as those in [12] or [13], emerges.

In conclusion, although there are useful and well-established techniques for the exploration of photos in association with time and geospace, many techniques focus only on one or two aspects rather than supporting the whole triplet of *space*, *time*, and *data contents* of photos; or they need further investigations for the visual exploration of photos through more visual patterns. In that regard, we take Peuquet's triad framework into account for the visualization of spatiotemporally referenced photos.

3   Visual Design

This section presents our general design as the basics for the contents presented in Section 4 and 5. The ideas are twofold with regard to (1) the presentation of the three aspects of photo data, and (2) visually communicating information in terms of combining different photo aspects.

3.1   The Three Aspects of Photo Data

We provide visualizations with regard to three aspects of photo data: (i) *what* - photo contents to be communicated through different levels of granularity (photo, photo thumbnail, tag, and numerical patterns), (ii) - *where* - geographical maps, and (iii) *when* - time plots and temporal visual patterns. The reason for such decision is that photo data are complex as connecting to geospace and time, and thus there would be no single view that can cope with all aspects.

What. To communicate photo contents, the imagery photos are to be exploited as used in any photo viewer tools. Besides, we show photos in form of thumbnails as in Google Panoramio (see Section 5). And, because photos on the Web are preferably linked with user-generated tags, tags are used for the communication of photo data as well. In Section 4, we discuss how tags are represented to show temporal dependencies. Lastly, inspired by the advancements in Information Visualization, numerical patterns extracted from photos are represented to communicate spatiotemporal references on maps.

Where. To present the geospatial aspect, usually geographical maps are used because they are effective means for geo-data communication (as seen in cartography and geovisualization). Therefore, we will also use maps to show the spatial context of photos (see Section 5). In this regard, photo data can be visually represented on maps, linked with maps, and interactively explored as maps are zoomed and panned.

When. To communicate the temporal aspect, such kind of data are usually represented through time plots, cyclic patterns, branch views, and so on [14]. This provides ways for users to discover temporal patterns as well as temporal relations amongst the explored data. In this work, we show photo tags as time plots (see Section 4), and use cyclic patterns to indicate the number of photos on geospace (see Section 5).

3.2   Visually Combining Photo Aspects

To aim the tasks of navigating through dataset and browsing for photos, we need specific visualization designs. Each stand-alone view of photo aspects, as presented in Section 3.1, can not communicate all information of photo data. And thus, visually combining photo aspects is the bottom line of our approach.

We benefit by the various represented levels of granularity of photo data to design visual combinations. For the representation of time-referenced photo tags (i.e., *when + what*), we show numerous tag sets, each associates with a specific time plot, to form a parallel tag clouds view (see Section 4). To present the combination of *where + what* or *where + when*, we show photos, thumbnails, and time glyphs on maps (see Section 5).

Those visual designs provide ways for the combinations of two aspects of photo data. And then, each of them are visually linked and explored in connection with the third aspect to tackle the situations S1-S3 (provided in Section 1). For situation S1, visual patterns of tags over time represented as parallel tag clouds view are visually linked with their geo-references on geographical maps. In doing so, user can easily explore photos in form of *what + when → where*. To deal with situation S2 (*what + where → when*), with the selected tags from the parallel tag clouds view, users zoom and pan on maps to find out temporal patterns of photos over geospace by time glyphs. Finally, with temporal patterns of photos on maps (i.e., through time glyphs), we support users to filter time data to search for photos. In this way, situation S3 (*when + where → what*) is answered.

4   Photo Tags with Temporal Frame of References

In this section, we present our design to support situation S1 (*what + when → where*), where photo tags are visualized in the context of their temporal frame of references.

With Flickr, Google Picasa, and many web-based photo applications, photos are typically tagged with textual tags. Normally a set of photos is linked with a set of tags. In
that regard, if examining photos with time references, we have different tag sets for different time points. This requires visualization to support the task of navigating through
tag sets in time for the exploration photo data.

To deal with time-dependent tags, there are recent developments such as time-
referenced Taggram [15], SparkClouds [16], or Parallel Tag Clouds [17]. In this work,
we introduce the enhancements of the Parallel Tag Clouds for the visualization of time-
referenced photo tags.

4.1   Time-Referenced Tag Clouds View

Derived from the ideas of tag clouds and parallel coordinates plot, Parallel Tag Clouds
is a technique developed for the exploration and analysis of tag clouds over axes of tags
[17]. This approach is applicable for the design of time-referenced photo tags: each axis
in the parallel tag clouds shows a set of photo tags at a time point, and the whole tag
cloud shows all tags over time. However, we have to enhance the basic approach to
allow large volumes of tags to be examined.

Our idea is to apply a fisheye lens to focus on axes of interest and tags of interest.
It means: (i) tag clouds' axes are visually abstracted in different ways to emphasize
different selected time points, and (ii) tags within each axis are displayed in different
sizes and positions with regard to their levels of interest.

Showing Axes of Interest. An axis of interest is displayed in the size that its tags are
readable, while for other axes, tags are resized much smaller to fit the display screen
(see Figure 1). Users are supposed to choose particular axes of interest, for example in
order to compare tags over a set of particular time points. Anyway, due to the limited
display area, just a limited number of axes can be shown with tags in readable sizes (e.g.,
in Figure 1, we show at most three selected axes). In this regard, the axes are updated
through user interactions: when users select an axis, its tags are readable and can be
further examined; when users deselect the axis, the tags are minimized. If users select
too many axes, the older axes will be marked as deselected and temporarily minimized.
They will be shown again when users deselect other axes.

Showing Tags of Interest. The tags shown on each axis are displayed in alphabetical
order for easy navigating. The heights of the tags indicate their weights (i.e., the number
of related photos). Each tag can be highlighted as hovered or selected through mouse
interactions. Color and background of the tags indicate their selected or hovered states.
We show the hovered tags in red with pink border, while the selected tags are colorized
with orange background (In Figure 2(a), tag "nature" is hovered and tags "myla"
and "nederland" are selected).

Because there could be much more tags than we can show, on each selected axis
just a subset of tags is displayed. Again, the idea of fisheye menu [18] is integrated.

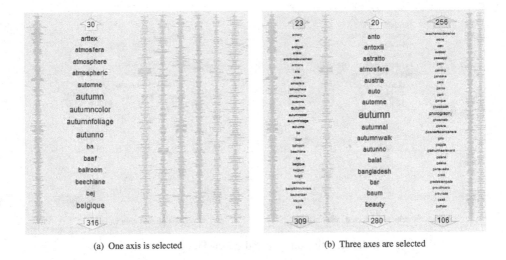

(a) One axis is selected   (b) Three axes are selected

Fig. 1. Tag clouds view with selected axes of interest and tags of interest

The tags in a selected range are displayed in full size (according to their weights), while those which are out of that range are minimized or removed from the axis' view (in this case, digits at the top and bottom of the axis indicate the numbers of unshown tags). The shown tags are updated through user interactions (i.e., by scrolling or paging up and down) on that axis. We also visually link tags over axes. Through user interaction, tags which are identical to the examined tag on the hovered axis (i.e., tag "nature") are highlighted with connected pink lines and red dots on other axes. The size of the dots are relative to weights of the tags through axes. If a linked tag is out of range on another selected axis, its range is updated (in Figure 2(a), tag "nature" is shifted to the bottom of axis 4 and to the top of axis 9). Users can select or deselect tags identical to the hovered one on all axes as well (selected tags on the minimized axes are encoded in orange color). Lastly, we support filtering tags in terms of their weights. Figure 2(b) shows tags with the updated weight range of [3, 16].

In doing so, tags with different characteristics in weights, colors, and positions on parallel time plots of tag clouds are visualized to represent temporal dependencies of photos (in form of *what + when*). In Section 6, we will see how this design is used for the exploration of photos on maps to satisfy situation S1.

5   Photos with Geospatial Frame of References

This section presents our design in dealing with situations S2 (*what + where → when*) and S3 (*when + where → what*). Photos are represented as thumbnails on maps to communicate spatial dependencies or as time glyphs to additionally show temporal dependencies (to support situations S2 and S3). In this regard, both tasks of navigating and browsing for photo data are to be carried out.

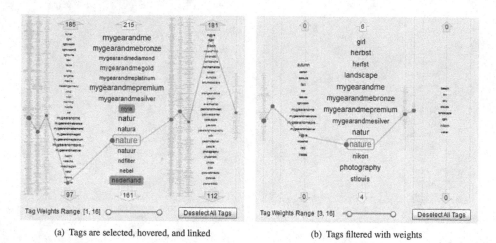

(a) Tags are selected, hovered, and linked   (b) Tags filtered with weights

Fig. 2. Presenting hovered and selected tags over axes

5.1 Thumbnails and Time Glyphs

Combining the *what* (or the *when*) with the *where* aspects of photos are accomplished through different levels of granularity of photo contents with respect to their geospatial frame of references. As thumbnails (the reduced-size versions for images representation) are typically used for recognizing and organizing large amount of photos in collections (e.g., as in the grid-based view of Google Picasa), they can be used to provide a glance view of photo distribution over geographical maps (see Figure 3). However, if we have many photos close together, showing all thumbnails would cause perceptual problems. In Figure 3(a), when thumbnails are shown in size of 40x40 pixels, they overlap each other. If they are shown in smaller sizes (e.g., by 14x14 pixels as in Figure 3(b)), the overlapping problem reduces, but the thumbnails are too small to comprehend. Therefore, alternative visual representations are needed.

Firstly, we suggest to selectively show a subset of thumbnails in comprehensible sizes (i.e., 40x40 pixels). For this purpose, we cluster photos based on their geocoordinates at each zooming level of the map. A cluster is composed of a list of photos within a local square region around a centroid photo. Each centroid (and then a new cluster) is created when a photo does not fall into any existing cluster. In Figure 3(c), photos from Figure 3(a) are clustered with square 80 x 80 pixels (the centroid is at position of pixel (40, 40)). The clusters will be located if the map changes its zooming level. With each cluster, we show the thumbnail for a photo of particular interest (e.g., the photo with specific tags). For clusters that contain more than one photo, a "stack"-background is added to the thumbnail. However, since photos are not evenly distributed on maps (i.e., they are condensed at some places and sparser at other places), thumbnails with stack-background do not adequately differentiate such information. Therefore, additional visual cues are added. For instance, numbers are added on the thumbnails to indicate how many photos are examined with that cluster (see Section 6). This design allows for the representation of *what + where* aspects.

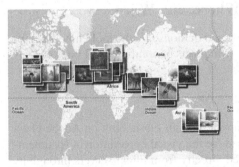

(a) showing 100 photo thumbnails on maps in size of 40 x 40 pixels

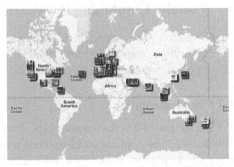

(b) those thumbnails are shown smaller in size of 14x14 pixels

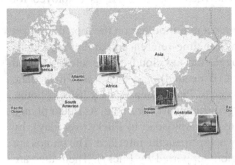

(c) thumbnails for clusters (80 x 80 pixels square)

(d) time glyphs for clusters (80 x 80 pixels square)

Fig. 3. Showing photos as thumbnails or time glyphs on geographical maps

Secondly, we further show temporal patterns of photos by time glyphs on maps. In doing so, we can provide insights about *where + when* patterns. Within each geo-referenced cluster of photos, there could be interesting information about their temporal references. For instance, some photos co-occur at specific days in week. Thus, for each cluster of photos, we design a time glyph with three main parts: (1) a center circle with a number indicating the number of photos in the cluster, (2) a ring with labels for cyclic temporal patterns (we developed 3 patterns: hours-in-day (numbers for hours such as 0, 6, 12, 18), days-in-week (abbreviated as M, T, W, Th, F, S, Su for Monday to Sunday - see Figure 3(d)), and months-in-year (abbreviated as J, F, M, A, M, J, J, A, S, O, N, D in consequence for consecutive months from January to December - see Figure 4(b))), and (3) arcs linked with the ring indicating the numbers of photos falling into the associated time slots. There, the length and lightness of an arc represent its number of photos.

In our implementation (see Section 6), photos are specifically selected for examination, we therefore colorize the arcs in orange for selected photos, and in blue to indicate the unselected ones. If an arc is too long (i.e., exceeding the space reserved for the time glyph), it is shortened and colorized darker (in Figure 3(d), the cluster in Europe is darker than those at the other places).

6   Visually Combining the What, Where, and When

In this section, we describe the implementation and demonstrate the tool PhotoTima for the exploration of spatiotemporal Flickr photos in terms of combining all three aspects to support all situations S1-S3.

6.1   Implementation

We implemented a web-based visualization application in Flash, built on Adobe Flash Builder 4.5. The application PhotoTima is used for the visual exploration of spatiotemporal Flickr photos. Flickr photos are retrieved directly from Flickr servers through its APIs (`www.flickr.com/services/api`), while Google Maps API (`code.google.com/apis/maps/documentation/flash`) is employed for the manipulation of geographical maps.

The application consists of three components: a main toolbar on the top, a viewport for geographical maps on the left, and a view for time-referenced parallel tag clouds on the right (Figure 4). We allow users to toggle the tag clouds view, select a period of time in the view, provide some initial tags (if needed), and then load Flickr data. Through Flickr API `flickr.photos.search`, PhotoTima loads a list of photos, each contains a set of tags, a taken time, and a geographical coordinate. As Flickr photos are too huge (e.g., in 2011, millions of photos are uploaded to Flickr everyday), by default we iteratively load 10 photos per query and refresh the interface. The photos are loaded from the most interesting ones (criterion supported by Flickr). Then, tags are grouped in various ways: per day, week, month, or year (options are provided on the tag clouds view, e.g., "months" is selected in Figure 4). Based on the selection, tags are accumulated for relevant time points (e.g., months) and then consequently visualized on the plots of the parallel tag clouds.

With options on the main toolbar, users choose whether to show photos as thumbnails or time glyphs on maps. The thumbnails or time glyphs are implemented as overlay objects added on Google Maps. They represent photos distributed over geospace and time. However, for photo browsing, users need to see the photos in detail as well (this is a necessary task in any photo viewer tool). In that regard, we do the same as Google Panoramio in showing photos on demand. Users click on a cluster's thumbnail or choose an arc on a time glyph, and a window is popped-up with detailed information about relevant photos. We show on the pop-up window: (1) title of the photo under examination, (2) its imagery content in size of max 240x240 pixels (Flickr photos' small size), (3) links to other photos (if existing) in the cluster or the examined arc, and (4) navigator link to the source photo (e.g., the photo on Flickr website with full descriptions, comments, etc.) (see Figure 4(c)).

6.2   Application

To explore Flickr photos in the context of situation S1 (*what + when → where*), users are supposed to specify photo tags and time points on the tag clouds view and examine them in correlation with geographical regions of interest. To demonstrate the procedure, we loaded 200 most interesting Flickr photos taken in the year 2010 (from Jan 01 to Dec 31) in terms of the tag "`poor`". The tool PhotoTima showed clusters with 51

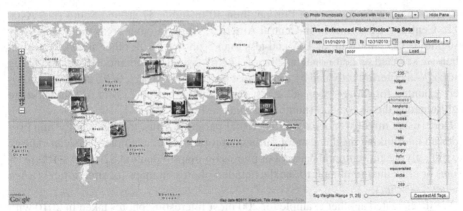

(a) searching Flickr photos with preliminary tag "poor" and highlighting patterns with tag "homeless"

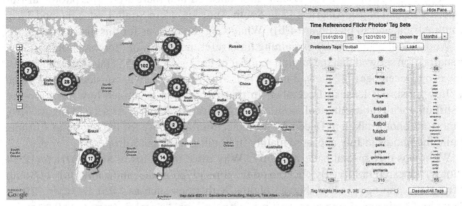

(b) with preliminary tag "football", time glyphs show the most number of photos in "July" for South Africa and Europe

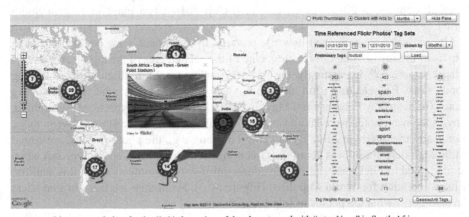

(c) pop-up window for detailed information of the photo tagged with "stadium" in South Africa

Fig. 4. Screenshots of the tool PhotoTima

photos (the most) in the area of Europe, then 40 in India, 37 around South East Asia, 30 in Central Africa, and 17 in Central America, while in other areas there were very few photos (15 photos in the US, and less than 5 photos on all other areas). However, when we selected an additional tag "homeless" (which is semantically related to tag "poor" - a criterion provided by Flickr) just 6 of 51, 5/40, 1/37, 0/30, and 3/17 photos were counted for those "poorest" areas, respectively, but up to 8 of 15 photos were highlighted at the area of US (numbers in pink in Figure 4(a)).

Here, users might wonder about the visual patterns. Thus, the tool PhotoTima provides an interlinking mechanism for further exploration. For example, users can explore the time glyphs for temporal patterns of photos on maps (situation S2: *what + where → when*) or click the thumbnails to see the detailed photos on maps for situation S3 (*when + where → what*).

We investigated another example for 200 most interesting photos taken in 2010 with initial tag "football". The visualization showed that there were 102 photos in Europe, 28 around North America, 17 in South America, 15 in South East Asia, and 14 in South Africa, and so on (Figure 4(b)). What were the reasons for this distribution?

We found the answers by examining time-referenced tags of "football" photos. The visualization showed that the highest number of tags is on July (552 tags) and the fewest one is on December (142 tags). It means that Flickr users seem to consider photos taken in July most, but least in December. In that regard, we examined how photos were distributed with time pattern of months over geographical maps. As seen in Figure 4(b), almost all photos taken in December were accumulated only for the region of Europe, while the photos in July appeared mainly in South Africa and Europe.

What was that special pattern of July? Why most of photos in South Africa (12/14 photos) appeared in July? By clicking on the time glyph's piece indicating July at South Africa, the pop-up window showed photos with titles such as "World Cup 2010 South Africa: Spain v Netherlands" or "World Cup 2010 South Africa: Spain v Germany". The answer was clear: the particular pattern about "football" photos in 2010 was about World Cup 2010 taken place in July in South Africa.

Alternatively, we examined how tag patterns in tag clouds view could be used to help us in finding out that information. One of the related tags of the tag "football" is tag "stadium". Interestingly, tag "stadium" appeared in all columns of the tag clouds view. By selecting it on all columns (i.e., for all photos), the two remaining photos (indicated by February and May) in South Africa's time glyph were highlighted. Why those two photos were about stadium? Could we find any relation between those photos and the others in July? By clicking on them, e.g., the photo in May, we found out that the description was about the Green Point Stadium I in Cape Town, and when we navigated to Flickr website, we saw descriptions and comments about this stadium in its preparation for World Cup 2010 (Figure 4(c)). From that, we thought that users can also guess what the photos in July were about.

7 Conclusions

In this paper, we have presented an approach for the visual exploration of Flickr photos in association with both geospace and time. We addressed the visualization of photos communicated through various granularity levels of data contents, geospace, and time displaying: (i) *what* - photos are explored through imagery photos, photo thumbnails, tags, and numerical patterns, (ii) *where* - geographical maps, and (iii) *when* - time plots and temporal visual patterns.

The representations of data aspects are visually combined to support the tasks of navigating and browsing for spatiotemporal photos. We combined *what* + *when* aspects of photos by a parallel tag clouds view (focused tags are shown-in-context by a fisheye lens). To communicate information with regard to *where* + *what* and *where* + *when*, we display thumbnails and time glyphs on geographical maps.

By brushing-and-linking the parallel tag clouds view and the maps view, we allow users to explore photos with regard to all three photo aspects. In doing so, our approach can simultaneously communicate the *what*, *where*, and *when* aspects of photos, and thus supporting all situations S1-S3.

The tool PhotoTima was developed for the exploration photos on Flickr. Comparing to Flickr photos, there are other Web media (such as video with Youtube - www.youtube.com, music with Last.fm - www.last.fm, and so on) that have similar data aspects; and thus, developing tools for the exploration of those media in terms of their spatiotemporal frame of references can be similarly considered. Hence, the prototype approach of PhotoTima can be applied for the development of similar tools for those media.

References

1. Peuquet, D.J.: It's about time: A conceptual framework for the representation of temporal dynamics in geographic information systems. Annals of the Association of American Geographers 84, 441–461 (1994)
2. Andrienko, N., Andrienko, G., Gatalsky, P.: Exploratory spatio-temporal visualization: an analytical review. Journal of Visual Languages & Computing 14, 503–541 (2003)
3. Porta, M.: Browsing large collections of images through unconventional visualization techniques. In: Proceedings of the Working Conference on Advanced Visual Interfaces, AVI 2006, pp. 440–444. ACM, New York (2006)
4. Bederson, B.B.: Photomesa: a zoomable image browser using quantum treemaps and bubblemaps. In: Proceedings of the 14th Annual ACM Symposium on User Interface Software and Technology, UIST 2001, pp. 71–80. ACM, New York (2001)
5. Ryu, D.S., Chung, W.K., Cho, H.G.: Photoland: a new image layout system using spatiotemporal information in digital photos. In: Proceedings of the 2010 ACM Symposium on Applied Computing, SAC 2010, pp. 1884–1891. ACM, New York (2010)
6. Liu, H., Xie, X., Tang, X., Li, Z.W., Ma, W.Y.: Effective browsing of web image search results. In: Proceedings of the 6th ACM SIGMM International Workshop on Multimedia Information Retrieval, MIR 2004, pp. 84–90. ACM, New York (2004)
7. Kristensson, P.O., Arnell, O., Björk, A., Dahlbäck, N., Pennerup, J., Prytz, E., Wikman, J., Åström, N.: Infotouch: an explorative multi-touch visualization interface for tagged photo collections. In: Proceedings of the 5th Nordic Conference on Human-Computer Interaction: Building Bridges, NordiCHI 2008, pp. 491–494. ACM, New York (2008)
8. Dubinko, M., Kumar, R., Magnani, J., Novak, J., Raghavan, P., Tomkins, A.: Visualizing tags over time. In: Proceedings of the 15th International Conference on World Wide Web, WWW 2006, pp. 193–202. ACM, New York (2006)

9. Huynh, D.F., Drucker, S.M., Baudisch, P., Wong, C.: Time quilt: scaling up zoomable photo browsers for large, unstructured photo collections. In: CHI 2005 Extended Abstracts on Human Factors in Computing Systems, CHI EA 2005, pp. 1937–1940. ACM, New York (2005)

10. Hilliges, O., Baur, D., Butz, A.: Photohelix: Browsing, sorting and sharing digital photo collections. In: Second Annual IEEE International Workshop on Horizontal Interactive Human-Computer Systems, TABLETOP 2007, pp. 87–94 (2007)

11. Toyama, K., Logan, R., Roseway, A.: Geographic location tags on digital images. In: Proceedings of the Eleventh ACM International Conference on Multimedia, MULTIMEDIA 2003, pp. 156–166. ACM, New York (2003)

12. Gomi, A., Itoh, T.: Miaow: a 3d image browser applying a location- and time-based hierarchical data visualization technique. In: Proceedings of the International Conference on Advanced Visual Interfaces, AVI 2010, pp. 225–232. ACM, New York (2010)

13. Peca, I., Zhi, H., Vrotsou, K., Andrienko, N., Andrienko, G.: Kd-photomap: Exploring photographs in space and time. In: 2011 IEEE Conference on Visual Analytics Science and Technology, VAST, pp. 291–292 (2011)

14. Aigner, W., Miksch, S., Muller, W., Schumann, H., Tominski, C.: Visual methods for analyzing time-oriented data. IEEE Transactions on Visualization and Computer Graphics 14, 47–60 (2008)

15. Nguyen, D.Q., Tominski, C., Schumann, H., Ta, T.A.: Visualizing tags with spatiotemporal references. In: 2011 15th International Conference on Information Visualisation, IV, pp. 32–39 (2011)

16. Lee, B., Riche, N., Karlson, A., Carpendale, S.: Sparkclouds: Visualizing trends in tag clouds. IEEE Transactions on Visualization and Computer Graphics 16, 1182–1189 (2010)

17. Collins, C., Viegas, F., Wattenberg, M.: Parallel tag clouds to explore and analyze faceted text corpora. In: IEEE Symposium on Visual Analytics Science and Technology, VAST 2009, pp. 91–98 (2009)

18. Bederson, B.B.: Fisheye menus. In: Proceedings of the 13th Annual ACM Symposium on User Interface Software and Technology, UIST 2000, pp. 217–225. ACM, New York (2000)

Mixed-Initiative Management of Online Calendars

L. Ardissono, G. Petrone, M. Segnan, and G. Torta

Dipartimento di Informatica, Università di Torino, Corso Svizzera 185, Torino, Italy
{liliana.ardissono,giovanna.petrone,marino.segnan,gianluca.torta}@unito.it

Abstract. Calendar management has been recognized as a complex, highly personal type of activity, which must take individual preferences and constraints into account in the formulation of satisfactory schedules. Current calendar management services are affected by two limitations: most of them lack any reasoning capabilities and thus cannot help the user in the management of tight schedules, which make the allocation of new tasks particularly challenging. Others are too impositive because they proactively schedule events without involving the user in the decision process.

In order to address such issues, we propose a mixed-initiative approach which enables the user to select the events to be considered, receive safe schedule suggestions from the system and select the preferred ones for revising a calendar. A peculiarity of our system is the fact that, in the suggestion of alternative schedules for an event, it searches for solutions which are very similar to the user's current schedule, with the aim of limiting changes to her/his daily plans as much as possible. Our calendar management service is based on the exploitation of well-known Temporal Constraint Satisfaction Problems techniques, which guarantee the generation of safe scheduling solutions.

Keywords: Calendar scheduling, mixed-initiative interaction, temporal reasoning.

1 Introduction

The recent adoption of Web-based calendars has empowered people to holistically handle their own life schedules by exploiting ubiquitous services for organizing their work and personal commitments; e.g., see [1] for a discussion on the importance of this issue. However, current calendar services are affected by limitations which reduce their usefulness: on the one hand, many services have no scheduling capabilities and thus leave the user alone in the resolution of timing conflicts, which may occur in tight schedules and are particularly difficult to handle, especially if they involve multiple actors. On the other hand, as discussed in [2], the fully or semiautomated scheduling systems developed so far "fail to account for the personal nature of scheduling, or they demand too much control of an important aspect of an individual's working world." A new, mixed-initiative scheduling model is thus needed to mediate between too little and too much proactivity: the idea is that of enabling the user to steer and control the system's operations, in order to receive a scheduling support that meets individual needs and preferences.

J. Cordeiro and K.-H. Krempels (Eds.): WEBIST 2012, LNBIP 140, pp. 167–182, 2013.

As a first step towards addressing this issue, we propose an intelligent, mixed-initiative scheduler supporting the management and revision of the user's calendar, given her/his commitments and those of the other actors involved in the shared activities. The main feature of our scheduler is its *mixed-initiative, conservative support*: besides the generation of complete schedule proposals, it helps the user to revise a schedule by suggesting alternative allocations of the events/tasks to be moved, having schedule stability as a priority.

- The mixed-initiative support is implemented as follows: by interacting with the rich user interface offered by our system, the user can select the events to be moved and explore their alternative allocations in order to decide which one should be applied.
- As far as stability is concerned, in the generation of the revision hypotheses, the system proposes conservative changes to the user's calendar in order to maintain previous commitments as originally planned or with minor temporal shifts.

Our scheduler, an initial version of which was presented in [3], is based on the exploitation of Temporal Constraint Satisfaction Problems (TCSP) techniques, used to generate safe full schedule proposals as well as to present all of the admissible intervals for the placement of specific tasks. At present, the system only offers a user interface for standard Web browsers, but we will soon develop an analogous one for mobile devices.

In the remainder of this paper, Section 2 provides some background on event scheduling and compares our work to the related one. Then, Section 3 describes a usage scenario and the features offered by our mixed-initiative scheduler. Section 4 describes the system and its underlying model. Section 5 provides some technical details and section 6 concludes the paper.

2 Background

The temporal allocation of events in calendars has been addressed from different viewpoints, offering more or less complex features for event scheduling, but the research on mixed-initiative interaction with the user has been rather limited so far. In the following, we briefly review the main types of support offered by commercial and research tools.

The simplest services are the to-do-list managers, such as Remember The Milk [4], which are connected to the user's calendar but typically do not provide any scheduling support. They only present the lists of items allocated in each time slot.

Most calendar management services (e.g., Google Calendar [5]) do not offer any scheduling function: they only help the user to identify free time slots for shared tasks and meetings by jointly visualizing the calendars of the actors to be involved, or by listing the free time slots to choose from (e.g., see the Google Calendar smart schedule feature). Other tools take actors and resources into account (e.g., Resource Central [6] supports the allocation of meeting rooms, etc.) but have no scheduling capabilities either.

Similarly, task managers such as Things [7], DoIt [8] and Standss Smart Schedules for Outlook [9] support the management of tasks, deadlines and task dependencies but they do not schedule any tasks.

Temporal reasoning and scheduling have been introduced in some process management tools to address their lack of capability to reason about time. In [10] the authors make use of the *Oz* multi-paradigm programming language [11] for solving scheduling problems with CLP techniques similar to the ones used in our work. Some process management tools, such as the one described in [12], offer a complementary feature with respect of our work: they estimate the dates of execution of future tasks to help the user preview the organization of pending commitments. Other tools, such as WorkWeb System [13], schedule multiple workflows by taking the availability of actors and resources (e.g., meeting rooms) into account. The main role of the actors' personal schedulers is that of automatically (or manually) accepting or rejecting new tasks and modifications proposed by other agents.

Complex schedulers plan the execution of tasks according to deadlines and to the surrounding context, e.g., in mission planning and/or robotic applications; for instance, see Pisces [14]. However, they are not suitable for managing the user's daily schedules, either because they are developed for very specific execution environments, or because they focus on allocating physical resources, without taking people's needs into account.

Opportunistic schedulers, typically based on planning technology, synchronously guide the user in the execution of activities according to the pending goals to be achieved. However, they do not provide the user with an overview of long-term schedules, do not manage the shared activities and are not mixed-initiative: they basically suggest opportunities of action, which the user may accept or ignore. For instance, see [15].

To the best of our knowledge, the only calendar management service which supports mixed-initiative scheduling is PTIME [2]. That system helps the user to organize personal and shared events by selecting high-level schedule generation criteria (e.g., favoring the robustness of the schedules, in terms of fault tolerance, or their tightness, and so forth). Our work differs in two ways with respect to PTIME:

- First, our system separates the selection of the scheduling policies to be applied from the identification of the portions of a calendar to be affected. It enables the user to revise a calendar by explicitly selecting the events and tasks to be rescheduled, and to preview the possible solutions (if any) to choose from.
- Second, our system supports the management of conservative schedule revisions which do not alter the relative order of the allocated tasks and events (except for the one selected for modifications). It proposes changes which involve sliding the other allocated items (e.g., postponing or anticipating them with respect to their current timing) and, as such, reduces the changes in the actors' calendars.

3   Sample Scenario

Let's consider the sample calendar in Figure 1, where a set of events has been allocated by user *U* using our mixed-initiative scheduler. As described later on, the user can (i) manually set events/tasks in the calendar; (ii) create events/tasks to be automatically allocated by the scheduler; (iii) select items to be moved to a different date and time (benefiting from the help of the system in such an activity).

The placement of tasks in the displayed calendar satisfies some constraints given by the user: for example, the Library meeting cannot take place at lunch time (13.00 to

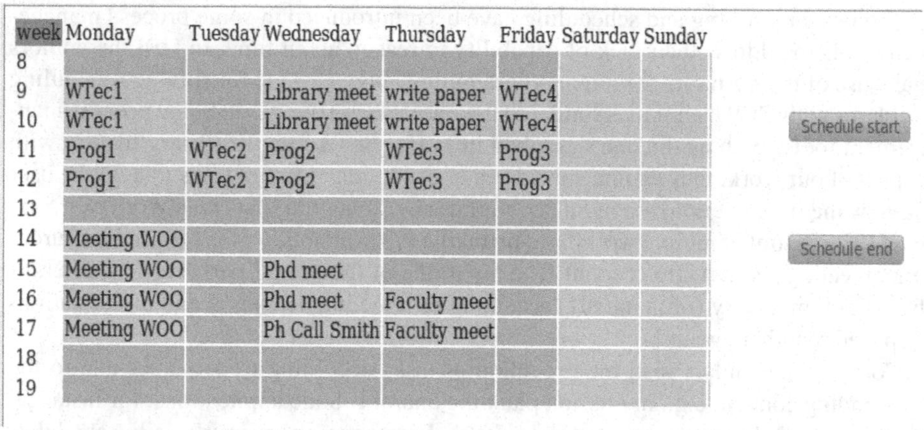

week	Monday	Tuesday	Wednesday	Thursday	Friday	Saturday	Sunday
8							
9	WTec1		Library meet	write paper	WTec4		
10	WTec1		Library meet	write paper	WTec4		
11	Prog1	WTec2	Prog2	WTec3	Prog3		
12	Prog1	WTec2	Prog2	WTec3	Prog3		
13							
14	Meeting WOO						
15	Meeting WOO		Phd meet				
16	Meeting WOO		Phd meet	Faculty meet			
17	Meeting WOO		Ph Call Smith	Faculty meet			
18							
19							

Schedule start

Schedule end

Fig. 1. User interface of our mixed-initiative scheduler: week calendar view

14.00; i.e., from 1pm to 2pm), nor after 17.00, and must end before Thursday 11.00. Moreover, the Ph.D meeting and the phone call must take place on Wednesday before 20.00 and the phone call must be done after the Ph.D meeting.

Let's assume that a new task arrives (e.g., meeting the plumber for fixing a leaking sink), that takes 3 hours and has to be performed on Wednesday before 18.00. It is easy to see that there is no free spot in the calendar where the new task can be placed. Then, the user can ask for the help of our scheduler: first, (s)he asks when the task can be allocated; in this case, the scheduler replies that it could start at 13.00, 14.00 or 15.00, since this would only require to anticipate or postpone the afternoon tasks, without affecting the *order* of the current ones. Indeed, if the new task is placed at 13.00 or 14.00, it is sufficient to delay a bit the Ph.D meeting and the phone call. Otherwise, if it is placed at 15.00, a solution can be found by anticipating the Ph.D meeting and deferring the phone call, and slipping the new task between them. If the user does not want to meet the plumber in the afternoon, (s)he can try to move the Library meeting to make room for the new task. For this purpose, the user points to the Library meeting task and asks the temporal reasoner for help. The reasoner replies that, considering only the user's tasks in the current schedule, the Library meeting can be moved to Wednesday at 8.00, 9.00, 14.00, 15.00 or to Thursday at 8.00 or at 9.00 (in which case, the write paper task should be anticipated to Wednesday afternoon).

Notice that if, after exploring several possibilities with the help of the scheduler, the user is still unsatisfied, (s)he can request a brand new schedule. However, this may cause many of the other tasks to change their times and their relative order.

4   Our Mixed-Initiative Scheduler

Our scheduler is integrated in a Collaborative Task Manager (CTM) service [16,17] that supports distributed collaboration by enabling users to synchronize with each other in the execution of their shared activities. The CTM manages task nets that regulate the execution of complex activities, possibly decomposed in simpler tasks which can be organized in patterns typical of workflow nets; e.g., sequence, parallel split, exclusive choice, synchronization, simple merge, etc. [18].

Our system manages calendar events and tasks which can involve multiple actors. In our view, the task concept subsumes the event one, as an event can represent a very simple "to-do", or an appointment not necessarily associated to the execution of specific operations. Thus, in the following we will only refer to tasks, assuming that events can be treated in the same way. The design of our scheduler has been driven by the following requirements:

- *Safe scheduling:* the proposed solutions must be consistent with the constraints imposed on the tasks in the user's calendar and with the commitments of the other involved actors; i.e., the scheduler must propose task allocations that are feasible for all the participants.
- *User control:* if the user wants to inspect the space of possible solutions, e.g., to allocate a new task, or to move an existing one, (s)he must be enabled to steer the system's behavior in order to select the paths to be explored. This is very important to impose personal scheduling preferences (e.g., by explicitly selecting the "victims" to be revised in order to solve a conflict).
- *Mixed-initiative:* even though the system has an important role in suggesting possible solutions to the existing conflicts, the user is in charge of exploring the available alternatives and selecting the preferred one. In other words, the user has an active role in guiding the scheduler's operations rather than being only responsible for accepting or rejecting the proposed solutions.
- *Conservativeness:* unless the user requests a new schedule, the system must search for solutions that are as conservative as possible with respect to the existing commitments in order to avoid a complete reorganization of the actors' daily schedules.
- *Collaboration support:* tasks are scheduled for all the involved actors, taking into account their calendars and the deadlines of their commitments.

Our mixed-initiative scheduler enables the user to define the tasks to be performed by specifying their actors, earliest start time, duration, deadline, and other types of information, such as, e.g., whether a task can be performed in parallel with other ones (i.e., it can overlap with other tasks). Even though some tasks have a fixed starting time, other ones can be scheduled at different time points and there is a safe starting time window which spans from the instant when they are enabled (earliest starting time) until the very last minute they have to be started to meet their deadline. In order to safely schedule a task, it has to be allocated within its safe starting time window. However, the specific allocation is not by itself a hard constraint to be met and can be modified for re-scheduling purposes. We thus model two main types of information: the basic constraints of tasks, which have to be met in any schedule proposal, and the specific configuration of a calendar, which represents the user's current decisions about how to organize the activities, but can be modified. The representation of tasks, and the temporal reasoning approach adopted in our work, reflect this idea.

As discussed later on, a critical aspect concerns the execution of shared tasks, whose scheduling affects multiple actors. Our current system fully addresses the management of a single calendar but provides a partial solution to the synchronization of multiple calendars, to be further developed in our future work.

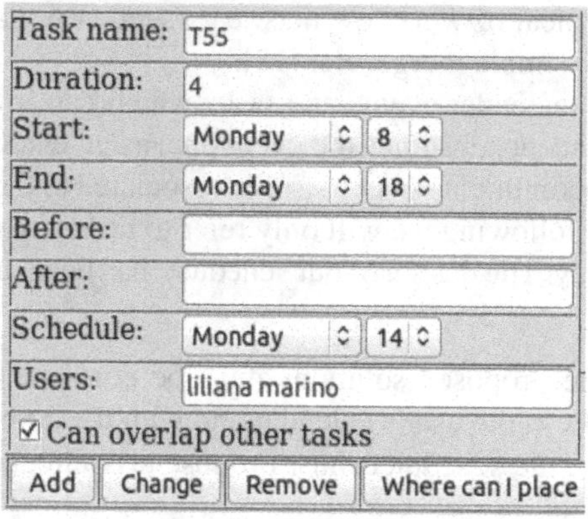

Task name:	T55
Duration:	4
Start:	Monday ⌄ 8 ⌄
End:	Monday ⌄ 18 ⌄
Before:	
After:	
Schedule:	Monday ⌄ 14 ⌄
Users:	liliana marino
☑ Can overlap other tasks	

Add	Change	Remove	Where can I place

Fig. 2. User interface of our mixed-initiative scheduler: event/task specification

4.1   User Interface

Figure 1 shows a portion of the user interface of our mixed-initiative scheduler. This user interface, currently only available for standard web browsers, is aimed at testing the scheduling capabilities of our prototype. We will restyle it, and develop another one supporting mobile access (mainly for tablets, as schedule revision is a rather difficult task to be performed using a smart phone), after having collected feedback from our users.

- An interactive calendar shows the user's schedule for the current week by displaying the names of the tasks in the time slots that have been associated with them.
- By clicking on a cell of the calendar the user can view and modify the details of the allocated task or delete it. Figure 2 shows the portion of the user interface offering this functionality (see the "Change" and "Remove" buttons).
- Figure 2 also shows the portion of the user interface supporting the definition of new tasks ("Add" button) and the rescheduling of tasks ("Where can I place this task?" button, partially displayed in the figure). If the user clicks on the "Where can I place this task?" button, the system visualizes in a pop-up window the safe task allocations that could be selected to revise the overall schedule, possibly by sliding other tasks in order to make room for the selected one. All such alternatives are handled as revision hypotheses and it is up to the user to decide whether applying one of them (thus updating the calendar) or not.
- In Figure 1, at the right of the calendar, the *Schedule start* and *Schedule end* buttons enable the user to request a new schedule following different task allocation policies. If at least one schedule solution exists, the *Schedule start* policy proposes one where tasks that can be started earlier are allocated before the others. Differently, the *Schedule end* policy produces a schedule where tasks are allocated depending on their urgency, i.e., those having earlier deadline are allocated before the others. The former policy produces tighter schedules, reducing the free time slots in the user's calendar. The latter is more cautious and generates more robust schedules by reserving time after the expected termination of tasks, which might be possibly exploited for recovery purposes.

4.2   Scheduling Modules

The mixed-initiative scheduling service offered by our system is based on the integration of two main software components:

- A basic scheduler (henceforth, scheduling module), which supports the generation of brand new schedules satisfying the temporal constraints of the existing tasks.
- A temporal reasoner suggesting alternative allocations for a specific task in the current calendar.

The scheduling module, given a set of tasks, their definition (e.g., duration, earliest start time and deadline) and the allocation policy selected by the user attempts to place the tasks in the calendars of the involved actors and proposes a solution, if any. Unless specified by the user by checking the "Can overlap other tasks" box in the task definition form (see Figure 2), we assume that tasks cannot be scheduled in parallel; e.g., the same person cannot attend two meetings at the same time. Thus, the scheduler sequentially allocates the non overlapping tasks.

The temporal reasoner, given the current schedule, the constraints imposed on the tasks and a problem to be solved (e.g., adding a task to the schedule or moving a task to a different time), searches for safe reallocation hypotheses concerning the problematic task. For this purpose, the execution of other tasks might be shifted back or ahead, within their start time windows, in order to reserve enough free time for it.

5   Mixed-Initiative Scheduling as a TCSP

5.1   Temporal Constraint Satisfaction Problems

As described later on in section 5.2, the constraints that must be satisfied by the tasks in a user's calendar can be represented as a Temporal Constraint Satisfaction Problem (TCSP) [19]. We thus briefly introduce this concept.

TCSPs are a class of Constraint Satisfaction Problems (CSPs) [20] tailored to the representation of temporal constraints.

A TCSP involves a set of variables $X_1, \ldots, X_n$ with continuous domains representing time points. Constraints can be unary or binary; a unary constraint:

$$(a_1 \leq X_i \leq b_1) \vee \ldots \vee (a_n \leq X_i \leq b_n)$$

constrains the value of one variable X_i to be in one of the intervals $[a_1, b_1], \ldots, [a_n, b_n]$. A binary constraint:

$$(a_1 \leq X_j - X_i \leq b_1) \vee \ldots \vee (a_n \leq X_j - X_i \leq b_n)$$

constrains the difference between two variables X_j, X_i to be in one of the intervals $[a_1, b_1], \ldots, [a_n, b_n]$.

As we shall see, TCSPs have the expressive power to capture all of the constraints of interest to this work. We solve TCSPs with a Constraint Logic Programming (CLP) solver; see Section 5.3.

For implementing some important features of our approach, we have to focus on a subclass of TCSPs, the Simple Temporal Problems (STPs) [19], where all of the constraints are binary and do not contain disjunctions:

$$(a \leq X_j - X_i \leq b)$$

This class of problems can be represented as a graph named Simple Temporal Network (STN) and has two important characteristics:

- checking whether a STN is consistent takes polynomial time [19,21]
- the same polynomial algorithm used for checking the consistency, also *minimizes* the STN; i.e., for each pair of variables X_i, X_j, it computes an interval $[a_{min}, b_{min}]$ such that in every global solution, the following holds:

$$a_{min} \leq X_j - X_i \leq b_{min}$$

and, vice versa, for each value $\delta \in [a_{min}, b_{min}]$ there is a global solution such that $X_j - X_i = \delta$.

We solve STPs with a specialized STN solver, as described in section 5.4.

5.2   Task Representation

We express the time constraints in the user's calendar as TCSP constraints. Starting from the basic constraints defined for a task (earliest starting time, duration, deadline, etc.), we associate two numeric variables T_s and T_e to the start and end time of each task T. For simplicity, we assume that the value of a variable T_s (resp. T_e) is the number of one-hour slots in our calendar between Monday 8.00 and the start (respectively the end) of task T.

Let us start by considering *deadlines*, *durations* and *precedences*, following the example schedule shown in Figure 1.

A *deadline*, such as "the Library meeting (LM) must take place before 11.00 on Thursday", is expressed as:

$$LM_e \leq 39$$

since in our calendar there are 39 one-hour slots between Monday 8.00 and Thursday 11.00 (see Figure 1). With a slight abuse, we use the term deadline also to indicate constraints on the exact end of a task; for example, the fact that the Prog2 class (P2) must end *exactly* on Wednesday at 13.00, is captured by:

$$P2_e = 29$$

which is equivalent to $29 \leq P2_e \leq 29$.

To express a *duration*, such as the fact that the Library meeting lasts 2 time slots, we simply write:

$$LM_e - LM_s = 2$$

A *precedence*, such as the fact that the Phone call to Mr. Smith (CS) must take place after the Ph.D meeting (PM), is expressed as:

$$CS_s - PM_e \geq 0$$

It is easy to see that all of the above constraints can be represented not only as a TCSP, but also as a Simple Temporal Network. However, there is an additional kind of constraints that is fundamental for computing an admissible schedule: the *non-overlapping* constraints. A typical non-overlapping constraint states that a task T cannot overlap with another task. For example, the fact that the Library meeting (LM) cannot overlap with the Prog2 class (P2) is expressed as:

$$P2_s - LM_e \geq 0 \lor LM_s - P2_e \geq 0$$

i.e., either LM ends before P2 starts, or vice versa. Clearly, there must be one of these constraints between each pair of non-overlapping tasks T, T' in the calendar.

There may be additional non-overlapping constraints. For example, in our scenario of section 3, the Library meeting must not take place at lunch time (i.e. from 13.00 to 14.00), nor after 17.00. In order to express this constraint on Monday, we write:

$$LM_e \leq 5 \lor LM_e \geq 8$$
$$LM_e \leq 9 \lor LM_e \geq 14$$

similar constraints must be added for each day of the week under consideration.

5.3   The Scheduling Module

Given the set of tasks to be allocated in the user's calendar, the scheduling module generates a schedule by handling the task definitions as constraints to be solved in a Constraint Satisfaction Problem. This type of activity has been largely explored in the research on Constraint Satisfaction; thus, we briefly describe it, leaving space for the temporal reasoning process, which is peculiar of our work.

If a task is not a precise appointment, its start and end times are time windows during which the task has to be executed (unless its duration is the same as the distance between such time points). The scheduling module thus represents the start and end time of each task as time intervals themselves, defining them as Finite Domain Variables whose domains represent the eligible time instants for starting/ending the task. For instance, if a task T must start after t0, end by t1 and its duration is d, its starting time window is [t0, t1-d].

Given the start and end Finite Domain Variables of the tasks to be scheduled and the existing non-overlapping constraints, the scheduling module performs a domain reduction on such variables in order to restrict their domains to the feasible values. If a solution exists (i.e., for each Finite Domain Variable, the domain is not null), the scheduling module explores the solution space for setting such variables to specific values, which represent the proposed allocation times. Otherwise, the scheduling module returns a "no solution" value, which describes the fact that the set of considered constraints is not satisfiable, i.e., a schedule addressing all the requirements specified by the user cannot be generated.

Different strategies could be applied in the exploration of the solution space, leading to different schedules. We selected two sample strategies to start with: allocating earlier tasks, or more urgent ones, before the others. Technically, such policies are implemented by selecting the order of the variables to be set during the exploration of the solution space (i.e., the set of possible configurations of the variables). In the *Schedule start* policy, the variables having the smallest minimum values in their domains are set before the others, which results in an early allocation of the tasks that can start earlier. In the *Schedule end* policy the variables having the smallest maximum values in their domains are set before the others, which results in an early allocation of the tasks that must end earlier.

In order to support an incremental mixed-initiative scheduling of tasks, and the possibility of reasoning on a subset of all the tasks to be considered, the scheduling module operates on a constraint set that is a clone of the original task specification. In this way, at each instant of time, the set of constraints to be considered can be reset or modified as needed. It is thus possible to create a history of the generated scheduling solutions and allow the user to navigate it and choose the preferred alternative.

It should be noticed that the constraints to be solved in the generation of a schedule might concern personal and shared tasks. Scheduling a shared task means allocating it in the calendar of all the involved actors. The scheduling module fully supports the allocation of shared tasks because the constraints belonging to the calendars of the involved users can be fused to search for a global solution by merging their constraints: in fact, even though each actor is committed to several tasks, those to be performed by different actors can overlap in the overall schedule; thus, task constraints can be merged to represent the complete set of activities to be scheduled.[1] If the overall set of constraints is not satisfiable (because there is no free slot where the involved actors can perform the task), the scheduling module returns a "no solution". However, if the failure is returned after the user has selected one of the (conservative) suggestions made by the temporal reasoner (see next section), it may still be possible to request a complete (non conservative) re-scheduling of all of the activities, to see if different solutions can be found which accommodate the new task.

5.4   The Temporal Reasoner

The deadlines, durations and precedences can be straightforwardly expressed without disjunctions, and therefore can be encoded in a Simple Temporal Network (STN). Figure 3 depicts the STN for the constraints of our running example regarding the Wednesday tasks. It shows the new task Meet Plumber (MP) to be inserted, as well as Library meeting (LM), Prog2 class (P2), Ph.D meeting (PM) and Phone Call to Smith (CS) (assuming that the tasks cannot be performed before Wednesday).

The z time point represents Monday 8.00, while the intervals on the arcs express the minimum and maximum distance between the connected time points; for example, interval $[26, 39]$ on the arc connecting z and LM_e represents:

$$26 \leq LM_e - z \leq 39$$

i.e., LM must end at most on Thursday 11.00, and at least on Wednesday 10.00. The dotted arc represents the precedence between PM and CS; its associated interval (omitted for readability) would be $[0, +\infty]$; i.e., CS_s must follow PM_e by at least 0 hours.

---

[1] If more than one actor is involved in a task to be re-scheduled, the task instances present in the various calendars are unified by imposing that their start and end times are equal.

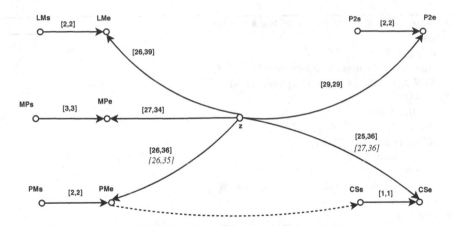

Fig. 3. Portion of the STN representing the basic constraints for the user tasks

The minimization of this STN only restricts the intervals of the arcs $z-PM_e$ and $z-CS_e$ (the restricted intervals are depicted in italics in the figure). In particular, the maximum value of PM_e (end of Ph.D meeting) becomes 35 (Wednesday 19.00) because there must be time for making the phone call to Mr. Smith afterwards. Similarly, the minimum value of CS_e becomes 27 (Wednesday 11.00) because there must be time for the Ph.D meeting before.

Note that this STN does not take the non-overlapping constraints into account and, in particular, its minimization does not affect the interval for the end PM_e of the new task (Meet plumber), which is still between 11.00 and 18.00 on Wednesday. Unfortunately, not all of the time points within this interval are admissible, as can be seen by considering, e.g., that the two time slots between 11.00 and 13.00 are rigidly allocated to the Prog2 class.

When the STN solver is invoked to show all the feasible time intervals for starting the Meet plumber task, we want it to return only admissible time points. Let us start by considering how we can take into account the non-overlapping between tasks (below, we will also discuss the non-overlapping between a task and certain time slots, such as lunch time for the Library meeting).

From the current schedule (Figure 1), we can infer the current order of the tasks that are already in the calendar. We make the assumption that the order of these tasks cannot change, while Meet plumber can be placed between any two of them.

Algorithm 1 implements this idea. It takes as inputs a new task T to insert, the sequence of the other tasks $(T_1, \ldots, T_k)$ in the order in which they appear in the current schedule, and an STN $\mathcal{N}$ encoding the basic deadline, duration and precedence constraints for $T_1, \ldots, T_k$ and T. Each possible positioning of T in the sequence determines a total order Ord among the tasks, including T). Such a total order is asserted as a set of precedence constraints into $\mathcal{N}$, and the resulting net is minimized, yielding an interval $[min_i, max_i]$ of possible values for the start T_s of T.

The algorithm returns a set $FInt$ containing all of such intervals. If the current order of the tasks is not allowed to change, the intervals in $FInt$ represent all of the possible choices for starting T.

Algorithm 1. Feasible intervals for adding a new task

---

input:
  new task T
  other tasks in current schedule order $(T_1, \ldots, T_k)$
  STN $\mathcal{N}$ (deadlines, durations, precedences)
$FInt \Leftarrow \emptyset$
for $i = 0 \ldots k$ **do**
  $Ord \Leftarrow (T_1, \ldots, T_i, T, T_{i+1}, \ldots T_k)$
  $\mathcal{N}' \Leftarrow$ assert order Ord in $\mathcal{N}$
  $\mathcal{N}' \Leftarrow$ minimize $\mathcal{N}'$
  $FInt \Leftarrow FInt \cup$
      $\{$ get interval $[min_i, max_i]$ for T_s from $\mathcal{N}'\}$
end for
return $FInt$

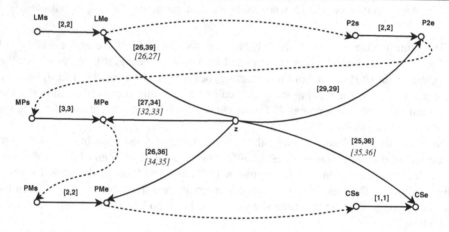

Fig. 4. STN for a specific task order

Going back to our example scenario, the new task is MP, the other tasks in the current scheduled order are $(LM, P2, PM, CS)$, and the basic STN $\mathcal{N}$ is the one depicted in Figure 3. Figure 4 shows the net $\mathcal{N}'$ computed by the algorithm at the 3rd iteration ($i = 2$), when the new task MP is placed between $P2$ and PM.

First of all, several intervals are restricted due to the minimization. In particular, the interval on the arc $z - MP_e$ is restricted to $[32, 33]$ (Wednesday from 16.00 to 17.00); when we ask the STN for the interval on the arc $z - MP_s$, we get $[29, 30]$ meaning that, if MP is placed between $P2$ and PM, it can start on Wednesday between 13.00 and 14.00.

The full execution of the algorithm yields the following set of intervals:

$$\begin{array}{ll} \emptyset & \text{when } MP \text{ is the first task} \\ \emptyset & \text{when } MP \text{ is between LM and P2} \\ [29, 30] & \text{when } MP \text{ is between P2 and PM} \\ [31, 31] & \text{when } MP \text{ is between PM and CS} \\ \emptyset & \text{when } MP \text{ is the last task} \end{array}$$

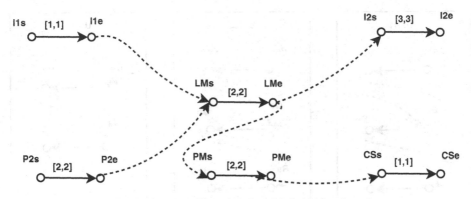

Fig. 5. STN for a specific task order with forbidden time slots

If we take the union of the overlapping intervals, we conclude that the meeting with the plumber can start on Wednesday from 13.00 to 15.00 (interval [29,31]).

Let us now show how the non-overlap constraint between a task and certain time slots can be handled by assuming that the user is not satisfied with the interval [29,31] for PM_s computed by Algorithm 1, because it would be preferable to meet the plumber in the morning. The user then attempts to make room for MP by selecting the Library meeting task and asking the STN solver to suggest where to move this task.

The computation of the possible start intervals of LM is made with an algorithm similar to Algorithm 1, which explores the effects of placing LM in each position within the current order of the other tasks $(P2, PM, CS)$. However, there is a parallel ordering to be explored; if we denote respectively as I1, I2 the lunch time (13.00 to 14.00) and the late afternoon (17.00 to 20.00) on Wednesday, the algorithm must also explore the placement of LM in each position within the order $(I1, I2)$. Figure 5 shows a portion of the STN where LM has been placed between P2 and PM in the order of tasks, and between I1 and I2 in the order of non-admissible slots.

The minimization of this particular network yields an interval [30,31] for starting LM (14.00 to 15.00). The algorithm also explores all the other combinations of the position of LM in the tasks order and in the non-admissible slots order, yielding the following admissible starting intervals:

> [24,25] LM first task before lunch
> [30,31] LM between P2 and PM after lunch
> [31,31] LM between PM and CS after lunch
> [36,37] LM on Thursday after Write paper

If we take the union of the overlapping intervals, we conclude that we can start LM on Wednesday from 8.00 to 9.00 or from 14.00 to 15.00, and on Thursday from 8.00 to 9.00. Going back to the user's goal, the Library meeting can be moved to Wednesday afternoon or Thursday morning, saving room for task Meet plumber on Wednesday morning.

It should be noticed that the described techniques could be extended to handle shared tasks. For example, after computing the slots where the Library meeting could be placed, we have only taken the current user's calendar into account. However, it might

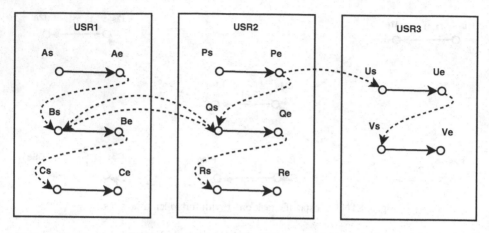

Fig. 6. Sample scenario involving multiple actors

be necessary or desirable to also take into account the calendars of the other people attending the meeting.

It is out of the scope of this paper to present the extended techniques that address this issue. In Figure 6 we give a hint of how a portion of STN encompassing multiple calendars may look like. There, tasks B and Q of USR1 and USR2 represent the same, shared task (e.g., a meeting), and this is expressed in the net by the fact that $B_s - Q_s \geq 0$ and $Q_s - B_s \geq 0$, i.e. $B_s = Q_s$. Moreover, task U of USR3 must follow task P of USR2, e.g., because the output of task P is an input for task U; this is expressed in the net by the link $U_s - P_e \geq 0$. The extensions needed to handle such an STN may benefit from distributed solving of the Simple Temporal Problem [22] and may involve negotiations among the schedules of different users (as partially done in [13], where a user affected by a change made by another user can accept or refuse it).

5.5 Technical Details

We implemented our mixed-initiative scheduler as a Java Web application. The scheduling module has been developed by integrating the JaCoP Constraint Solver [23], while the temporal reasoner has been implemented in Perl using the Graph.pm extension module [24] for representing and manipulating STNs; in particular, the minimization of the STNs is performed by invoking the implementation of the Floyd-Warshall algorithm included in Graph.pm.

The Java Web application calls the temporal reasoner as a local REST (REpresentational State Transfer) service via the HTTP protocol. The user interface is developed as a rich interface, based on the Google Web Toolkit (GWT [25]).

6   Conclusions

Calendar scheduling is a complex type of activity, which can dramatically benefit from automated support, especially in tight schedules where the allocation of new events and tasks can generate non-trivial timing conflicts to be addressed. At the same time, it cannot be reduced to the identification of solutions satisfying all the existing constraints: in fact, users handle scheduling problems in a very personal way, taking into account individual preferences, as well as information about the other involved participants. Moreover, any change which drastically modifies an existing schedule might be confusing for the involved actors because it would strongly change their daily plans. For such reasons, calendar management should support the user in finding solutions which are under her/his control and have schedule stability as a priority.

The work described in this paper follows this concept: we described a mixed-initiative calendar scheduler which proposes safe schedules and suggests conservative revisions on demand. Our system helps the user to solve scheduling conflicts but also to reschedule specific events by suggesting the time slots where they might be allocated without breaking any existing temporal constraints in the respect of the commitments of the other involved actors.

At the current stage, our mixed-initiative scheduler handles personal tasks but it only partially supports the management of shared tasks: while it generates global schedules if at least one solution satisfying the overall set of constraints exists, it cannot repair scheduling failures. In our future work we will extend the system to deal with such situations by improving the temporal reasoner that supports task re-allocation and by developing an interaction protocol that helps the involved users to reach an agreement on schedule modifications. Our future work will also be devoted to testing the scalability of our scheduler and its usability with end-users, as well as to developing its user interface for mobile access.

References

1. Grimes, A., Brush, A.: Life scheduling to support multiple social roles. In: Proceedings of CHI 2008, Florence, Italy, pp. 821–824. ACM (2008)
2. Berry, P., Gervasio, M., Peintner, B., Yorke-Smith, N.: PTIME: Personalized assistance for calendaring. ACM Transactions on Intelligent Systems 2, 40:1–40:22 (2011)
3. Ardissono, L., Petrone, G., Torta, G., Segnan, M.: Mixed-initiative scheduling of tasks in user collaboration. In: Proc. of WEBIST 2012 - Eight International Conference on Web Information Systems and Technologies, Porto, Portugal, pp. 342–351 (2012)
4. Remember The Milk: The best way to manage your tasks. never forget the milk (or anything else) again (2011), http://www.rememberthemilk.com/
5. Google: Google calendar (2010),
   https://www.google.com/accounts/ServiceLogin?service=cl
6. Bi101: Resource central - simplified resource management for meeting & event planners (2012), http://www.bi101.com/solutions/resource-central/
7. Cultured Code: Things Mac (2011), http://culturedcode.com/things/
8. DoIt.im: Doit anywhere, any time! (2011), http://www.doit.im/
9. Standss: Standss smart schedules for outlook (2012),
   http://www.standss.com/smartschedules/default.asp
10. Senkul, P., Toroslu, I.: An architecture for workflow scheduling under resource allocation constraints. Information Systems 30, 399–422 (2005)
11. Wurtz, J.: Constraint-based scheduling in oz. Selected Papers of the Symp. on Operational Research, pp. 218–223 (1996)

12. Eder, J., Pichler, H., Gruber, W., Ninaus, M.: Personal Schedules for Workflow Systems. In: van der Aalst, W.M.P., ter Hofstede, A.H.M., Weske, M. (eds.) BPM 2003. LNCS, vol. 2678, pp. 216–231. Springer, Heidelberg (2003)

13. Tarumi, H., Kida, K., Ishiguro, Y., Yoshifu, K., Asakura, T.: WorkWeb system - multi-workflow management with a multi-agent system. In: Proc. of Int. ACM SIGGROUP Conference on Supporting Group Work, New York, NY, pp. 299–308 (1997)

14. Berry, P., Moffitt, M., Peintner, B., Yorke-Smith, N.: The design of a user-centric scheduling system for multifaceted real-world problems. In: Proc. of ICAPS 2007 Workshop on Moving Planning and Scheduling Systems into the Real World, Providence, RI (2007)

15. Horvitz, E., Koch, P., Subramani, M.: Mobile Opportunistic Planning: Methods and Models. In: Conati, C., McCoy, K., Paliouras, G. (eds.) UM 2007. LNCS (LNAI), vol. 4511, pp. 228–237. Springer, Heidelberg (2007)

16. Ardissono, L., Bosio, G., Goy, A., Petrone, G., Segnan, M., Torretta, F.: Collaboration support for activity management in a personal cloud. International Journal of Distributed Systems and Technologies 2, 30–43 (2011)

17. Ardissono, L., Bosio, G., Goy, A., Petrone, G., Segnan, M.: Integration of cloud services for web collaboration: A user-centered perspective. In: Models for Capitalizing on Web Engineering Advancements: Trends and Discoveries, pp. 1–19. IGI Global (2012)

18. van der Aalst, W., Ter Hofstede, A., Kiepuszewski, B., Barros, A.: Conformance checking of service behavior. ACM Transactions on Internet Technology (TOIT), Special Issue on Service-oriented Computing 8, art. 13 (2008)

19. Dechter, R., Meiri, I., Pearl, J.: Temporal constraint networks. Artificial Intelligence 49, 61–95 (1991)

20. Dechter, R.: Constraint networks (survey). In: Encyclopedia of Artificial Intelligence, 2nd edn. John Wiley & Sons (1992)

21. Planken, L., de Weerdt, M., van der Krogt, R.: Computing all-pairs shortest paths by leveraging low treewidth. In: Proceedings of the 21st Int. Conf. on Automated Planning and Scheduling, ICAPS 2011 (2011)

22. Boerkoel, J., Durfee, E.: A comparison of algorithms for solving the multiagent simple temporal problem. In: Proceedings of the 20th Int. Conf. on Automated Planning and Scheduling, ICAPS 2010 (2010)

23. JaCoP: JaCoP - Java Constraint Programming solver (2011),
    http://www.jacop.eu/

24. Hietaniemi, J.: Graph-0.94 (2010),
    http://search.cpan.org/~jhi/Graph-0.94/

25. Google: Google Web Toolkit (2010),
    http://code.google.com/intl/it-IT/webtoolkit/

Part III
Society, e-Business and e-Government

Knowledge Discovery:
Data Mining by Self-organizing Maps

Everton Luiz de Almeida Gago Júnior, Gean Davis Breda,
Eduardo Zanoni Marques, and Leonardo de Souza Mendes

School of Electrical and Computer Engineering, University of Campinas, Campinas, SP, Brazil
{elagj,gean,emarques,lmendes}@decom.fee.unicamp.br

Abstract. Due to the characteristics offered by automated management systems, municipal administrations are now attempting to store digital information instead of keeping their physical documents. One consequence of such fact is the generation of large volume of data. Usually, these data are collected by ICT technologies and then stored in transactional databases. In this environment, collected data might have complex internal relationships. This may be an issue to identify patterns and behaviors. Many institutions use data mining techniques for recognize hidden patterns and behaviors in their operational data. These patterns can assist to future activities planning and provide better management to financial resources. Intelligent analysis can be realized using the Support Tools and Support Decision Making (STSDM). These tools can analyze large volume of data through previously established rules. These rules are presented for STSDM in the training phase, and the tool learns about the patterns that should look. This paper proposes a model to support decision making based on self-organized maps. This model, applied to electronic government tools, can recognize patterns in large volume of data without the set of rules for training. To perform our case study, we use data provided by the city of Campinas, Sao Paulo.

Keywords: Business intelligence, Data mining, e-Government, Self-organizing maps.

1 Introduction

The results offered by Information and Communication Technologies (ICT) make the public and private organizations get rid of physical documents and store their information digitally [1]. The Electronic Government (e-gov) has emerged as a popular word in the public administration to classify the use of ICTs as tasks, activities and events management tools. The ICTs are utilized in the public sector aiming to help the organizations manage the resources by monitoring the results of the implementation of public policies in the society [2].

One of the consequences of using the ICTs is the production of large amounts of data with complex relationships amongst them. This large volume of data makes difficult for the public administrators and people in charge of making decisions identify patterns and behaviors derived from the data [3]. Another aggravating is that a big

J. Cordeiro and K.-H. Krempels (Eds.): WEBIST 2012, LNBIP 140, pp. 185–200, 2013.

deal of public departments and organizations uses distinctive databases. This hampers not only the exchange of data between departments but also the interpretation of this information [1]. This way, the public organizations demand software solutions that can help the identification of deficiencies and business opportunities based on the intelligent analysis of operational data [4]. The intelligent analysis of data originated from the public institutions can be carried out through data mining techniques [5].

The data mining techniques are divided into two groups: supervised learning and non-supervised learning. The supervised learning needs previous knowledge of the data to be mined. This knowledge is employed to train the data mining algorithms. The non-supervised learning algorithms exempt the previous knowledge of data, once these algorithms operate on the basis of characteristics and similarities existing in the records. In general, the non-supervised learning techniques seek for frequent behaviors and events hidden in the operational data of the institutions [6].

The use of data mining techniques has been intensified in more developed countries. The North-American government finances private institutions for processing information in order to identify evidences of violation, e.g., the overuse of government credit by public servants and tax evasion. The data mining is also employed by the North-American military sector in the search for evidences of terrorist attacks, and even in the selection of young people for military service.

Braga [7], Oliveira [8] and Mourady [2] show that the support platform to public planning and data mining can contribute to economical, fiscal and tributary development of public institutions. Kum [9] shows that data mining can also be utilized to self-evaluate the performance of these institutions, providing better use of financial, human and technological resources. The work of Kum [9] demonstrates that the data mining enables the enhancement of processes and speeds up the back and forth of administrative paperwork and protocols of public institutions.

Several studies are carried out with the purpose of improving the management of public resources. These works employ supervised learning techniques which depend on controlled vocabulary and thesauruses.

The data mining done through supervised learning techniques raises the operational cost, as it needs ontologies and analyses of patterns that will be used during the training of data mining algorithms. This kind of solution makes difficult the gathering of new information, as the data will be explored in accordance with pre-established rules. In these cases, the algorithms of data mining are restricted to classify the data bearing known labels, leaving unnoticed some new information.

1.1   Objectives

This paper proposes a Generic Model for Representation of Samples and Extraction of Knowledge (GMRSEK) which enables the identification of unknown patterns by mining the operational data of the public institutions. To identify unknown patterns in large volume of data, we shall use a non-supervised classification technique called self-organizing maps.

Self-organizing maps are neural networks of competitive learning. On this kind of network the processing units, called neurons, compete with one another for the right of representing an input datum. The neuron whose distance is shorter, regarding to the input datum, wins the competitive process. The winner neuron and its neighbors are adapted towards the input datum; however, these contiguous neurons are adapted with less intensity [7].

By using this data mining technique, it is expected to get data gatherings which show similar information between them, so that, it is possible to find classes of logs and possible patterns existing in the data. The patterns and gatherings found after exploratory analysis of the data will be treated as knowledge. The knowledge got through the exploratory analysis must be stored in the GMRSEK which provides an organized structure, enabling the generation of reports and the use of this information by electronic government systems.

2   Electronic Government

Many countries throughout the world stimulate reforms in the public institutions due to growing expectations of citizens, regarding to their governors. The success of public management is measured based on the benefits they assure to society. Private organizations, communities and citizens demand efficiency and accountability in public resources management, as well as, ensure the delivery of better services and results.

In this new scenario, the countries seek to revitalize their public administrations by innovating their structures and procedures, and qualifying their human resources. In this context, the utilization of Information and Communication Technologies (ICT) has a fundamental role in managing and creating an environment propitious to social and economic growth, leading to the achievement of these goals [2].

2.1   Structure of e-Gov

To establish and regulate the standards of integration and exchange of services between government, companies and citizens, it is important to define the e-Gov structure. This structure makes easy to understand the implementation process of the electronic government and the implications of this process [1].

The generic structure of e-Gov proposed by Ebrahim [1] is divided into four layers, as we can see in Fig. 1:

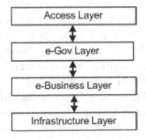

Fig. 1. Structure of e-Gov [1]

The access layer provides the means for distribution of services, products and information provided by e-Gov. These means consist of on-line access channels, such as portals that can be accessed via computer or mobile devices [1].

The e-Gov layer can be seen as a repository, where all the services offered by the government are allocated. The purpose of this layer is to establish a single entry point for users, enabling the search and utilization of services.

The e-Business layer is where the IT data an services of different agencies and public departments can be integrated. In this layer, the common data and services between different agencies and public institutions should be shared through a distributed interface, allowing the various public departments to access information from a single point [4].

On the other hand, the infrastructure layer concentrates the hardware solutions, which enable to provide information and services via on-line access channels.

We can list as elements of infrastructure layer the application servers, routers and other pieces of equipment which clears the way for distribution of services via Internet, Intranets and Extranets [1].

2.2   Classification of e-Gov

E-Gov systems have broad applications and hold users of distinctive needs and profiles. In order to group the services offered to each class of users, it comes the necessity of classifying the electronic government systems. The e-Gov systems are classified as follows: Citizen to e-Gov, Business to e-Gov, Government to e-Gov, Internal Efficiency Applications, and Effectiveness and Global Infrastructure [4].

The Citizen to Government system class concentrates the services offered to the citizens. In general these services are communication channels which permit the citizen to ask the public institutions for the execution of a given task, for instance, cleaning and mowing a park, or simply issuing a form copy of a document, such as IPTU (tax for urban territorial property), or a debt clearance certificate [4].

The Business to Government system class holds part of the services offered to the companies, such as, printing forms, copying taxation documents, thus, facilitating communication between government and business. Among the services offered to entrepreneurs, it is usual, in this class of electronic government, the occurrence of electronic bids, where competitive propositions are made for getting the right of taking over a public enterprise or a service bound to be outsourced [3].

The Government to Government class deals with the services which must be shared between the various agencies and departments of the government itself. In general, governmental agencies and departments do not adopt a single solution for software and data storage; on the contrary, pieces of information are kept in separate and distinctive environments. In this scenario, the sharing of information and services is a challenge for the public institutions, which demand software and hardware solutions that can lead to the solution of this problem [4].

The class of systems called Internal Efficiency and Effectiveness deals with applications that aim to improve quality and efficiency of internal processes in governmental agencies and departments. To exemplify these applications, one can mention the work of [9], which proposes a system of knowledge discovery for self-evaluation on the results achieved from public departments and agencies, allowing to monitor the implementation results of public policies in the society.

The class of global infrastructure comprises matters concerned to interoperability of e-Gov applications, providing quality and assurance of services. The solutions employed in this class of systems put together hardware and software resources. As an example of global structure, one can mention the work of Mendes [10], which establishes communication networks, enabling the integrations of governmental agencies and departments through the distribution of services via on-line service channels [10].

3   Business Intelligence

Business Intelligence (BI) comprises a set of techniques which permit to identify behavior trends from a frame of events. These trends can help the process of decision making in business. With the fast-evolving computing sector and the enhancement of data storage mechanisms, organizations turned to store all pieces of information coming from their daily activities, such as sending protocols and documents, recording activities performed by clients, like ordering, purchasing, and so on [2].

The organizations begin to see these data as source of information that could guide their evolution and development just by utilizing the information concealed in the large volume of data stored during long periods of gathering. The growing competition between organizations and the demand for better services by clients prompted the development of more efficient techniques which permit to analyze large volumes of data in an intelligent way. The BI has emerged as a popular expression to cover these needs and is classified as systems for supporting the decision [9].

The large amount of data and the complexity of its relations make difficult the understanding and extraction of useful information for decision-making. Thus, there is the need of storing these data in simplified environments where the degree of relationship among the data is lower, leading to better performance in queries and cross-checking information. To meet these requirements it comes the Data Warehouse's concept (DW), which are multidimensional data bases with a lower level of standardization compared to transactional databases. In data warehouse, queries can be done more quickly and the data do not suffer from having constant modification [9]. Fig. 2 displays the BI environment and technologies involved in it:

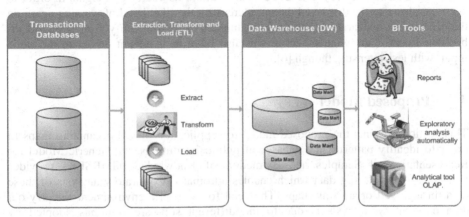

Fig. 2. BI environment

As we can see in Fig. 2 the DW is fed by data coming from transactional data bases. The insertion of data in the DW is done by tools called Extraction, Transformation and Load – ETL. The data in the DW are in a suitable format for exploration through supporting tools for decision, without duplicities and integrated as for terminologies and formats [2].

3.1   Data Mining

Data mining is the analysis of large volumes of data in order to recognize new patterns and trends coming from information of an organization. Generally, these data are cached in transactional databases or in DW, and data mining uses techniques of pattern recognition which searches for existing similarities among the data under analysis. These patterns are characterized based on recurrent events, for instance, several people get the same disease in a given time of the year. If this event occurs again in the following years, it can be considered a pattern. Data mining can identify this kind of behavior by eliminating those less cyclical facts [9].

Data mining enables knowledge discovery, i.e., it gets unknown information among the data. When there is no previous knowledge about the data to be mined, it is used, in general, techniques of non-supervised exploratory analysis. The self-organizing maps are examples of these techniques, not requiring any previous knowledge about the data, i.e., they operate on large amount of non-classified data, of unknown types, classes and groups [9].

The self-organizing maps are competitive neural networks which are organized into two layers: the input-layer and the output-layer. Each neuron of the input-layer is connected to all the neurons of the output-layer through the vectors of weights [6]. The completion of these neural networks supposes the presence of a set of data, taken randomly and in a repetitive way in which every neuron has a weight vector associated with each input of the total of inputs. There is competition among all neurons to win the right of representing the data displayed in the network. The neuron whose vector is closer to the input datum wins the competition and gets the name of Best Matching Unit (BMU) [6]. The BMU neuron alters its vector of weights in order to get even closer to the displayed datum, increasing the likelihood of winning again on the occasion of appearance of the same datum. In order to identify groups, the neighbor's neurons of the winner neuron will also have their weight driven to the same input, with less intensity, though [6].

4   Proposed Model

This section presents the proposed model for application of self-organizing maps in order to identify patterns in databases of public institutions. the Generic Model for Representation of Samples and Extraction of Knowledge (GMRSEK) provides mechanisms for storing data which enables automated exploratory analysis of these data through self-organizing maps. The need for a generic environment to carry out data exploratory analysis is due to the different software solutions adopted by Brazilian municipalities. The GMRSEK is capable of storing an undetermined number of samples made up of dimensions and values that, after being submitted to the self-organizing map, results in a set of new pieces of information which, hereafter, we call knowledge.

The expected results from data mining are concentrations of data, whose meaning can be represented by the GMRSEK through a hierarchical structure. Fig. 3 presents the Extraction Process of Knowledge:

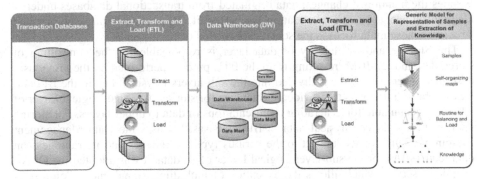

Fig. 3. Extraction process of knowledge

As we can see in Fig. 3 data originated from transactional databases go through a process of transformation and are stored in a Multidimensional Conceptual Model (MCM). In the MCM, the data must be in an appropriate format for the application of exploratory analysis, without duplicities and integrated, as for the different terminologies existing in the transactional databases. Although data stored in the MCM are in a suitable format for exploratory analysis, public organizations, in general, have distinctive environments, turning the data mining process difficult, due to the need of integration and utilization of specific routines for data mining. In this scenario, the GMRSEK is capable of storing an undetermined number of samples coming from the MCM, and, further, submit them to a self-organizing map.

4.1   Multidimensional Model

The MCM to be used in the extraction process of knowledge as showed in Fig. 3 is the model proposed by Marques [3]. Marques proposes a Multidimensional Conceptual Model (MCM) of business intelligence application in electronic government. In his work, he describes the application of the MCM for analyzing operational data in the Social Assistance area. Marques' MCM comprises the integration of different tools and open sources technologies which regards from data gathering and transformation to availability of tools for end users to analyze and deal with pieces of information stored in the MCM, according to a model of intuitive use. Marques uses a structure divided into three layers: ETL layer, Storage and Availability of Data Visions, and End Users Applications Layer.

The ETL layer is responsible for the process of extraction, transformation and load of data in the repositories of operational data to the database of MCM. In this structure the ETL process is divided into sub-layers: Motor ETL and Middleware.

To implement the ETL Engine sub-layer, it was adopted a tool called Talend Open Studio, which is specialized in integration and migration of data. To choose this tool,

Marques has taken into account the available documentation and the facility of providing exports routines in .jar extensions [3]. Diversely, in the Middleware sub-layer it was adopted the JDBC driver. The changes applied to the data include the removal of duplicated records, integration of terminologies and values, such as, monetary values, dates and profile data, like gender, types of disabilities, race, color, and so on. Besides the mentioned changes, data originated from transactional databases undergo a structural adequacy, accommodating the pieces of information in an issue-oriented structure whose main focus is the social care carried out to citizens.

The Storage and availability of data layer is responsible for the controlling of stored data in the MCM, resulting from the ETL process performed by the previously described layer. This layer is divided into the sub-layers Physical data in the BI databases, whose function is to provide mechanisms for storing data, and Logical Layer of BI data, accountable for generating representations of data to upper layers. For storing data in the sub-layer Physical data in BI databases, [3] uses the Data Management System MySQL, for its support to the various types of indexes and its rapidness on data loading. As for the sub-layer Logical Layer of BI data, it was adopted the OLAP Mondrian server, which allows the execution of multidimensional queries on a relational database. Along with the server, the Mondrian Schema Workbench tool is released to help the multidimensional mapping of relational data, facilitating the completion of the mapping files in XML format [3].

The End Users Applications Layer has as its objective to provide solutions that allow users to intuitively analyze available data in BI environment through pre-defined visions. The OpenI tool has been sorted out for this purpose. The OpenI tool allows users to check BI data through a WEB application where the results are presented in form of multidimensional tables and graphs [3].

4.2   Generic Model for Representation of Sample and Extraction of Knowledge

The Generic Model for Representation of Samples and Extraction of Knowledge (GMRSEK) offers a centralized environment capable of storing a large volume of data, made up of an undetermined number of dimensions and values. The GMRSEK consists of a set of entities in charge of storing data which will be utilized by data mining process, and summarizes knowledge obtained through this process in a hierarchical structure.

The tables of the GMRSEK are fulfilled with the data brought from the MCM. These data are extracted by an ETL routine, which associates numeric values to the data before storing them in the GMRSEK. The numeric values will be presented to the self-organizable map during the data mining phase.

The numeric values associated to the data should be normalized in the open interval between 0 and 1. This normalization is necessary, for the activation function utilized by the self-organizable map has better convergence when these values are within this interval [6].

The ETL routine that extracts the data from the MCM and stores them in the GMRSEK should also reduce the amount of variables of some dimensions. This reduction will increase the similarity amongst the records and will ease the convergence of the self-organizable map. Not all the dimensions need to have their variables reduced. This reduction must be employed only on the dimensions that can hamper the

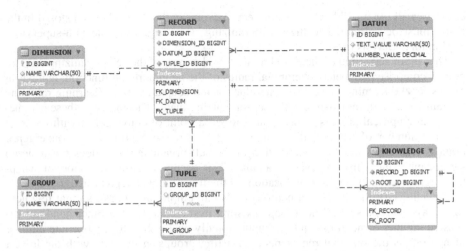

Fig. 4. Generic model for representation of samples and extraction of knowledge

separation of the data into large groups. The age dimension, for instance, can have its values reduced to child, teenager, adult and elderly.

In Fig. 4 we can see the existence of six entities: Dimension, Record, Datum, Group, Tuple and Knowledge. The entity Dimension stores columns of a sample, identified in a single way, while the entity Datum stores different values that each dimension can take. It stores, along with the descriptive value, a numeric constant which will be used by the self-organizing map while running data mining. This numeric constant will be utilized to calculate the similarity between topological regions of the self-organizing maps and the input data.

The entity Record relates to a value of the entity Datum, where the dimension and the datum belong to the same input. Each input has a record in the entity Tuple, which relates to the entity Record, as well. The entities Dimension, Datum, Tuple and Record are Entities of Sample Representation (ESR), in charge of storing all the data to be submitted to the data mining process through the self-organizing map.

The ESRs will be fulfilled with data stored in the MCM proposed by Marques [3]. These data will be extracted from the MCM through a specific conversion routine and recorded in the GMRSEK. The extraction, Transformation and Load process (ETL) must be done through a specific routine which reads the data of the multidimensional model, changing these data to be stored in the entities of sample representation of the GMRSEK.

The option for using the MCM proposed by Marques [3] took place due to being the data converted into a suitable format for the mining process, with a possible reduction of the number of variables, which summarize and integrate the data to be submitted to the extraction of knowledge. The dimensions of MCM proposed by Marques [3] used by the routine of load are: gender, race, social program, location, education and disability.

The mining of data will be accomplished through a self-organizing map, due to its capability of non-supervised classification and identification of groups based on the similarities of data. The option for this technique lies on the fact of not previously knowing the data to be mined, so that it is not possible specify a set of training which comprises all the possible classes of objects existing in the data. The data stored in the ESRs must be submitted to the self-organizing map, triggering the non-supervised exploratory analysis process.

The parameterization of the neural network and choice of the self-organizing map topology comprise parameters like: initial radius of the neighborhood function, number of events for the learning process, initial value for the adaptation pace (learning rate) and the number of neurons existing in the self-organizing maps. The choice of these parameters is an empirical process whose goal is to get a point of convergence with the least possible number of neurons, thus, minimizing the processing time. The convergence point is reached when the configuration of the self-organizing map does not undergo significant changes from an event to another. This occurs because the vectors of synaptic weights reached the minimum locations of the function to be represented [6].

The choice of the number of neurons is also an empirical process, so that few neurons may not represent all the groups existing in the data. On the other hand, an excessive number of neurons can be computationally costly. So, the appropriate number of neurons is the one that represents all existing groups in the data with the lowest number of units in the self-organizing map. The interpretation of results from the self-organizing map can be presented through a graphical representation by the Unified Distance Matrix (U-Matrix) and through analytical representation by assessing the relation between the records stored in the entity Knowledge, of the GMRSEK. It follows the routine for training routine self-organizing map.

```
w_{i,j} = weight.start();
r = network.getSize();
α = null;
δ = 0.9;
k = 0;
som  (V_1{v_1, v_2 ... v_n}, V_2{v_1, v_2 ... v_n}, V_n{v_1, v_2 ... v_n}){
while(((α=null||α<>0)&(k < 10000){
```

$$d_{i,j}(t) = min\sqrt{\sum |v_i - w_j|};$$

$$\alpha(t) = \exp - \left(|n_i - d_{i,j}|^2/2.r^2(t)\right);$$

$$w_j(t+1) = w_j(t) + \delta(t).\alpha(t).\left[v_i(t) - w_j(t)\right];$$

```
neighbors.reduce();
knowledge.reduce();
α = som(t) - som(t + 1);
k = k + 1;
}
}
```

As it can be seen in the routine previously described, the synaptic weights $w_{i,j}$, between the input layer and the network neurons are initialized at random. The neighborhood radius of neurons, represented by the variable r, is initially as large as the network but it is reduced in all learning iterations. The variable α stands for the difference of the map in the time status $t - 1$ and when this difference is equals zero we say there was data convergence. The conditions for stopping neural network come through either data convergence or through a number k, which limits the iterations in case of no convergence.

The learning rate must be initiated by having a fixed value; in the example, the learning rate δ starts in 0.9, but must be gradually reduced as the network learning goes on. The variable $d_{i,j}(t)$ stands for the winner neuron that is the closest one to the input provided to the network. In the sequence, the neighborhood function is calculated, which affects the degree of adaptation of the neuron and its neighbors. After concluding the data mining by the self-organizing map and identification of the groups by the entity Group, the hidden information concerned to the data is already in the GMRSEK.

Although the knowledge is stored, reaching these pieces of information may be a costly task under the computational point of view, once the set of stored data in the GMRSEK may be big. There is, then, the need of a structure which leans the information, making knowledge available in an agile and unique access channel. This channel allows other applications of electronic government which makes use of knowledge achieved through the data mining process for decision-making, therefore, enhancing quality of reports and information provided to users.

As it can be seen in Fig. 4. The entity Knowledge has self-relationship, featuring a hierarchical structure, in such a way that enables interdependent relationship among the entities Data, Dimensions and Tuples. Hierarchical structures are known by their representative capability and access agility, however, the performance during the access to these structures is closely related to data balancing represented by them. The data must be distributed, so that, the information tree does not grow indiscriminately in just one side. If this occurs, the access performance will be like a list and not like a tree.

In the sequence, it is presented the Routine for Balancing and Load which summarizes the knowledge achieved by data mining in the hierarchical structure comprised by the entity Knowledge of the GMRSEK:

```
gi = groups.getAll();
dimensions.order();
for each i of g do {
tk = gi.getTuples();
for each k of t do {
rm = tk.getRecords();
integer j = 0;
for each m of r do {
if (m < 1) then {
knowledge.save();
}
else {
knowledge.save(r, rm-1);
}
}
}
}
```

As it can be seen in the above routine, to load all the data in the entity Knowledge to the entities Dimension, Record, Datum, Group and Tuple, they have to be fulfilled in. The loading process of these entities starts with getting all the groups found after mining data, along with the organization of the set of samples. The dimensions of the set of samples must be organized in accordance with the number of variations of their sides, in such a way that the dimension with the lowest number of variations must be presented first. We also notice that in the first iteration of each record r, the entity Knowledge refers to the record r. In the other iterations, the entity Knowledge refers to the record r and to the record r[t - 1], where t - 1 stands for the previous iteration record.

5   Case Study

This section presents the results achieved from a real case study applied to data gathered from services rendered to beneficaries of social programs from the city of Campinas, SP, Brazil.

5.1   Operacional Data Source

The Brazilian Federal Government holds the control on the service addressed to the beneficiaries of social programs by using a data gathering tool in order to characterize the status of families called Family Development Index (FDI) [11]. Although this data gathering tool is established by the Federal Government, public institutions look for complementary solutions which can bring bigger efficiency to the management of operational data, thus, allowing visualization of managerial reports and graphs regarding to social services. The SIGM is a good example of these solutions. It is a software focused on the need of municipal management, providing mechanism for dealing with all services, records of citizens, process management and other relevant data for municipal administration. This system is developed on the structure of multiple layers, by using the EJB technology for distributing the business objects, and managing relational database system for data storage [3]. For managing operational data, Marques [3] has adopted the SIGM module for Social Management by loading in its MCM all bits of information from the SIGM transactional database. Throughout the ETL process, the data underwent a format change in order to fit the MCM. This change leads to the redistribution of information in the dimensions of multidimensional model and the elimination of duplicated records, with no integration of values, as the data come from a unique source, that is, from the SIGM transactional base.

In the MCM by Marques [3] there are around 21,000 social care records, of which 1,621 were loaded to the ESRs of GMRSEK. Only the most consistent data records were sorted out, taking in consideration the logs of the following pieces of information: Gender, Race, Disability, Education, Attends School, Type of social benefit and metropolitan region. These dimensions were selected because they can portrait individuals and are capable of characterizing them without interfering in their privacy.

5.2   Loading Data in the GMRSEK

While loading data from the MCM to the GMRSEK, some dimensions had their values grouped into broader classes aiming to provide closer data similarity. For this reason, some different disabilities were not considered, making this dimension to be a Boolean one, that is, only saying whether the person is disabled or not. Nevertheless, the item Education had its various levels grouped into four categories: None, Low, Fair, and High. The kind of social care, likewise, had a reduction of variables, packing the different benefits into five types. They are: Income transference, Housing benefit, Social-educative benefit, Child and Teen Care and Youth-addressed Programs. The reduction for these variables was necessary to bring bigger similarity in the data set, once the similar social programs benefit citizens with the same features.

5.3   Data Mining

During the exploratory analysis carried out through the self-organizing map, it was possible to notice that the free parameters of the neural network and the choice of the number of neurons have directly influenced the convergence of results, sometimes, even the results themselves. Initially, the self-organizing map had been defined with many neurons, having 841 processing units, that is, a grid of 29 x 29 neurons. This is a generous estimative, taking in consideration the number of available data. It took the exploratory analysis 15 hours to reach the convergence point, and, in the end, it was possible to identify the existence of five groups of data. By decreasing the number of neurons to 64 units, the convergence time has dropped to approximately 90 minutes; however, only four groups have come to evidence, being the fifth one embodied to the others. In the trial of establishing an intermediate value, a grid of 100 processing units was then defined.   In this last configuration, it was possible to obtain the same five groups resulting from the first execution with fewer processing units and to shorten the convergence time to around 12 hours.

For achieving convergence of results, the neural network had to go through several learning events. One could notice that when modifying the pace of adaptation of the neural network, the number of necessary events to convergence had been different. Taking the 100-neuron grid, with the learning pace starting at 0.9, it was necessary about 2300 events to have the occurrence of convergence of results. Nevertheless, by initiating at 0.3, it was necessary around 1000 events for having convergence of results. A third trial was carried out with the same 100-neuron grid, but with the adaptation pace at 0.6. This way the convergence point was reached with about 700 events. Fig. 5. shows the U-Matrix which illustrate the 100 neurons of the self-organizing map and the groups found:

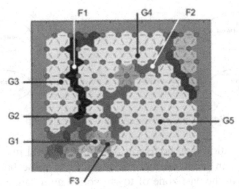

Fig. 5. U-Matrix

Fig. 5 is a graphical representation of the groups found by the data mining process through the U-Matrix. In it, we can notice the division of the input data into five different groups. Between one group and another there is a delimitation done by frontiers of bigger or smaller intensity. The darkest frontiers F1 and F2 are those representing smaller similarity among the groups. This way the clearest frontier F3 represents bigger similarity among the groups. It is possible to notice the existence of a small group G1 made up of just one hexagon, surrounded by clearer frontiers, at the bottom left of the image. This group has little difference from G5 and G2 groups. It is important to highlight that there is smaller similarity between G5 and G2 groups, bordered by the darkest frontier F2 between them. Other two groups G3 and G4 can be seen on the top of Fig. 5. The frontier F1 between them shows that there is little similarity between the two groups.

5.4   Balancing and Load

After the end of the automatic exploratory analysis carried out by the self-organized map, the five groups found had already been identified in the entity Group of the GMRSEK. Although the groups were associated with the tuples, that is, to the inputs which generated them, the big volume of data made difficult the understanding of results in an analytical way. The results, in their analytical form, were better understood after having summarized the knowledge, representing the results through a hierarchical structure provided by the entity Knowledge of the GMRSEK. This was possible thanks to Balancing and Load Routine. The data summarized by the balancing and load routine show that people who claim for programs addressed to the young public are generally of female gender.

The young female, deficiency holders, have a high level of education and are no longer attending school and live in the east zone of town. Nevertheless, the young female, non-deficiency holders, have medium education level and are still attending school, usually downtown, as shown in Fig. 6:

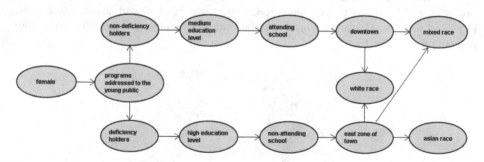

Fig. 6. Descriptive representation of groups

This piece of information may be useful for the municipal institutions, as it allows the actions to be taken in order to improve services to these beneficaries. The case study has shown that, in the east zone of town, social attendance points must provide accessibility to disabled people beyond forwarding the most qualified beneficiaries to the job market, assuring that other people can be helped in this region.

6   Conclusions

This piece of work has shown that the implicit information in the operational data of the institutions is a valuable component concerning to decision-making act in the public administration. The administration of the knowledge and the data mining permits to obtain information derived from the operational data, thus benefitting the institutions and the society.

For the private institutions the administration of the knowledge is a competitive differential, but, on the other hand, for the public institutions the administration of the knowledge can change the way the government interact with the society and the economy, when meeting the citizens' needs. For this matter, the electronic government can enable the inter-operability between its systems and provide intelligent analyzes on their operational data. The self-organizable map has shown that it is possible to identify concealed patterns in the operational data, even without a training set. These patterns can be used further in future investigations about the same operational data.

We can sort out the groups found by the self-organizable map and assess the behavior of variables not yet considered along the data mining, for instance, the family per capita income. If there is likeness in the family per capita income of all the elements of that group, this variable can have some influence on the condition of those people. Possibly, a change in this variable can contribute for those people to leave that classification. Although the self-organizable map has grouped the logs from the existing similarities in the data, the visualization of these groups through the U-Matrix is not very clear. The U-Matrix shows just the topologic distribution of the groups and it is not able to show the characteristics of these groups. These characteristics become more evident by using the GMRSEK as it can associate each log to the correspondent group.

Even if the GMRSEK associates the logs to the groups, understanding the characteristics of these groups can be difficult when there is a large volume of data. These characteristics can be better understood after the summary obtained by the balancing routine and load. This routine organizes the data in a tree-like structure that ease the understanding and allows a good perception of the results got from the data mining. For having the convergence of data, the self-organizable map had to be submitted to several learning epochs, that is, a set of data was presented many times to a neural network. It was possible to notice that the network adaptive pace may influence the amount of epochs necessary for the convergence. When this pace is very big, the algorithm may overtake the function convergence point and be forced to step back. Nevertheless, if this pace is too small, the algorithm may delay and reach the convergence point. In the case study carried out, the most satisfactory results were obtained when we started the adaptive pace in an intermediate value, and, we gradually reduced this pace after each learning epoch of the map.

New studies can be developed in order to identify the variables correlate to each group obtained by the PEC. These variables can have their values changed, and simulate, through projections, the behavior of operational data. This would allow previewing the results of an action even before executing it.

References

1. Ebrahim, Z., Irani, Z.: E-government adoption: structure and barriers. Business Process Management Journal 11(5) (2005)
2. Mourady, A., Elragal, A.: Business Intelligence in Support of eGov Healthcare Decisions. In: European, Mediterraneam & Middle Eastern Conference on Information System, Athens, Greece (2011)
3. Marques, E.Z., Miani, R.S., de Almeida Gago Júnior, E.L., de Souza Mendes, L.: Development of a Business Intelligence Environment for e-Gov Using Open Source Technologies. In: Bach Pedersen, T., Mohania, M.K., Tjoa, A.M. (eds.) DaWaK 2010. LNCS, vol. 6263, pp. 203–214. Springer, Heidelberg (2010)
4. Yan, P., Guo, J.: Researching and Designing the Structure of E-government Based on SOA. In: Proceedings of the 2010 International Conference on E-Business and E-Government (2010)
5. Mohammed, A., Goo, S.K.: Government Increasingly Turning to Data Mining. The Washington Post (2006),
http://www.washingtonpost.com/wp-dyn/
content/article/2006/06/14/AR2006061402063.html (access: January 9, 2012)
6. Haykin, S.: A Comprehensive Fundation. Pearson Education, McMaster University Hamilton, Ontario, Canada (1999)
7. Braga, C.V.: Rede Neural e Regressão Linear: Comparativo entre Técnicas Aplicadas a um Caso Prático na Receita Federal. Dissertação de Mestrado. Faculdade de Economia e Finanças IBMEC (2010)
8. Oliveira, T.P.S.: Sistemas Baseados em Conhecimento e Ferramentas Colaborativas para Gestão Pública: Uma proposta ao Planejamento Público Local (2009)
9. Kum, H., Duncan, D.F., Stewart, C.J.: Supporting self-evaluation in local government via Knowledge Discovery and Data Mining. Government Information Quarterly (2009)
10. Mendes, L., Bottoli, M.L., Breda, G.D.: Digital cities and open MANs: A new communications paradigm. In: IEEE Latin-American Conference on Communications, LATINCOM 2009 (2009)
11. Ministério do Desenvolvimento Social (2011),
http://www.mds.gov.br/programabolsafamilia/noticias/aplicati
vo-do-indice-de-desenvolvimento-da-familia-ja-esta-
disponivel/

The Use of Social Media in Arab Countries: A Case of Saudi Arabia

Sanaa Saleh Askool

Informatics Research Centre, University of Reading, Reading, U.K.
s.s.askool@pgr.reading.ac.uk, saskool@gmail.com

Abstract. Social media or what is called social websites has become a crucial method for communication development and a key driver in the way individuals and organisations across the globe create a collaborative environment. Despite the fact that social media are broadly used among individuals, it is not well understood how cultural issues and individuals motivations influence their social and professional use. This paper aims to explore and examine the use of social media among individuals in Saudi Arabia using a quantitative approach to investigate and understand the effect of cultural restrictions on individual's motivation, users' attitude, intention behaviour and their actual use. Based on the study findings, individuals' attitude and behaviour towards the use of social media are discussed followed by suggestions for future work.

Keywords: Social media, Social websites, Web 2.0, Saudi arabia, Developing countries.

1   Introduction

The fast growth of Web 2.0 technologies that have been observed over the past few years is changing the daily life of many people around the world. What attract individuals to use social media are the ease of connection, communication, participation and collaboration, as well as avoidance of restriction for meeting people who are in different places. They also provide people with new and different ways to interact over the Internet; using their PCs or mobile devices. At the same time, the engagement with these tools creates potential benefits as well as concerns about the ways people are using them. Similar to other communications tools, social media services include certain social norms, rules and principles which users have to follow.

Web 2.0 platforms have become one of the main methods of social connection and interaction, whether among individuals, business or governments [1]. The civil movement in Tunisia and Egypt between December 2010 and January 2011 are examples of the growth and shift in the use of social websites by citizens. Attitudes towards social media and their impacts have been studied by researchers in the developed countries [2, 3]. However, to the best of our knowledge, there are limited studies that focus on peoples' behaviour towards using social media tools in the Middle East, in particular in Saudi Arabia [4]. The kingdom of Saudi Arabia currently is experiencing a rapid social change as a result of wealth created by its oil and the government's commitment to modernization. It is also facing population growth coupled with the

J. Cordeiro and K.-H. Krempels (Eds.): WEBIST 2012, LNBIP 140, pp. 201–219, 2013.

young-age structure of the Saudi population [5]. As a result, we believe that it is important to study the effects of social media on Saudi society and its people's attitude and behaviour towards using them.

The survey conducted look at the social media that are used by Saudi society. It aims to understand how people are using these sites and their attitudes and behaviours towards this form of communication tools. This paper draws on a quantitative research method; using a questionnaire for people in Saudi Arabia who are using these websites in their everyday lives and activities. One of the purposes of this paper is to see whether the growth of social media can be considered as a positive approach to develop social and business relationships and as a widely used source of information.

2   Background

2.1   Social Media / Web 2.0

Social media and Web 2.0 are two terms that are often used interchangeably which refer to highly interactive technologies that emphasise human interaction, collaboration and connectivity [6]. Blogs, microblogging, wikis, podcasts, social networking services (SNS), video and RSS feeds are the most common types of social media. In this paper we will try to cover some of those tools:

Blogs or WebBlogs are online journals where entries appearing in reverse chronological order saving into an archive which is easy to browse or search [7, 8]. Many different messages can be found in blogs such as long essays, personal diaries or links to other website. The various   types of blogs include [8]: (1) Personal Blogs (2) Political Blogs 3) Business Blogs and 4) Mainstream Media Blogs.

Microblogging is a new type of real-time communication publishing that combines social networking with bite-sized blogging where messages are limited to less than 200 characters. Short contents are distributed online or over the mobile network [9]. Twitter is the most popular and fastest growing service in this area [9].

Social Networking Services (SNS): Personal web pages that focus on building online communities and interacting with others in order to share information, interests and activities [10]. It is a new way to communicate and share information that is used regularly by millions of people. The most famous social network websites are MySpace, Facebook and LinkedIn. Facebook is enabling people to develop applications and run them free of charge and this is one of features that makes Facebook popular [11]. LinkedIn is a site for business people to build connections with other business professionals. It enables people to look for jobs, looking for experts in a specific field, or connect with other members through chain of trusted connections.

Social Bookmarking are services that allow users to classify online resources by using folksonomies or keyword categorisations, to tag and share frequently used or interesting online resources. del.icio.us is a popular bookmarking site [12].

Wikis: enable a group of people to co-author and interact by adding or editing articles online [13]. Wikis have many-to- many information exchanges that enable people to contribute to a communal document [14]. Wikipedia is the most famous websites in this area that has significantly grown, edited by users globally. [15]. It is a simple virtual collaboration platform [15] and can be considered as a source for getting information and knowledge.

All of these tools can be used within a firm to support or replace their current communication, cooperation, collaboration and connections efforts.

Over the past few years, these social media tools have spread widely among individuals [16] and have attracted attention of practitioners and researchers. According to Nielsen's [17] report almost three quarters (74%) of internet users around the world are using SNS/blogging sites while the average hours of using these sites equals six hours per month. In the US, the use of social media has increased significantly and the age group increasing their use quickest of all are the over 30s and the number of users on SNSs almost doubled over a year for the 50 and over age group [18]. It is clear that a massive growth can be highlighted and using these tools is not limited to younger generations. At the same time, almost 40% of Web 2.0 platforms users accessed these websites from their mobile phones [19].

Nielson [20] revealed that the global use of SNS has dramatically increased from December 2007 to December 2008; the SNS have attracted close to 67% of the total online global population, up from 61% the previous year. Members use these websites for interacting, managing relationships and keeping friends updated on their lives by sharing status updates, photos and video [20]. The main reason for this widespread attention can be attributed to the fact they have attracted millions of people who use them as their preferred communication channel. While a wide range of tools are coming under the list of social media, in this paper we will cover the most common ones.

People use social media tools for personal and professional use [21]. Several attractive factors that encourage people to join these websites were discussed by Dinev [2] and Wu et al. [3]. Social media tools allow groups of people to interact with each other or with other interested members, with people from other disciplines with similar interests, and with industry professionals and mentors. They are easy and effective tools to create and manage their relationships [21]. More individuals have been encouraged to be a part of these social and professional networks as a result of the development of the infrastructure of these tools [21]. In summary, all of these tools can be used within an enterprise to support or replace their current communication, cooperation, collaboration and connection efforts.

2.2   Saudi Arabia and Internet Usage

The Kingdom of Saudi Arabia is the largest country among the Gulf States [5]. It had estimated population of 24.39 million in 2010, growing at relatively high rate of 3.2% between 2004 and 2010 [22].

To understand the impact of social media on Saudi life, it is important to examine the Saudi Arabian culture. One of the key factors that affect not only Saudi social life but also business is the family: the most important social institution in community because of the importance of family ties is based on Islam [23]. The religion of Saudi Arabia is Islam, a Muslim must keep in contact with other members in the extended family at all times and offer them anything considered as a way of keeping ties with them [23]. Therefore, Saudis prefer building social and business relationships with family members rather than others [24]. However, rapid modernisation and increased interaction with the outside world resulted in changing in the Saudi community.

In terms of business, most of Saudi firms are family businesses that are owned and operated by the dominance of a family and the senior executive positions are filled by wealthy and well-educated immediate family members [24]. A family firm is considered as the social welfare safety net that assists all members of the extended family. Conversely, social networks have an impact on business; given a good relationship with the right person, it will help a firm to sell their product [25]. Therefore, it seems that Saudis have a different way of doing business and managing relationships.

At the same time, the growing number of educated people in Saudi Arabia, who are now participating in the different roles of technical, professional, and managerial positions, has been accompanied by a fast growth in Internet usage from around 1 million in 2001 to an estimated 11.4 million and the penetration rate increased to 43.6% at the mid of 2011 [26]. In addition, Saudi Arabia is considered as one of the fastest growing Internet markets and as the best country among Arab countries in broadband speed with average 3.53Mb/s [27]. According to the CITC [28], a remarkable increase in the number of broadband subscriptions from 2.75 million to 4.4 million between 2009 and 2010. This growth was due to an exceptional grow in wireless and wireless broadband and connections; grew by more than 100% over 2009 which representative to two-thirds of full broadband connections. In the mean time, competition in the mobile telecommunications market has resulted in main improvements in service offerings, quality of service, customer care, reduced prices, and subscriber growth in using online services. A study in using information technology (IT) in Middle East shows that usage behaviours are often different from those reported in the West due to cultural differences [29]. In Saudi Arabia, culture continues to provide an important contribution to the business environment; there are tightly interwoven personal relationships, thus, social networks are expected to play a more significant role in various aspects of the community including business [24].

The social media revolution in Arab world has been viewed either negatively or positively by contributing to economic growth globally [1]. It has also indicated that social media tools have the potential to promote social inclusion and create opportunities for employment, entrepreneurship and development [1]. Morrison [30] states that based on The Facebook Global Monitor Data From Inside Face Gold report, Saudi Arabia achieved an impressive growth of 13.4% in active users between March and April 2010 and, with its relatively low penetration rate, there are more opportunities for growth in the future. It seems that social media have attracted young people in Saudi Arabia and freed them from some restrictions, giving them chance to express themselves and communicate with others.

3   Research Questions and Methodology

The literature review suggested that different external factors influence the use of technology and may be experienced differently by different users. Culture has been highlighted to be an external factor that influences the use of technology and information system (IS)—which leads the question of how society culture influence the behaviour intention and in turn the actual use of such a system. Straub et al. [31] proposed a model called Cultural Influence Model and found that cultural beliefs have great impact on resistance to IT transfer in Arab countries. Loch et al. [32] tested this model to investigate how culture-specific beliefs and values can enable and impediment the use of Internet in Arab countries. They revealed that both social norm and the degree of technological culturation influence both individual and organisational use and acceptance of the Internet. On the other hand, it has also suggested that motivation plays great roles in forming the user attitude and behaviour towards new technology [33]. Two types of motivation were highlighted: intrinsic motivation and extrinsic motivation. Davis et al. [33, p.112] defined extrinsic motivation as "the performance of an activity because it is perceived to be instrumental in achieving valued outcomes that are distinct from the activity itself, such as improved job performance, pay, or promotions". Intrinsic motivation refers to "the performance of an activity for no apparent reinforcement other than the process of performing the activity per se" [33, p.112]. Despite the fact that both types of motivation have effect on the user intention to use technology, different impacts across different users may be found. Accordingly, limited studies investigate the influence of cultural restrictions on users' motivation, attitude towards the use of a technology, behavioural intention and finally the actual use. This leads to the following research questions: How do cultural restrictions in Saudi society affect the use social media?

A conceptual model (Figure 1) was developed including some factors drawn from literature in technology use and acceptance such as motivation, attitude, and behavioural intention to use a technology. This proposed model guided data collection and analysis to understand how it does relate to cultural restrictions, users' motivation, behavioural intention and actual use in both social and business.

A quantitative approach was applied in this study for collecting the data in order to validate the model. An online survey method was used for collecting the data with a total sample of 600 people who were pre-selected from the Saudi community. The survey was conducted between 1st June and 15th July 2010. Most of the respondents were participants of social websites. A total of 362 valid responses were collected, yielding a response rate of 60.1% (362/600).

3.1   Survey Administration

A questionnaire was designed for this purpose in English, translated to Arabic. To confirm the validity of the instrument, two academics who were knowledgeable in instrument development and in the field of internet technology use reviewed the survey. Then, the survey was initially sent to some IS experts for review and feedback and then pr-tested with ten people located in Saudi Arabia. The feedback in general was positive; only some questions were rewarded to improve their clarity. An online survey was preferred to attract interested Web users and due to the fact that social media usage attitudes and behaviour was the object of the study. The participants were asked which of listed communication and interactive tools they used, including, SNS, instant messaging (IM), blogs, wikis, podcast, audio and video tools, and for what purposes. They were also asked if they know the terms "social media and social networking sites".

In the survey, we defined a cultural restriction as any issue or fear related to Saudi culture that influences their use of social media due to the fact that culture is one of the most key factor that play major roles in Saudis' social and business life. As the survey were developed to capture the perceptions of cultural restrictions, users' motivation, behavioural intention and the use of social media, participants were asked to express their level of agreement on a five-point Likert scale ranging from 1 (strongly disagree) to 5 (strongly agree). Table 2 summarises the final survey items used to measure each construct.

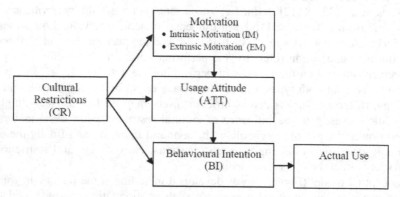

Fig. 1. A conceptual model for understanding social Media usage

3.2   Measurement Scale Reliability

Measurement items were developed based on literature review or were identified from thorough consultation with IS experts to ensure their validity and reliability. Then, to correct any issues related to the survey questions, a pilot test of the final survey was conducted on 10 participants randomly selected and questionnaire statements were updated accordingly before the distribution process. The reliability of the pre-test survey achieved the Cronbach's alpha value of 0.81; an α greater than 0.7 is often used as the threshold for reliability [34].

4   Statistical Results

Data was analysed using SPSS 17.0 statistical software packages.

4.1   Demographic Characteristics

Because the paper focuses on individuals' attitudes and behaviour towards the use of social media, demographic information was a part of the survey. Table 1 shows the distribution of the demographic characteristics of the respondents. Only employed respondents were broken down into five groups (sales & marketing, customer services, information technology, human resources, public relations, research and development, and education) based on their nature of job, i.e. students were excluded from these groups.

Table 1. Profile of survey sample

Respondents Characteristics	Number of respondents (n=362)	Percentage (%)
Age		
Under 20	47	13.0
20 to less than 30	157	43.4
30 to less than 40	105	29.0
40 to less than 50	36	9.9
50 and more	17	4.7
Gender		
Male	218	60.2
Female	144	39.8
Education		
High school	70	19.3
Diploma	12	3.3
Bachelor's degree	152	42.0
Master's degree	102	28.2
Doctoral degree	26	7.2
Occupation		
Employee-government firm	71	19.6
Employee-private firm	152	42.0
Self employed	43	11.9
Student	93	25.7
Unemployed	3	0.8
Department		
Sales & Marketing	53	14.6
Customers Services	18	5.0
Information Technology	78	21.5
Human Resource	31	8.6
Public Relations	26	7.2
Research & Development	18	5.0
Education	45	12.4
Other	93	25.7

4.2   The Use of Social Media

The survey shows that people in Saudi Arabia are aware of the term social media and social networking sites, i.e., where users can share their thoughts and experiences and leave comments on each others' profiles. 80.4% were knowledgeable with these terms and only 19.6% were not familiar. In addition, the survey indicates that people tend to use the sites' brand names such as Facebook rather than the generic term. Figure 2 presents the awareness of these terms based on age groups.

In terms of main social media tools that are used by Saudi society, it was found that a different combination of tools are used for both work and social/leisure purposes. YouTube is the most popular tool used by Saudi society for social life with 92.3%. However, only 44.5% of them used it for work. In terms of SNS, Facebook is used for social, leisure purpose and for professional purpose as well more than LinkedIn. This could be because the aim of LinkedIn is to create professional network rather than a social one or simply that Facebook is more popular than other SNS. Wikipedia and Google Docs are considered appropriate for professional work more than for personal and social life. This may be due to the fact that around 43.1% of respondents were students and employees who are working in educational sectors. Conversely, while

Twitter is well known in Saudi society, the percentage of people who are using this service for professional activities was only around 40% and 62% for social purpose. A significant number of people (more than 82%) stated that they never used or heard about social bookmarking services such as Digg in addition to other sites such as MySpace and Google Wave.

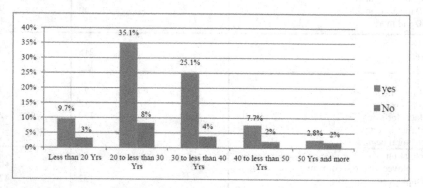

Fig. 2. Awareness of social media and social networking sites terms based on age groups

Based on the responses, it was reported that people are using some alternative sites and they also emphasised that local web forums in Saudi Arabia are widely used as social networking tools. Overall, a person uses at least 3-4 applications from the list provided in the survey. An adult usually uses a variety of social media sites; it is common to have a profile on two or three social media sites with the main ones being Facebook and Twitter.

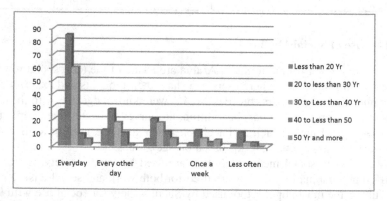

Fig. 3. Respondents age breakdown of their frequency of visiting social media sites

Two questions were asked to determine the survey participants' usage time and experience. The first is how long have you been using social media? followed by how often do you visit any of the social media sites? A significant 84.3% of people surveyed are using social media for at least one year and 46.4% represents people who are using these tools from three to more than five years which may gives indication that nearly half of the sample are aware about these tools and its functions.

The survey also indicated that respondents are used these tools frequently, with 95% accessing social media at least once a week, and more than half of all users access social media every day. Not surpassingly, as we can see in figure 3 it is clear that people who are between 20-40 years old are more addicted to social media sites than other groups. Therefore, it could be said that there is a direct link between how long people in Saudi Arabia have been using social media and their weekly time commitment.

The level of activity on social media varied among the respondents. Based on the participants answers, more than half (58%) of respondents are either partially (36 %) or actively (23%) contributing to these sites and most active users are employees in private organisations and students with 31 percent and 25 percent respectively (see figure 4).

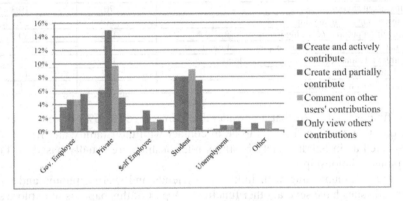

Fig. 4. Users' contribution on social media sites based on their occupation

4.3   Users Segments

According to respondents, there are a number of complex factors impacting the use of social media. The majority of comments were positive about using social media. Moreover, privacy and safety on social media did not come as 'top of mind' for most participants. Intellectual rejecters were the smallest group in the survey sample. These people see social media as waste of time or they do not see the point of using them with 11% and 9.9% respectively.

Accordingly, people who have concerns or were not welling to use social media can be categorised as follow:

- People who have concerned about safety online in particular making their personal information available online,
- People who have low level of confidence in their ability to use these tools.
- People who have no time or interest in social media and look to them as a waste of time.

4.4   Other Functions for Social Media Tools

The research sought to understand the usage of social media in business through the analysis of their actual usage on various business activities. The participants were provided with twelve different social and business activities (Table 2) and their views sought on how they use these social media tools. The respondents were asked to select more than one reason if applicable.

Table 2. Reasons for using SM sites

Reasons	Frequencies	Percentage (%)
Communicating with family, friends or colleagues	317	87.6
Communicating about recent local or world news	181	50.0
Planning Events	125	34.5
Engaging in social issues	174	48.1
Engaging in political issues	43	11.9
Talking about shopping	70	19.3
For advertising and marketing	80	22.1
For recruiting purpose / Seeking job	112	30.9
Information mining about other people to explore	161	44.5
For public relations /corporate communications	118	32.6
Knowledge Transfer	167	46.1
Engagement with customers	76	21.0

The findings indicated that a considerable percentage (87.6%) of respondents revealed that they use social media to be in contact with their family and friends. This was expected as in Saudi society business relationships are usually based on family and personal relationships.

Beyond communicating with family and friends and sharing photos and videos, social media sites have several other functions. A part of this paper is to explore some other potential functions that can be achieved through these kinds of communication tools. It seems that social media tools can be an ideal way of engaging in social issues in Saudi Arabia. 48.1% of respondents indicated that they use social media for 'engaging in social issues' which may have a positive effect on social change. One example of the power of social media in social issues is "Rescue Jeddah", a group in Facebook boasts more than 9,000 members. This group was acted like an umbrella for relief efforts and a gathering point for volunteers. However, very few participants (11.9%) used these sites for taking part of political issues.

Following from this position, 46.1% or respondents used these tools in knowledge transfer. This is may be due to the fact that 32.6 and 10.5% of respondents are students and employees who are working in education field respectively. Almost 31% of the respondents used these tools for recruitment purpose. The low percentage of other business activities may be because the rate of workers is only around 47% of the total respondents.

People also may use these sites to explore, look for and collect information of people for several reasons. These reasons may be for recruitment purposes, looking up for candidates employees or for illegal reasons such as identify theft. 44.5% revealed social media is useful tools to explore and collect data about people.

In addition, some respondents mentioned that they are using social media sites for targeting and reaching new customers (22.1%) and build strong relationships with their current customers (21%). One respondent gave an example of how he use Twitter for a small-scale commercial purpose. He stated "I use also Twitter.com for both personal interest or to build some relations with some people who I know I want to target in future sales". Even though the percentages are considered as low, organisations cannot ignore these behaviours and will need to bear this in mind.

The above results show that this could be important tools to create relationships with others. Heavy users are more extensively for interaction with their friends, family and sometimes for work.

5   Data Analysis

Structural equation modelling (SEM) was performed using AMOS (Version 17.0) software to test the overall fit of the model in addition to evaluating the internal consistency reliability and validly of each construct used. It helps in constructing tests of the psychometric properties of the scales applied to determine the parameters of structural model.

5.1   Measurement Scale Validation

In order to test the validity of the measures, a two phase approach suggested by Anderson and Gerbing [35] were applied. This approach includes the test of the measurement model by performing confirmatory factor analysis followed by the evaluation of the structural relationships among latent constructs. According to Fornell [36], it is important to estimate the internal consistency reliability, the convergent and discriminate validly of the research instrument in the first step as they indicate strength measures used to examine the proposed model. Three types of measures were employed to assess scale reliability: internal reliability, convergent validity and average variance extracted (AVE). The final instrument includes 30 items presented in Table 3 with a Cronbach's alpha (α) reliability of 0.780. This instrument includes: eight items for capturing cultural restrictions (CR) with $\alpha=0.721$); nine items for measuring motivation determinants with $\alpha=0.772$ (Intrinsic (IM): 0.766 and extrinsic (EM): 0.719); four items for users' attitude (ATT) with $\alpha=0.891$, and behavioural intention (BI) determinants with $\alpha=0.792$. As we can see in table 3, the Cronbach's Alpha (α) value of all measures were above the acceptable level which means that all constructs were reliable to use.

Moreover, Fornell and Larcker [37] mentioned that convergent validity is used to assess the validity across multiple operationalisations and achieving an average variance extracted (AVE) of a least 0.5 is recommended. Conversely, discriminant validity describes to what extent measurement scales differ from one another. The square root of AVE has to be greater than the correlation among any pair of latent variables in order to achieve acceptable discriminant validity [37]. Table 4 illustrates the discriminant validity of latent constructs including the square root of AVE on the diagonal. The statistical analyses results showed the convergent and discriminate validity and of this study constructs. Moreover, in Table 3, we can notice that the factor loadings for each construct are high; the lowest factor loading was 0.740. Overall, the results of statistical analysis show an adequate reliability for each group of items.

Table 3. Constructs reliability and validity

Constructs	Items	Measure	Loading	Cronbachs Alpha (α)	Average Variance Extracted (AVE)
Cultural Restrictions (CR)	CR1	Restrictions around meeting new people	0.771	0.721	0.620
	CR2	Restrictions around giving out personal details	0.767		
	CR3	Rules around meeting people you met on social media sites in person	0.745		
	CR4	Only add others as friends if I know them before	0.762		
	CR5	Restrictions around posting photos	0.793		
	CR6	Restrictions around posting video	0.824		
	CR7	Rules in privacy settings	0.815		
	CR8	I am not familiar with social media tools	0.771		
Intrinsic Motivation (IM)	IM1	Keeping in touch with family members	0.787	0.766	0.589
	IM2	Keeping in touch with friends	0.831		
	IM3	Managing existing relationships	0.820		
	IM4	Sharing ideas, photos and video	0.787		
Extrinsic Motivation (EM)	EM1	Meeting new people	0.815	0.719	0.580
	EM2	Creating new social networks	0.796		
	EM3	For communication and general discussion with others	0.794		
	EM4	Looking for Professional/business networking	0.814		
	EM5	For collaborative business work	0.823		
Attitude towards the Use (ATT)	ATT1	Social media development will support our social activities	0.842	0.891	0.753
	ATT2	Social media development will support our professional activities	0.822		
	ATT3	I will encourage my network members the use of social media in business	0.740		
	ATT4	In general, my attitude towards the use of social media is positive	0.800		
Behavioural Intention (BI)	BI1	I do not have interest in using social media tools	0.849	0.792	0.645
	BI2	I prefer to rely on face-to-face of using social media	0.825		
	BI3	I communicate with people in other ways	0.685		
	BI4	Using social media is waste of time	0.795		

Table 4. Discriminant validity of construct

Correlation Matrix SQUARED	CR	IM	EM	ATT	BI
CR	**0.78**				
IM	0.51	**0.77**			
EM	0.49	0.51	**0.75**		
BI	0.39	0.48	0.54	**0.72**	
AU	0.33	0.36	0.42	0.57	**0.71**

Note: Diagonal elements (in bold) are the square root of average variance extracted (AVE) and off-diagonal elements are the correlations among constructs.

5.2   Model Fit

In order to test the proposed model and the hypothesised relationships, SEM was applied. It is a useful method for studying a set of dependence relationships at the same time, in particular, when direct and indirect effects are expected among the constructs [38]. AMOS software and Generalised Least Squares procedure were employed to execute the evaluation of the research model as the data were non-normally distributed. In the SEM, the sample size has to be considered as it is playing a major role in the reliably of the test. While a minimum sample size of 200 is recommended by Anderson and Gerbing [35], Hair et al. [38] argued that 150 can be an adequate sample size if a study includes five or fewer factors with more than three items each and high item communality of 0.60 or above. Accordingly, the sample size (362) of this research is satisfactory for this purpose.

Table 5. Model fit results

Measure Type	Fit Index (Statistic)	Recommended Level of Fit	Proposed Model Value	Acceptable?
Absolute Fit Measures	CMIN (χ^2)	-	1546.045	-
	DF	-	743	-
	$\chi2 / df$	< 5.00	2.169	Acceptable
	GFI	1.000 = Perfect	0.896	Marginal
	AGFI	>0.800	0.897	Acceptable
	RMSEA	0.050 – 0.080	0.065	Acceptable
Incremental Fit Measures	CFI	>0.800	0.602	-
	TLI	>=0.80	0.482	-
Parsimony Measures	PRATIO	>0.600	0.964	Acceptable
	PCFI	>0.500	0.573	Acceptable

A range of indices were created to measure the model fit and to examine if the data support the proposed model [39, 40]. The value of some of these indices is usually between 0.00-1.00. Minimum discrepancy (CMIN) is the only statistical measure of goodness-of-fit which is represented by chi-square (χ^2) has no acknowledged value for this variable. However, CMIN divided by the degree of freedom with a value less than 5 indicates acceptable fit. Other indices were also recommended: Goodness of Fit (GFI), Adjusted Goodness of Fit (AGFI), Root Mean Square Error of Approximation (RMSEA), the Comparative Fit Index (CFI) and Parsimony Ratio (PRATIO) [39]. Table 5 shows each value of these indices satisfied the recommended level of acceptable value except incremental measure fit, i.e. Tucker-Lewis index (TLI) and the comparative fit index (CFI). West et al. [41] argued that non-normality can cause fairly underestimated fit index for example TLI and CFI. Accordingly, even though incremental measure fit was not achieved the suggested level, a good fit of the model was accomplished.

5.3   Examination of Research Hypotheses

The results related to the proposed model will be discussed in this section. The path coefficients beta weight (β) will be used to evaluate the structural model which represent the level of strength of the relationships between dependent and independent variables, and the amount of variance explained by independent variables which is referred to by R^2 value. The path coefficients and R^2 value show how the model is performing. The predictive power of the model can be tested by R^2 which will be analysed in the same way of normal regression analysis. Chin [42] recommended that the standardised level of path coefficients (around 0.20 and ideally above 0.30) has to be obtained in order to be considered as meaningful. Table 6 presents the results of the statistical analysis of the research model. The results found that 4 variables have a significant statistical support.

Table 6. Hypothesis testing results

No	Hypothesis Path	β	S.E.	C.R. (t-value)	P	R^2	Supported?
H1	CR → IM	.737	.085	9.793	***	0.574	Yes
H2	CR → EM	.482	.078	5.201	***	0.309	Yes
H3	CR → ATT	.731	.090	9.132	***	0.667	Yes
H4	CR → BI	.786	.111	7.978	***	0.464	Yes
H5	IM → ATT	.122	.080	1.386	.166	0.101	No
H6	EM → ATT	.691	.104	4.002	***	0.453	Yes
H7	ATT → BI	.886	.087	4.433	***	0.768	Yes
Note: *** $p < 0.01$							

We argued that there are relationships between cultural restrictions (CR) and users' motivation (IM and EM), attitude (ATT), and behavioural intention (BI) to the use of social media. The statistical analysis indicated that cultural restrictions and concerns had effects on users' motivation, attitude and usage behaviour with positive coefficient paths 0.737, 0.482, 0.731, and 0.786 respectively; this means that hypotheses from H1 to H4 were supported. We suggested that H5 and H6, i.e. IM and EM could have positive influence on attitude towards the use of social media; however it was found that IM had no effect on attitude (β = 0.122). This non-significant path indicates that hypothesis H5 was not supported. Hypothesis H6 which suggested that EM has a positive impact on ATT was supported with positive pat coefficients (β = 0.691). The strongest relationship was between attitude and BI as expected with (β = 0.886), this showed a strong support with H7.

6   Discussion

The growth in the use of social media websites has encouraged individuals and enterprises to improve their personal and business relationships in addition to employing them in business activities such as marketing, sales, recruitment and others. As more and more people use these tools, it is necessary to understand their attitudes towards usage of these technologies. This paper investigated several significant issues impacting users' attitude and behaviour towards these tools in the context of Saudi Arabia including reasons for using these sites, factors that encouraging them to use it and issues related to safety and security. This study achieved as significant explanatory power (R^2) which explain approximately 77% (R^2 = 0.768) of the variance in behavioural intention (BI). Hernandez et al. [43] argued that if the model have R^2 value that are far from 100%, this mean that the proposed subject is not correct. Accordingly, our study showed that the model correctly explains the role of cultural restriction on the use of social media.

It was found that survey respondents are well aware of these tools and they are using them for social and leisure purposes more than business activities. YouTube, Facebook, and Twitter were the top three tools used by Saudi society, in that order. iTunes was ranked of highest interest, followed closely by Twitter. In terms of professional activities, Wikipedia, Google docs and LinkedIn websites were the most popular tools. However, while there are factors that encourage people to use these communication tools, some cultural restrictions were reported, as well as, issues related to individuals' perceptions towards these tools. As individuals' attitude and behaviour towards such a new innovation usually has an impact on usage and acceptance behaviour [44, 45], the findings may help system designers when designing tools or software in order to satisfy users and allow them to have a greater control in managing their accounts. For example, while some respondents are more open to sharing their personal information, other make full of use of set privacy level features and they ask for more control.

It was also found that social websites are most popular with young adults aged from 20-40 years old. They are using them to communicate, whether through their PC or their mobile phone. An adult usually uses a variety of social media sites; it is common to have a profile on 2-3 social websites with the main ones being Facebook and LinkedIn.

It is interesting to find that in terms of gender, the male used a greater number of social media tools and features and they are more active than female. This finding is similar to the results from previous study [46, 47]. This is indicative of the fact that females have more concerns towards using social media than male because of the social and cultural issues around the Saudi society. A study revealed that 68% of Saudi girls prefer to conceal their family name on their profiles, and 32% of them have accounts in Facebook under an alias or false name compared to 80% of Saudi boys who are members of Facebook under their own full name [48]. It is also common for Saudi women to publish photos of their father, a cartoon, or a drawing rather than posting photos of themselves [48]. It is clear that gender has a strong influence on decisions regarding the use of social media. In addition, cultural restrictions and users' concerns have been considered as they tend to have direct effect on their attitude and attitude towards the use of social media.

As Saudi society is considered as very conservative community the survey highlights the major concerns and restrictions of the use of social media in Saudi Arabia which is presented in Table 3. These factors have been regarded as they tend to have direct effect on their usage behaviour. One of the answers emphasized the privacy issue: "*I think the main issue for most people would be privacy. I have seen people in America (Saudis [in America]) and Americans) talk about Facebook or Twitter as a threat to our lives. So by time and experience people will figure whether they will be (or not) involved in such social/communication websites*".

On the other hand, other issues were reported by respondents such as issues related to information quality in these websites mentioning that "*I limit my interaction online, beyond practical uses of social media ... I find twitter and immediate status posts on Facebook ... the height of arrogance and self importance. I find it irritating that I could be bombarded by useless information continuously.*" Another issue is related to internet speed, a respondent stated that "*to use social media tools effectively, high internet speed is required which I think is an issue here.*"

According to the results of SEM test, relationships were found between cultural restrictions, motivation, attitude, and behavioural intention. For example, relationships were found between these restrictions and users' motivation to use social media in creating social networks. We can argue that as Saudi Arabia is a very conservative society, these restrictions could have affects on using these tools in terms of creating personal relationships rather than on building business relationships. This also confirms that Saudi culture is facing a cultural shift with regards to business and social media will create change in Saudi society and will open new business opportunities. A respondent indicated that social media websites become her "*second life world that dedicated to my creativity, which inevitably blur the boundaries.*" Another respondent stated that "*use of social media is a must in the current time we are living ... I can see that in coming years, more and more social media tools will come up and Saudis will definitely use them.*"

Conversely, cultural restrictions have more impact on behavioural intention than other constructs. This could be due to the fact that Saudis still prefer to use other ways to be in touch with their relatives or friends or even when creating business, such as face-to-face and through phone calls. One of the respondents emphasised that people in Saudi Arabia "*still rely on their mobile and SMS to communicate with others*".

Overall, the research results show that social media could be valuable tools to create relationships with others for both social and business life. A limitation of this research is that it based only on a survey method that was limited to the people who are currently using social media. Another limitation of our analysis was the relatively small size of the sample compare to the total population of Saudi Arabia.

7   Conclusions

The paper mainly investigated how and why individuals in Saudi Arabia are using social media, as well as their attitude, and behaviour towards them. A model for exploring and predicting the role of cultural restriction on the users' motivations, attitude, and behaviour towards use social media has been developed in this paper. The measures used in this study were created based on various existing work in order to validate the model. The findings of this study point to a need for thorough understanding of the influence of culture in order to encourage the use and acceptance of social media. As the result of this paper was based on descriptive analyses and SEM tests, future work will include a further statistical analysis to investigate the relationships between privacy and security concerns, and trust in social media and other different issues that were examined in the survey. Furthermore, a qualitative approach could be used to investigate and look at the attitudes, behaviours, and wider issues that arise from survey results. Carrying out interviews with some survey respondents may help to present rich insights around users' attitude and behaviour towards social media.

References

1. Arab Social Media Report, Facebook Usage: Factors and Analysis. Dubai School of Government, Dubai (2011)
2. Dinev, T., Xu, H., Smith, H.J.: Information Privacy Values, Beliefs and Attitudes: An Empirical Analysis of Web 2.0 Privacy. In: The Proceedings of 42nd Hawaii International Conference on System Sciences, HICSS 42, Big Island, Hawaii, pp. 1–10 (2009)
3. Wu, M.-Y., et al.: A Study of Web 2.0 Website Usage Behavior Using TAM 2. In: Asia-Pacific Services Computing Conference, APSCC 2008. IEEE (2008)
4. Askool, S.: An Investigation of Social Media Use in Saudi Arabia. In: The 8th International Conference on Web Information Systems and Technologies, WEBIST 2012. SciTe-Press, Porto (2012)
5. Ministry of Economy and Planning Report. About Saudi Arabia (2009),
   http://www.mep.gov.sa/index.jsp;jsessionid=84857681F85783BC1
   A36562608CF6196.alfa?event=ArticleView&Article.ObjectID=8
   (cited April 11, 2010)
6. Burns, K.S.: A historical Examination of the Development of Social Media and its Application to the Public Relations Industry. In: ICA Preconference, Montreal, Quebec, Canada (2008)
7. LIoyd, G.: Are Weblogs Really ECM Lite? AIIM E-DOC 19(3), 42–44 (2005)
8. Mayfield, A.: What is Social Media? iCrossing (2006)
9. Akshay, J., et al.: Why we twitter: understanding microblogging usage and communities. In: Proceedings of the 9th WebKDD and 1st SNA-KDD 2007 Workshop on Web Mining and Social Network Analysis. ACM, San Jose (2007)
10. Kolbitsch, J., Maurer, H.: The Transformation of the Web: How Emerging Communities Shape the Information We Consume. Journal of Universal Computer Science 12(2), 187 213 (2006)
11. Boyd, D.M., Ellison, N.B.: Social Network Sites: Definition, History, and Scholarship. Journal of Computer-Mediated Communication 13(1), 210–230 (2008)
12. Yusuke, Y., et al.: Can social bookmarking enhance search in the web? In: Proceedings of the 7th ACM/IEEE-CS Joint Conference on Digital Libraries. ACM, Vancouver (2007)
13. Ebersbach, A., et al.: Wiki Web Collaboration (2006)
14. Tredinnick, L.: Web 2.0 and Business: A pointer to the intranets of the future? Business Information Review 23(4), 228–234 (2006)
15. Ebersbach, A., SpringerLink: Wiki Web collaboration (2008),
    http://dx.doi.org/10.1007/978-3-540-68173-1 (cited)
16. Chui, M., Miller, A., Roberts, R.P.: Six Ways to Make Web 2.0 Work. McKinsey Quarterly (2), 64–73 (2009)
17. Nielsen Online. 2010: Media Industry Fact Sheet (2010),
    http://blog.nielsen.com/nielsenwire/press/
    nielsen-fact-sheet-2010.pdf (cited August 11, 2010)
18. Madden, M.: Older Adults and Social Media: Social Networking Use Among those Ages 50 and Older Nearly Doubled Over the Past Year. Pew Research Center, Washington, D.C. (2010)
19. Nielsen Online. State of the Media: The Social Meida Report (2011),
    http://www.nielsen.com/content/dam/corporate/us/en/reports-
    downloads/2011-Reports/nielsen-social-media-report.pdf (cited
    November 08, 2011)

20. Nielsen Online. Global Faces and Networked Places (2009), `http://blog.nielsen.com/nielsenwire/wp-content/uploads/2009/03/nielsen_globalfaces_mar09.pdf` (cited December 11, 2009)
21. O'Murchu, I., Breslin, J.G., Decker, S.: Online Social and Business Networking Communities. DERI Technical Report (August 11, 2004), `http://www.deri.ie/fileadmin/documents/DERI-TR-2004-08-11.pdf` (cited July 25, 2009)
22. CDSI. Key indicators (2010), `http://www.cdsi.gov.sa/english/index.php` (cited April 14, 2011)
23. Al-Saggaf, Y.: The effect of Online Community on Offline Community in Saudi Arabia. Journal of Information Systems in Developing Countries (EJISDC) 2, 1–16 (2004)
24. Long, D.E.: Culture and customs of Saudi Arabia. Greenwood Press, Westport (2005)
25. Rodenbeck, M., Wells, C.: The Complete Idiot's Guide to Understanding Saudi Arabia. The New York Review of Books 51(16), 22 (2004)
26. Internet World Stats. Internet Usage and Population Statistics (2011), `http://www.internetworldstats.com/` (cited October 07, 2011)
27. Kassar, T.: The top broadband speed countries in the Arab World. Interactive Middle East (2010), `http://interactiveme.com/index.php/2010/04/the-top-broadband-speed-countries-in-the-arab-world/` (cited April 20, 2010)
28. CITC, CITC Annual Report 2010, Communications and Information Technology Commission, Riyadh (2010)
29. AlSukkar, A., Hasan, H.: Toward a model for the acceptance of Internet banking in developing countries. Information Technology for Development 11(4), 381–398 (2005)
30. Morrison, C.: Saudi Arabia Leads the Middle East With High Growth in March. Inside Facebook (2010), `http://www.insidefacebook.com/2010/04/15/saudi-arabia-leads-the-middle-east-with-high-growth-in-march/` (cited April 16, 2010)
31. Straub, D.W., Loch, K.D., Hill, C.E.: Transfer of information technology to the Arab world: a test of cultural influence modeling. In: Advanced Topics in Global Information Management, pp. 141–172. IGI Publishing (2003)
32. Loch, K.D., Straub, D.W., Kamel, S.: Diffusing the Internet in the Arab World: The Role of Social Norms and Technological Culturation. In: Leidner, D.E., Kayworth, T.R. (eds.) Global Information Systems the Implications of Culture for IS Management, pp. 143–177. Elsevier Butterworth-Heinemann, Amsterdam (2008)
33. Davis, F.D., Bagozzi, R.P., Warshaw, P.R.: Extrinsic and Intrinsic Motivation to Use Computers in the Workplace1. Journal of Applied Social Psychology 22(14), 1111–1132 (1992)
34. Hair, J., et al.: Multivariate data analysis, 5th edn., xx, 730, 12 p. Prentice Hall, Englewood Cliffs (1998)
35. Anderson, J., Gerbing, D.: Structural Equation Modeling in Practice: A Review and Recommended Two-Step Approach. Psychological Bulletin 103(3), 411–423 (1988)
36. Fornell, C.: A Second generation of multivariate analysis. Praeger, New York (1982)
37. Fornell, C., Larcker, D.F.: Evaluating Structural Equation Models with Unobservable Variables and Measurement Error. Journal of Marketing Research (JMR) 18(1), 39–50 (1981)
38. Hair, J.F.J., et al.: Multivariate data analysis. Pearson Prentice Hall, New Jersey (2006)

39. Blunch, N.J.: Introduction to structural equation modelling using SPSS and AMOS. SAGE, Los Angeles (2008)
40. Kline, R.B.: Principles and practice of structural equation modeling. Guilford Press, New York (2005)
41. West, S.G., Finch, J.F., Curran, P.J.: Structural Equation Models with nonnormal variables. In: Hoyle, R.H. (ed.) Structural Equation Modeling: Concepts, Issues, and Applications. Sage Publications, Thousand Oaks (1995)
42. Chin, W.W.: Issues and Opinion on Structural Equation Modeling. MIS Quarterly, 1 (1998)
43. Hernández, B., Jiménez, J., Martín, M.J.: Extending the technology acceptance model to include the IT decision-maker: A study of business management software. Technovation 28(3), 112–121 (2008)
44. Davis, F.D., Bagozzi, R.P., Warshaw, P.R.: User Acceptance of Computer Technology: A Comparison of Two Theoretical Models. Management Science 35(8), 982–1003 (1989)
45. Venkatesh, V., et al.: User Acceptance of Information Technology: Toward A Unified View. MIS Quarterly 27(3), 425–478 (2003)
46. Eyrich, N., Padman, M.L., Sweetser, K.D.: PR practioners' use of social media tools and communication technology. Public Relations Review 34(4), 412–414 (2008)
47. Curtis, L., et al.: Adoption of social media for public relations by nonprofit organizations. Public Relations Review 36(1), 90–92 (2010)
48. Khaddaf, I.A.: 68 Percent of Saudi Girls Drop Last Name on Facebook (2010), http://www.aawsat.com/english/news.asp?section=7&id=19572 (cited May 01, 2011)

Service-Coordinated Emergency Response Community

Alexander Smirnov, Tatiana Levashova, Nikolay Shilov, and Alexey Kashevnik

St. Petersburg Institute for Informatics and Automation of the Russian Academy of Sciences,
39, 14th line, St. Petersburg, 199178, Russian Federation
{smir,tatiana.levashova,nick,alexey}@iias.spb.su

Abstract. The research aims to exploit facilities provided by smart spaces, Web-services and Web-based communities in order to organize resources of a smart space into an emergency response community. Organization of such a community is coordinated by Web-services, which represent different kinds of smart space's resources. The Web-services coordinate efforts on planning emergency response actions and on involving acting resources as well as people that are in the emergency situation into a Web-based community. The community's members communicate on making decisions on action plans and exchanging the actual information during the response actions. The applicability of the ideas behind the research is demonstrated by a simulated case study on organization of a fire response community.

Keywords: Web-based community, Smart space, Web-services, Service-oriented architecture, Emergency response.

1 Introduction

Recently, technologies of smart space environments, Web-services, and Web-based communities have received much attention due to facilities offered by them. The smart environments provide efficient facilities for organization of their resources in a context-aware way to assist people in their needs [1], [2]. Web-services offer advantages of seamless information exchange between the resources of smart environments [3] and a potential for lower integration costs and greater flexibility [4], [5]. Web-based communities are beneficial in instant information exchange and online decision making.

The present research aims to exploit facilities provided by the technologies above. The paper proposes a framework that incorporates concepts of smart space, Web-based communities, and Web-services. The framework is intended to organize resources of a smart space into a community aiming to emergency response. Various sensors, actuators, electronic devices with computational capabilities, etc. as well as humans and organisations are considered as various kinds of resources comprising the smart space.

The organization of resources is proposed to be coordinated by Web-services. In this direction, real-world resources of the smart space are replaced with their service-based representations. As a result of this replacement, the emergency response community is made up of Web-services representing resources that would provide emergency response services.

J. Cordeiro and K.-H. Krempels (Eds.): WEBIST 2012, LNBIP 140, pp. 220–234, 2013.

The emergency response community is organized based on an emergency response plan, which is a result of solving planning problem by Web-services. Emergency responders that are in this plan and people involved in emergency are enabled to use Web-based interface for exchanging the actual information during the response actions and making decisions on action plans. In this way the emergency responders constitute a Web-based community.

The rest of the paper is structured as follows. Section 2 presents a brief survey of related research. Section 3 introduces the framework intended for organisation of emergency response communities in smart spaces. Service-oriented architecture used in the framework and interactions of Web-services are discussed in Section 4. Section 5 demonstrates the applicability of the framework by a simulated case study on organization of a fire response community. Main concluding remarks are summarized in the Conclusion.

2   Related Research

There is no extensive literature on the subject of organization of Web-based communities in smart spaces or involvement of members of such communities in joint actions. An example of coordination of different users doing collaborative activities from diverse locations through different devices is the use of a hypermedia model to describe and support group activities in intelligent environments [6].

The role of social media and online communities is being thoroughly investigated within the research area of crisis informatics [7]. Online forums [8], Web portals [9], Tweeter [10], [11], micro-blogging [12], social networks [13], [14], and other forms of social media are believed to be powerful tools enabling collaboration of different parties to respond more effectively to emergencies.

To some extent potentialities of smart spaces in emergency have been used in an architecture that intends to improve the collaboration of rescue operators in emergency management via their assistance by a Process Management System [15]. This system is installed on the smart phones and PDAs of the rescue operators. It manages the execution of emergency-management processes by orchestrating the human operators with their software applications and some automatic services to access the external data sources and sensors.

The idea close to the integration of Web-services into an emergency response community has been studied in research addressing the investigation of effectiveness of actor-agent communities in context of incident management [16]. Although the preliminary research results are inconclusive, they allow ones to suggest that agents, at least, can efficiently support humans in achieving a common goal.

The idea beyond the present research of treating emergency response as the problem of planning emergency response actions in an efficient manner is shared by many studies, e.g. [17], [18], and many others.

The approaches above address different aspects of organisation of communities of actors (including emergency response communities) sharing a common goal. They integrate various emerging technologies to achieve their goals. But no one of them investigates jointly both the problems of planning response actions and involvement of the participants of these actions into Web-based communities.

3   Framework

The proposed framework is intended to coordinate operations of various resources of a smart space in context aware way to assist people in attaining their objectives. The framework distinguishes two kinds of resources in the smart space: information and acting. The information resources are various kinds of sensors and electronic devices that provide data & information and perform computations. Particularly, some information resources are responsible for problem solving. The acting resources are people and/or organizations that can be involved in the response actions, i.e., emergency responders.

3.1   Emergency Response Community

As known from e-Government practice, participation of different stakeholders in e-Government's activities can result in broader (integrated) solutions [19], [20]. So, the framework assumes partnerships of different stakeholders in emergency response actions. It integrates emergency services the smart space provides and voluntary sector as the partnerships (Fig. 1). It is considered that the smart space provides emergency response services on first aid, emergency control, and people evacuation. The services on first aid and emergency control are services rendered by professional emergency responders, whereas the evacuation services are provided by the voluntary sector. This sector is represented by car drivers – they are the volunteers ready to evacuate the potential victims.

    Access to the emergency response services is achieved through wire or wireless Internet-accessible devices. Communications between the participants of emergency response actions are supported by Web-based interface. In this way these participants organize a Web-based community.

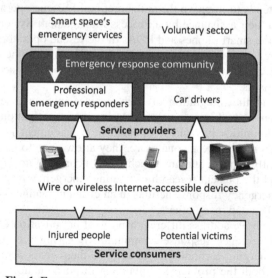

Fig. 1. Emergency response community in smart space

The professional emergency responders and the volunteers make up the emergency response community. They use Web-based interface to make decisions on action plans, to exchange information during the response actions, and to communicate with victims.

3.2   Generic Scheme of Framework

The idea behind the framework is to represent the resources of the smart space, emergency responders, and people in any way involved in the emergency by sets of Web-services. Each of the listed objects is characterized by its profile. A profile, besides typical information characterizing an object (object's name, address, etc.), holds a set of context sensitive properties, e.g. the object's location, its availability, role, etc. The Web-services provide data stored in the profiles and implement the resources' functionalities. As a result of the representation used, the emergency response community comprises Web-services representing emergency responders taking the response actions.

The framework guides the emergency response as follows (Fig. 2). Whenever an emergency event occurs, resources of the smart space recognize the type of event and determine other event characteristics (the location, intensity and severity of the event, etc.). Based on the type of emergency and knowledge represented in an application ontology of the emergency management domain, special developed services create an *abstract context*. This context is an ontology-based model of the emergency situation of the given type at the abstract (non-instantiated) level. It represents knowledge relevant to the emergency situation, i.e. kinds of services required in the given emergency situation and other knowledge related to these services.

The abstract context is instantiated by resources of the smart space. The resources continuously fill up the abstract context with real-world information characterising the emergency situation. In this way an *operational context* is produced, which is a model of the emergency situation representing fully-instantiated real-world objects relevant to it. Particularly, the operational context contains information about the locations of potential emergency responders along with some other their characteristics (their availabilities, capacities, etc.).

The operational context serves as the basis for producing a plan of response actions. An emergency response plan is a set of emergency responders with transportation routes for the mobile responders, required helping services, and schedules for the responders' activities. The problem of plan producing is solved as a constraint satisfaction problem, the result of which is a set of feasible action plans.

From the set of feasible plans an efficient plan is selected. For this, some efficiency criteria are applied. For professional emergency responders the following efficiency criteria are provided for: minimal time of arriving of professional emergency responders at the emergency location, minimal time and cost of transportation of injured people to hospitals, and minimal number of mobile teams involved in the response actions. For car drivers efficiency criteria are minimum evacuation time and maximum evacuation capacity.

The efficient plan is displayed on the Internet-accessible devices of emergency responders that are in this plan for making decisions if they are ready to act according to the plan or not. The procedure of making decisions is provided for two reasons.

Firstly, emergency situations are rapidly changing ones – something may happen between the moment when a plan is selected and time when the possible community members receive this plan. Secondly, resources of the smart space may be disabled in emergency and because of this operational information may be not available; therefore the operational context may not meet the real state of the situation.

The approved plan is thought to be the guide for the response actions. The emergency responders scheduled in this plan organise the emergency response community.

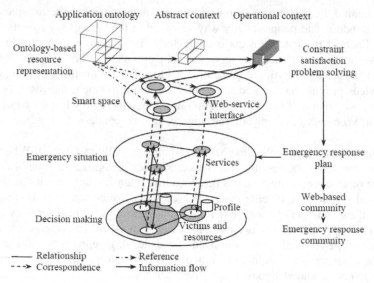

Fig. 2. Generic scheme of the framework

3.3   Decision Making

Decisions on action plans are made online using Internet-accessible devices and Web-based interface. But procedures of making decisions by professional emergency responders and volunteers are different.

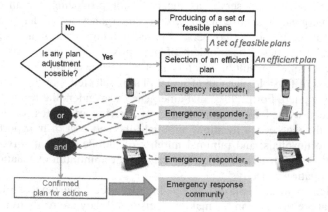

Fig. 3. Decision making by professional emergency responders

For the professional emergency responders an emergency response plan is a set of professional emergency responders (emergency teams, fire brigades, rescue parties, hospitals, etc.), a set of services these responders have to provide in the emergency situation (fire extinguishing, transportation, first aid, etc.), a set of transportation routes to go to the emergency location and to transport injured people to hospitals, and schedules for the responders' activities.

The procedure of making decisions by professional emergency responders is as follows (Fig. 3). If the plan is approved by all the responders this plan is supposed to be the plan for actions. Otherwise, either this plan is adjusted (so that the potential participant who refused to act according to the plan does not appear in the adjusted plan) or another set of plans is produced.

The plan adjustment is in a redistribution of the actions among emergency responders that are contained in the set of feasible plans. If such a distribution does not lead to a considerable loss of time (particularly, the estimated time of the transportation of the injured people to hospitals does not exceed "The Golden Hour") then the adjusted plan is submitted to the renewed set of emergency responders for approval. If a distribution is not possible or leads to loss of response time a new set of plans is produced, from which a new efficient plan is selected and submitted to approval.

For the car drivers the emergency response plan is a plan for evacuation of potential victims from the dangerous area. Potential victims here are people who have been out of danger so far or got themselves out of the dangerous area. Plan for a car driver is a ridesharing route and transportation schedule.

Decision making on an evacuation plan is in making agreement between the driver and the evacuee to go according to the scheduled ridesharing route (Fig. 4). In case, when there is no agreement between a driver and an evacuee, another car for evacuation of this passenger is sought for. At that, the confirmed routes are not revised.

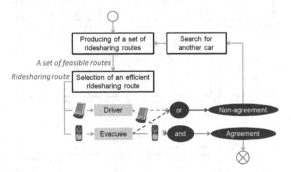

Fig. 4. Decision making by car drivers and evacuees

The emergency responders that are in the approved plan intended for professional emergency responders and the drivers participating in the evacuation organise the emergency response community.

4   Service-Oriented Architecture

To coordinate the interactions of Web-services, the framework deals with, service-oriented architecture has been designed.

4.1   Architecture Components

The architecture comprises three groups of services (Fig. 5). The first group is made up of core services responsible for the registration of the Web-services in the service register and producing the real-world model of the emergency situation, i.e. the creation of the abstract and operational contexts. Services belonging to this group are as follows:

- *registration service* registers the Web-services in the service register;
- *application ontology service* provides access to the application ontology;
- *abstract context service* creates, stores, maintains, and reuses the abstract contexts;
- *operational context service* produces the operational contexts.

Web-services comprising the second group are responsible for the organization of an emergency response community. This group contains:

- *emergency response service* integrates information provided by the city's resources;
- *routing service* generates a set of feasible plans for emergency response actions;
- *smart logistics service* implements functions of the ridesharing technology;
- *decision making service* selects an efficient plan from the set of feasible plans and coordinates the (re)planning procedure.

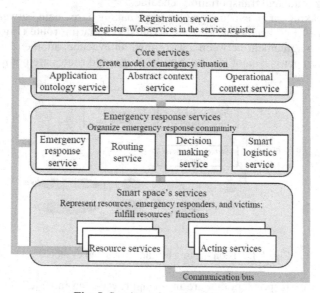

Fig. 5. Service-oriented architecture

The third group comprises sets of services responsible for the representation of the smart space's resources, implementation of their functions, and representation of emergency responders and people in any way involved in the emergency. This group includes:

- *resource services* provide data stored in the profiles of information resources and implement functions of these resources;

- *acting services* provide data stored in the profiles of acting resources (emergency responders) and other people involved in emergency.

4.2   Service Interactions

Service interactions in Web-based community are demonstrated by two scenarios. These scenarios introduce the service interactions in making decisions on the plan for actions intended for professional emergency responders.

Fig. 6 shows Web-service interactions when all the emergency responders agree to participate in the joint actions according to the plan selected by *decision making service* (in the figure the emergency responders are represented by vehicles that they use – ambulance, fire truck, and rescue helicopter). It is seen that *decision making service* sends simultaneous messages to all the emergency responders with the plan for each responder, waits their replays on plan acceptance (Ready), and sends them simultaneous messages to take the response actions (Start).

Fig. 7 demonstrates Web-service interactions in case when all the ambulances selected for the response actions are not ready to participate in them and *routing service* does not manage to adjust the selected plan. Two ambulances (Ambulance 1 and Ambulance 2) replay "Not ready" to the messages of *decision making service*. This replay is accompanied with the messages to *decision masking service* and *operational service* with the reasons of their refusals. Examples of such reasons are the road has been destroyed, the ambulance has blocked, etc.

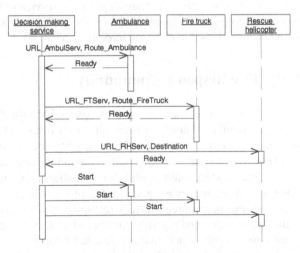

Fig. 6. Emergency responders accept emergency response plan

Decision making service duplicates the messages with the reasons for *operational service*. The duplication is a guarantee that *operational service* will receive information that it was unaware of up to this moment. As well *decision making service* sends the message on excluding the two ambulances from the list of available emergency responders to *routing service*.

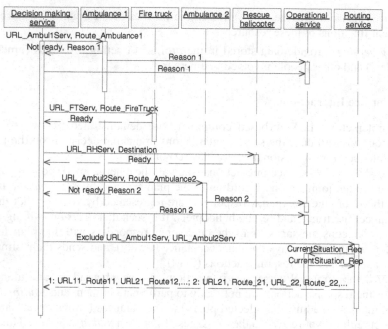

Fig. 7. Plan regeneration

Operational service corrects the operational context according to the information contained in the reasons. *Routing service* requests *operation service* of the operational context that represents the up-to-date information of the emergency situation, generates a new set of plans, and sends it to *decision making service*.

5   Case Study: Fire Response Community

An applicability of the proposed framework is demonstrated via the organization of an emergency response community aiming to response to a fire event happened in a smart space. The event was simulated using an internal platform that supports a GIS-based simulation. The platform is capable to generate random failures and locations of emergency responders, and random route availabilities; it allows ones to input contextual information on types of emergency events, number of victims, etc.

According to the framework resource services recognize the fire event, fix the fire location, classify the fire severity, and registers number of victims to be transported to hospitals. In the test case it is simulated that the fire has happened in a building, its level of severity is low, 9 injured people have to be transported to hospitals. This information is sent to emergency response service. This service concludes that to extinguish the fire 1 fire brigade is required.

Based on the type of emergency (fire) abstract context service creates an abstract context. This context represents the following kinds of response services required in the fire situation: fire service, emergency service, and transportation service. These services are provided by the following kinds of emergency responders: fire brigades, emergency teams, hospitals, and car drivers. Besides the listed knowledge, the abstract context represents various kinds of vehicles that may be used by the emergency responders, and kinds of roles of the individuals involved in the fire situation (e.g. leader of a team, driver, victim, passenger, etc.).

Operational context service instantiates the kinds of concepts represented in the abstract context and produces in that way an operational context. For the instantiation *operational context service* uses the information provided by the resource services and acting services:

- the location and severity of the fire event;

- the number of victims;

- the current locations, availabilities, and capacities of the mobile emergency responders, i.e., fire brigades, emergency teams, and car drivers;

- the types of vehicles the mobile emergency responders use;

- the addresses, contact information, availabilities, and free capacities of the hospitals;

- the destinations of cars passing by the fire place and the cars' properties (free capacities, availabilities of baby car seats, etc.);

- the current locations of the uninjured people to be evacuated from the fire area;

- the transportation network, the route availabilities, and the traffic situation.

Operational context service passes the operational context to *routing service*. *Routing service* analyses types of routes (roads, waterways, etc.) that the emergency teams and fire brigades can follow depending on the vehicles they use. Then, *routing service* selects feasible fire brigades, emergency teams, and hospitals that can be involved in the response operation. They are selected depending on 1) their availabilities; 2) the types of vehicles they use and 3) the routes available for these types; and 4) the hospitals' free capacities.

In the simulated area 7 available fire brigades, 8 emergency teams, 5 hospitals having free capacities for 4, 4, 2, 3, and 3 patients correspondingly are found; 6 fire trucks and 1 fire helicopter are allocated to the fire brigades, 7 ambulances and 1 rescue helicopter are allocated to the emergency teams.

For the found emergency responders *routing service* generates a set of feasible plans for actions. A plan for actions produced for the emergency teams supposes that one vehicle can house one injured person.

Routing service passes the operational context and the set of plans to *decision making service*. The latter selects an efficient plan (Fig. 8). At that, minimal time of victim transportations is used as the efficiency criterion. In Fig. 8 the big dot denotes the fire location; dotted lines depict routes to be used for transportations of the emergency teams and fire brigades.

As it is seen from the figure, the set of emergency responders comprises 1 fire brigade going by 1 fire helicopter, 7 emergency teams allocated to 1 rescue helicopter and 6 ambulances, and 3 hospitals having free capacities for 4, 2, and 3 patients. 1 ambulance (encircled in the figure) and the rescue helicopter are planned to go from the fire location to hospitals twice. The estimated time of the operation of transportations of all the victims to hospitals is 1h. 25 min.

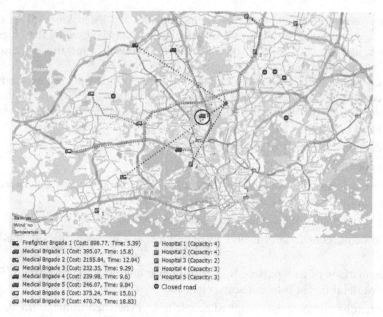

Firefighter Brigade 1 (Cost: 898.77, Time: 5.39)   Hospital 1 (Capacity: 4)
Medical Brigade 1 (Cost: 395.07, Time: 15.8)   Hospital 2 (Capacity: 4)
Medical Brigade 2 (Cost: 2155.84, Time: 12.94)   Hospital 3 (Capacity: 2)
Medical Brigade 3 (Cost: 232.35, Time: 9.29)   Hospital 4 (Capacity: 3)
Medical Brigade 4 (Cost: 239.98, Time: 9.6)   Hospital 5 (Capacity: 3)
Medical Brigade 5 (Cost: 246.07, Time: 9.84)   Closed road
Medical Brigade 6 (Cost: 375.24, Time: 15.01)
Medical Brigade 7 (Cost: 470.76, Time: 18.83)

Fig. 8. Plan for actions for fire brigades and emergency teams

Decision making service submits the plan to the emergency responders that are in it for making decisions on this plan. The plan is displayed on the Internet-accessible devices of these responders. The view of the plan depends on the roles the emergency responders fulfill in the current emergency situation. Fig. 9 shows part of the plan displayed on the Tablet PC of the leader of an emergency team.

In the test case all the emergency responders represented in Fig. 8 are supposed to agree on the plan and therefore have become the members of the emergency response community.

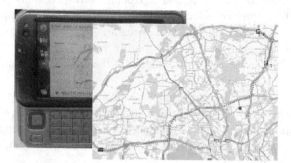

Fig. 9. Plan for actions for an emergency team

Concurrently with the planning of the response actions activities on evacuation of people from the fire area are undertaken. Persons who need to be evacuated from the fire area invoke *smart logistics service*. This service scans cars passing the person locations. Based on the information about the person locations and destinations, and the locations and destinations of the found cars, *routing service* produces a set of feasible ridesharing routes for the person transportations. *Decision making service* selects efficient routes.

The selected efficient routes are displayed on Internet-accessible devices of the drivers and the evacuees to confirm their intentions to go according to the proposed to them ridesharing routes. Besides the routes, the passengers are informed of the model, color, and license plate number of the car intended for their transportation.

As the drivers and the passengers confirm the evacuation plans, *smart logistics service* sends appropriate signals to the drivers included in the agreed plans. Examples of ways routed for a driver and a passenger and displayed on their smart phones are given in Fig. 10 and Fig. 11. For the passenger the walking path to the locations where the drivers are offered to pick his/ her up is displayed. The encircled car in the figures shows the location where the driver is offered to pick up the passenger.

In the simulated example 26 persons are supposed to have to be evacuated from the fire area. The results obtained for this are as follows: 22 persons have been driven directly to the destinations by 16 cars whereas for 4 persons no cars have been found. These 4 persons are informed through their mobile devices that they can be evacuated by taxis. If they agree, *smart logistics service* makes orders for taxi.

The Web-based community organized in the test case comprises 1) the professional emergency responders scheduled in the fire response plan (Fig. 8) in the persons of the leaders of the emergency teams and fire brigades as well as the administrators of the hospitals; 2) the cars' drivers participated in the confirmation of the ridesharing routes and 3) the evacuees. The emergency teams, fire brigades, hospitals, and car drivers constitute the emergency response community.

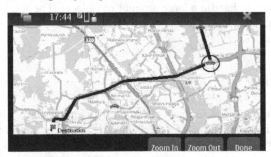

Fig. 10. Ridesharing route: driver's view

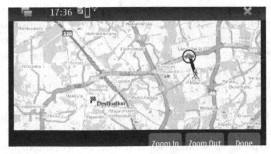

Fig. 11. Ridesharing route: passenger's view

The Smart-M3 platform [21] was used in the scenario execution. Tablet PC Nokia N810 (Maemo4 OS), smart phone N900 (Maemo5 OS), and different mobile phones served as the user devices. Personal PCs based on Pentium IV processors and running under Ubuntu 10.04 and Windows XP were used for hosting other services.

Table 1. Execution results

Number of emergency responders	Number of victims	Total number of objects	Time of plan generations, s.
10	10	20	4.85
10	20	30	9.12
20	20	40	17.51
30	30	60	37.93
40	40	80	66.13
50	50	100	101.29

In the experiments with different datasets the execution time from the moment the emergency event was registered to the moment of producing the operational context took around 0.0007 s. The time taken to generate the sets of action plans for different datasets is shown in Table 1. The approximating equation is quadratic for the total amount of objects involved in the response actions. The experimentation showed that the system already takes a reasonable time for result generation. Presented results are based on the usage of a research prototype running on a desktop PC. In a production environment the system is aimed to be run on dedicated servers and it is expected to be responsive enough to handle a large amount of objects. The future development of Smart-M3 up to the production level with a higher capacity could also contribute to the system performance.

6   Conclusions

The problem of integration of services provided by a smart space with the purpose of service-coordinated organization of emergency response communities was investigated. A framework that serves to integrate concepts of smart space, Web-services and Web-based communities has been proposed. The framework supports seamless information exchange between the resources of the smart space, allows the members of an emergency response community to make online decisions on plans for their actions and to communicate during these actions for coordination of their activities, enables Web-based communications between the emergency responders and emergency victims, supports access the emergency services that the smart space provides using any wire and wireless Internet-accessible devices.

An original feature of the way the response actions are planned is in involvement of ridesharing technology in planning evacuation activities.

Some limitations of the developed framework are worth mentioning. The framework does not take into account cases when it is not found enough available professional emergency responders or when some resources become disabled at time of the response actions. As well, the framework does not address the problem of lack of passing cars for evacuation of people from the fire area and the problem of searching for a route with changes if there are not any cars nearby the fire area going directly to the person destination. The listed limitations as well as real-life testing and implementation will be subjects for future research and activities.

Acknowledgements. The present research was supported partly by projects funded by grants 10-07-00368, 11-07-00045, 11-07-00058, 12-07-00298 of the Russian Foundation for Basic Research, the project 213 of the research program "Information, control, and intelligent technologies & systems" of the Russian Academy of Sciences (RAS), the project 2.2 of the Nano- & Information Technologies Branch of RAS, and the contract 14.740.11.0357 of the Ministry of Education and Science of Russian Federation.

References

1. Lamorte, L., Venezia, C.: Smart Space a New Dimension of Context. In: Proc. Symp. at the AISB 2009 Convention, Edinburgh, Scotland, pp. 20–25. The Society for the Study of Artificial Intelligence and Simulation of the Behaviour (2009)
2. Özçelebi, T., Lukkien, J., Bosman, R., Uzun, Ö.: Discovery, Monitoring and Management in Smart Spaces Composed of Very Low Capacity Nodes. IEEE T. Consum. Electr. 56(2), 570–578 (2010)
3. Schroth, C.: The Internet of Services: Global Industrialization of Information Intensive Services. In: Proc. 2nd Intl. Conf. on Digital Information Management, ICDIM 2007, Lyon, France, vol. 2, pp. 635–642 (2007)
4. Web Services Integration. Microsoft Corporation (2003), http://msdn.microsoft.com/en-us/library/aa478995.aspx
5. Mahmoud, Q.H.: Service-Oriented Architecture (SOA) and Web Services: the Road to Enterprise Application Integration (EAI). Oracle (2005), http://www.oracle.com/-technetwork/articles/javase/soa-142870.html
6. Arroyo, R.F., Gea, M., Garrido, J.L., Haya, P.A., Carro, R.M.: Authoring Social-Aware Tasks on Active Spaces. J. Univers. Comput. Sci. 14(17), 2840–2858 (2008)
7. Hagar, C.: Introduction to Special Section on Crisis Informatics. Bulletin of the American Society for Information Science and Technology 36(5), 10–12 (2010)
8. Palen, L., Starr, R.H., Liu, S.: Online Forums Supporting Grassroots Participation in Emergency Preparedness and Response. Commun. ACM 50(3), 54–58 (2007)
9. Mandel, L.H., McClure, C.R., Brobst, J., Lanz, E.C.: Helping Libraries Prepare for the Storm With Web Portal Technology. Bulletin of the American Society for Information Science and Technology 36(5), 22–26 (2010)
10. Starbird, K., Palen, L.: "Voluntweeters": Self-Organizing by Digital Volunteers in Times of Crisis. In: Proc. ACM CHI 2011 Conf. on Human Factors in Computing Systems, Vancouver, Canada, pp. 1071–1080 (2011)
11. Starbird, K., Palen, L.: (How) Will the Revolution be Retweeted?: Information Propagation in the 2011 Egyptian Uprising. In: Proc. 2012 ACM Conf. on Computer Supported Cooperative Work, Bellevue, USA, pp. 7–16 (2012)

12. Vieweg, S., Hughes, A., Starbird, K., Palen, L.: Microblogging During Two Natural Hazards Events: What Twitter May Contribute to Situational Awareness. In: Proc. ACM 2010 Conf. on Computer Human Interaction, Atlanta, USA, pp. 1079–1088 (2010)
13. Armour, G.: Communities Communicating With Formal and Informal Systems: Being More Resilient in Times of Need. Bulletin of the American Society for Information Science and Technology 36(5), 34–38 (2010)
14. Krakovsky, A.: The Role of Social Networks in Crisis Situations: Public Participation and Information Exchange. In: Proc. 7th Intl. Conf. on Information Systems for Crisis Response and Management, ISCRAM 2010, pp. 52–57 (2010)
15. Catarci, T., Leoni, M., Marrella, A., Mecella, M.: The WORKPAD Project Experience: Improving the Disaster Response through Process Management and Geo Collaboration. In: French, S., Tomaszewski, B., Zobel, C. (eds.) Proc. 7th Intl. Conf. on Information Systems for Crisis Response and Management, ISCRAM 2010, Seattle, USA (2010),
    http://www.iscram.org/ISCRAM2010/Papers/136-Catarci_etal.pdf
16. Gouman, R., Kempen, M., Wijngaards, N.: Actor-Agent Team Experimentation in the Context of Incident Management. In: French, S., Tomaszewski, B., Zobel, C. (eds.) Proc. 7th Intl. Conf. on Information Systems for Crisis Response and Management, ISCRAM 2010, Seattle, USA (2010),
    http://www.iscram.org/ISCRAM2010/Papers/179-Gouman_etal.pdf
17. Ling, A., Li, X., Fan, W., An, N., Zhan, J., Li, L., Sha, Y.: Blue Arrow: a Web-based Spatially-Enabled Decision Support System for Emergency Evacuation Planning. In: Proc. 2009 IEEE Intl. Conf. on Business Intelligence and Financial Engineering, pp. 575–578. IEEE Computer Society (2009)
18. Ng, C.W.W., Chiu, D.K.W.: E-Government Integration with Web Services and Alerts: a Case Study on an Emergency Route Advisory System in Hong Kong. In: Proc. 39th Hawaii Intl. Conf. on System Sciences, HICSS 2006, vol. 4, p. 70.2. IEEE Computer Society (2006)
19. Chourabi, H., Mellouli, S.: E-government: Integrated Services Framework. In: Proc. 12th Annual Intl. Digital Government Research Conf. on Digital Government Innovation in Challenging Times, pp. 36–44. ACM, New York (2011)
20. Rainford, S.: e-Sri Lanka: An Integrated Approach to e-Government Case Study. Regional Development Dialogue 27(2), 209–218 (2006)
21. Honkola, J., Laine, H., Brown, R., Tyrkko, O.: Smart-M3 Information Sharing Platform. In: IEEE Symposium on Computers and Communications, pp. 1041–1046. IEEE Computer Society (2010)

Part IV
Web Intelligence

Ranking Location-Dependent Keywords to Extract Geographical Characteristics from Microblogs

Satoshi Ikeda, Nobuharu Kami, and Takashi Yoshikawa

Cloud System Research Laboratories, NEC Corporation, Kawasaki, Japan
s-ikeda@fd.jp.nec.com, n-kami@ak.jp.nec.com,
yoshikawa@cd.jp.nec.com

Abstract. The spread of microblogging services, such as Twitter, has made it possible to extract geographical characteristics such as keywords specific to a geographical region, with fine granularity. The results of content analysis of microblogging services are easily affected by users who post excessive messages. In addition, because geographical granularity of users' interests differs, it is preferable to support multiple levels of granularity for usability. Thus, we propose a ranking method of location-dependent keywords based on a term frequency-inverse document frequency method to extract geographical characteristics. In our method, ranking scores are weighted by diversity of information sources so that the effect of loud users is mitigated. Multiple zoom levels of geographical areas are supported by approximation while databases at only several zoom levels are maintained. We evaluated our ranking method with a real dataset from Twitter and showed its effectiveness. We also describe a prototype implementation of a system using our ranking method.

Keywords: TF-IDF, Context awareness, Keyword ranking.

1 Introduction

Microblogging services, such as Twitter, have been spreading worldwide in recent years. A characteristic of users frequently updating their status has made it possible to obtain users' context information with fine granularity in real time.

Accordingly, user content from microblogging services has been widely leveraged as a research object of user context[13,3]. In particular, context based on geographical location information, *location-dependent context*, is notable since users' activities are closely related to their location. Moreover, the popularization of smartphones equipped with GPS receivers has encouraged research on location-dependent context. In fact, many studies analyzing content from microblogging services based on geographical location information have been conducted[1,9].

One way to express location-dependent context is to extract and rank *location-dependent keywords*, which characterize a geographical region by analyzing content from microblogging services. In content analysis of microblogging services, the impact of advertisement messages must be taken into consideration. Since microblogging services are also used as advertisement tools, malicious users may try to compromise the analysis result by posting a large number of messages. Though spam filtering with a

J. Cordeiro and K.-H. Krempels (Eds.): WEBIST 2012, LNBIP 140, pp. 237–251, 2013.
© Springer-Verlag Berlin Heidelberg 2013

Bayesian filter[8] would be considered effective to determine whether a message is an advertisement or not, it requires training using sample messages in advance. Moreover, it is difficult to determine what should be filtered out as malicious since an advertisement message may be useful if it contains context related to its location. Hence, it is not adequate to filter out all advertisement messages. Additionally, the granularity of geographical areas with which location-dependent context is analyzed is important. For instance, an application that analyzes and visualizes location-dependent keywords should use geographical areas with appropriate granularity based on the zoom level of a map because sizes of geographical areas in which users are interested may differ. Therefore, it is preferable to support multiple levels of granularity with a method that can reduce computational cost and database size, because a naive approach must calculate and store ranking scores for all zoom levels.

We propose a ranking method of location-dependent keywords, which enhances a term frequency-invert document frequency (TF-IDF) method [10]. Diversity of information sources is taken into consideration with our method. Specifically, by penalizing keywords with low diversity of users, the impact of excessive repeating of messages by a few users is mitigated. Additionally, our ranking method supports multiple zoom levels of geographical areas by TF-IDF approximation. With this approximation, we need not to calculate and store TF and DF values for all zoom levels because values for only several zoom levels are stored and TF-IDF values for the intermediate zoom levels are interpolated. From evaluations using an actual dataset from Twitter, we show the effectiveness of user diversity and the accuracy of TF-IDF approximation. We also introduce a prototype implementation of a system using our ranking method.

The rest of this paper is organized as follows. Section 2 introduces our ranking method of location-dependent keywords. Section 3 describes the prototype implementation of a system using our ranking method. Section 4 discusses the evaluation of the effect of user diversity and approximation used in our ranking method. Related work is discussed in Section 5, and Section 6 gives the conclusions.

2   Ranking Method

In this section, we introduce our location-dependent keyword ranking method that enhances a TF-IDF method. In our method, diversity of information sources is utilized to suppress the impact of loud users. Moreover, our method supports multiple zoom levels of geographical areas by TF-IDF approximation.

2.1   Application of TF-IDF

The basic idea for extracting location context is to apply a TF-IDF method to ranking location-dependent keywords.

In contrast to original TF-IDF for determining how important a word is to a document in a collection of documents, the purpose of our approach is to determine how important a word is to a geographical area. For this purpose, we regard a collection of messages posted in a geographical area as a document of the TF-IDF method. A geographical point, latitude and longitude, tagged in a message is converted into a location label representing an area the point is located in. An area represented by a location label is one cell of a square grid on the Mercator projection of the earth. The size of an area is determined by zoom level. Specifically, a single cell covers almost the whole earth at zoom level 0 and is divided into four cells for each additional zoom level.

To label geographical points, we use tile coordinates, which are used in the Google Maps API [5] and reference a specific tile on a map at a specific zoom level. The tile coordinates (x, y) at zoom level z are determined from a geographical point with latitude φ and longitude λ as follows:

$$x = \left\lfloor 2^z \cdot \frac{\pi + \lambda}{2\pi} \right\rfloor, \quad y = \left\lfloor 2^z \cdot \frac{\pi - \ln(\tan\varphi + \sec\varphi)}{2\pi} \right\rfloor.$$

For instance, tile coordinates $(0, 0)$ at zoom level 0 includes almost the whole earth.

We consider a TF-IDF-based keyword ranking method for each area whose location is expressed in the tile coordinate system. A TF-IDF value for a word w in an area with a location label l of tile coordinates (x, y) at a specific zoom level is calculated as follows:

$$tfidf_{w,l} = tf_{w,l} \cdot idf_w \tag{1}$$

where $tf_{w,l}$ is the number of occurrences of w in l. The inverse document frequency idf_w is defined as:

$$idf_w = \log_2 \frac{N}{n_w} \tag{2}$$

where n_w is the number of areas where w occurs at least once.

To accurately rank location-dependent keywords, we need to pay attention to a definition of N, which is simply the number of all areas in the case of the original TF-IDF method. Some words are given an unexpectedly high ranking score especially when a zoom level is high in which the minimum and maximum DF values tend to be close if we simply select the number of all areas for N. If we instead take the number of "active" areas that accommodate at least one word, this unexpected ranking problem is mitigated since we can exaggerate the difference in the location-dependence of words by enlarging the difference between the minimum and maximum DF values. Yet, there is still room for improvement and we propose to use $\max_w(n_w)$ instead of these candidates of N. By adopting the maximum DF value as N, IDF values of location-independent keywords come closer to zero than when the number of active area is used as N. Consequently, location-independent keywords are expected to be placed at lower ranks without lowering ranks of location-dependent keywords.

2.2 User Diversity Weighting

Microblogging services are also leveraged for commercial advertisements and announcements from public institutions. For instance, some restaurants provide time-limited coupons and some fire departments announce information on responses to 911 calls. In such cases, the frequency of posts from such services is relatively high on a constant basis such as tens of posts a day. Moreover, since these services usually use message templates, the messages have a strong tendency to include specific words related to the services or the users. As a consequence, TF values of such user specific keywords tend to increase, as well as TF-IDF values. This indicates that malicious users can easily juggle keyword ranking simply by posting a large number of messages with target keywords.

To prevent such user-specific keywords from becoming too influential, we introduce using a diversity index of each keyword, which is a measure that represents how many users equally originate a keyword, for penalizing the ranking scores of those keywords.

There are several diversity indices such as Shannon's diversity index and Simpson's diversity index. We use Simpson's due to its simple definition. The user diversity index for a word w in an area l is defined as follows:

$$D_{w,l} = 1 - \sum_{u \in U} \left(\frac{n_{w,l,u}}{n_{w,l}} \right)^2$$

where U is a set of users, $n_{w,l}$ is the number of occurrences of w in l, and the user term frequency $n_{w,l,u}$ is the number of occurrences of w from a user u in l.

We use the user diversity index to lower the ranking of keywords from malicious users. This index ranges from zero to one and approaches one when a word is uniformly posted by many users. Because of these characteristics, the ranking of keywords from malicious users is lowered simply by multiplying TF-IDF values by the user diversity index. We define diversity-weighted TF-IDF (DTF-IDF) as follows:

$$dtfidf_{w,l} = D_{w,l} \cdot tfidf_{w,l}.$$

2.3   Zoom Support

It is preferable to provide rankings for each zoom level for usability since the granularity of interest may differ among users. Because a change in zoom level alters the geographical partitioning, the simplest solution is to calculate and store TF-IDF values for each zoom level. However, this requires a huge database whose size is approximately proportional to the number of TF entries. Moreover, the computational cost is also roughly proportional to these entries. Figure 1 shows the number of TF entries for each zoom level for a dataset of actual tweets collected from Twitter, which is described in detail in Section 4. If we maintain TF tables at each zoom level from 7 to 16, we need to keep about 15 million TF entries. Additionally, calculation of the user diversity index in real time needs to maintain the number of occurrences of words at all areas for each user. The total database size required for the dataset was about 1.3 GB.

To reduce the database size, we introduce an approximation approach for calculating TF-IDF values. Instead of maintaining calculated results for all zoom levels, calculated results are stored for several zoom levels to the database and TF-IDF values for the omitted zoom levels are approximated from the stored zoom levels. This approximation approach also has another advantage in that it supports various sizes of a target area. An approximated TF-IDF value for an area consisting of 3×3 sub-areas, for example, can be calculated with this approximation approach even if partitioning with 3×3 sub-areas is not supported.

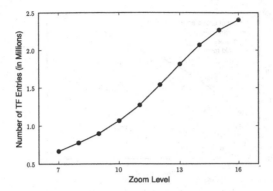

Fig. 1. Number of TF entries at each zoom level

IDF Approximation. For approximating TF-IDF values, IDF values for the omitted zoom levels must be estimated. This can be accomplished by interpolating DF values.

In general, location dependency of keywords varies according to the size of the target areas. For instance, if the size is large enough, a name of a nationwide chain store would have least location-dependency (IDF value) since the name would be posted in almost all areas. In contrast, in a small area, the name would have a relatively high dependency since it would be posted within a narrow range near the stores. Hence, we cannot simply use an IDF value for other zoom levels available in a database as the value for the target zoom level. Therefore, appropriate DF values should be used for TF-IDF approximation.

While one might think variations in DF values for all words have similar tendency to the number of areas, this is not the case. Figure 2 shows variations in DF values of some words and the number of active areas. The DF values monotonically increase as the zoom level increases. The shapes of the curves, however, differ from each other including "# of active areas". The DF value of "aid response" increases quickly from zoom level 13 to 16. In contrast, the DF value of "san francisco" increases gradually in this range.

The tendency seen in Figure 2 is that the segments that result from splitting the curves several ways are roughly approximated by straight lines in linear-log space. Hence, some interpolation approaches in linear-log space are used to yield good approximation results. With linear interpolation in linear-log space, we store DF values for K zoom levels $\{\xi_1, \xi_2, \ldots, \xi_K\}$ with $\xi_i < \xi_{i+1}$. The DF value df_z at zoom level $z \in (\xi_i, \xi_{i+1})$ is interpolated by the following equation:

$$df_z = df_{\xi_i} \left(\frac{df_{\xi_{i+1}}}{df_{\xi_i}} \right)^{\frac{z - \xi_i}{\xi_{i+1} - \xi_i}}.$$

A maximum DF value used for calculating IDF values is also approximated by this equation.

TF Approximation. Precise TF values are calculated from those at a larger zoom level by just summing up TF values in all sub-areas included in a target area for each word.

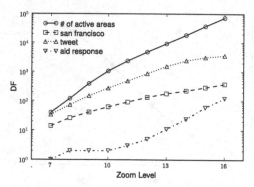

Fig. 2. DF values for some words for each level. Line with "# of active areas" is number of areas having at least one word.

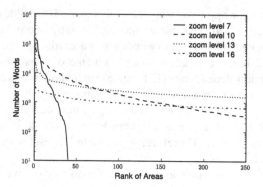

Fig. 3. Number of words in top 250 areas in decreasing order

The user diversity indices are also calculated by aggregating user term frequencies in all sub-areas.

However, the computational cost of calculating TF-IDF values from TF and DF tables is not negligible since aggregation is required per query. Figure 3 shows the number of words in the top 250 areas in decreasing order for zoom levels 7, 10, 13, and 16.

There were 144,251 words in the area with the largest number of words at zoom level 7. If the naive approach is taken, it requires aggregation for all the words per query for accuracy. Because of this, it is not realistic to calculate precise values for such areas with a large amount of words.

Hence, approximation is taken for TF aggregation to reduce the computational cost in areas with thousands of words. Our approximation approach limits the number of words taken from each sub-area, that is, for some integer k, only the words with top k TF values in each sub-area are taken for aggregation and the others are ignored.

While this approximation may yield TF-IDF rankings with less accuracy, the choice of k can improve accuracy. Undoubtedly, a large enough k results in precise TF values, while it increases the computational cost. The effect on rankings of this approximation is evaluated in Section 4.4.

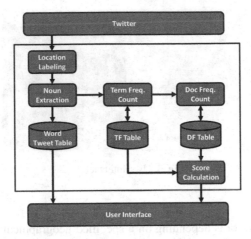

Fig. 4. Architecture of our ranking system

3 Implementation

With the ranking method described above, we implemented a ranking system for location-dependent keywords. In this section, we briefly introduce our ranking system.

3.1 Architecture

The system architecture is shown in Figure 4. Our system collects geotagged tweets from Twitter using the Streaming API [14], making it possible to collect tweets within a specific geographical area in real time.

When the system receives a tweet via the Streaming API, the geographical point (latitude, longitude) of the tweet is converted to a location label (tile coordinates) which represents a geographical area. Next, nouns (or noun phrases) in the tweet are extracted as candidate keywords. We use a part-of-speech (POS) tagger for noun extraction. To show tweets that contain such nouns, the mapping between a tweet and the nouns are stored in a database. Then, the number of occurrences of nouns are updated and stored into the TF table. At the same time, user term frequencies are also stored for calculating user diversity indices. If a noun is found to be the first occurrence in the area in the TF counting process, the DF value of the noun is also updated and stored in the DF table. Thus, the TF and DF tables are kept updated in real time. A ranking is generated per request by calculating DTF-IDF scores using the approximation described in Section 2.

On a machine with Intel Xeon 3.1 GHz and 4 GB memory, the response time per request is shorter than 300 milliseconds even for areas with a large number of words if the database is in memory. In contrast, it is shorter than 100 milliseconds for rural areas with not many words. The response time is considered to be improved by caching generated rankings for areas that requests concentrate on.

Fig. 5. User interface

3.2 User Interface

Our system ranks keywords depending on a specified geographical area by analyzing tweets with geographical information. Figure 5 shows a user interface of the ranking system. When a user clicks at a point on the map, a keyword ranking in an area that contains the clicked point is displayed on the right side. While only the top 13 keywords are shown in Figure 5, the ranking area is scrollable and the top 100 rankings are calculated by default. A user can look at tweets that contain a keyword by selecting it if he or she wants to know why the keyword is rated highly. The zoom level of tile coordinates used to specify a target area is basically one zoom level larger than that of the map. In other words, the size of a target area varies by the zoom level of the map. This makes it possible for users to specify a target area with granularity of interest.

Although the prototype system simply provides a keyword ranking, the ranking can be used also for keyword recommendation or completion. When one inputs a text with a smartphone out the door especially at a location that he or she visit for the first time, its content should relate closely his or her geographical context. By recommendation or completion of location-dependent keywords, he or she would be able to notice the excitement at the location which is usually passed over unnoticed.

4 Evaluation

We obtained 866,420 geotagged tweets via the Twitter Streaming API from Sept. 3 to Sept. 16, 2011. The geographical area covering the west coast of the United States was specified as the query parameter. The south-west and north-east corners of the area were respectively (32.0, -125.0) and (49.0, -114.0).

4.1 Comparison among IDF Candidates

As discussed in Section 2.1, what to use as N in IDF computation (Eq.(2)) is important since it has a significant impact on rankings of location-dependent keywords. We compared three candidates for N in IDF computation: the number of all area, the number of active areas, and the maximum DF value.

Figure 6 plots these candidates for N against various zoom levels for the dataset. If the number of all areas is selected as N at zoom level 16, the IDF value of a word with

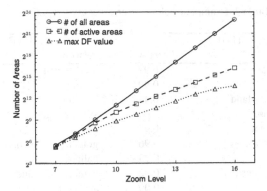

Fig. 6. Candidates for N in IDF computation

Table 1. Comparison among candidates for N in IDF computation

	# of all areas		# of active areas		max DF value	
rank	keyword	score	keyword	score	keyword	score
1	love	1884	anaheim	1435	anaheim	1070
2	time	1716	disneyland	1205	angel stadium	885
3	anaheim	1685	angel stadium	1052	disneyland	828
4	day	1483	santa ana	838	santa ana	667
5	disneyland	1471	love	811	star tours	400
6	work	1169	time	739	orange	269
7	angel stadium	1166	work	717	mickey	233
8	need	1128	need	692	class	212
9	today	1018	day	639	winrt	207
10	right	979	today	625	brea	203

the maximum DF value is about 9.3 and the IDF value of a word that occurs at a single area is about 23.0. This means that, for least and most location-dependent keywords w_L and w_M, w_L is ranked higher than w_M if w_L occurs only thrice of w_M. On the other hand, if the number of active areas is selected as N, the IDF values respectively change to 2.5 and 16.2. By adopting the maximum DF value as N, IDF values for the least location-dependent keywords are zero. Consequently, a least location-dependent keyword is always ranked lowest.

Table 1 lists an example rankings with TF-IDF scores generated by using these candidates. These are top ten rankings in a section of Anaheim, CA, in which there are very famous spots such as the Disney Resort and Angel Stadium of Anaheim. Thus, keywords related to these spots are expected to be placed high in a ranking. However, when the number of all areas was used as N, location-independent keywords, such as love, time, and day, were highly ranked. As a result, the ranks of keywords related to the location were relatively low. By employing the number of active areas as N, the ranking was improved, but not remarkably. The ranking still contained location-independent keywords while location-dependent keywords rose in the ranking. On the other hand, by using the maximum DF value, the ranking was significantly improved. As you can

Table 2. Example results of user diversity weighting

rank	TF-IDF keyword	diversity	DTF-IDF keyword	diversity
1	arts festival	0.97	arts festival	0.97
2	seattle	0.99	seattle	0.99
3	bainbridge island	0.48	bumbershoot	0.97
4	aid response	0.00	space needle	0.96
5	bumbershoot	0.97	keyarena	0.93
6	space needle	0.96	golden gardens park	0.92
7	keyarena	0.93	ballard	0.95
8	golden gardens park	0.92	bainbridge island	0.48
9	new listing	0.00	alki beach	0.92
10	e 21	0.00	woodland park zoo	0.74

see, almost all location-dependent keywords dropped from the top 10 ranking. Therefore, using the maximum DF value as N is effective to filter out location-independent keywords.

In the evaluations below, the maximum DF value was used as N in IDF computation.

4.2   Effect of User Diversity Weighting

Table 2 lists the example results of the effect of user diversity weighting. These are top ten rankings of location-dependent keywords with and without user diversity weighting in the area with tile coordinates $(163, 357)$, a section of Seattle, WA, at zoom level 10.

The TF-IDF ranking without user diversity weighting contained keywords of 'aid response', 'new listing' and 'e 21'. Of these keywords, 'aid response' and 'e 21' were a part of announcements related to 911 calls posted by one user, and 'new listing' was a part of advertisements from a real-estate agency. Though they are indeed location-dependent in the sense that they have large IDF values, the ranks are considered to be overrated due to one user's massive tweets.

With user diversity weighting, the ranking is adjusted so that the impact of loud users are mitigated. The keywords above were filtered out by the user diversity index of 0.00. At the same time, keywords posted by many users can maintain higher ranks. For instance, the keyword 'bumbershoot', a name of a festival, which was posted by 40 users, had a user diversity index of 0.97 and its rank rose from 5th to 3rd.

4.3   Effect of IDF Approximation

Cubic interpolation in linear-log space also promises a better outcome than linear interpolation since it yields smooth and continuous curves that linear interpolation can not yield. In this section, we compare the linear interpolation of DF values described in Section 2.3 with cubic interpolation. The comparison results show that the two interpolations of DF values in linear-log space did not show significant differences in errors of approximated IDF values.

Table 3. Comparison of approximation errors

precise IDF	Linear		Cubic		rate (%)
	RMSE	MAE	RMSE	MAE	
< 2.0	0.082	0.065	0.090	0.071	1.3
< 4.0	0.150	0.122	0.154	0.123	8.9
< 6.0	0.235	0.185	0.225	0.178	19.3
< 8.0	0.257	0.182	0.270	0.196	24.9
8.0 ≤	0.261	0.213	0.255	0.209	45.6
ALL	0.245	0.190	0.244	0.190	

There were 432,132 words in the dataset, and 374,992 words of them had the same DF values at zoom levels 7 and 16. Since such words yield no errors by the interpolations, these words were excluded from the evaluation. We evaluated the error in IDF values of the remaining 57,140 words. We used DF values at zoom levels 7, 10, 13 and 16 and approximated IDF values at the six intermediate levels.

Errors of approximated IDF values are summarized in Table 3. The errors are classified by the range of precise IDF values (*precise IDF*). In both interpolation methods, the errors tend to decrease as IDF values decrease. The fact of low errors for words with small IDF values indicates that approximation can keep location-independent words as they are.

Another finding is that there is no significant difference in both Rooted Mean Squared Errors (RMSEs) and Mean Absolute Errors (MAEs) between linear and cubic interpolations. In both methods, RMSE and MAE were respectively about 0.24 and 0.19.

From the evaluation results, the approximation by cubic interpolation had no significant advantages compared with linear interpolation. In contrast to linear interpolation requiring only two zoom levels, cubic interpolation requires at least four zoom levels. This would increase database access and computational cost. For this reason, we chose linear interpolation for approximation.

4.4 Effect on Rankings

As mentioned above, for ranking location-dependent keywords, it is not necessarily required to calculate precise TF-IDF values for all candidate words. The important thing is to provide precise ranking against perfect ranking which is obtained from precise TF-IDF calculations.

For evaluation of rankings by the approximation described in Section 2.3, we used the normalized discounted cumulative gain nDCG_k [6]. nDCG_k for a top-k ranking is defined as:

$$\text{nDCG}_k = \frac{\text{DCG}_k}{i\text{DCG}_k}$$

where $\text{DCG}_k = R_1 + \sum_{i=2}^{k} (R_i / log_2 i)$. R_i is the relevance value of a word at rank i, which takes a large value if the word strongly depends on the location, and $i\text{DCG}_k$ is DCG_k for perfect ranking. From this definition, nDCG_k is such a value that the more similar a ranking is to an ideal one, the closer it is to one. Thus, if nDCG_k for an approximated ranking is close to one, the approximation is considered to be highly accurate. We use precise TF-IDF values of a word at rank i as relevance R_i since a word with a higher TF-IDF value is considered to be strongly dependent on a geographical area.

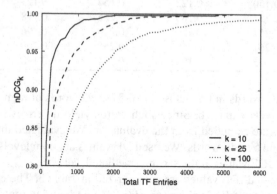

Fig. 7. Evaluation of TF approximation at zoom level 8 by aggregating TF entries at base zoom level 10

In the evaluation below, the results in Figures 7, 8 and 9 are the average nDCG$_k$ values of the top ten areas with a large number of words at a specified zoom level.

Figure 7 shows the evaluation results for TF approximation at zoom level 8 using TF values at the base zoom level of 10. The x-axis represents the number of TF entries used in the approximation. If it is 1,600, for instance, the top 100 TF entries for each sub-area are collected since there are 16 sub-areas to aggregate. In this evaluation, we used the precise IDF values without approximation and ranked by TF-IDF instead of DTF-IDF values, without user diversity weighting, to evaluate the effect of TF approximation.

The number of entries per sub-area to achieve a highly accurate ranking is not large. There were about 275,000 words on average in the top ten areas at zoom level 8. For $k = 10$, 25, and 100, respectively, about only 70, 140, and 310 TF entries per sub-area were needed to achieve nDCG$_k$ over 0.99. Since the average number of words per area is less than that at smaller zoom levels, TF entries required to achieve this accuracy are considered to be less than these results for a zoom level larger than 8.

The differences among base zoom levels at which TF values were used to approximate TF values at zoom level 8 are shown in Figure 8. Similar to the evaluation above, we used TF-IDF rankings with precise IDF values and the approximated TF values without user diversity weighting. For $z_b = 8$, approximation was performed simply by ignoring words with low TF values. For base zoom levels $z_b = 9$ and $z_b = 10$, there were respectively 2×2 and 4×4 sub-areas to aggregate.

The results show that the total number of TF entries required for equivalent accuracy is not proportional to the number of sub-areas. For nDCG$_{100} \geq 0.99$, the required total entries doubled or tripled when the base zoom level increases by one while the number of sub-areas increases to four times.

In the next evaluation, the effect of IDF approximation is taken into consideration. Figure 9 shows nDCG$_k$ values with and without IDF approximation.

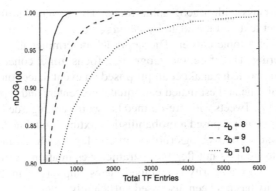

Fig. 8. Evaluation of approximation for different base zoom levels z_b

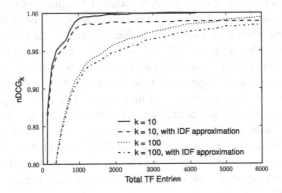

Fig. 9. Effect of IDF approximation

With IDF approximation, the $nDCG_k$ takes small values compared to the case without approximation regardless of k. This is because the errors in IDF approximation make perfect ranking impossible. To be more precise, in a TF-IDF result ranking with IDF approximation, since the approximated TF-IDF values are not necessarily the same as the precise ones, it is impossible to generate a perfect ranking even if all TF entries for each sub-area are aggregated. However, our approximation is considered to have good accuracy since the differences in $nDCG_k$ between the cases with and without IDF approximation are less than 0.02.

5   Related Work

Many studies have been conducted for analyzing content in microblogging services and leveraged geographical location context. Arakawa et al. introduced an extraction method of location-dependent keywords by extracting grids with high density of specific keywords using breadth-first search[1]. It needs to specify a target keyword to calculate its dependency and is suitable for detecting locations the keyword depends on. On the other hand, it is not suitable for ranking keywords that depend on a specific location. TwitterStands[11] is a news processing system that analyzes tweets and detects late breaking news with a geographic focus. The geographic focus, which is determined from tweet text and metadata by *geotagging*, is calculated by ranking the geographic locations in a topic cluster. The approach determines the geographic focus after topic clustering. Therefore, the geographic focus might concentrate in areas where many tweets are posted. Sakaki et al. proposed an event detection scheme using a Kalman filter in real time and estimated earthquake epicenters and typhoon trajectories from Twitter data[9]. Tweets with pre-defined keywords are regarded as sensor data of a target event. Mei et al. proposed a probabilistic mixture model and analyzed spatiotemporal theme patterns on weblogs (not on microblogs) with the model[7]. Since the granularity of a location is not flexible, parameter estimation of the model must be reperformed when the granularity is changed. Thus, support of multiple levels of geographical granularity has not been discussed sufficiently.

TF-IDF methods are widely used in analysing tweets. TwitterStands uses TF-IDF for weighting important words to cluster topics. Eddi[2] assigns topics to a tweet using TF-IDF-style key terms obtained from search results of nouns in the tweet. Chen et al. studied URL recommendation on Twitter[3]. In their approach, the recommendation is made based on a user profile which is a TF-IDF vector generated from his/her tweets. A set of tweets from a user is regarded as a document; in contrast, a set of tweets in an area is regarded as a document in our approach. Our user diversity weighting is applicable for recommendation to mitigate the impact of malicious users.

Diversity of users in a geographical area is useful also for purposes other than mitigating the impact of loud users. Cranshaw et al. examined connection between an online social network and the location traces of its users[4]. They showed that users who visit a location with high diversity tend to have more connections in the social network. Toch et al. showed that users appear more comfortable sharing their presence at locations with high diversity[12].

6   Conclusions

We proposed a location-dependent keyword ranking method for microblogging services, which adopts a TF-IDF method to geographical location context, and described the prototype implementation of a keyword ranking system. Our ranking method penalizes keywords with low user diversity and supports multiple zoom levels of geographical granularity by using TF-IDF approximation. The evaluation results showed that user diversity weighting is effective in mitigating the effect of excessive posts from a few users and approximation can yield a highly accurate ranking in terms of similarity to precise TF-IDF ranking without approximation. We plan to extend our method for spatiotemporal analysis so that it can track trends and the spread of location-dependent keywords.

References

1. Arakawa, Y., Tagashira, S., Fukuda, A.: Extraction of Location Dependent Words from Twitter Logs. IPSJ SIG Technical Reports 2010-MBL-55(10), 1–6 (2010) (in Japanese)
2. Bernstein, M., Suh, B., Hong, L., Chen, J., Kairam, S., Chi, E.: Eddi: Interactive Topic-based Browsing of Social Status Streams. In: UIST 2010: 23rd Annual ACM Symposium on User Interface Software and Technology, pp. 303–312 (2010)

3. Chen, J., Nairn, R., Nelson, L., Bernstein, M., Chi, E.: Short and Tweet: Experiments on Recommending Content from Information Streams. In: CHI 2010: 28th International Conference on Human Factors in Computing Systems, pp. 1185–1194 (2010)
4. Cranshaw, J., Toch, E., Hong, J., Kittur, A., Sadeh, N.: Bridging the Gap between Physical Location and Online Social Networks. In: UbiComp 2010: 12th ACM International Conference on Ubiquitous Computing, pp. 119–128 (2010)
5. Google Inc.: Google MAPs JavaScript API V3 (2009), http://code.google.com/intl/en/apis/maps/documentation/javascript/ (retrieved October 2011)
6. Järvelin, K., Kekäläinen, J.: Cumulated Gain-based Evaluation of IR Techniques. ACM Transactions on Information Systems 20(4), 422–446 (2002)
7. Mei, Q., Liu, C., Su, H., Zhai, C.: A Probabilistic Approach to Spatiotemporal Theme Pattern Mining on Weblogs. In: WWW 2006: 15th International Conference on World Wide Web, pp. 533–542 (2006)
8. Sahami, M., Dumais, S., Heckerman, D., Horvitz, E.: A Bayesian Approach to Filtering Junk E-mail. In: AAAI 1998 Workshop on Learning for Text Categorization (1998)
9. Sakaki, T., Okazaki, M., Matsuo, Y.: Earthquake Shakes Twitter Users: Real-time Event Detection by Social Sensors. In: WWW 2010: 19th International Conference on World Wide Web, pp. 851–860 (2010)
10. Salton, G., Buckley, C.: Term-Weighting Approaches in Automatic Text Retrieval. Information Processing & Management 24(5), 513–523 (1988)
11. Sankaranarayanan, J., Samet, H., Teitler, B., Lieberman, M., Sperling, J.: Twitterstand: News in Tweets. In: ACM SIGSPATIAL GIS 2009: 17th ACM SIGSPATIAL International Conference on Advances in Geographic Information Systems, pp. 42–51 (2009)
12. Toch, E., Cranshaw, J., Drielsma, P., Tsai, J., Kelley, P., Springfield, J., Cranor, L., Hong, J., Sadeh, N.: Empirical Models of Privacy in Location Sharing. In: UbiComp 2010: 12th ACM International Conference on Ubiquitous Computing, pp. 129–138 (2010)
13. Tumasjan, A., Sprenger, T., Sandner, P., Welpe, I.: Predicting Elections with Twitter: What 140 Characters Reveal about Political Sentiment. In: ICWSM 2010: 4th International AAAI Conference on Weblogs and Social Media, pp. 178–185 (2010)
14. Twitter Inc.: Streaming API — Twitter Developers (2010), https://dev.twitter.com/docs/streaming-api (retrieved October 2011)

Using W-Entropy Rank as a Unified Reference for Search Engines and Blogging Websites

Li Weigang and Zheng Jianya

TransLab, Department of Computer Science, University of Brasilia-UnB, Brasilia, Brazil
weigang@unb.br, darcy_zheng@hotmail.com

Abstract. Baidu, Sogou and Google are three main utilized search engines in China reported by Chinese Internet Date Centre (CNZZ) recently. There are significant differences among the search rank indexes such as Baidu weight, Sogou rank and PageRank. As a result, the sequence of the search lists is totally different for a same keyword. On the other hand, some valuable articles in Web as blog in ScienceNet.cn are ignored by Baidu, Sogou and others. It is impossible to unify these ranking systems to a same level due to the business models from multi-enterprises. This paper studies the difference of ranking indexes of these search engines by analyzing 42 websites from 4 sectors in China. Using information theory, W-entropy rank index is proposed as a search ranking reference. With the analyses of the correlation among the ranking indexes, the proposed index demonstrates the ranking reality of Chinese websites. The paper also described the application of W-entropy rank index to measure the influence of the blogs on the Internet. TOP10 of the most important blogging websites in China is listed as the preliminary study.

Keywords: Baidu weight, Blogging website, Information theory, Sogou rank, PageRank, W-entropy rank.

1 Introduction

According to the recent monthly report from Chinese Internet Date Centre (CNZZ) [1], Baidu, Sogou and Google are three main search engines with 93.50% using rate in China. At the same time, some statistic results show that 70% of people use search engines to find the product or service that they want to buy; and 90% of web searchers never make it to the second page of search results. This means that to get a potential business and a better propagation in the Internet, it is important to be listed at the top of the major search engines. There is no doubt, in Baidu, Sogou and Google.

Every search engine has proper criteria and evaluation system to rank the feature of web pages, such as Baidu weight (by Baidu search), Sogou rank (by Sogou search), and PageRank (by Google search [2]) and so on. However, the difference of the ranking algorithms and criteria systems makes the same web page have the different importance values by above search engines. In some especially situations, the Baidu weight and Sogou rank are lower than PageRank for universities and research institutions and Google has lower PageRank than others for Chinese financial institutions.

J. Cordeiro and K.-H. Krempels (Eds.): WEBIST 2012, LNBIP 140, pp. 252–266, 2013.

As a result, the sequence of the search results is totally different even for the same keyword. Some valuable articles in web, such as blog papers by some famous scientists in ScienceNet.cn [3] may be not well classified and further propagated on the Internet, even not be indexed by Baidu and Sogou search engines.

In order to adjust the inequality of the inquiry from different search engines, this paper firstly analyzes the ranking indexes such as Baidu weight, Sogou rank and PageRank for 42 websites from 4 categories institutions in China: Internet media, universities and research institutions, financial institutions and some enterprises to show the problems. Then it uses statistical method to find out the correlation between every two search engines, such as Baidu weight with PageRank, etc. And further it establishes the mean index among these three ranks and weighted index based on statistic result by CNZZ. The paper also describes the model of W-entropy rank using the information theory and the application for the 42 websites mentioned above.

The W-entropy rank is proposed as a reference to adjust the gap among the Baidu weight, Sogou rank and PageRank. With the property analyses, this new index demonstrates the ranking reality of Chinese websites. After the publication of our main idea in our blog of ScienceNet.cn, Baidu and Sogou adjusted their ranking indexes achieving a better matching with the result of W-entropy rank and the reality.

Another application of W-entropy rank is proposed to measure the influence of the blogging websites. The basic factors related to this influence are analyzed. The Weighted PageRank (WPR) is defined initially as one of these factors. Using the W-entropy rank, the paper gives the TOP10 ranking list of Chinese blogging websites.

The paper is organized as following. Section 2 explains the problem of the heterogenic ranking indexes of search engines in China. Section 3 analyzes the different search engines return the different results for the same query keywords using the example of a blog article in ScienceNet. Section 4 studies the correlation among the ranking indexes from these search engines by comparing various website samples. In section 5, the paper presents the information theory briefly and proposes a new index called W-entropy rank to unify the existed search ranking indexes as a reference. And in section 6, the new index is used as a reference for the search engines. The application results of W-entropy Rank for blogging websites are illustrated in section 7 and the section 8 is the conclusion of the paper.

2   Heterogenic Ranking Indexes of Search Engines

As mentioned by the report from CNZZ, in October 2011[1], Baidu search engine remained in the top shot with a commanding 81.10% market share in China, Sogou earned 7.52% share and the third place Google had 5.49% share. This paper takes these three most popular search engines to study the ranking index, a measurement of importance of the web pages.

Table 1 shows the rank indexes by the search engines for some websites in China and there are two rank values in the last columns: Averaged rank is the average of rank indexes from these three search engines. Another is weighted rank, where every search engine is assigned a different weight in accordance of market share. Baidu is weighted as 81.10%, Google and Sogou both are weighted as 9.45%. The distribution of the weights is still a research topic. It may use the Analytic Hierarchy Process – AHP [4] to further study the effective weights to reflect the reality.

Table 1. Rank indexes of Baidu, Sogou, Google for related web sites (2011-11-14)

Website	URL	Field	Baidu Weight	Sogou Rank	Google PR	Averaged Rank	Weighted Rank
Baidu	baidu.com	search	9	9	9	9	9
Google	google.com	search	8	9	10	9	8.28
Sogou	sogou.com	search	9	9	7	8.33	8.81
Zhejiang U.	zju.edu.cn	education	4	6	9	6.33	4.66
CAS	cas.cn	science	4	6	8	6	4.57
ICBC	icbc.com.cn	financial	8	9	7	8	8
Unipay	unionpay.com	financial	2	1	7	3.33	2.38

1. The website of Baidu gets 9/10 score from every one of these three engines. For Google's site, 8 score was weighted by Baidu, ranked 9 by Sogou, and PageRank 10 by itself, so the Averaged rank of Google is 9, but its Weighted rank is 8.28. For Sogou's site, the rank index from both Baidu weight and Sogou rank is 9, its PageRank is 8, the Averaged rank of Sogou is 8.33 and Weighted Rank is 8.81. These data present the basic scenario of Chinese search engines and the market share distribution.
2. From the collected data, Baidu weighted 4/10 score for the websites of both Zhejiang University and Chinese Academy of Science (CAS). Sogou rank is 6 for them. However, Google's PageRank for Zhejiang University is 9, and for Chinese Academy of Science is 8. This result shows the Baidu search engine classified the websites of the most universities unreasonable systematically till now.
3. There is also some inequality classification for the web sites of financial institutions. For the website of Industrial and Commercial Bank of China – ICBC, its Sogou rank is 9; Baidu weight is 8; Google's PageRank is only 7. In an especial case, Baidu just weighted the website of Unipay, the biggest credit card company in China, as 2, and 1 by Sogou rank. It should be mentioned that, Unipay is the biggest credit card company in China. This situation shows the importance to develop a unify index system as a reference for these search engines in China.

3   Different Search Engines, Different Ranks

In this section, ScienceNet is presented firstly and then, the propagation and search results of a famous paper in the Internet are discussed to show the situation of the different search engines with the different ranking list.

3.1   ScienceNet

Besides timely and reliable science news, abundant and valuable classified information, ScienceNet [3] hosts the most active and high-profile virtual community of Chinese-speaking scientists. This site is co-sponsored by Chinese Academy of Sciences (CAS), Chinese Academy of Engineering (CAE) and National Natural Science Foundation of China (NSFC).

Since 2007, there have been 900,000 registered users, in which 50,000 are renowned scientists registered under their real names. ScienceNet is a virtual society with the most well-known science media in Chinese research institutes, universities as well as many Chinese science communities scattered around the world.

According to the statistic data from Alexa [11], Table 2 presents the user stream in ScienceNet. The blog.sciencenet has 42.71% of accesses, a PR value of 6 and a Baidu weight of 4. The page of news.sciencenet has 22.86% of accesses and a PR of 7. BBS.sciencenet is placed third in accesses, 18.15% and a PR of 7. The homepage sciencenet.cn has a PR of 9, Baidu weight of 6, and 10.66% of accesses. Table 2 also shows other related information.

Table 2. User steam in the different channels of ScienceNet (2011-11)

Channels	User stream (%)	PR
Blog	42.71	6
News	22.86	7
BBS	18.15	7
Homepage	10.66	9
Talent	1.49	7
Paper	0.94	7
Group	0.85	6
Talk	0.66	5
Meeting	0.43	7
Others	1.25	7

ScienceNet is managed by the cooperation of a group of bloggers who are within the top 100 bloggers in terms of number of visits, and among the top 100 bloggers whose blogs have had the most page views. This system is a very democratic, promoting the direct participation of its members.

3.2   Propagation of a Blog Paper

Shi Yigong, a famous scientist from Tsinghua University, published an article "How to be an excellent PhD student?" [5] in ScienceNet, in September 9th, 2011. Using the title of the article as the keyword to search in Baidu, Sogou and Google, there are some interesting results to be analyzed:

1. The first three results listed in the first page of Baidu search engine are respectively: a) the article re-published by Baidu Online Library; b) the article re-published by Douban online community; c) the article re-published by Dingxiang forum. This sequence basically is ordered by the Baidu weight, a rank index of Baidu to classify the importance of websites. The website of both of Baidu Library and Douban online community is with 9 of the Baidu weight and Sogou rank; and the website of Dingxiang is with 6. Even the version of the article was re-published in Baidu Library by someone rather than the original author, Baidu indexed very fast and took the snapshot on September 14th. Whereas the original version from the blog of SicenceNet, was listed in 24th place on the third page and didn't take the snapshot until November 13th.

2. In Sogou search engine, the first three results were listed as: a) the article re-published by the Sina iask site; b) the article re-published by Baidu Online Library; c) the article published in the 1000plan net. For Sina iask site, the Sogou rank is 5, for Baidu Library and 1000plan, both of them is 4. Although in the first 8 search pages (with 80 results), all the links are totally with the re-published version of the article, and there is no exist the original version from ScienceNet. It can be explain reasonable, Sogou ranked 2 for the website of the blog of ScienceNet.

3. The results from Google search engine are: a) the original version of the article in the blog of ScienceNet; b) the related article "How to be a good PhD student (continue)" (Shi, 2011) in the ScienceNet; c) the article republished by Sina iask site. Google classified ScienceNet as PR 9 and the blog of ScienceNet as 7. According to this high ranking index, the original version and the related article are certainly listed in the first two lines by Google, see figure 1.

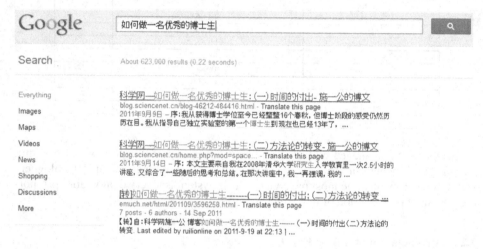

Fig. 1. The search result of "How to be a good PhD student" by Google

Compare with the results of this example, it can be found that the different ranking indexes are main reason of the scenario of heterogenic search results. The search engines of Baidu and Sogou focus on the popular sites and Google gives more weight to the innovation pages.

4   Correlation between Different Rank Indexes

As mentioned above, the different search engines with different search reports. How about the relation among the ranking criteria from the different search engines? Correlation coefficient (R) [6] is used as an indicator to measure the relationship among these indicators. The range of R is [-1, 1], the abstract value of R bigger, the correlation between these variables stronger, otherwise the correlation is weaker. Usually when the |R| >0.8, it is considered that these two variables have strong correlation.

Table 3 listed the ranking indexes from Baidu, Sogou and Google for some websites of the Internet media in China. The data were collected in Nov. 14, 2011.

The correlation is defined syntactical by 5 levels: |R| between 0~0.2 is no correlation, 0.2~0.4 is little correlation, 0.4~0.6 is ordinary correlation, 0.6~0.8 is fine correlation, 0.8~1.0 is linear correlation. Table 4 shows the correlation among the ranking indexes form Baidu, Sogou and Google search engines. It is also analyzed the correlation among the ranking indexes with the Averaged Rank and Weighted Rank indexes. The |R| between Baidu weight and Sogou rank is 0.0663, so there is no correlation between the ranking indexes from these two search engines; also they don't have correlation with PageRank of Google, the |R| values are 0.1768 and 0.1406 respectively. Baidu weight has little correlation with the Averaged Rank, but has linear correlation with the Weighted Rank, obviously the reason is that the weight of the ranking index of Baidu is 81.1% when calculation the Weighted Rank value. Sogou rank has linear correlation with the Averaged Rank value and ordinary correlation with the Weighted Rank value; Google has ordinary correlation with Averaged Rank value and has no correlation with the Weighted Rank value.

Table 3. The ranking indexes for some websites of the Internet media (2011-11-14)

Website	URL	Baidu Weight	Sogou Rank	Google PageRank	Averaged Rank	Weighted Rank
Baidu	baidu.com	9	9	9	9	9
Sohu	sohu.com	9	9	8	8.67	8.91
Sogou	sogou.com	9	9	7	8.33	8.81
Google	google.com	8	9	10	9	8.28
Sina	sina.com	9	9	8	8.67	8.91
Tencent	qq.com	10	9	8	9	9.72
Sina micro-blog	weibo.com	9	1	8	6	8.15
Net Ease	163.com	9	9	8	8.67	8.91
Youku	youku.com	10	8	8	8.67	8.62
Tianya	tianya.cn	9	8	8	8.33	8.81
Douban	douban.com	9	8	7	8	8.72
Mop	mop.com	8	7	7	7.33	7.81

Table 4. The correlation analyses among the ranking indexes from Baidu, Sogou and Google

	Baidu Weight	Sogou Rank	PageRank	Averaged Rank	Weighted Rank
Baidu Weight	-	0.0663	0.1768	0.2311	0.8978
Sogou Rank	No	-	0.1406	0.9329	0.4749
PageRank	No	no	-	0.4085	0.0447
Averaged Rank	Little	Linear	Ordinary	-	-
Weighted Rank	Linear	Ordinary	No	-	-

Table 5 listed the ranking indexes from Baidu, Sogou and Google for some websites of the education institutions in China. The data were collected in Nov. 14, 2011. In table 5, USTC is the abbreviation of the University of Science and Technology, and SJTU is the Shanghai Jiaotong University. And RUC is the People's University.

Table 6 presents the analyses of the correlation among the ranking indexes from Baidu, Sogou and Google for the websites of some Chinese education institutions. Baidu weight has no correlation with Sogou rank, the |R| between them is 0.0709; it has ordinary correlation with Google PageRank (0.4737), fine correlation with Averaged rank value (0.6947) and linear correlation with Weight rank value. Sogou rank has ordinary correlations with PageRank of Google and Averaged rank, little correlation with the Weighted rank value. Google PageRank has linear correlation with Average rank value and fine correlation with Weighted rank value.

Table 5. The ranking indexes for some websites of the education institutions (2011-11-14)

Website	URL	Baidu Weight	Sogou Rank	Google PageRank	Averaged Rank	Weighted Rank
Tsinghua U.	tsinghua.edu.cn	5	7	9	7	5.57
Peking University	pku.edu.cn	6	7	9	7.33	6.38
USTC	ustc.edu.cn	5	5	8	6	5.28
Nanjing U.	nju.edu.cn	6	5	9	6.67	6.19
Fudan University	fudan.edu.cn	5	6	9	6.67	5.47
Zhejiang U.	zju.edu.cn	4	6	9	6.33	4.66
SJTU	sjtu.edu.cn	4	7	9	6.67	4.76
RUC	ruc.edu.cn	5	6	8	6.33	5.38
Sun Yet-Sen U.	sysu.edu.cn	6	5	8	6.33	6.09
CAS	cas.cn	4	6	8	6	4.57
ScienceNet	sciencenet.cn	6	5	9	6.67	5.38
1000plan	1000plan.org	3	4	7	4.67	3.47

Table 6. The correlation analyses among three search engines

	Baidu Weight	Sogou Rank	PageRank	Averaged Rank	Weighted Rank
Baidu Weight	-	0.0709	0.4737	0.6947	0.9874
Sogou Rank	No	-	0.6285	0.7326	0.2204
PageRank	Ordinary	Fine	-	0.8798	0.5890
Averaged Rank	Fine	Fine	Linear	-	-
Weighted Rank	Linear	Little	Ordinary	-	-

Analyzing above studies, some interesting points should be mentioned:

1. Heterogenic sequences of presentation the search results of the same keyword from the different search engines should be noted in Chinese Internet search scenario. The main reason is that every search engine has its own criterions and algorithms to determine the rank of web pages. This is a difficulty factor in the Search Engine Optimization.

2. The Averaged rank indexes of Tencent, Baidu and Google are 9, but distribution manner of ranking index from the every search engine is different. For example, for Tencent, its Baidu weight is 10, its Sogou Rank is 9 and its Google PageRank is 8. The Weighted rank index can distinguish this difference.

3. According to the correlation analyses, in Averaged rank case, Baidu weight has linear correlation with the Averaged rank, and Sogou rank too. Google PageRank has little correlation with Averaged rank. In Weighted rank case, only the Baidu weight has linear correlation with Weighted rank index. Sogou rank has fine correlation with Weighted rank value and Google PageRank has no correlation with it. So, there is a necessary to develop a new ranking index with the advantage from both of Averaged rank and Weighted rank.

5   Information Theory and the Definition of W-Entropy Rank

The information theory is introduced firstly in this section. Based on this theory, W-entropy rank is defined.

5.1   Brief Introduction of Information Theory

The concept of Shannon's entropy [7] is the central role of information theory sometimes referred as a measurement of uncertainty. Let X be a discrete random variable taking a finite number of possible values $x_1, x_2...x_n$ with probabilities $p_1, p_2...p_n$ respectively such that $\Delta n = \{P = (p_1, p_2...p_n) : p_i \geq 0, \sum p_i = 1, i = 1, 2...n\}$. Let h be a function defined on the interval $(0, 1]$ and $h(p)$ be interpreted as the uncertainty associated with the event $X = x_i, i = 1, 2...n$. For each n, a function $H_n(p_1, p_2...p_n)$ is defined as the average uncertainty associated with the event $\{X = x_i\}$, given by

$$H_n(p_1, p_2, \cdots, p_n) = \sum_{i=1}^{n} p_i * h(p_i) \tag{1}$$

Let $H_n:\Delta n \rightarrow IR\ (n \geq 2)$ be a function satisfying the following axioms:
(a) $H_n(p_1, p_2... p_n)$ is a continuous function of $p \in [0, 1]$.
(b) $H_n(p_1, p_2... p_n)$ is a symmetric function of its arguments.
(c) $H_n(p_1, p_2... p_n) = H_{n-1}(p_1, p_2... p_n) + (p_1 + p_2)*H_2(p_1/(p_1 + p_2), p_2/(p_1 + p_2)), p_1 + p_2 > 0.$

Then $H_n(p_1, p_2...p_n)$ is the formula as Shannon defined:

$$H_n(p_1, p_2, \cdots, p_n) = -C \sum_{i=1}^{n} p_i \log_b{}^{p_i} \tag{2}$$

Where $C > 0, b > 1$, with $0*log_b0 = 0$.
   Weigang presented a practical application of the entropy, where the entropy of information was applied to measure the degree of disorder and an application algorithm was proposed [8], also adopted this theory to measure the influence of individual among the different social networks [9,10].

5.2   Definition of W-Entropy Rank

Suppose a ranking index for a web page is $P_j, j = 1...n$, there are n these indexes from related search engines. The weights of these indexes are $\{a_1, a_2...a_n\}$, $\sum a_j = 1$, which are selected as $1/n$ for every search engines as mentioned in section 4. Because the ranking index is usually divided in 10 levels, so there is $p_j = P_j/10$.

Then the Averaged rank index of this web page is:

$$m = \sum_{j=1}^{n} a_j p_j \tag{3}$$

The Averaged rank is a very simple and intuitive method to present the unified rank index for a web page. As discussed in section 4, it cannot identify the difference cases between the distribution of rank indexes in 10, 9, 8, and in 9, 9, 9. The entropy concept of information theory can be employed to quantify this distribution. Firstly, there is a transformation for p_j to q_j.

$$q_j = p_j /(n+1) \quad j=1,2...n \tag{4}$$

$$q_{(n+1)} = 1 - \sum_{j=1}^{n} q_j \tag{5}$$

Where q_j presents a numeric value of the information of j_{th} ranking index from j_{th} search engine. On the other hand, $q_{(n+1)}$ is a percent that presents an absence of information of all n ranking indexes of the related search engines. The entropy is defined as a correction coefficient to reflect the distribution of the ranking indexes of these related search engines, in briefly distribution coefficient:

$$h(q_1, q_2, \cdots, q_{n+1}) = -\sum_{j=1}^{n+1} q_j \log_{n+1} q_j \tag{6}$$

Based on the formulas (3) and (6), *W-entropy Rank*, a new index to class the importance of a web page can be defined as:

$$W\text{-}entropy\ Rank = h * m \tag{7}$$

In order to simplify this formula for application purposes, the value from formula (7) was scaled in relation to maximum *W-entropy Rank*, and multiplied by 100, which results in the following equation:

$$W\text{-}entropy\ Rank_{relative} = \frac{W\text{-}entropy\ Rank}{W\text{-}entropy\ Rank_{max}} \tag{8}$$

Generally, the Relative W-entropy rank index is simply presented as W-entropy rank.

6   W-Entropy Rank for Search Engines

This section presents the application of W-Entropy rank to the web sites of the Internet media and education institutions of China. There is some difference of the ranking indexes of Baidu, Sogou between tables 3 and 7 (5 and 8 too) because the companies of these search engines changed the ranking indexes during this period.

6.1   W-Entropy Rank for Some Websites of the Internet Media

Table 7 shows the W-entropy rank indexes for some websites of the Internet media in China. For the website of Baidu, its ranking index is 9/10 by Baidu, Sogou and Google. The Averaged rank index is 9 too. The distribution coefficient h is 0.9863, the absolute W-entropy rank index is 8.88. This is the largest value in this moment, so, the relative W-entropy rank index of Baidu is defined as 100.

In case of Google, its website is classified by Baidu as 8, Sogou as 9 and proper as 10, The Averaged rank index is 9 too. The distribution coefficient h is 0.9829, the absolute W-entropy rank index is 8.85. According to Baidu, the relative W-entropy rank index of Google is defined as 99.78.

As in table 7, for websites of Tencent and Youku, Baidu changed the weight for them from 10 to 9, which is the maximum Baidu weight value in China now. So, the relative W-entropy rank index of Tencent together with Sina, NetEase and Sohu is 95.48, Youku is 90.91 together with Tianya.

In an especial case, Baidu re-classified Unipay's website from 2 to 4, the adjustment reflected the affection of our proposal. As the result, the relative W-entropy rank index of Unipay is defined as 28.41.

Table 7. W-entropy rank for some websites of the Internet media (2011-12-01)

Website	URL	Baidu Weight	Sogou Rank	Google PR	Averaged Rank	W-Entropy Rank
Baidu	baidu.com	9	9	9	9	100
Google	google.com	8	9	10	9	99.78
Tencent	qq.com	10/9	9	8	8.67	95.48
Sina	sina.com	9	9	8	8.67	95.48
NetEase	163.com	9	9	8	8.67	95.48
Sohu	sohu.com	9	9	8	8.67	95.48
Youku	youku.com	10/9	8	8	8.33	90.91
Tianya	tianya.cn	9	8	8	8.33	90.91
Sogou	sogou.com	9	9	7	8.33	90.70
Douban	douban.com	9	8	7	8	86.10
Mop	mop.com	8/9	7	7	7.67	81.79
Sina weibo	weibo.com	9	1	8	6	52.40
Visa China	visa.com.cn	1	5	6	4	28.71
ChinaUnipay	unionpay.com	2/4	1	7	4	28.41

6.2 W-Entropy Rank for Some Websites of Education Institutions

As an indicial study in table 5, Baidu and Sogou classified the websites of education institutions with lower indexes. In the later of November, these search engines changed the rank indexes for these websites. As presented in table 8, the Baidu weight of the websites of Shanghai Jiaotong University and Zhejiang University were re-classified from 2 to 4. And the websites of Tsinghua University, People's University of China, Nanjing University, Sun Yat-sen University and University of Science and Technology of China ware modified from 5 to 6. For Chinese Academy of Science, its Baidu weight was also increased from 4 to 5.

As the results, in the Shanghai Jiaotong University, Peking University and Tsinghua University, their websites were classified by Baidu as 6, Sogou as 7 and Google as 9, The Averaged rank index is 7.33. The distribution coefficient h is 0.9309, the absolute W-entropy rank index is 6.83. According to Baidu, the relative W-entropy rank index of them is defined as 76.28.

The Fudan University, Nanjing University and Zhejiang University shared fourth place with the W-Entropy rank index 71.33. Sun Yat-sen University, Chinese Academy of Science, University of Science and Technology of China, ScienceNet are also listed in the same level with the W-Entropy rank index more or less 62.

Comparing the results in table 8 and the Internet traffic records of Alexa [11], the rank sequence of the websites is listed as the Shanghai Jiaotong Unviersity, Fudan University, ScienceNet, Tsinghua University, Peking University, Nanjing University, and Zhejiang University. This means that, probably, Baidu and Sogou search engines adjusted the classification for this institutions using W-entropy rank as a reference.

Table 8. W-entropy rank for some websites of education institutions (2011-12-01).

Website	URL	Baidu Weight	Sogou Rank	Google PR	Averaged Rank	W-Entropy Rank
SJTU	sjtu.edu.cn	4/6	7	9	7.33	76.28
Tsinghua U.	tsinghua.edu.cn	5/6	7	9	7.33	76.28
Peking U.	pku.edu.cn	6	7	9	7.33	76.28
Fudan University	fudan.edu.cn	5/6	6	9	7	71.33
Nanjing U.	nju.edu.cn	6/6	5/6	9	7	71.33
Zhejiang U.	zju.edu.cn	4/6	6	9	7	71.33
People' s U.	ruc.edu.cn	5/6	6	8	6.67	66.81
CAS	cas.cn	4/5	6	8	6.33	61.78
Sun Yet-sen U.	sysu.edu.cn	6/6	5	8	6.33	61.78
USCT	ustc.edu.cn	5/6	5	8	6.33	61.78
Science Net	sciencenet.cn	6/5	5	9	6.33	61.22
1000plan	1000plan.org	3	4	7	4.67	38.15

6.3   Correlation Analyses of W-Entropy Rank with Others

In this section, 42 websites from some Internet media, education, research, finance institutions and telecommunication enterprises were selected to analyze the correlation between the W-entropy rank index and the rank indexes from every individual search engine. The indicial results are presented in table 9 and there are following observations:

Table 9. Correlation analyses of W-Entropy rank with the indexes of Baidu, Sogou and Google

	Baidu Weight	Sogou Rank	PageRank	Averaged Rank	Weighted Rank	W-entropy rank
Baidu Weight	-	0.5648	0.1530	0.8796	0.9957	0.8657
Sogou Rank	Ordinary	-	0.1044	0.8438	0.6297	0.8647
PageRank	No	No	-	0.3442	0.1968	0.3402
Averaged Rank	Linear	Linear	Little	-		
Weighted Rank	Linear	Fine	No	-	-	-
W-entropy Rank	Linear	Linear	Little	-	-	-
The average of correlation coefficients between each search engine and different rank value				0.6956	0.6074	0.6902

1. With the comparison, the correlation between W-entropy rank index and Baidu weight is 0.8657, i.e, linear correlation. For Sogou rank, the correlation coefficient is 0.8647 and also as linear correlation. For the PageRank of Google, the correlation coefficient is 0.3402, even it is with little correlation, but is still better than PageRank with Weighted rank. This result reduces the gap between the PageRank with other two ranking indexes.

2. Comparing the correlation study among the Baidu weight, Sogou rank and Google PageRank with the Average rank, Weighted rank and W-entropy rank in table 9. The sum of the column of the correlation coefficient of Average rank is 0.6956, the sum of the column of W-entropy rank is 0.6094 and the Weighted rank is 0.6074, this result shows that the W-entropy rank index has a better presentation.

3. The W-entropy rank index is developed to synchronize the information distribution of the ranking indexes from the different search engines. In case of the websites of Baidu and Tencent, both of them get 9 in Average rank, but Baidu is also with a better distribution of the classification: 9, 9, and 9 by Baidu, Sogou and Google. As the result, the distribution coefficient h is 0.9863, the absolute W-entropy rank index is 8.88, and, the relative W-entropy rank index of Baidu is 100. Otherwise, in case of Google, the ranking indexes are classified as 8, 9 and 10, the distribution coefficient is 0.9829, so W-entropy rank index is 99.78, lesser than Baidu.

7   W-Entropy Rank for Blogging Websites

This section presents the application of W-entropy rank to measure the influence of the blogging websites on the Internet. The Weighted Page Rank (WPR) is proposed initially in this analysis. For more cases, the Baidu weight, Sogou rank and others can also be applied as the basic indexes.

7.1   Definition of the Weighted Page Rank

In the study of the influence of the blogging websites, the Weighted PageRank (WPR) of a website is related to two factors: 1) The PR value of the website, noted as PRs, for example, the ScienceNet is with PR 9; 2) The PR values of the different channel's, noted as PRc(i). Table 2 shows the PR values of different channels of ScienceNet, such as blog.sciencenet with 6 and 42.71% accesses.

Based on the data from table 2, the Weighted PageRank (WPR) is defined as:

$$WPR = \sum_{i=1}^{n} PRc(i) \qquad (9)$$

where n is the number of the channels within this website. Alexa provides the user stream in different channels, in percentage, see table 2.

This percentage is used as a weight $\gamma(i)$ to measure the quality of the channel of a webpage and the importance of the visitors from Internet:

$$WPR = \sum_{i=1}^{n} \gamma(i) PRc(i) \ /1000 \qquad (10)$$

where n is the number of the channels of the website, $\sum\gamma(i)\,)/100 = 1$. In this paper, the first 10 channels were considered. The other percentages were summed into the 10th.

7.2 Influence Factors of the Social Networks

Based on the study of the typical blogging websites in China, three factors are selected to measure the influence of this kind of social networking platforms.

1. Index of the visit traffic flow of the website, noted as P_1. The percentages of global Internet users who visit the website by Alexa are used. Also this factor can take the indicator of the number of people per million by China Internet Network Information Center (CNNIC) [12]. The weight of this factor is proposed as 40% in this moment.

2. Index of the quality of the site and the importance of the visitors, noted as P_2. The Weighted Page Rank (WPR) of the website is used as indicate of this factor. The weight for this part is 30%.

3. Index of the number of the new pages indexed by a search engine, noted as P_3. Baidu Indexed pages of the website are considered in this paper. It can also take in consideration the data from Google search engine. The weight of this part is 30%, too.

In some cases, such as Starcount [13] in ranking the influence of the members over Facebook, Twitter and YouTube, the mean of indexes of these factors is simple calculated without considering the distribution of information over above platforms.

7.3 Ranking Blogging Websites by W-Entropy Rank

A new concept of W-entropy Rank can also be used to serve as a measurement for the influence of blogging websites. TOP10 blog-based social networks in China are listed including Baidu Tieba, Sina Blog and Sina Weibo (micro-blog) etc.

According to the theory and analysis above, table 10 listed TOP10 Blog, Microblog and BBS based social networks in China. Baidu Tieba, a typical BBS, is in the first place. There are 0.73% of the global In-ternet users visiting Tieba.baidu.com. In the recent month it has been indexed 25.4 million new pages by the Baidu search engine and the W-entropy Rank value of this site is 0.8376. Hence the average coefficient is 0.6862 and the coefficient of the distribution is 0.9755. Its relative W-entropy index is the biggest with the relative value 100.

Sina Blog is a popular blog in China in the second position. There are 0.93% of the global Internet users visiting blog.sina.com. In the recent month it has been indexed 15.7 million pages by Baidu and the WPR value of this site is 0.7850. With the calcu-lation, the average coefficient is 0.5932 and the coefficient of the distribution is 0.9468. Its relative W-entropy index is 96.13.

Sina Weibo, a micro-blog, is in the third position with the W-entropy index 91.76. There are 2.18% of the global Internet users visiting the weibo.com. In the recently month it has been indexed 14.8 million pages by Baidu and the WPR value of this site is 0.7352. The average coefficient of this site is 0.6380 and the coefficient of the distribution is 0.7611.

Tianya is in the fourth position with the w-entropy index 90.14. There are 0.73% of the global Internet users visiting tianya.cn. In the recent month it has been indexed

14.6 million pages by Baidu and the WPR value of this site is 0.7009. The average coefficient is 0.5174 and the coefficient of the distribution is 0.8955. There is more information of other social networks in the TOP10, see table 10.

Table 10. Top 10 social networking websites in China

Social Networks	Average Coefficient	Coefficient of the distribution	W-entropy Rank Index	Rank
Baidu Tieba	0.6862	0.9755	100	1
Sina Blog	0.5932	0.9468	96.13	2
Sina Weibo	0.6380	0.7611	91.76	3
Tianya	0.5174	0.8955	90.14	4
Baidu Space	0.3726	0.6737	63.30	5
Mop	0.3400	0.6845	59.79	6
Tencent Blog	0.3403	0.6564	57.92	7
China	0.2905	0.6167	48.34	8
Sohua Blog	0.2740	0.5130	39.05	9
Netease Blog	0.2691	0.5212	38.98	10

There is also another list of China Webmaster [14] who ranked the TOP10 blog-related social networks in China. Comparing with these two lists, there is 70% similarity. Analyzing their list, there are three questions for discussion:

1. The scores of TOP6 website from that list all are 98. The aim of the list is to rank a sequence of the sites by the influence to assist the user make decision which one they will choose. If the result of the list is almost the same thing, this is useless for administer and Internet users.

2. The position of the site spaces.live.com in the TOP10 is not consistent. It is in 35176th places all over the world and 33697th place in the China by Alexa. Recently this website already closed so Google didn't have its PR value, also didn't have the new pages indexed by Baidu search. Why this site can still be listed at the 9th place?

3. In that list, Sina micro-blog is listed at the 10th place, when the PR value was 0. Now the PR value of this site is 8, so where will it come in the new list of them?

Considering ScienceNet, 0.02% of the global Internet users visited this site, in the recent month it has been indexed 0.165 million pages by Baidu. The WPR value of this site is 0.6764. By the calculation, the average coefficient is 0.2080 and the coefficient of the distribution is 0.3556. Its relative W-entropy index is 21.29.

8   Conclusions

As the national Internet search engines, Baidu, Sogou and Soso take the main market share in China. There is still a space for Google search too. In order to adjust the gaps among the Baidu weight, Sogou rank and PageRank and other search engines, a new concept, W-entropy rank was proposed as a reference. This index unified the rank indexes from above research engines to smooth the gaps among them. It is also better than simple use the averaged rank because of using the entropy concept of the information theory to reflect the distribution of the information from different ranking indexes of the related platforms.

Based on the study of 42 websites from 4 sectors such as Internet media, education/research, finance institutions and telecommunication enterprises, the sequence of these websites according the W-entropy rank is well listed comparing with the Internet traffic rank list by Alexa.

It should be mentioned that, the W-entropy rank is not proposed to substitute the existed ranking indexes, but just to be a reference for all search engines in China. After the publication the main idea in our blog in ScienceNet.cn about this reference, Baidu, Sogou and Google adjusted their criteria and methods of the ranking indexes, especially for education and research institutions.

W-entropy rank was used to rank the websites according to their influence index. The paper listed the TOP10 of the important blogging websites of China to show the application.

The further study of the research is to develop an automated system to produce frequently a W-entropy rank list to cover the important websites in China even worldwide to establish a public domain for reference to any kinds of the users, especially, search engines. It is very important with a democracy and quality in the website ranking by any search engine over the Internet.

References

1. CNZZ (Chinese Internet Date Centre), Monthly report of the using rate of Chinese Internet search engines (2011), http://data.cnzz.com/main.php?s=engine
2. Brin, S., Page, L.: The anatomy of a large-scale hyper-textual web search engine. Computer Networks and ISDN Syst. 30, 107–117 (1998)
3. ScientNet (2011), http://www.sciencenet.cn
4. Saaty, T., Alexander, J.: Conflict Resolution: The Analytic Hierarchy Process. Praeger, New York (1989)
5. Shi, Y.: How to be an excellent PhD student (2011),
   http://bbs.sciencenet.cn/home.php?mod=space&uid=46212&do=blog&id=484416
6. Pearson, K.: Mathematical contributions to the theory of evolution, III: regression, heredity and panmixia. Philos. Trans. Roy. Soc. London Ser. A 187, 253–318 (1896)
7. Shannon, C.E.: A Mathematical Theory of Communication. Bell System Technical Journal 27, 379–423, 623–656 (1948)
8. Weigang, L.: An Algorithm for Negative Entropy-The Sequence of the Complex System Structure. Systems Engineering Theory & Practice 8(4), 15–22 (1988)
9. Li, W., Zheng, J., Li, D.L.: W-entropy Index: The Impact of the Members on Social Networks. In: Gong, Z., Luo, X., Chen, J., Lei, J., Wang, F.L. (eds.) WISM 2011, Part I. LNCS, vol. 6987, pp. 226–233. Springer, Heidelberg (2011)
10. Weigang, L., Jianya, Z., Daniel, L.: Analysis of W-entropy Index: the Impact of Members on Social Networks. In: The Proceedings of IADIS International Conference WWW/INTERNET, Best Paper Awards, Rio de Janeiro, Brazil, pp. 171–178 (2011b)
11. Alexa, Internet Information website, http://alexa.com/ (retrieved in 2011)
12. China Internet Network Information Center (CNNIC), http://chinarank.org.cn (retrieved in 2011)
13. Starcount, http://www.starcount.com (retrieved in 2012)
14. China Webmaster, http://top.chinaz.com (retrieved in 2011)

Extracting Term Relationships from Wikipedia

Brigitte Mathiak[1], Víctor Manuel Martínez Peña[2], and Andias Wira-Alam[1]

[1] GESIS - Leibniz Institute for the Social Sciences, Cologne, Germany
[2] Institute for Web Science and Technologies, University of Koblenz-Landau, Germany
{brigitte.mathiak,andias.wira-alam}@gesis.org

Abstract. When looking at the relationship between two terms, we are not only interested on how much they are related, but how we may explain this relationship to the user. This is an open problem in ontology matching, but also in other tasks, from information retrieval to lexicography. In this paper, we propose a solution based on snippets taken from Wikipedia. These snippets are found by looking for connectors between the two terms, e.g. the terms themselves, but also terms that occur often in both articles or terms that link to both articles. With a user study, we establish that this is particularly useful when dealing with not well known relationships, but well-known concepts. The users were learning more about the relationship and were able to grade it accordingly. On real life data, there are some issues with near synonyms, which are not detected well and terms from different communities, but aside from that we get usable and useful explanations of the term relationships.

Keywords: Relationship extraction, Wikipedia, Ontology matching.

1 Introduction

The purpose of semantic relatedness measures is to allow computers to reason about written text. They have many applications in natural language processing and artificial intelligence [1], and have consequently received a lot of attention from the research community. In ontology matching [2] standard measures have been used to find likely partner based on labels.

However, the pure measure of relatedness in numbers is not very helpful to normal users. These people are not so much interested in the quantity of relatedness, but the quality. We use a modified standard method to measure relatedness between Wikipedia entries based on a combination of link analysis and text analysis, which evaluate comparably to other similar measures. We leverage information used by these methods to find text snippets on Wikipedia, which are significant for the relationship and describe it in a human-readable way.

The goal of these snippets is to inform the user of the quality of the relationship, especially in the case of an information gap. For evaluation, we have made a user study using Mechanical Turk. We have first asked the participants what they know about the relation between two concepts, such as Barack Obama and Chicago and then present them with a number of snippets extracted with our method. The general feedback was very positive, with most participants finding most of the snippets helpful. The learning

J. Cordeiro and K.-H. Krempels (Eds.): WEBIST 2012, LNBIP 140, pp. 267–280, 2013.
© Springer-Verlag Berlin Heidelberg 2013

effect was also quite visible, while in one group 58 % of the participants felt there was a relationship between both, only 22 % could specify that relationship precisely, while the others were either very general ("both in America") or plainly wrong ("He was the governor the State of Illinois"). Yet, they quickly accepted the connections made by the application as meaningful.

The next step was to evaluate our method on real life data. We chose the prepared data set from an ontology matching challenge, in order to find snippets that explain the relationships between some of the term pairs. While the recall on those term pairs, in terms of snippets found, were not as high as we expected, we could show that the snippets we did find gave adequate descriptions of the underlying relationships.

2 Related Work

Current research explores two fundamentally different ways to compute semantic relatedness between two terms. The first is *link-based*. In a hierarchical structure, usually a taxonomy, this typically applies to the shortest path between the two concepts. This is often modified with other parameters, such as the depth of the term in the taxonomy, weights derived from the semantics of the taxonomy and so on [3,4]. This can also be applied to Wikipedia, through the use of categories, like is done with WikiRelate [5]. More accuracy is gained by exploiting the link structure between the articles, such as in [6], simply because there are many more links than categories per page. Beyond the very simple distance of counting the shortest path, in [7] the anchor texts of links and link structure itself is used to find. They use link counts weighted by the probability of the link occurring on the page (inspired by tf-idf) as a vector representation of the article while calculating the cosine similarity on the vectors for the similarity measure. This may look very similar to our approach, but we use tf-idf on the terms not the links as well as a directly computable measure for the link structure, so we can calculate our measure online with only two requests to the Wikipedia API. Thus, we combine a link-based measure with the second category of text based measures.

Text based measures take an example corpus of documents that are known to relate to the two terms and then calculate the semantic distance between the two document sets, thereby splitting the problem of relatedness between terms into two problems: choosing a suitable data set and calculating the semantic distance between the documents. There are large numbers of semantic distances to choose from: Lee distance, tf-idf cosine similarity [8], Jaro-Winkler distance, and Approximate string matching [9], just to name a few. In [6], the Semantic Text Similarity (STS) has been developed as a variety of the Longest Common Subsequence (LCS) algorithm and a combination of other methods. It is optimized on very short texts, such as single sentences and phrases. This method was evaluated by using definitions from a dictionary.

The *Explicit Semantic Analysis* ESA [10] uses Wikipedia, just like our approach, and calculates a complete matrix of term to concept relatedness, which can be further refined by introducing human judgments. Unlike our approach, however, it requires the processing of the whole of Wikipedia in a non-linear process, which is very expensive and has not been replicated on the scale since.

There are other approaches to mix both link and text analysis, such as [11] which extracts explicit relationships such as Apple is Fruit, Computer is Machine, Colorado is U.S. state. The goal of this paper, however, is not to use Wikipedia to find relationships which conform to established standards and semantics, but quite the opposite, to produce explanatory text suited for unusual relationships.

When looking at explanation for term matches in complex domains, these are most often based on the structural properties of the domain [12] or the arithmetical relationship of the instances [13]. In [14] a matchability score is given to the user as feedback. The system introduced in [15] allow users to collaborate on descriptions of label-to-label mappings, but does not suggest descriptions on its own.

The problem of explaining matchings on domain models is widely recognized. It is a recurring theme in [2,16]. In [17] it has been suggested that good explanations and usability are more valuable for the quality of data mappings than slightly better matching algorithms.

3   Relationship Extraction

3.1   Architecture

The RelationWik Extractor was built as a web information system. From a user's point of view, it's function it quite simple. The articles for which a relationship is sought and a few parameters are input over a web site and the system will show the results as both a score and snippets illustrating the connection from both sides.

The Wikipedia articles are then downloaded directly via the Wikipedia API. The text is then scanned for additional information such as links, templates, etc. and stripped of its Wikipedia syntax. Both text and meta-information is stored in a database cache. The results of the algorithms are visualized with PHP and the Google Chart API.

3.2   Calculating Relatedness

For the actual calculation of the relationship, two differently approaches are used. One is based on the link structure and the other on the textual closeness of the texts. A third approach is a mixture of both.

The first algorithm measures the connectedness of the terms, by studying inlinks and outlinks. When looking at connections that go over several hops, it becomes clear that the connection can be quite thin. For example, Banana and Berlin are connected by an enzyme that occurs in the Banana and was identified in Berlin. This gets worse when looking at connections with even more connectors in between. Therefore, we decided to ignore all connections involving more than one intermediary. The connections with one intermediary that made the most sense occurred in the scenario where both articles link to the same article. This occurs, for example, when both of the given articles A and B are connected to a category or another larger super-concept by linking to it. Also, in terms of computation time, it is the fastest possible link analysis since outlinks are the easiest to extract from.

Following that argumentation, we only look at articles that either have intersecting outcoming links or have a link from A to B or from B to A. Any other pairs are given a relatedness of zero. Connected articles A and B receive a base relatedness b of 0.5

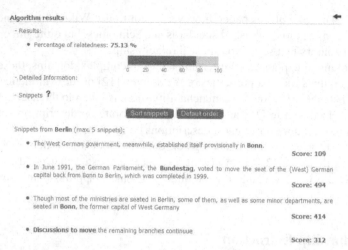

Fig. 1. The result page of the Relationship Extractor with the terms Bonn and Berlin. The algorithm is set to sentence-sized snippets. The Score given next to the snippets is a relevance measure based on the terms used in both documents.

and are given a boost of 0.1 for additional connections (e.g. 0.7 when A and B link to each other and link to at least one third article). This base value is further modified by the number of backlinks of the linked-to article in relation to the links from the other article. And, if applicable, by the ratio between common outlinks c and total outlinks $l_{A\rightarrow}$ respective of $l_{B\rightarrow}$.

$$Rel_{AB} = b - \frac{l_{A\rightarrow B} + l_{B\rightarrow A}}{l_{total}} + \frac{c}{2l_{A\rightarrow}} + \frac{c}{2l_{B\rightarrow}} \tag{1}$$

It was originally planned to optimize the choice of b and introduce weighting factors, but the initial choices performed quite well in the evaluation and so no further optimization was necessary and might have introduced overfitting.

For the second algorithm, we use a standard cosine similarity between the articles. The articles are preprocessed by stripping wikisyntax, punctuation and symbols, removing stop words and unique terms and using only basic stemming by removing plurals. The term vectors A and B are calculated with tf idf.

$$\cos(\theta) = \frac{\sum_{i=1}^{n} A_i \times B_i}{\sqrt{\sum_{i=1}^{n} (A_i)^2} \times \sqrt{\sum_{i=1}^{n} (B_i)^2}} \tag{2}$$

As our third method, we average the results of the two similarities above. Again weighing was considered, but since our goal is not to optimize the relationship score, but to present human-readable snippets, the exact optimal ratio, was of no consequence to us.

4   Evaluation

For the evaluation of the relatedness score, we use the WordSimilarity-353 Test Collection [18]. It contains 353 English word pairs with human-assigned similarity judgments.

It contains antonyms, synonyms and similar words and connected terms, such as Film and Popcorn. Not all terms from the dataset can be used directly, e.g. keyboard was mapped to the Wikipedia article Computer keyboard, Plane to Fixed-wing aircraft, etc. The mappings were constructed by using the Wikipedia search engine and choosing the first entry. A few terms had to be removed, such as Diego Maradona, because of errors on the page. The similarity scores from all three algorithms were tested on the data set by using a Pearson linear correlation coefficient [19]. The results are shown in Table 1.

Table 1. Pearson-correlation

Algorithm	r-Pearson coefficient
links	0.65
cosine	0.55
combined	0.69
[5]	0.49
[10]	0.75
[7]	0.69

On closer inspection, we can observe that the cosine similarity tends to judge too low on somewhat similar articles, such as Radio, Computer or Internet. The links similarity on the other hand is vulnerable to over judging relatedness due to singular rogue links and has problems in general with articles containing only few links. On average, both effects seem to dampen each other.

The combined score is competitive with other methods such as described in [5], [10] and later in [7], but it is very fast, without needing any pre-processing and is able to work online. The wait time mostly depends on the speed of downloading both articles. All three other methods work on a Wikipedia dump, which is more or less extensively pre-processed. With the pre-processed data-set however, they achieve much faster response times. We rarely go beyond 10 seconds for any given pairs of terms, though this depends on the current traffic on the Wikipedia server. A caching mechanism has been implemented to alleviate the effect, lowering response times to much lower numbers.

We have not addressed some of the serious questions in the field, such as how to match search terms from the evaluation set to the Wikipedia articles. Since we expect user interaction, the disambiguation can be done with Wikipedia-specific means. Alternatively, methods, as outlined in the above-mentioned publications can be employed.

The terms, we are most interested in, are not generally found in evaluation data sets. And with good reason: they are terms, which have hidden or not commonly known relationships. Human judges would give varying degrees of relationship, depending on whether they happen to know the details about the relationship or not. Terms, such as Belarus and Ukraine[1] are blindly judged as completely unrelated by 28.8 % of the participants, yet our algorithms judge the relationship as high. We believe the algorithm is right and that the information gap is something to be closed.

---

[1] Two neighboring countries that used to be part of the USSR.

5 Snippets

We assume that a common user is not so much interested in how much two terms are related, but rather how they are related. As we have shown above, the connections that we find are positively correlated to the human-perceived relation between two terms. This offers us a connection point between the terms. For the linking algorithm it is rather simple. The links themselves serve as a direct connection. For intersecting outlinks the links to the intersecting articles are a connection point. The cosine algorithm also gives us a measure of which terms are most highly relevant for the similarity and we can use those a connector. Those connection points are then transformed into snippets and shown to the user. All three can be mapped to one or more specific text positions inside of Wikipedia articles. The corresponding snippet is generated from there, choosing either paragraph, sentence or a fixed-size window. Since there can be more than one link on a page and terms can be mentioned several times, we receive a large number of snippets. The remaining questions are: What is the optimal window? What is best way to rank? And most importantly, is the method beneficial in the first place?

5.1 Methodology of the User Study

We offered 0.25 US$ at Amazon Mechanical Turk to 40 participants to answer a short survey on our snippets. We chose 10 pairs of terms (ref. 2). The last 4 term pairs are taken from the WordSimilarity-353 test set as a control group. The first 6 were chosen based on a lesser known connection. We were striving to take into account a variety of connections, such as biographical events, historical similarity, recent news, spatial closeness, same super-category and part-of. Also, we were trying to find term pairs in which at least one term should be known by the participants, and preferably both.

Table 2. Term pairs used for the user study

Term 1	Term 2	connection
Barack Obama	Chicago	Where he went to law school
Bonn	Berlin	Both were capital of Germany at some point
Google	Apple	Recent law suit concerning Motorola
Belarus	Ukraine	Neighboring countries; ex-USSR
German language	English language	Both indogermanic languages
Dave Mustaine	Metallica	Founding member; guitarist
Radio	Television	
Cat	Tiger	
Sex	Love	
Student	Professor	

For the study, we first asked the participants to rate the relationship between the terms between 0 and 10, without using any secondary information sources, such as the Internet. We then presented up to five snippets for each pair and asked for an evaluation of each individual snippet on a scale ranging from not good to very good (description of the relationship). Then we asked again for a rating of the relationship between the two terms.

Table 3. Ratings before the snippets were shown and after. Numbers are (in order): Median, simple mean

Term 1	Term 2	before	after
Barack Obama	Chicago	7, 7.0	8, 7.2
Bonn	Berlin	5, 5.4	7, 6.7
Google	Apple	6, 5.3	6, 5.2
Belarus	Ukraine	6, 5.9	7, 6.1
German language	English language	5, 5.0	6, 5.7
Dave Mustaine	Metallica	5, 5.5	7, 6.7
Radio	Television	6, 6.2	7, 6.8
Cat	Tiger	7, 6.7	8, 7.2
Sex	Love	7, 6.7	7, 6.5
Student	Professor	8, 7.1	7, 6.9

As a control mechanism, we asked the participants to give us a catchword description of the relationship from their point of view, in order to understand why they would rate in a certain way. This was checked both on the initial rating and after the snippets had been given.

Final methodological note: As one of the participants pointed out to us (a self-proclaimed MS in Resource Economics), we did not offer an "opt-out" button on our rating scales. This introduces bias towards stating an opinion even if there is no informational basis for this opinion. The participants have to answer the question to gain the monetary incentive, even if they do not in fact know anything about the subject matter, thus (in economical theory) they are prone to answer randomly[2]. We have pondered this issue, but since our aim is to measure how much they know in the first place, giving them an easy way out seemed like losing too much information and thus introducing a bias against the uninformed. We assume they will not answer randomly, but choose something on the low end of the scale. The data seems to corroborate our assumption. There is a strong gap between the relationship rating in the first 6 pairs between before the snippets and after, although with a large spread, which could be a result of the random choices.

5.2 Experiences from the User Study

There were no technical difficulties with the Amazon Mechanical Turk platform. However, setting up a suitable survey was a bit tricky for non-psychologists (see above for some pitfalls). We were forced to change the procedures quite a bit, before finding a method to adequately measure what we were interested in. Still, some participants simply did not play by the rules, e.g. one participant wrote in the general comments "(...)we can complete this survey easily using search engines like Google(...)", although we

---

[2] The literature on this is in fact extensive and not as clear-cut as that. While the general opinion, such as [20] seems to be that it is better to avoid forced-choice answer sets as it puts extra strain on the participants, they are common practices for special purposes like memory tasks [21]. In [22], it has been shown that forced-choice increases both the time spent on answering the question and the quality of the data in a web scenario similar to ours.

Table 4. Ratio of relationships rated as zero

Term 1	Term 2	before	after
Barack Obama	Chicago	18.2	3
Bonn	Berlin	28.8	1.5
Google	Apple	18.2	1.5
Belarus	Ukraine	28.8	0.0
German language	English language	27.3	0.0
Dave Mustaine	Metallica	36.4	7.8
Radio	Television	13.6	0.0
Cat	Tiger	9.1	0.0
Sex	Love	13.6	1.5
Student	Professor	13.6	1.5

Table 5. Rating that most participants agreed upon

Term 1	Term 2	before	after
Barack Obama	Chicago	0	10
Bonn	Berlin	0	8
Google	Apple	0	6
Belarus	Ukraine	0	7
German language	English language	0	7
Dave Mustaine	Metallica	0	8 &10
Radio	Television	8	8
Cat	Tiger	7	8
Sex	Love	10	10
Student	Professor	10	7

stated twice and in large letters that the Internet was not to be used. Overall the general comments were very helpful in designing better versions of the survey.

There were some complaints concerning for example money or a lack of understanding about the purpose of the survey. However, we decided it was not wise to explain what we were looking for in order to avoid the interviewer-compliance bias as much as possible. Some treated it as a game and wondered whether they had won.

Quite a lot (37%) of the participants did not complete the survey, for unknown reasons. We did not raise the incentive to test for lack of incentive. Some of the drop-outs can probably be explained by participants being annoyed with the forced-choice answers. Many of the participants that eventually dropped-out gave mocking answers to the open-ended questions.

We did award the incentive to everyone who answered more than a few questions and claimed to be finished and used answers from unfinished questionnaires for the analysis.

5.3 Learning Effect

When looking at the median or mean differences in the relationship rating the difference seems slight, comparable to the variance in the control group (cf. table 3). Now, when looking at the ratio of zero relationship votes (cf. table 4), we can see a pronounced change between before and after. What is surprising, though, is that the values also drop significantly for the control group.

One part of this effect is that the snippets show new information between well known concepts such as Cat and Tiger, two concepts that both belong to the same animal class. A look at the catchwords that were provided by the participants to explain their relationship rating confirms this view. New information from the snippets was incorporated there allowing the participants to waver from their belief that there was no connection at all. However, while some new information led to upgrades in the relationship rating, it often led to downgrades as well.

One reason for this was misinformation. A number of participants wrongly stated that Barack Obama used to be the governor/senator of Illinois. After they read the snippets, they revised this opinion and accordingly downgraded the relationship level. On the other hand, most of the participants rating the relationship between the President and Chicago as zero, gave only general catchwords, such as "America" and later upgraded their rating when they learned more. For other term pairs (Apple, Google), they digested the new information, but did not see any reason to adjust their rating. For some pairings, such as Bonn, Berlin and Dave Mustaine, Metallica, there was quite a shift in the mean rating, but mostly, it seemed, to account for the fact that many did not know of Bonn or Dave Mustaine beforehand.

What is interesting, though, is that the knowledge of the participants concerning the numerical relationship rating was somewhat stable, regardless of additional information. This is a good sign that relationship ratings tend to become clearer with more information; the variance gets lower, and especially the extreme statement of "not related" gets rarer. This trend for humans to rate more gradual with more information is especially visible when looking at which rating category received the most "votes" (cf. table 5). For the pairs with hidden information this jumped from 0 to the mean, while for the control group it remained stable.

5.4 Sentences vs. Paragraphs

Apart from the general learning effect gained from the snippets, we also investigated which type of snippets (paragraph or sentence) were favored and why. For each set of snippets we asked the participants, which they found most useful. They were split into two control groups, each alternating sentence and paragraph. Overall, 40 participants chose 112 sentences and 89 paragraphs as the best description, almost an equal number. The slight bias does not allow a conclusive choice. We therefore decided to integrate a user choice into the web interface.

Still, distribution was not equal. For "Barack Obama" and "Chicago", the top choices were a paragraph with 25% and a sentence with 17.5% of the votes. However, both were from the same connection point, telling the story about the career of Barack Obama with some timeline. For "Dave Mustaine" and "Metallica", the participants again chose the same connection point about the career history, regardless of paragraphs or sentences. The connection itself was the criteria for voting the best snippets. In the paragraph scenario, they just happened to be more interesting than the alternatives. For the other pairs, we had a consistent bias towards sentences.

Curiously, we found that the characteristics of a "best" snippet is not so much tied to length, but to containing interesting bits of knowledge, regardless of the information content to the relationship. For example, in the snippets for "German language" "English language", the snippet "English replaced German as the dominant language of science Nobel Prize laureates during the second half of the 20th century." was chosen as best by the majority. However, the snippet does not so much add to the knowledge of the relationship, as it is simply an interesting piece of trivia. In a similar vain, the sentence "Television sends the picture as AM and the sound as AM or FM, with the sound carrier a fixed frequency (4.5 MHz in the NTSC system) away from the video carrier." won the majority vote for "Radio" and "Television".

We conclude that users prefer interesting snippets over relevant ones and that length does not seem to be important. Therefore, the vote of which snippet is best cannot be used as a direct measure to which snippet educated the user best about the relationship. This can only be determined indirectly (e.g. through the analysis of catchwords).

6   Limitations of the Approach

Partial information is not the only limitation when it comes to reliably judging the relationsship between two terms. The use case that immediately springs into mind is translation between languages and its weaker twin problem: translation between different domains. For the later problem, a domain expert of one domain needs to find a similar or ideally identical term to best describe his concept in another domain, sometimes freely, sometimes from a fixed set or vice versa. Typical real-life use cases include ontology matching, cross-link generation between controlled vocabularies and many practical applications in interdisciplinary project, such as software engineering for non-computer scientists. Unlike for automatic translation, there are not many good test data sets, which have translations between domains side-by-side. An exception are cross-walks between thesauri.

A thesaurus serves to classify literature in a library thematically, but since they often used in web retrieval systems they typcially include synonyms and other relationsships between terms. Domain specific libraries typically use domain specific thesauri, but since these want to share book entries between them, especially if the domains overlap, they define mappings, called cross-walks to find the term with the highest relationship to the term they are looking at.

With our method, we looked at cross-walks manually created by domain experts, between TheSoz, a thesaurus from the German Social Sciences[3], and STW, a thesaurus for German Economics[4] as described in the Ontology Matching challenge of the OAEI[5]. Since both ontologies contain links to DBPedia, it seemed like a perfect opportunity. And indeed, much can be learned.

---

[3] http://lod.gesis.org/thesoz/
[4] http://zbw.eu/stw/versions/latest/about
[5] http://web.informatik.uni-mannheim.de/oaei-library/2012/

6.1 Lost in Translation

When looking at our snippets, some oddities occur. As a starting point, we looked at term pairs that were manually labeled as exactMatch. And indeed, for the two terms Limited_liability_company and Corporation, we found a relation ship score of 7.6 (out of ten). Yet, one of our snippets suggested that in Brazil a Limited_liability_company is a special case of a Corporation, another confirms this for the US, but the cross-walk labels it as exactMatch. This is not surprising, when we look at the original German term, which is the exact same for both thesauri: Kapitalgesellschaft. Apparently, in Germany, there is no such clear distinction, so each expert team chose another term as translation and used it as a basis for the DBPedia links. Unfortunately, this is not an isolated incident. Assuming a 90% interrater-agreement[6] on translations and DBPedia mappings, we reach a 35% error rate not accounting for the errors the algorithm itself may have.

6.2 Context of Terms

Another problem is the point of view from the different domains. Information_retrieval and Online_search are marked as exactMatch, and although these are vastly different from a computer scientist point of view, both sociologists and economists felt them to be identical. Unfortunately, Wikipedia does not have a lot of articles sorted by context, so the articles are written from the computer scientist view, which does not link both terms at all. This effect becomes more pronounced when one term is very special to one domain.

"Aggression, in its broadest sense, is behavior, or a disposition, that is forceful, hostile or attacking. It may occur either in retaliation or without provocation. In narrower definitions that are used in *social sciences* and behavioral sciences, aggression is an intention to cause harm or an act intended to increase relative social dominance." (Wikipedia, retrieved 22.6.12, italics added). Here it is explicit that the social sciences use aggression in a different scope than one would normally expect. The economists do not have such a special attachment, so they crosslink it to violence, which is also studied in a socio-economic background, but by a different community. Both articles have no links towards each other, although Wordnet defines violence as "an act of aggression".

We can conclude that the Wikipedia corpus is not optimal when it comes to connecting terms typically used in different context but meaning similar things, especially compared to sources specialized in precisely this task, such as synonym dictionaries or dictionaries in general. This impression is enforced when looking at terms which are obviously similar just on a linguistical/syntactical basis (Professional_ethics vs. Work_ethic, Journalism vs. Journalists, etc.), but do surprisingly not share any links. This is not an isolated phenomenon, only 26% of the exact match term pairs can be connected with our algorithm, and only 19% have extractable snippets. This is compared to

---

[6] This is actually optimistically high for a translation. Each dictionary typically gives 2 or more terms. We take into account that given the synonymic nature of translations and mappings, it is likely that the mapping may cancel out a translation problem or vice versa. When looking at exact matches, we find that only 59.9% link to the same DBPedia entity, the rest are split up between grammatical variants, near synonyms and probable mistakes e.g. Martial_law exactMatch war_crime.

a 60% discovery rate when using Levensthein distance combined with a standard synonym dictionary and stemming. However, it must be said that the comparison method is bound to produce a higher rate of false positives, which we have not investigated here. Also, our method does find relationships, the other does not find.

6.3 Snippets Are a Good Indicator for the Relationship

Ironically, Wikipedia is much more helpful in finding and describing the relationship of term pairs not labeled as exact match, but as related match. The discovery rate raises to 37% with 30% for snippets, while the linguistical method remains stable at 62%. Although globalization and global_change are rated only 5 on the relationship score, the snippets provide a good description of globalization being an example of global_change. The snippets usually give a good and often even succinct description of the relationship. Example: A *pedastrian* is a person who is *walking* on a road, pavement or path. Although some (17%) of the snippets rather explain one of the subject rather than the relationship, in our sample, these never occured exclusively, meaning that at least one of the extracted snippets gave the actual relationship. However, it must be noted that the relationship is not very useful to readers that are not familiar with the concepts of the term pairs. Example: The *marginal utility* of a good or service is the utility of its *marginal use*.

While sometimes a tradionally used label for the relationship can be derived from the snippets (e.g. partOf, belongsTo, etc.), more often the relationship seems simple, but not easy to grasp within controlled vocabulary, like with Declaration_of_war and war, conflict_resolution and conflict, faith and religion.

7   Conclusions and Future Work

By showing text snippets around the connectors, the user gets a good overview on the nature of the relationship between any two given terms, especially in those cases in which the relationship is usually not well known (e.g. Berlin and Bonn). Please try yourself on http://multiweb.gesis.org/RelationShipExtractor/.

Applied on real data, we observe difficulties when dealing with full-fledged synonyms or translations between domains, probably because the generative process of Wikipedia articles discourages separate articles on synonyms, unless the article writers are ignorant of each other. We plan to address this issue by incorporating basic linguistic analysis and a synonym dictionary in future versions of our service. Also, we plan to give a special weight to the case when we do find the other term in the article, just not as a link.

For the application on real-life data, we also need to pay special attention to the matching between the original term and article. Relying on pre-made crosslinks to DB-Pedia can point in the wrong direction, as these crosslinks are not always suitable for our use case, due to cascading information loss. This matching is a separate problem that has been addressed among others in [7]. It is functionally similar to the matching step for Entity Recognition and needs to be addressed by us to allow for greater applicability.

We believe that with the analysis of thesauri, we can make good progress towards the goal of matching general domain descriptions, such data schemata and ontologies and supplementing them with additional relationship-oriented information.

References

1. Budanitsky, A.: Lexical semantic relatedness and its application in natural language processing. Technical report, Department of Computer Science, University of Toronto (1999)
2. Pavel, S., Euzenat, J.: Ontology matching: state of the art and future challenges. IEEE Transactions on Knowledge and Data Engineering, 1 (2011)
3. Leacock, C., Miller, G.A., Chodorow, M.: Using corpus statistics and wordnet relations for sense identification. Comput. Linguist. 24, 147–165 (1998)
4. Slimani, T., Ben Yaghlane, B., Mellouli, K.: A new similarity measure based on edge counting. World Academy of Science, Engineering and Technology 23, 34–38 (2006)
5. Strube, M., Ponzetto, S.P.: Wikirelate! computing semantic relatedness using wikipedia. In: Proceedings of the 21st National Conference on Artificial Intelligence, vol. 2, pp. 1419–1424. AAAI Press (2006)
6. Islam, A., Inkpen, D.: Semantic text similarity using corpus-based word similarity and string similarity. ACM Trans. Knowl. Discov. Data 2, 10:1–10:25 (2008)
7. Milne, D., Witten, I.H.: An effective, low-cost measure of semantic relatedness obtained from wikipedia links. In: Proceedings of the First AAAI Workshop on Wikipedia and Artificial Intelligence, WIKIAI 2008, pp. 25–30 (2008)
8. Ramos, J.: Using tf-idf to determine word relevance in document queries. Department of Computer Science, Rutgers University, Piscataway, NJ (2003)
9. Navarro, G.: A guided tour to approximate string matching. ACM Comput. Surv. 33, 31–88 (2001)
10. Gabrilovich, E., Markovitch, S.: Computing semantic relatedness using wikipedia-based explicit semantic analysis. In: Proceedings of the 20th International Joint Conference on Artifical Intelligence, IJCAI 2007, pp. 1606–1611. Morgan Kaufmann Publishers Inc., San Francisco (2007)
11. Nakayama, K., Hara, T., Nishio, S.: Wikipedia link structure and text mining for semantic relation extraction. In: Workshop on Semantic Search (SemSearch 2008) at the 5th European Semantic Web Conference (ESWC 2008), pp. 59–73 (2008)
12. Shvaiko, P., Giunchiglia, F., da Silva, P.P., McGuinness, D.L.: Web Explanations for Semantic Heterogeneity Discovery. In: Gómez-Pérez, A., Euzenat, J. (eds.) ESWC 2005. LNCS, vol. 3532, pp. 303–317. Springer, Heidelberg (2005)
13. Dhamankar, R., Lee, Y., Doan, A., Halevy, A., Domingos, P.: imap: discovering complex semantic matches between database schemas. In: Proceedings of the 2004 ACM SIGMOD International Conference on Management of Data, pp. 383–394. ACM (2004)
14. Chai, X., Sayyadian, M., Doan, A., Rosenthal, A., Seligman, L.: Analyzing and revising data integration schemas to improve their matchability. Proceedings of the VLDB Endowment 1, 773–784 (2008)
15. Noy, N.F., Griffith, N., Musen, M.A.: Collecting Community-Based Mappings in an Ontology Repository. In: Sheth, A.P., Staab, S., Dean, M., Paolucci, M., Maynard, D., Finin, T., Thirunarayan, K. (eds.) ISWC 2008. LNCS, vol. 5318, pp. 371–386. Springer, Heidelberg (2008)
16. Shvaiko, P., Euzenat, J.: Ten Challenges for Ontology Matching. In: Meersman, R., Tari, Z. (eds.) OTM 2008, Part II. LNCS, vol. 5332, pp. 1164–1182. Springer, Heidelberg (2008)

17. Bernstein, P., Melnik, S.: Model management 2.0: manipulating richer mappings. In: Proceedings of the 2007 ACM SIGMOD International Conference on Management of Data, pp. 1–12. ACM (2007)
18. Finkelstein, L., Gabrilovich, E., Matias, Y., Rivlin, E., Solan, Z., Wolfman, G., Ruppin, E.: Placing search in context: the concept revisited. ACM Trans. Inf. Syst. 20, 116–131 (2002)
19. Rodgers, J.L., Nicewander, W.A.: Thirteen ways to look at the correlation coefficient. The American Statistician 42, 59–66 (1988)
20. Dillman, D.A., Bowker, D.K.: The Web Questionnaire Challenge to Survey Methodologists, pp. 159–178. Pabst Science Publishers (2001)
21. Martin, R.C., Bolter, J.F., Todd, M.E., Gouvier, W.D., Niccolls, R.: Effects of sophistication and motivation on the detection of malingered memory performance using a computerized forced-choice task. Journal of Clinical and Experimental Neuropsychology 15, 867–880 (1993)
22. Smyth, J.D., Dillman, D.A., Christian, L.M., Stern, M.J.: Comparing check-all and forced-choice question formats in web surveys. Public Opinion Quarterly 70, 66–77 (2006)

Growing Hierarchical Self-organizing Maps and Statistical Distribution Models for Online Detection of Web Attacks

Mikhail Zolotukhin, Timo Hämäläinen, and Antti Juvonen

Department of Mathematical Information Technology,
University of Jyväskylä, Jyväskylä, FI-40014, Finland
{mikhail.m.zolotukhin,timo.t.hamalainen,antti.k.a.juvonen}@jyu.fi
https://www.jyu.fi/it/laitokset/mit/en/

Abstract. In modern networks, HTTP clients communicate with web servers using request messages. By manipulating these messages attackers can collect confidential information from servers or even corrupt them. In this study, the approach based on anomaly detection is considered to find such attacks. For HTTP queries, feature matrices are obtained by applying an n-gram model, and, by learning on the basis of these matrices, growing hierarchical self-organizing maps are constructed. For HTTP headers, we employ statistical distribution models based on the lengths of header values and relative frequency of symbols. New requests received by the web-server are classified by using the maps and models obtained in the training stage. The technique proposed allows detecting online HTTP attacks in the case of continuous updated web-applications. The algorithm proposed is tested using logs, which were acquired from a large real-life web service and included normal and intrusive requests. As a result, almost all attacks from these logs are detected, and the number of false alarms remains very low.

Keywords: Intrusion detection, Anomaly detection, n-Gram, Growing hierarchical self-organizing map, Single-linkage clustering.

1 Introduction

In modern society, the use of computer technologies, both for work and personal use, is growing with time. Unfortunately, computer networks and systems are often vulnerable to various forms of intrusions. Such intrusions are executed manually by a person or automatically with engineered software and can use legitimate system features as well as programming mistakes or system misconfigurations [1]. That is why computer security becomes one of the most important issues when designing computer networks and systems.

Some of the most popular attack targets are web-servers and web-based applications. Since web-servers are usually accessible through corporate firewalls and web-based applications are often developed without following security rules, attacks which exploit web-servers or server extensions give rise to a significant portion of the total number of vulnerabilities. Usually, the users of web-servers and web-based applications request and send information using queries, which in HTTP traffic are strings containing a set

J. Cordeiro and K.-H. Krempels (Eds.): WEBIST 2012, LNBIP 140, pp. 281–295, 2013.

of parameters having some values. It is possible to manipulate these queries to create requests which can corrupt the server or collect confidential information [2]. In addition, a HTTP request message contains header fields, which define the operating parameters of an HTTP transaction. Such fields usually contain information about user agent, preferred response languages, connection type, referer, etc. The attacker can inject malicious code to these fields to construct various kinds of attacks based on HTTP response splitting or malicious redirecting [25].

One way to ensure the security of web-servers and web-based applications is to use Intrusion Detection Systems (IDS). As a rule, IDS gathers data from the system under inspection, stores this data to logfiles, analyzes the logfiles to detect suspicious activities and determines suitable responses to these activities [3]. There are many different IDS architectures, which continue to evolve with time [4,5]. IDSs can also differ in audit source location, detection method, behaviour on detection, usage frequency, etc.

There are two basic approaches for detecting intrusions from the network data: misuse detection and anomaly detection [6,7]. In the misuse detection approach, the IDS scans the computer system for predefined attack signatures. This approach is usually accurate, which makes it successful in commercial intrusion detection [7]. However, the misuse detection approach cannot detect attacks for which it has not been programmed, and, therefore, it is likely to ignore all new types of attack if the system is not kept up to date with the latest intrusions. The anomaly detection approach learns the features of event patterns which form normal behaviour, and, by observing patterns that deviate from the established norms (anomalies), detects when an intrusion has occurred. Thus, systems which use the anomaly detection approach are modelled according to normal behaviour and, therefore, are able to detect zero-day attacks. However, the number of false alerts will probably be increased because not all anomalies are intrusions.

To solve the problem of anomaly detection, different kinds of machine learning based techniques can be applied, for example Decision Trees (DTs), Artificial Neural Networks (ANNs), Support Vector Machines (SVMs). As a rule, anomaly detection IDSs for web-servers are based on supervised learning, which trains the system by using a set of normal queries. On the other hand, unsupervised anomaly detection techniques do not need normal training data, and therefore such techniques are the most usable.

To find code injections in HTTP headers, we apply statistical distribution models based on the length of header values and relative frequency of non-alphanumeric symbols, whereas, to detect intrusive HTTP queries, the approach based on Growing Hierarchical Self-Organizing Maps (GHSOMs) is employed. For analyzing and visualizing high dimensional data, a regular Self-Organizing Map (SOM) based on the unsupervised learning neural network model proposed by Kohonen can be used [9]. SOMs are able to discover knowledge in a data base, extract relevant information, detect inherent structures in high-dimensional data and map these data into a two-dimensional representation space [8]. Despite the fact that the approach based on self-organizing maps has shown effectiveness at detecting intrusions [10,11], it has two main drawbacks: the static architecture and the lack of representation of hierarchical relations. A Growing Hierarchical SOM (GHSOM) can solve these difficulties [12]. This neural network consists of several SOMs structured in layers, the number of neurons, maps and layers being determined during the unsupervised learning process. Thus, the structure of the GHSOM is automatically adapted according to the structure of the data.

The GHSOM approach looks promising for solving the problem of detecting network intrusions. In [13], a GHSOM model with a metric which combines both numerical and symbolic data is proposed for detecting network intrusions. An IDS based on this model detects anomalies by classifying IP connections into normal or anomalous connection records, and, if they are anomalies, into the type of attack. An adaptive GHSOM-based approach is proposed in [14]. The suggested GHSOM adapts online to changes in the input data over time by using the following enhancements: enhanced threshold-based training, dynamic input normalization, feedback-based quantization-error threshold adaptation and prediction confidence filtering and forwarding. The study in [15] investigates applying GHSOM for filtering intrusion detection alarms. GHSOM clusters these alarms in a way that helps network administrators to make decisions about true or false alarms.

In this research, we aim to detect anomalous HTTP request messages by applying an approach that is based on adaptive growing hierarchical self-organizing maps and statistical distribution models. The remainder of this paper is organized as follows: Section 2 describes the process of data acquisition and feature extraction from network logs; in Section 3 we show how to apply adaptive GHSOM and statistical distribution models for detecting anomalies; experimental results are presented in Section 4; and Section 5 concludes this paper.

2 Data Model

Let us consider some network activity logs of a large web-service of some HTTP server. Such log-files can include information about the user's IP address, time and time zone, the HTTP request, which includes the resource and parameters used, the server's response code, the amount of data sent to the user, and the web-page which was requested and used by a browser software. Here is an example of a single line from an Apache server log file. This information is stored in a combined log format [24]:

```
127.0.0.1 - frank [10/Oct/2000:13:55:36 -0700]
"GET /resource?parameter1=value1&parameter2=
value2 HTTP/1.0"
200 2326 "http://www.example.com/start.html"
"Mozilla/4.08 [en] (Win98; I ;Nav)"
```

Here the focus is on analysis of HTTP header fields and HTTP queries, which are strings containing a set of attributes having some values. We do not focus on static HTTP queries because they do not contain any parameters. It is not possible to inject code via static requests unless there are major deficiencies in the HTTP server itself. Dynamic queries, which are handled by the web applications of the service, are more interesting for this study, because all static queries are normal. Let us assume that most request messages which are coming to the HTTP server are normal, i.e. they use legitimate features of the service, but some obtained requests are intrusions. All HTTP requests are analyzed to detect the anomalous ones.

A HTTP query can be expressed as a composition of the path to the desired web resource and a string which is used to pass parameters to the referenced resource and identified by a leading '?' character. To extract features from each query, an n-gram model is applied. N-gram models are widely used in statistical natural language processing [16] and speech recognition [17]. An n-gram is a sub-sequence of n overlapping items (characters, letters, words, etc) from a given sequence. For example, a 2-gram character model for the string '/resource?parameter1=value1&parameter2=value2' is '/r', 're', 'es', 'so', 'ou', 'ur', ..., 'lu', 'ue', 'e2'.

An n-gram character model is applied to transform each HTTP query to a sequence of n characters. Such sequences are used to construct an n-gram frequency vector, which expresses the frequency of every n-character in the analyzed request. To obtain this vector, ASCII codes of characters are used to represent the sequence of n-characters as a sequence of arrays, each of which contains n decimal ASCII codes, and the frequency vector is built by counting the number of occurrences of each such array in the analyzed request. The length of the frequency vector is 256^n because every byte can be represented by an ASCII value between 0 and 255. For example, in the previous example the following sequence of decimal ASCII pairs can be obtained: $[47, 114]$, $[114, 101]$, $[101, 115]$, $[115, 111]$, $[111, 117]$, $[117, 114]$, ..., $[108, 117]$, $[117, 101]$, $[101, 50]$. The corresponding 256^2 vector is built by counting the number of occurrences of each such pair. For example, the entry in location $(256 \times 61 + 118)$ in this vector contains a value equal to 2 since the pair $[61, 118]$, which corresponds to pair '=v' can be seen twice. Thus, each HTTP query is transformed into a 256^n numeric vector. The matrix consisting of these vectors is called the feature matrix and it can be analyzed to find anomalies.

To extract features from HTTP headers, the lengths of header values and all non alphanumeric symbols used are counted and stored separately for different HTTP header types. These vectors of length and sets of non-alphanumeric symbols can be used to train the system and find code injections in the header fields of HTTP request messages.

3   Method

The algorithm proposed can be considered as a set of two classifiers. The first of these is based on transforming the query strings into numeric vectors by applying an n-gram model, and constructing and training GHSOMs using the feature matrices obtained. The second one analyzes HTTP headers and searches for code injections using statistical distribution models based on the length of header values and relative frequency of non-alphanumeric symbols. If a request is defined as anomalous at least by one of these classifiers then this request is classified as an intrusion.

3.1   Detecting Anomalous HTTP Query Strings

In this study, adaptive growing hierarchical self-organizing maps are used to find anomalous HTTP queries. A self-organizing map is an unsupervised, competitive learning algorithm that reduces the dimensions of data by mapping these data onto a set of units set up in a much lower dimensional space. This algorithm allows not only to compress high dimensional data but also to create a network that stores information in such a way that any topological relationships within the data set are maintained. Due to this, SOMs are widely applied for visualizing low-dimensional views of high-dimensional data.

SOM is formed from a regular grid of neurones, each of which is fully connected to the input layer. The neurons are connected to adjacent neurons by a neighbourhood relation dictating the structure of the map. Associated with the i-th neuron of the SOM is a d-dimensional prototype (weight) vector $w_i = [w_{i1}, w_{i2}, \ldots, w_{id}]$, where d is equal to the dimension of the input vectors. Each neuron has two positions: one in the input space (the prototype vector) and the other one in the output space (on the map grid). Thus, SOM is a vector-projection method defining a nonlinear projection from the input space to a lower-dimensional output space. During the training, the prototype vectors move so that they follow the probability density of the input data.

SOMs learn to classify data without supervision. At the beginning of learning, the number of neurons, the dimensions of the map grid, the map lattice and the shape should be determined. Before the training, initial values are given to the prototype vectors. A SOM is very robust with respect to the initialization, but properly accomplished initialization allows the algorithm to converge faster to a good solution. At each training step t, one sample vector $x(t)$ from the input data set is chosen randomly and a similarity measure (distance) is calculated between it and all the weight vectors $w_i(t)$ of the map. The unit having the shortest distance to the input vector is identified as the best matching unit (BMU) for input $x(t)$. The index $c(t)$ of this best matching unit is identified. Next, the input is mapped to the location of the best matching unit, and the prototype vectors of the SOM are updated so that the vector of the BMU and its topological neighbours are moved closer to the input vector in the input space:

$$w_i(t+1) = w_i(t) + \delta(t)N_{i,c(t)}(r(t))\left(x(t) - w_i(t)\right), \tag{1}$$

where $\delta(t)$ is the learning rate function and $N_{i,c(t)}(r(t))$ is the neighbourhood kernel around the winner unit, which depends on the neighbourhood radius $r(t)$ and the distance between the BMU having index $c(t)$ and the i-th neuron.

The most important feature of the Kohonen learning algorithm is that the area of the neighbourhood shrinks over time. In addition, the effect of learning is proportional to the distance of the node from the BMU. As a rule, the amount of learning fades over distance, and, at the edges of the BMUs neighbourhood, the learning process has barely any effect.

The SOM has shown to be successful for the analysis of high-dimensional data in data mining applications such as those used for network security. However, the effectiveness of using traditional SOM models is limited by the static nature of the model architecture. The size and dimensionality of the SOM model is fixed prior to the training process, and there is no systematic method for identifying an optimal configuration. Another disadvantage of the fixed grid in SOM is that traditional SOM can not represent hierarchical relations that might be present in the data.

The limitations mentioned above can be resolved by applying growing hierarchical self-organizing maps. GHSOM has been developed as a multi-layered hierarchical architecture which adapts its structure to the input data. It is initialized with one SOM and grows in size until it achieves an improvement in the quality its representation of data. In addition, each node in this map can be dynamically expanded down the hierarchy by adding a new map at a lower layer for a further-detailed representation of data. The procedure of growth can be repeated in these new maps. Thus, the GHSOM architecture is adaptive and can represent data clearly by allocating extra space as well as uncover the hierarchical structure in the data.

The GHSOM architecture starts with the main node at the zero layer and a 2×2 map at the first layer trained according to the SOM training algorithm. The main node represents a complete data set X, and its weight vector w_0 is calculated as the mean value of all data inputs. This node controls the growth of the SOM at the first layer and the hierarchical growth of the whole GHSOM. The growth of the map at the first layer and the maps at the next layers are controlled with the help of quantization error. This error for the i-th node is calculated as follows

$$e_i = \sum_{x_j \in C_i} ||w_i - x_j||, \tag{2}$$

where C_i is the set of input vectors x_j projected to the i-th node and w_i is the weight vector of the i-th node. The quantization error E_m of map m is defined as

$$E_m = \frac{1}{|U_m|} \sum_{i \in U_m} e_i, \tag{3}$$

where U_m is the subset of the m-th map nodes onto which the data is mapped, and $|U_m|$ is the number of these nodes of the m-th map.

When E_m reaches certain fraction α_1 of the e_u of the corresponding parent unit u in the upper layer, the growing process is stopped. The parent node of the SOM at the first layer is the main node. The parameter α_1 controls the breadth of maps, and its value ranges from 0 to 1. After that, the most dissimilar neighbouring node s is selected according to

$$s = \max_j(||w_e - w_j||), \text{ for } w_j \in N_e, \tag{4}$$

where w_j is the weight vector of the error node, N_e is the set of neighbouring nodes of the e-th node, and w_i is the weight vector of the neighbouring node in set N_e. A new row or column of nodes is placed in between the nodes e and s. The weight vectors of the newly added nodes are initialized with the mean of their corresponding neighbours.

After the growth process of the SOM is completed, every node of this SOM has to be checked for satisfying of the global stopping criterion [12]:

$$e_i < \alpha_2 e_0, \tag{5}$$

where $\alpha_2 \in (0, 1)$ is the parameter which controls the hierarchical growth of GHSOM, and e_0 is the quantization error of the main node, which can be found as follows:

$$e_0 = \sum_{x_j \in X} ||w_0 - x_j||. \tag{6}$$

The nodes not satisfying this criterion (5), and therefore representing a set of too diverse input vectors, are expanded to form a new map at the subsequent layer of the hierarchy.

Similarly to the creation of the first layer SOM, a new map of initially 2×2 nodes is created. This maps weight vectors are initialized to mirror the orientation of the neighbouring units of its parent. For this reason, we can choose to set four new nodes to the means of the parent and its neighbours in the respective directions [18]. The newly added map is trained by using the input vectors which are mapped onto the node just expanded, i.e., the subset of the data space mapped onto its parent. This new map will again continue to grow, and the whole process is repeated for the subsequent layers until the global stopping criterion given in (5) is met by all nodes. Thus, an ideal topology of a GHSOM is formed unsupervised and based on the input data, and hierarchal relationships in the data are discovered.

The anomaly detection algorithm which is proposed in this study is based on the use of GHSOM. The algorithm consists of three main stages: training, detecting and updating. In the training phase, server logs are used to obtain a training set. The logs can contain several thousands of HTTP requests, which are gathered from various web-resources during several days or weeks. These logs can include unknown anomalies and real attacks. The only condition is that the quantity of normal requests in the logs used must be significantly greater than the number of real intrusions and anomalous requests. HTTP queries from these logs are transformed to a feature matrix by applying an n-gram model.

When the feature matrix is obtained, a new GHSOM is constructed and trained based on this matrix. The zero layer of this GHSOM is formed by several independent nodes, the number of which corresponds to the number of different resources of the web-server. For each such node, a SOM is created and initialized with four nodes. Requests to one web-resource are mapped to the corresponding parent node on the zero layer and used for training the corresponding SOM. These SOMs form the first layer, and each of these maps can grow in size by adding new rows and columns or by adding a new map of four nodes at a lower layer, thus providing a further detailed representation of data. For each parent node on the zero layer, the quantization error which controls the growing process of the maps on the first layer is calculated and the GHSOM is hierarchically grown.

The aim is not to find intrusions in the logs which were used as the training set but to detect attacks among new requests received by the web-server. Each new query is transformed to a frequency vector by applying the n-gram model. After that, this vector goes to one of the parent node according to its resource and is mapped to one of the nodes on the corresponding map by calculating the best matching unit for this query. To determine whether the new request is an attack or not, the following two criteria are used:

- If the distance between a new request and its BMU weight vector is greater than the threshold value, then this request is an intrusion, otherwise it is classified as normal;
- If the node which is the BMU for the new request is classified as an "anomalous" node, then this request is an intrusion, otherwise it is classified as normal.

The threshold for the first criterion is calculated based on the distances between the weight vector of the node, which is the BMU for the new query, and other queries from the server logs already mapped to this node at the training stage. Assume that the new query is mapped to the node which already contains l other queries mapped to this node during the training phase. Denote the distances between the node and these l queries as $e_1, e_2, \ldots, e_l$. Let us assume that the values of these distances are distributed more or less uniformly. In this case, we can estimate maximum τ of continuous uniformly distributed variable as follows [19]:

$$\tau = \frac{l+1}{l} \max_l \{e_1, e_2, \ldots, e_l\}. \tag{7}$$

Obtained value τ can be used as the threshold value for the node considered, and a new request message is classified as an intrusion if the distance between its query and the node is greater than τ.

To find "anomalous" nodes, a U^*-matrix [20] is calculated for each SOM. U^*-matrix presents a combined visualization of the distance relationships and density structures of a high dimensional data space. This matrix has the same size as the grid of the corresponding SOM and can be calculated based on U-matrix and P-matrix.

U-matrix represents distance relationships of queries mapped to a SOM [21]. The value of the i-th element of an U-matrix is the average distance of the i-th node weight vector w_i to the weight vectors of its immediate neighbours. Thus, the i-th element of the U-matrix $U(i)$ is calculated as follows:

$$U(i) = \frac{1}{n_i} \sum_{j \in N_i} D(w_i, w_j), \tag{8}$$

where $n_i = |N_i|$ is the number of nodes in the neighbourhood N_i of the i-th node, and D is a distance function, which for example can be Euclidean distance. A single element of U-matrix shows the local distance structure. If a global view of a U-matrix is considered then the overall structure of densities can be analyzed.

P-matrix allows a visualization of density structures of the high dimensional data space [22]. The i-th element of P-matrix is a measure of the density of data points in the vicinity of the weight vector of the i-th node:

$$P(i) = |\{x \in X | D(x, w_i) < r\}|, \tag{9}$$

where X is the set of queries mapped to the SOM considered and radius r is some positive real number. A display of all P-matrix elements on top of the SOM grid is called a P-matrix. In fact, the value of $P(i)$ is the number of data points within a hypersphere of radius r. The radius r should be chosen such that $P(i)$ approximates the probability density function of the data points. This radius can be found as the Pareto radius [23]:

$$r = \frac{1}{2} \chi_d^2(p_u), \tag{10}$$

where χ_d^2 is the Chi-square cumulative distribution function for d degrees of freedom and $p_u = 20.13\%$ of the number of requests contained in the data set X. The only condition is that all points in X must follow a multivariate mutual independent Gaussian standard normal density distribution (MMI). It can be enforced by different preprocessing methods such as the principal component analysis, standardization and other transformations.

The U^*-matrix which is the combination of a U-matrix and a P-matrix combines distance relationships with density relationships and can give an appropriate clustering. The i-th element of the U^*-matrix is equal to $U(i)$ multiplied with the probability that the local density, which is measured by $P(i)$, is low. Thus $U^*(i)$ can be calculated as follows:

$$U^*(i) = U(i)\frac{|p \in P|p > P(i)|}{|p \in P|},\tag{11}$$

i.e. if the local data density is low, $U^*(i) \approx U(i)$ (this happens at the presumed border of clusters), and, if the data density is high, then $U^*(i) \approx 0$ (this is in the central regions of clusters). We can also adjust the multiplication factor such that $U^*(i) = 0$ for the p_{high} percent of the P-matrix elements which have greatest values.

Since we assumed that most of the requests are normal, intrusions can not form big clusters but will be mapped to nodes which are located on cluster borders. Thus, "anomalous" nodes are those which correspond to high values of U^*-matrix elements. In this research, the following criterion for finding anomalous nodes is used: if the difference between $U^*(i)$ and $U^*_{average}(i)$ (average value of all elements of U^*-matrix) is greater than difference between the $U^*_{average}(i)$ and minimal value of U^*-matrix, then the i-th neuron is classified as "anomalous", otherwise this neuron is classified as "normal". If a node of a GHSOM is classified as "normal" but has a child SOM, then all the nodes of this child SOM should also be also checked by calculating new U^*-matrix for this SOM to find out whether they are "normal" or "anomalous".

Web-applications are highly dynamic and change on a regular basis, which can cause noticeable changes in the HTTP requests which are sent to the web-server. This can lead to a situation where all new allowable requests will be classified as intrusions. For this reason, the GHSOM should be retrained after a certain period of time T to be capable of classifying new requests.

Let us assume that the number of requests sent to the web-server for this period T is much less than number of requests in the training set. We update the training set by replacing the first requests from this set by requests obtained during the period T. After that, the GHSOM is retrained by using the resulting training set. During the update phase the structure of the GHSOM can be modified. The update of the GHSOM structure starts from the current structure. Parameters τ and matrices U, P and U^* should be recalculated. The update phase can occur independently from the anomaly detection. During retraining, requests obtained are classified using the old GHSOM, and, once the GHSOM retraining is completed, the classification of new requests continues with the updated GHSOM.

Countermeasures are necessary against attackers who try to affect the training set by flooding the web-server with a large number of intrusions. It can be enforced for example by allowing a client (one IP address) to replace a configurable number of HTTP requests in the training set per time slot. In order to address the threat of botnets, it is also possible to restrict the globally allowed replacements per time slot independent of the IP addresses.

3.2 Detecting Anomalous HTTP Headers

Usually header fields have a finite set of possible values, therefore to solve the problem of finding anomalous headers it is reasonable to apply simple statistical distribution models. In this research, we analyze the lengths of header fields and non-alphanumeric symbols used in them [26]. All different header types are supposed to be analyzed separately. Similarly to the previous scheme, for the second classifier we define three stages: training, detecting and updating.

In the training stage, headers of the request messages which have been employed for constructing GHSOMs are used. For each header type, we construct the vector of its lengths $(l_1, l_2, \ldots, l_M)$. Since we assume that some HTTP requests from the training set can be attacks, some filtering can be applied to remove outliers and build the pattern of normal user behaviour. As proposed in study [26], we define the following distance function: $d(l_i, l_j) = p(l_i \text{ is normal}) - p(l_j \text{ is normal})$, where $p(x \text{ is normal})$ is the probability that length x is normal and can be found as follows:

$$p(x \text{ is normal}) = \begin{cases} \frac{\sigma^2}{(x-\mu)^2}, & \text{if } x \geq \mu + \sigma, \\ 1, & \text{if } x < \mu + \sigma, \end{cases} \tag{12}$$

where μ and σ^2 are the mean and the variance, respectively. In this case, the distance d between a normal pattern and an outlier pattern is expected to be higher than the distance d between two normal patterns or two outlier patterns. Thus, it is easy to divide all the lengths into two clusters, i.e. normal lengths and outliers, by using a simple clustering algorithm, e.g. a single-linkage clustering [27]. All outliers are removed from the model and all normal lengths are used for detecting anomalies. For header type k we denote the cluster of normal lengths as L_k^n and the number of entries contained in this cluster as $|L_k^n|$.

In addition, during training all non-alphanumeric symbols are counted for each header type. The distance function between the different symbols s_i and s_j is defined as $d(s_i, s_j) = p(s_i \text{ is normal}) - p(s_j \text{ is normal})$ where $p(x \text{ is normal})$ is the probability that symbol x is legitimate and can be found as the relative frequency of symbol x in the training set:

$$p(x \text{ is normal}) = \frac{N_x}{N}, \tag{13}$$

where N_x is the number of appearances of non-alphanumeric symbol x in the training set and N is the total number of non-alphanumeric symbols there. Similarly to the previous model, all outliers can be removed by applying a single-linkage clustering, where the distance between two symbols is defined as $d(s_i, s_j)$ and the number of clusters is two. All the remaining non-alphanumeric symbols are considered as legitimate to use. Let us denote the set of legitimate symbols for header type k as S_k^l.

In the detecting stage, the following criterion is used to find anomalous requests. Let a new request message received by the web server contain the following header fields $\{h_1, h_2, \ldots\}$. If for any header value h_k of this request at least one of the following conditions:

1. length of $h_k > \frac{|L_k^n|+1}{|L_k^n|} \cdot \max(L_k^n)$, where $\max(L_k^n)$ is maximal element of L_k^n,

2. $\exists$ non-alphanumeric symbol $s \in h_k : s \notin S_k^l$.

is satisfied, then this new request message is classified as an intrusion, otherwise it is legitimate.

Similarly to the first part of the algorithm, all these criteria are supposed to be updated with time. We update the training set by replacing the first requests from this set by requests obtained during the period T. For the updated training set for each header type we find a new cluster of normal lengths, recalculate the threshold value, and update the set of legitimate non-alphanumeric symbols. Just as in the case for detecting anomalous HTTP queries, countermeasures against attackers trying to affect the training set by flooding the web server with a large number of intrusions are supposed to be applied here also.

4 Simulation Results

The proposed method is tested using logs acquired from a large real-life web service. These logs contain mostly normal traffic, but they also include anomalies and actual intrusions. The logfiles are acquired from several Apache servers and stored in a combined log format. The logs contain requests from multiple web-resources. Since it is not possible to inject code via static query strings unless there are major deficiencies in the HTTP server, HTTP query strings without parameters are considered as normal.

In our simulation, request messages to twenty-five most popular web resources of the server are analyzed. The training set is created at the beginning and it contains 20000 requests. By using this training set, twenty five GHSOMs are trained (one for each web resource) based on dynamic query strings and for each header type the cluster of legitimate lengths as well as the set of legitimate non-alphanumeric symbols are formed. New requests are chosen from logfiles and classified one by one to test the technique proposed. The number of requests in the testing set is equal to 100000 and 9679 of them are attacks. During the testing stage, the system is updated after each processing of 5000 requests.

To evaluate the performance of the proposed technique, the following characteristics are calculated in our test:

- True positive rate: the ratio of the number of correctly detected intrusions to the total number of intrusions in the testing set;
- False positive rate: the ratio of the number of normal requests classified as intrusions to the total number of normal requests in the testing set;
- True negative rate: the ratio of the number of correctly detected normal requests to the total number of normal requests in the testing set;
- False negative rate: the ratio of the number of intrusions classified as normal requests to the total number of intrusions in the testing set;
- Accuracy: the ratio of the total number of correctly detected requests to the total number of requests in the testing set;
- Precision: the ratio of the number of correctly detected intrusions to the number of requests classified as intrusions.

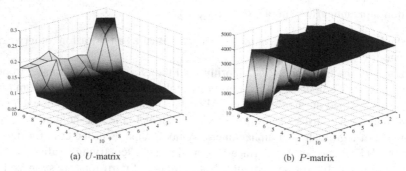

(a) U-matrix   (b) P-matrix

Fig. 1. U-matrix and P-matrix after the training stage

Let us consider one of the web resources, which allows users to search a project by choosing the appropriate category of the projects or initial symbols of the project name. Thus, query strings of all those HTTP requests have one of the two different attributes which can be used by attackers to inject malignant code. When the GHSOM training is completed, U-matrix, P-matrix and U^*-matrix are constructed. In Figure 1, U-matrix and P-matrix are shown. As one can see, some nodes on one of the map edges are distant from all others (Figure 1 (a)), and at the same time the density of data inputs in these nodes is very low (Figure 1 (b)). These facts make these nodes candidates to "anomalous" ones.

The U^*-matrix for this GHSOM is plotted in Figure 2. We can notice that there are two big clusters corresponding to the queries in which different methods of searching a required project are used: by specifying the project category or the initial symbols of project name. The nodes on one of the map edges are classified as "anomalous". The technique proposed does not allow us to define the intrusion types, but we can check manually the nodes which have been classified as "anomalous" and make sure that requests mapped to those nodes are real intrusions: SQL injections, buffer overflow attacks and directory traversal attacks, as shown in Figure 2.

After constructing the U^*-matrix and building statistical distribution models for each header type, the detection process is started. Query strings of new requests are mapped to the GHSOM one by one and classified as intrusions if the distance between a new request and its BMU weight vector is greater than the threshold value or if the node which is the BMU for this new request is anomalous. In addition, the lengths of header fields and non-alphanumeric symbols used in them are checked according to the scheme proposed.

During the detection phase, the system is retrained periodically when a certain number of requests are processed. After the system update, all threshold values, GHSOMs and statistical distribution models are modified to allow detection of new request messages.

the results of the detection phase are shown in Table 1. As one can see, almost all real attacks are correctly classified as intrusions by using the proposed technique. At the same time, the false positive rate is about zero on average, which means that the number of false alarms is very low. The accuracy of the method is close to one hundred percent.

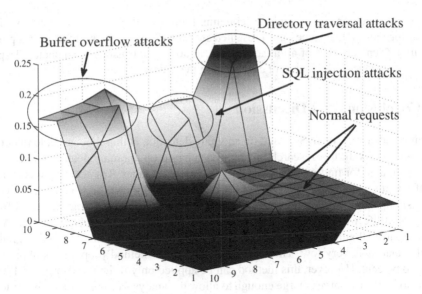

Fig. 2. U^*-matrix after the training stage

Table 1. Performance metrics values

True positive rate	False positive rate	True negative rate	False negative rate	Accuracy	Precision
99.56 %	0.00 %	100.00 %	0.44 %	99.96 %	100.00 %

Table 2. The simulation results for different types of attacks

Attack type	Total number of attacks	Number of detected attacks	Proportion of detected attacks
SQL injection	484	484	100 %
Directory traversal	488	469	96.11 %
Buffer overflow	488	486	99.59 %
Cross-site scripting	1011	1011	100 %
Double encoding	471	471	100 %
Common gateway interface scripting	401	392	97.76 %
Shell scripting	114	112	98.25 %
XPath injection	510	510	100 %
HTTP response splitting	2530	2529	99.96 %
Cache poisoning	117	117	100 %
Eval injection	377	369	97.88 %
String formatting	238	238	100 %
Cross-User defacement	246	246	100 %
Session fixation	2204	2204	100 %
Total	9679	9638	99.57 %

In our simulation, the testing set contains fourteen different types of attack. The results for these attack types are presented in Table 2. We can see that the proposed algorithm found 99.57% of all attacks. Thus, almost all intrusions are detected despite the fact that some of them are not contained in the training set.

5   Conclusions and Discussion

The main advantage of IDSs based on anomaly detection is that they are able to detect zero-day attacks. In this research, the approach based on anomaly detection is considered as suitable for finding intrusive HTTP request messages. The technique proposed is self-adaptive and allows detection of HTTP attacks in online mode in the case of continuously updated web-applications. The method was tested using logs acquired from a large real-life web-service. These logs include normal and intrusive requests. As a result, almost all attacks from these logs are detected and at the same time the number of false alarms is very low. Thus, the accuracy of the method proposed is about one hundred percent. However, this method can be applied only if the number of HTTP requests to a web-resource is large enough to allow the analysis of normal user behaviour. Sometimes, attackers try to access the data stored on servers or to harm the system by using holes in the security of less popular web-resources, for which it is difficult to define which requests are "normal". In the future, we are planning to develop an anomaly detection based system which can solve this problem.

References

1. Mukkamala, S., Sung, A.: A comparative study of techniques for intrusion detection. In: Proc. 15th IEEE International Conference on Tools with Artificial Intelligence, pp. 570–577 (November 2003)
2. Nguyen-Tuong, A., Guarnieri, S., Greene, D., Shirley, J., Evans, D.: Automatically Hardening Web Applications Using Precise Tainting. In: Sasaki, R., Qing, S., Okamoto, E., Yoshiura, H. (eds.) Security and Privacy in the Age of Ubiquitous Computing. IFIP AICT, vol. 181, pp. 295–307. Springer, Boston (2005)
3. Axelsson, S.: Research in intrusion-detection systems: a survey. Department of Computer Engineering, Chalmers University of Technology, Goteborg, Sweden, Technical Report, pp. 98–117 (December 1998)
4. Patcha, A., Park, J.M.: An overview of anomaly detection techniques: Existing solutions and latest technological trends. Computer Networks: The International Journal of Computer and Telecommunications Networking 51(12) (August 2007)
5. Verwoerd, T., Hunt, R.: Intrusion detection techniques and approaches. Computer Communications - COMCOM 25(15), 1356–1365 (2002)
6. Kemmerer, R.A., Vigna, G.: Intrusion Detection: A Brief History and Overview. Computer 35, 27–30 (2002)
7. Gollmann, D.: Computer Security, 2nd edn. Wiley (2006)
8. Kohonen, T.: Self-organizing map, 3rd edn. Springer, Berlin (2001)
9. Kohonen, T.: Self-organized formation of topologically correct feature maps. Biological Cybernetics 43(1), 59–69 (1982)
10. Kayacik, H.G., Nur, Z.-H., Heywood, M.I.: A hierarchical SOM-based intrusion detection system. Engineering Applications of Artificial Intelligence 20 (2007)

11. Jiang, D., Yang, Y., Xia, M.: Research on Intrusion Detection Based on an Improved SOM Neural Network. In: Proc. of the Fifth Intl Conference on Information Assurance and Security (2009)
12. Rauber, A., Merkl, D., Dittenbach, M.: The growing hierarchical self-organizing map: exploratory analysis of high-dimensional data. IEEE Transactions on Neural Networks 13(6), 1331–1341 (2002)
13. Palomo, E.J., Domínguez, E., Luque, R.M., Muñoz, J.: A New GHSOM Model Applied to Network Security. In: Kůrková, V., Neruda, R., Koutník, J. (eds.) ICANN 2008, Part I. LNCS, vol. 5163, pp. 680–689. Springer, Heidelberg (2008)
14. Ippoliti, D., Xiaobo, Z.: An Adaptive Growing Hierarchical Self Organizing Map for Network Intrusion Detection. In: Proc. 19th IEEE International Conference on Computer Communications and Networks (ICCCN), pp. 1–7 (August 2010)
15. Shehab, M., Mansour, N., Faour, A.: Growing Hierarchical Self-Organizing Map for Filtering Intrusion Detection Alarms. In: International Symposium on Parallel Architectures, Algorithms, and Networks, I-SPAN 2008, pp. 167–172 (May 2008)
16. Suen, C.Y.: n-Gram Statistics for Natural Language Understanding and Text Processing. IEEE Transactions on Pattern Analysis and Machine Intelligence PAMI-1(2), 164–172 (1979)
17. Hirsimaki, T., Pylkkonen, J., Kurimo, M.: Importance of High-Order N-Gram Models in Morph-Based Speech Recognition. IEEE Transactions on Audio, Speech, and Language Processing 17(4), 724–732 (2009)
18. Chan, A., Pampalk, E.: Growing hierarchical self organising map (ghsom) toolbox: visualisations and enhancements. In: 9th Int'l Conference Neural Information Processing, ICONIP 2002, vol. 5, pp. 2537–2541 (2002)
19. Johnson, R.W.: Estimating the Size of a Population. Teaching Statistics 16(2), 50–52 (1994)
20. Ultsch, A.: Clustering with SOM: U*C. In: Proc. Workshop on Self-Organizing Maps (WSOM 2005), Paris, France, pp. 75–82 (2005)
21. Ultsch, A., Siemon, H.P.: Kohonen's Self Organizing Feature Maps for Exploratory Data Analysis. In: Proc. Intern. Neural Networks, pp. 305–308. Kluwer Academic Press, Paris (1990)
22. Ultsch, A.: Maps for the Visualization of high-dimensional Data Spaces. In: Proc. WSOM, Kyushu, Japan, pp. 225–230 (2003)
23. Ultsch, A.: Pareto Density Estimation: A Density Estimation for Knowledge Discovery. In: Innovations in Classification, Data Science, and Information Systems - Proc. 27th Annual Conference of the German Classification Society (GfKL), pp. 91–100. Springer, Heidelberg (2003)
24. Apache 2.0 Documentation (2011), http://www.apache.org/
25. Klein, A.: Detecting and Preventing HTTP Response Splitting and HTTP Request Smuggling Attacks at the TCP Level. Tech. Note (August 2005), http://www.securityfocus.com/archive/1/408135
26. Corona, I., Giacinto, G.: Detection of Server-side Web Attacks. In: Proc of JMLR: Workshop on Applications of Pattern Analysis, pp. 160–166 (2010)
27. Jain, A., Murty, M., Flynn, P.: Data clustering: a review. ACM Computing Surveys 31(3), 264–323 (1999) ISSN 0360-0300

Mining Product Features from the Web:
A Self-supervised Approach

Rémi Ferrez[1], Clément de Groc[1,2], and Javier Couto[1,3]

[1] Syllabs, Paris, France
[2] Univ. Paris Sud & LIMSI-CNRS, Orsay, France
[3] MoDyCo, UMR 7114, CNRS-Université de Paris Ouest Nanterre La Défense, France

Abstract. Mining information available on the Web to automatically build knowledge bases is a field of interest for academic research as well as industry. Existing wrapper induction approaches require manual annotations or aim to build domain-specific extractors that usually do not cope with template changes. In this paper, we tackle the problem of large scale product feature extraction from e-commerce web sites. We propose a novel self-supervised approach that relies on visual clues and a small knowledge base to automatically annotate product features. Our approach does not need an initial set of labeled pages to learn extraction rules and is robust to web site changes. Experimental results with product data extraction from 10 major French e-commerce web sites (roughly 1 000 web pages) show that the proposed method is promising. Moreover, experiments have shown that our method can handle web site template changes without human intervention.

Keywords: Product feature extraction, Wrapper induction, Information extraction, Web mining.

1   Introduction

Product feature extraction is a popular research area given the vast amount of data available on the Web and the potential economic implications. In this paper we focus on mining commercial product features from large e-commerce web sites, such as best-buy.com or target.com. Given a product, we want to extract its features represented as a set of related pairs (feature name, value). For example, for the "Apple MacBook Pro MD311LL/A" product, we would like to extract the information that the product color is silver, that its maximal display resolution is 1920x1200 pixels, its RAM size 4GB and so forth. The massive extraction of product features can be useful to a variety of applications including product or price comparison services, product recommendation, faceted search, or missing product features detection.

Our goal is to develop a method that allows mining product features in a self-supervised way (i.e. a semi-supervised method that makes use of a labeling heuristic), with a minimal amount of input. Moreover, the method should be as domain-independent as possible. In this paper, we present a method that relies on a small set of web pages (typically 5 to 10), few examples of product features, and visual clues.

J. Cordeiro and K.-H. Krempels (Eds.): WEBIST 2012, LNBIP 140, pp. 296–311, 2013.

The input examples can be the output of a previous data processing, given by a human, or chosen from an existing Knowledge Database such as Icecat [1].

Using visual clues such as spatial position, instead of relying on HTML tags, brings robustness to the method and independence from specific HTML structure. Consider tables for instance: various HTML tags can be used to present information in a tabular way. On the other hand, the <table> tag is sometimes used to visually organize web pages. Therefore, relying on the HTML <table> tag to identify tabular information is unsure. In addition to robustness, a good degree of domain-independence is achieved, as our method does not depend on text content, but only relies on visual clues. This is a major difference with similar work (see Section 2).

We have evaluated our system on 10 e-commerce web sites (1 000 web pages). Results show that the proposed approach offers very high performances. Further evaluations should be done to validate the method over e-commerce web sites which are using less templated web pages. Although these cases don't fully satisfy our hypotheses, our method should be adjustable to this type of web sites (less homogeneous due to the partial use of templates). However, as Gibson et al. pointed out [1], about 40-50 % of the content of the web is built using templates. Thus, it seems to us that the results obtained are promising.

The article is structured as follows: in Section 2, we survey existing methods regarding wrapper induction and product feature extraction. In Section 3, we describe the proposed approach. In Section 4, we evaluate our approach on a panel of 10 web sites (1 000 web pages). We conclude in Section 5.

2 Related Work

The proposed method is close to two research fields in web mining: *Wrapper Induction* and *Product Feature Extraction*.

Wrapper Induction refers to the generation of extraction rules for HTML web pages. Introduced by Kushmerick [2], wrapper induction methods rely on the regularity of web pages from the same web site, mostly due to the use of Content Management Systems (CMS).

While early work relied on human-labeled examples [2], recent approaches, known as unsupervised wrapper induction, have been proposed in order to avoid this step. Those new approaches are typically applied to two types of web pages: list-structured web pages displaying information about multiple products [3,4,5,6] and product web pages [7,8,9]. However, unsupervised methods require a post-processing step, as attribute names are usually unknown [9].

To the best of our knowledge, the use of prior knowledge to improve wrapper induction has been little studied. Knowledge is provided to the system using different formalisms such as concepts [10,11] or facts/values [12,13]. Moreover, such methods usually aim at extracting a small number of specific features about a particular type of product (e.g. camera, computer, books). Our work is thus significantly different from

---

[1] http://icecat.us is an IT-centered multilingual commercial database created in collaboration with product manufacturers. Part of this database, Open Icecat is freely available but very incomplete.

previous work as we propose a self-supervised and domain-independent method that relies on a preexisting knowledge base and visual clues.

On the other hand, *Product Feature Extraction* methods directly extract product features, without generating wrappers.

Wong et al.'s work [14] focuses on three *structural contexts* (or visual layouts): two-column tables, relational tables and colon-delimited pairs. Once the structural context of their data has been heuristically identified, they apply a set of rules in order to handle the variable length of the data structures. Part of our method was inspired by this article, however the use of visual hypotheses instead of heuristics, allows us to handle more HTML structures displayed with the same appearance.

Wong et al. [15] propose a method that considers each page individually and can retrieve an unlimited number of features. The probabilistic graphical model used in their paper considers content and layout information. Therefore, relying on textual content implies that their model is domain-dependant.

Our work is closely related to that of Wu et al. [16]. The main idea of their work is to first discover the part of the web page which contains all features, and then to extract them. The first step is performed using a classifier, and each NVP (Name Value Pair) discovered by this classifier receives a confidence score. The complete data structure is then located by taking the subtree with the best confidence score according to heuristic rules. A tree alignment is used to discover the remaining NVPs. This method can discover an unlimited number of features, but the initial classifier still needs to be trained on human-labeled examples. Moreover, as the previously discussed method [15], the classifier is trained for only one kind of product.

Our method inherits some ideas from these previous works, while investigating a different path based on visual information and an external knowledge base:

- A minimal knowledge base is provided to the system instead of human-labeled examples
- Visual clues avoid making assumptions about the HTML structure. As a result, features formatted with any kind of HTML structure but displayed as a table can be extracted
- The number of features extracted for one product is unlimited
- The extraction rules induced by our method can be applied to any type of product provided that the web site is built using templates

3 Our Method

3.1 Overview

The different aspects of template-generated web pages used in the whole process include content redundancy (site invariant features), visual/rendering features and structural regularities. All these aspects lead to different steps applied to a set of web pages in two different approaches: page-level (local) and site-level (global) analyses (the site is represented by a sample of web pages, "site-level" is used instead of "page-set-level" for clarity). Page-level analyses refer to algorithms that consider each page taken individually, whereas site-level analyses benefit from having multiple pages from the same site.

Wrapper Induction

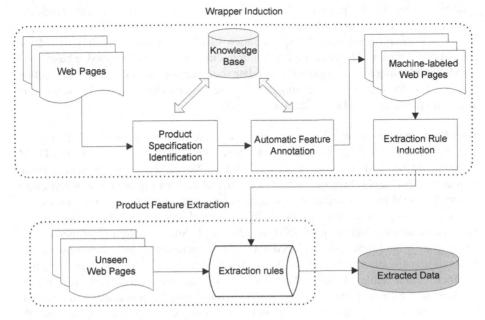

Fig. 1. Complete product feature extraction framework

The whole process (see Figure 1) is iterative, and alternates steps at page- and site-level.

Taking as input a small set of product web pages:

1. product specifications are located using a combination of page- and site-level information (section 3.2)
   (a) content redundancy is evaluated using site-level information
   (b) an estimation of known feature coverage is computed per page
   (c) according to a) and b), every part of the pages is scored and ranked
   (d) product specification are located using a site-level vote
2. on each page, product feature names and values are automatically annotated (section 3.3)
   (a) a partial feature matching is performed to identify some feature names and values
   (b) more examples are inferred by relying on the specification block layout
3. extraction rules are induced using all annotated features (section 3.4)
4. rules are applied to unrendered web pages from the same web site to extract features from any type of product

3.2 Specification Block Detection

The first step of our method is to detect the block containing all the product features that we would like to extract (which we call "product specification" block).

Web pages generated from a particular template share common blocks of HTML. These parts are considered site-invariant. On the contrary, some elements depend on the product presented in the page, like feature tables, descriptions, prices, related products, ads, etc... Those site-variant features will give us a clue to identify the specification block. A distinction between the specification block and other variable parts of the pages is later achieved by crossing information with the external knowledge base.

After explaining how we generate candidate specification blocks (section 3.2, section 3.2), we describe a method for scoring and ranking each block (section 3.2) and a voting algorithm to select a final candidate (section 3.2).

Web Page Segmentation. Web pages can be cut into multiple parts of different sizes. These parts are called segments or blocks, and correspond to a subtree in the DOM (Document Object Model) tree of the whole page. We studied segments instead of all displayed elements in the page (which is the trivial case of segmentation when every leaf in the DOM tree is a segment) in order to identify whole data structure blocks.

Web page segmentation is another field of research but advanced methods are not required in our case. Indeed, the CSS (Cascading Style Sheets) "display" property gives a very good hint of how content placed under a node is rendered by a web browser. We base our segmentation on this attribute and filter out all segments whose value is neither a "block", nor a "table". Keeping these two values guarantees that we don't restrain the method and we can potentially extract well structured data formatted with other HTML tags. Strictly speaking, this method is not a web page segmentation method, mostly because the segments obtained are nested. In the context of this work, this is not a problem because our scoring algorithm will cope with this aspect.

Block Identification. A major issue when trying to evaluate the variable aspect of segments from different web pages, is how to identify these segments and how to locate them within each page. Two considerations should be taken:

1. each identifier should locate a unique segment (a sub-tree of the whole DOM tree) of the web page, for every page in the set
2. the same segment in each web page of the set should share the same identifier regardless of HTML optional elements

An example of the second item is when we can clearly see that a table displayed in every page of the set is the same, but the strict path (from the root of the DOM tree to the table) is not the same in all web pages. We refer to "strict path" as the concatenation of HTML tags from root to any node, with the position of each tag specified at every level. The position is computed as follows: the first occurrence of a tag under a node has the first position and for every sibling node with the same tag, we increment the position by 1. On the other hand, we call "lazy path" the concatenation of HTML tags from root to an element without positional information. However such path cannot cope with condition 1 and thus may identify multiple segments on the web page.

These considerations led us to use a more flexible path, based on the XPath formalism.

As already mentioned, at this point of the method, we want each path to be robust against optional DOM nodes but strict enough to locate candidate blocks in all pages of the set. Hence, we start with a lazy path, and progressively add HTML attributes ("class", "id") or position information so that each path locates a unique node in the page set. HTML attributes such as "class" and "id" often refer to the visual or functional purpose of DOM nodes ("blue-link", "feature-name", "page-body", ...). Using such information in our formalism generates more "semantic" or interpretable paths.

Block Scoring and Ranking. In this section, we describe how the simultaneous use of content redundancy and a knowledge base can help to distinguish which block contains the features regardless of how they are displayed.

We first analyze how text fragments are distributed within the set of pages, aiming at separating variable from invariable content. We later cross information between our knowledge base and pages in the set to isolate the variable segment we want to extract.

Entropy-based Redundancy Analysis.
There are different methods to evaluate content variability for the segments we have created. We used an entropy-based approach as proposed by Wong and Lam [12]. In the following, we refer to each segment by its root node in the DOM tree. We define $\mathbb{W}$ as the set of words occurring in this block. Then, we define the probability to find a word $w \in \mathbb{W}$ in the text content located under node N as:

$$P(w, N) = \frac{occ(w, N)}{\sum_{w_i \in \mathbb{W}} occ(w_i, N)} \tag{1}$$

where $occ(w, N)$ is the number of occurrences of word w in the text content located under node N.

We directly define an entropy measure for node N on page p as:

$$E_p(N) = - \sum_{w_i \in \mathbb{W}} P(w_i, N) log P(w_i, N) \tag{2}$$

Taking one of the pages as a reference, we compute the difference of entropies between this page and other pages from the set in order to evaluate the content variability for all segments.

Actually, the measure defined in equation 2 can be computed for a unique page, or for multiple pages. In this case, the text content under the node N is not taken on one page but on all pages. The set of words is directly computed as the union of all sets.

Wong and Lam took as reference, one of the pages from the set. We believe that it is hard to find the most representative page of the set. Moreover, we won't be able to evaluate all paths since the reference page only contains a limited number of paths. However, as our set of pages is small, a complete scoring is tractable and can be achieved by taking each page as the reference page once.

Formally, we define a measure of word dispersion, the information $\mathfrak{I}$ for node N, computed by:

$$\mathfrak{I}(N) = \frac{1}{|\mathbb{P}|} \sum_{p \in \mathbb{P}} |E_p(N) - E_{\substack{\forall p' \in \mathbb{P} \\ p' \neq p}}(N)| \tag{3}$$

where $\mathbb{P}$ is the set of pages.

For every node which contains invariant text content, $\mathfrak{I}$ will be null. On the contrary, when the text content varies a lot (the set of words located under node N is very large), $\mathfrak{I}$ will be high.

Because we are interested in segments which contain a lot of informative nodes (feature values are expected to be very different from one product to another), this measure gives a good hint for identifying potential specification block.

At this point, we need a threshold to differentiate variable blocks from invariable ones. However, identifying the specification block by solely relying on the variability criterion $\mathfrak{I}$ proved difficult. For instance, the specification block was often blended with other variable segments, like customer reviews or product descriptions.

Feature Matching and Final Score.
The easiest way to differentiate feature-rich sections from other variant sections is to look at the coverage of a reference feature set. This can be achieved by relying on our knowledge base. Moreover, this knowledge base can be completed when new data are extracted. During our test, we used a free product feature database, Icecat which provides a large multilingual product feature source.

The feature coverage FC can be computed using a standard bag-of-words model, defined as:

$$FC(N) = \frac{|\omega_N \cap \omega_f|}{|\omega_f|} \tag{4}$$

where ω_f is the set of words computed on feature values in the reference set, and ω_N is the set of words in the text content of node N.

Finally, we can combine equations (3) and (4) to compute a final Specification Block Score SBS:

$$SBS(N) = (1 - \lambda)\mathfrak{I}(N) + \lambda FC(N) \tag{5}$$

where $\lambda \in [0; 1]$ is automatically computed according to the feature coverage in the text of the whole page FC_p. The fewer FC_p is, the bigger λ is for every node. In fact, feature coverage should be a strong indication of where the specification block is located. A small value of FC_p indicates differences on presentation text for a lot of features, and FC should be more weighted than $\mathfrak{I}$. On the contrary, if this value is too high, this may indicate either lots of matching in other parts of the page or less differences in how presentation text is written. In this case, weights of FC and $\mathfrak{I}$ are balanced because FC value is less reliable.

Candidate Block Selection. At this stage, we have a ranked list of blocks for each page in the set. We now want to decide which block designates the specification one.

Instead of averaging values of the SBS score for each block over all web pages, we use a voting method, more robust to the fact that SBS scores are simultaneously very small and close to each other.

For example, a typical case we try to overcome is when a web page contains a product description written in plain text and composed of many product features. Using an average SBS value usually leads to a wrong final ranking.

Fig. 2. First step - specification block identification

Therefore, we have evaluated two preferential voting methods: Borda count and Nanson's method. The difference between those two is that Nanson eliminates choices that are below the average Borda count score at every ballot. Initial tests have shown that Nanson's method yields better results and is robust enough to deal with our most ambiguous cases.

The final result of the product specification block detection is illustrated in Figure 2. The specification block is colored in light grey.

3.3 Data Structure Inference

After locating the product specification block, we need to find how features are presented in order to annotate them. Recall that each feature we want to extract is composed of two elements: its name and its corresponding value.

For each page of our set, we first use the knowledge base to identify both elements for each feature in the data structure. We obtain a partial matching due to the fact that our knowledge base is incomplete. Moreover, due to language variability, several feature names and values will mismatch or not match at all. Consider for instance matching a camera sensor resolution. Our database contains a "Megapixel" feature name and a corresponding value of "18 MP". However, depending on the web site, this same value

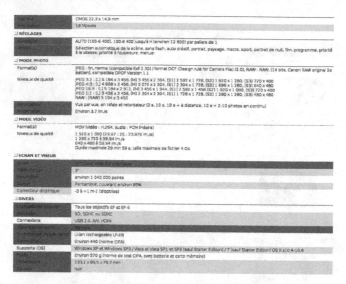

Fig. 3. Second step - partial feature matching

may be written as "18 MP", "18 Mpx", "18 million px", "18 million pixels", "18 mega pixels" or even "18 000 000 pixels". Matching such values with our knowledge base without normalization rules is a difficult task. In this work, we rely on a simple edit distance to match our knowledge base entries to web page elements which means we will have to handle a lot of mismatches.

To cope with silences and errors, we use visual clues and hypotheses about how these features are displayed. We finally obtain a valid and large set of machine-labeled examples.

Partial Feature Matching. If we consider a product web page and a reference set of features for this product, we can assume to match some features in the web page, even if there is a lot of variation about how feature names and values are written.

We use the Damerau-Levenshtein distance to match each text fragment (corresponding to a leaf in the DOM tree) with reference feature names and values. Each text fragment is assigned to the feature name or value that minimizes the distance (normalized between 0 and 2). An empirically fixed threshold[2] is used to avoid matching unrelated text fragments and reference features.

This partial feature matching is illustrated in Figure 3. Feature names and values are respectively colored in dark and light grey.

Data Structure Generalization. The current machine-labeled examples (both feature names and values) are incomplete and noisy, for multiple reasons:

- some values (resp. names) in the web page are considered as feature names (resp. values) in the reference feature set
- some text fragments are neither a feature name nor a value
- some text fragments have been mismatched

---

[2] A value of 1.35 was used throughout our experiments.

Thus, we need to clean these examples in order to:

1. remove as much noise as possible
2. maximize the number of examples without adding extra web pages

We can achieve these goals by making hypotheses about how features are displayed. We use visual-based hypotheses (after rendering the page) instead of tree-based ones because it gives us a complete independence towards the underlying HTML structure.

We distinguish two kinds of practices used when presenting data in a table-like structure that justify the use of visual-based hypothesis.

First, we find every method used for displaying each feature:

- different formatting tags (<b>, <i>, <big>, <em>...) for cells of the same table
- some of the values or feature names are links
- images are used to clarify some features (typically for features that take few values and are key features for selling the product, for example sensor resolution of a camera)

Web developers can employ other formatting methods (non-table tags combined with CSS properties) to display features as a table. Moreover, W3C recommendations are not always followed when using proper table tags. All those facts lead us to various situations:

- each table row contains another table structure, giving a nested table tree
- labeling cells (namely our feature names) should be encoded using the "TH" tag, but are more often seen with the "TD" tag
- the entire table is formatted using nested "DIV" tags or HTML definition lists ("DL"/"DT" tags)

Having the DOM tree after rendering instead of the usual DOM tree based only on the HTML file, gives direct access to geometric and HTML attributes. Every node of the HTML tree is rendered as a box and geometric attributes can be retrieved (i.e. absolute positions and sizes). This process is quite expensive in time, because we need to fetch images and run scripts on every page. However, we conceived our framework to limit the rendering process to input pages only, thus making the rendering cost acceptable.

The two hypotheses that we make are:

1. features should be displayed in a table-like structure
2. based on the first hypothesis, feature names and values should be aligned vertically or horizontally

We applied these hypotheses to name and value rendered box center coordinates. Experiments show that they are robust enough to tackle real life issues. A sample application to our previously shown example is presented in Figure 4. As before, feature names and values are respectively colored in dark and light grey.

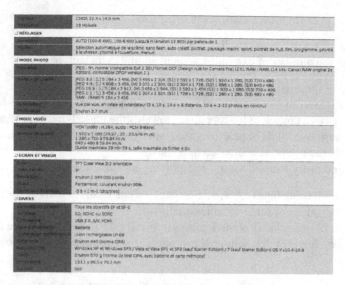

Fig. 4. Third step - visual alignement

Name-Value Association. The last step of our method is to associate each marked feature name with its corresponding value.

We use again visual clues instead of tree-based clues to avoid issues described in the previous section (formatting tags, improper HTML table tags, ...). We believe that visually closest names/value pairs should be associated together. We resort to a euclidean distance between the coordinates of the box centers.

3.4   Extraction Rule Induction

We have shown how we generate machine-labeled examples, and replace the laborious manual work of human labeling.

The data structure recognition process yields a large set of samples (pairs of feature names and values) from a small set of pages. The major drawback is that all visual clues are given by a rendering engine. In practice, we don't want to render all product pages of the e-commerce web sites, so we chose a different format for the extraction rules. Different methods have been employed for the induction of wrappers based on labeled examples, including string-based extraction rules [17], regular-expressions [9], or tree automata [18]. We prefered to use XPath rules instead because of its wide use in web information systems as well as its flexibility.

Based on previously machine-labeled examples we can automatically induce extraction rules in three parts:

1. *XPath 1*: Path to the product specification block
2. *XPath 2*: Path to all feature pairs, relative to *XPath 1*
3. *XPath 3*: Path to feature name and value for each feature pair, relative to *XPath 2*

Splitting XPath in three parts offers greater flexibility as it allows us to manually correct a specific step of the process (for instance, one could annotate the specification block manually), but also keeps track of the association between feature names and values.

Instead of building a strict XPath as described in section 3.2, we can take advantage of the flexibility of the XPath language which can handle HTML attributes for node localization. The failure of a strict XPath rule caused by the existence of optional elements can be avoided in most cases with this method. Thus, if a node has a unique "id" or "class" attribute, we use this information and use strict position numbers as a last resort.

Although the formalism is the same, the method used for the automatic induction of these rules is different from the one we used in the section 3.2. The previous formalism was constrained by the fact that each path had to locate only one segment per page. At this stage of the procedure, the XPath is not restricted for the same purpose (identifying a unique node) because we want more genericity for the following reasons:

1. extracting an unlimited number of features. In particular the *XPath 2* can match multiple nodes in each page
2. being able to handle unseen pages

For these reasons, for each rule, we try to induce an XPath which can validate as much machine-labeled examples as possible. This can be achieved by using disjunction over HTML attributes usually used for CSS classes as demonstrated in the following example:

```
.../TABLE/TR[@class='allparams even' OR @class='allparams odd']
```

Using one of these attributes is not always possible. The worst case is when we have a different strict XPath for each node. In this case, the system builds multiple rules. However, this case never happened on the web sites from our evaluation set.

4 Evaluation

4.1 Corpus

To the best of our knowledge, there is no available dataset to evaluate product feature extraction from semi-structured product specifications found in recent e-commerce web sites. We have considered evaluating the proposed approach using a cross-validation method and the Icecat knowledge base. However due to text variability (as discussed in section 3.3), this proved difficult, leading us to produce our own manual annotations.

We have created a novel collection of product features by downloading a sample of nine major French e-commerce web sites: boulanger.fr, materiel.net, ldlc.fr, fnac.com, rueducommerce.fr, surcouf.com, darty.fr, cdiscount.com and digit-photo.com. The ldlc.fr web site changed its page template during our experiments so we evaluated our method on the first and second version of this web site (resp. ldlc.fr (v1) and ldlc.fr (v2)). This emphasizes an interesting aspect of our method which is its robustness to structure changes: even if extraction rules change, product features are usually kept as is. Thus, our method can readily induce new rules without human intervention.

For each web site, we have applied a clustering algorithm in order to group web pages built from the same template (i.e. lists, search results, product details, etc...). Following Gottron [19], we have extracted "bag of paths" features from each web page (here, we consider "lazy paths" as described in section 3.4). Then, we have clustered documents using the Mean Shift algorithm. For the purpose of this evaluation, we manually selected the cluster containing product web pages from the set of clusters. Finally, a gold standard was produced by randomly sampling 100 web pages from all categories (e.g. Movies & TV, Camera & Photo, . . .) and annotating product features (name and corresponding value).

The final corpus is composed of 1 022 annotated web pages containing 19 402 feature pairs.

4.2   Experimental Settings

For each web site, we ran our method as follows:

- We randomly chose 5-10 unseen web pages from randomly chosen categories
- We retrieved the corresponding feature sets from the Icecat knowledge base. Association between a web page and a feature set was achieved automatically by looking at the product name and the page title
- We applied the proposed method and induced XPath extraction rules
- Finally, we applied those rules to our gold standard web pages in order to extract product features

We have used standard metrics to assess the quality of our extractions:

- precision, defined as the ratio of correct features extracted to the total number of features extracted
- recall, defined as the ratio of correct features extracted to the total number of all available features.

4.3   Results

As shown in Table 1, our method offers very high performance. Most of the time, the system gives a perfect extraction, due to a good *templateness* and little variability in the whole web site. This proves that our initial hypotheses and the choice of the XPath formalism were relevant. Actually, our custom formalism derived from XPath correctly captures what is regular in templated web pages: HTML structure (tags) and attributes (such as the "class" attribute which provides rendering clues sometimes). Moreover, dividing our extraction rules in three parts (see section 3.4) allows us to extract features precisely and robustly which leads to high precision. Our sequential approach (specification block detection, data structure generalization, name-value association) is a major difference with previous methods that considered all text fragments in web pages. However, as it is clearly iterative, failure of one step of the method is irrecoverable which is exactly why extractions on web sites 8 and 10 failed.

More interestingly, we observe mixed results on web sites 6 and 7. The lower recall for web site 6 can be explained by a misrepresentative sample. The extraction rules do not cover all existing HTML attributes that locate the specification block due to the absence of examples while inducing the rules. The noise extracted for web site 7 is due to the alignment hypothesis. In-depth analysis reveal that several table cells, aligned

Table 1. Evaluation of product feature extraction

		Input pages	Pages	Features	Precision	Recall
1	boulanger.fr	5	100	1 390	1.00	1.00
2	materiel.net	5	100	2 960	1.00	1.00
3	ldlc.fr (v1)	5	102	1 324	1.00	1.00
4	ldlc.fr (v2)	5	102	1 498	1.00	1.00
5	fnac.com	5	101	1 856	1.00	1.00
6	rueducommerce.fr	5	140	2 190	1.00	0.723
7	surcouf.com	5	102	2 125	0.76	1.00
8	darty.fr	5	127	2 917	#	0.00
9	cdiscount.com	5	48	1 271	1.00	1.00
10	digit-photo.com	5	100	1 871	#	0.00
	Total	#	1 022	19 402	0.97	0.77

Table 2. Impact on recall of increasing the number of input pages

		Input pages	Pages	Features	Precision	Recall
6	rueducommerce.fr	10	140	2 190	1.00	0.723
8	darty.fr	9	127	2 917	1.00	0.94
10	digit-photo.com	10	100	1 871	#	0.00
	Total (for all sites)	#	1 022	19 402	0.97	0.87

with product feature names or values, are mislabeled. For instance, all features relative to a computer screen are preceded by a "Screen" cell erroneously labeled as a feature name.

We tried to overcome some of those problems by providing more input pages for these sites. We decided to limit the number of input pages to 10 in order to respect our initial goal to use few input pages. In fact, we made the hypothesis that SBS scores on these sites were wrong due to a lot of differences in the DOM trees. The use of more pages gives a more precise evaluation of text variability and increases the probability of finding known features on web pages. Results shown in Table 2 and in-depth analyses confirm this hypothesis.

On site 8, when providing only 5 pages as input, a block containing a lot of features written in plain text was selected instead of the specification block. This problem was avoided when more pages were provided. On site 6, recall did not increase which means that there are still cases which we did not capture from our automatically labeled examples.

Results for site 10 show another issue, which cannot be handled by our method regardless of how many pages we use as input. The main context which leads to the failure of the specification block detection is when we cannot compare the same segments on all pages. Manual analysis of each step for this web site show that this case happened here. In fact, we don't have any specific HTML attributes (the usual "id" and "class") for locating web page segments, and there are different optional elements on each page too. The combination of both leads to the comparison of different parts of the web pages, thus giving a wrong measure of content variability. Moreover, the vote cannot be done because equivalent blocks don't have the same identifier on all web pages. Even if this case shows a clear disadvantage of our pipeline approach, average results indicate that the idea behind the construction of a path based on the XPath formalism is still relevant.

5 Conclusions

In this paper, we have tackled the problem of product feature extraction from e-commerce web sites. Starting from a small set of rendered product web pages (typically 5 to 10), our novel method makes use of a small external knowledge base and visual hypotheses to automatically produce feature annotations. The proposed method, designed as a pipeline, is composed of three subtasks: product specification identification, feature matching and data structure recognition, and, finally, extraction rule induction. Those extraction rules are then applied to extract new product features from unseen web pages. We have carried out an evaluation on 10 major French e-commerce web sites (roughly 1 000 web pages) and have reported interesting results.

We are considering several leads for future work. First, as the proposed approach is built as a pipeline, it offers high precision and no noise but a single failure leads to a complete failure of the method. Thus, we will explore more global approaches which could avoid such effect. In particular, as results show the importance of having a *representative* set of web pages for inducing the extraction rules, we will develop a method for building such sets. Secondly, we would like to induce feature value normalization rules from several knowledge bases built from multiple web sites. Finally, while the method is domain independent, which is an interesting property for large and cross-domain web sites, we will focus our work on small web sites such as small specialized portals.

Acknowledgements. We would like to thank Mickaël Mounier for his contribution on the rendering engine and the annotation tool. We also gratefully acknowledge Marie Guégan for her helpful comments on the first version of this paper. This work was partially funded by the DGCIS (French institution) as part of the Feed-ID project (no. 09.2.93.0593).

References

1. Gibson, D., Punera, K., Tomkins, A.: The volume and evolution of web page templates. In: Special Interest Tracks and Posters of the 14th International Conference on World Wide Web, pp. 830–839. ACM (2005)
2. Kushmerick, N.: Wrapper induction for information extraction. PhD thesis, University of Washington (1997)
3. Chang, C., Lui, S.: Iepad: information extraction based on pattern discovery. In: Proceedings of the 10th International Conference on World Wide Web, pp. 681–688. ACM (2001)
4. Liu, B., Grossman, R.: Mining data records in web pages. In: Proceedings of the Ninth ACM SIGKDD International Conference on Knowledge Discovery and Data Mining, pp. 601–606. ACM (2003)
5. Wang, J., Lochovsky, F.: Wrapper induction based on nested pattern discovery. World Wide Web Internet and Web Information Systems, 1–29 (2002)

6. Zhao, H., Meng, W., Wu, Z., Raghavan, V., Yu, C.: Fully automatic wrapper generation for search engines. In: Proceedings of the 14th International Conference on World Wide Web, pp. 66–75. ACM (2005)
7. Arasu, A., Garcia-Molina, H.: Extracting structured data from web pages. In: Proceedings of the 2003 ACM SIGMOD International Conference on Management of Data, pp. 337–348. ACM (2003)
8. Chang, C.H., Kuo, S.C.: Annotation Free Information Extraction from Semi-structured Documents. Engineering, 1–26 (2007)
9. Crescenzi, V., Mecca, G., Merialdo, P., et al.: Roadrunner: Towards automatic data extraction from large web sites. In: Proceedings of the 27th International Conference on Very Large Data Bases, pp. 109–118 (2001)
10. Rosenfeld, B., Feldman, R.: Using Corpus Statistics on Entities to Improve Semi-supervised Relation Extraction from the Web. In: Proceedings of the 45th Annual Meeting of the Association for Computational Linguistics, pp. 600–607 (2007)
11. Senellart, P., Mittal, A., Muschick, D., Gilleron, R., Tommasi, M.: Automatic wrapper induction from hidden-web sources with domain knowledge. In: Proceedings of the 10th ACM Workshop on Web Information and Data Management, pp. 9–16. ACM (2008)
12. Wong, T., Lam, W.: Adapting web information extraction knowledge via mining site-invariant and site-dependent features. ACM Transactions on Internet Technology (TOIT) 7 (2007)
13. Zhao, S., Betz, J.: Corroborate and learn facts from the web. In: Proceedings of the 13th ACM SIGKDD International Conference on Knowledge Discovery and Data Mining, pp. 995–1003. ACM (2007)
14. Wong, Y., Widdows, D., Lokovic, T., Nigam, K.: Scalable attribute-value extraction from semi-structured text. In: Proceedings of the 2009 IEEE International Conference on Data Mining Workshops, pp. 302–307. IEEE (2009)
15. Wong, T., Lam, W., Wong, T.: An unsupervised framework for extracting and normalizing product attributes from multiple web sites. In: Proceedings of the 31st Annual International ACM SIGIR Conference on Research and Development in Information Retrieval, pp. 35–42. ACM (2008)
16. Wu, B., Cheng, X., Wang, Y., Guo, Y., Song, L.: Simultaneous product attribute name and value extraction from web pages. In: Proceedings of the 2009 IEEE/WIC/ACM International Joint Conference on Web Intelligence and Intelligent Agent Technology, vol. 7, pp. 295–298. IEEE Computer Society (2009)
17. Muslea, I., Minton, S., Knoblock, C.: Hierarchical wrapper induction for semistructured information sources. Autonomous Agents and Multi-Agent Systems 4, 93–114 (2001)
18. Kosala, R., Van den Bussche, J., Bruynooghe, M., Blockeel, H.: Information Extraction in Structured Documents Using Tree Automata Induction. In: Elomaa, T., Mannila, H., Toivonen, H. (eds.) PKDD 2002. LNCS (LNAI), vol. 2431, p. 299. Springer, Heidelberg (2002)
19. Gottron, T.: Clustering Template Based Web Documents. In: Macdonald, C., Ounis, I., Plachouras, V., Ruthven, I., White, R.W. (eds.) ECIR 2008. LNCS, vol. 4956, pp. 40–51. Springer, Heidelberg (2008)

Capturing User's Interest from Human-Computer Interaction Logging

Vincenzo Deufemia, Massimiliano Giordano, Giuseppe Polese, and Genoveffa Tortora

Università di Salerno, Via Ponte don Melillo, Fisciano(SA), Italy
{deufemia,mgiordano,gpolese,tortora}@unisa.it

Abstract. Mining user's expectations and interests has become the focus of many Internet-based application providers, such as those operating in the areas of social networks, search engines, e-commerce, and so forth. This is often accomplished by means of explicit feedbacks requested to end-users, which might yield distorted results due to the intrusive nature of this kind of approach. Thus, it would be desirable using implicit feedbacks, provide that they faithfully reflect user's habits and expectations. In this paper we propose an approach to capture user's feedbacks from their interaction actions while processing a document, with particular emphasis on web documents. To this end, we propose a new model to interpret mouse cursor actions, such as scrolling, movement, text selection, while reading web documents, aiming to infer a *relevance* value indicating how the user found the document useful for his/her purposes. We have implemented the proposed model through light-weight components, which can be easily installed within major web browsers as a plug-in. The components log mouse cursor actions that we have used as experimental data in order to validate the proposed model. The experimental results show that the proposed model is able to predict user feedbacks with an acceptable level of accuracy.

1 Introduction

Nowadays, the goal of many internet application providers is to collect feedbacks from their users. Thus many modern internet applications frequently inquire their users asking them to provide feedbacks on the quality of provided services, or their trends and expectations to help providers meet their needs.

However, this has often resulted in a continuous spoiling of users daily work, which can potentially affect the accuracy by which they provide the requested feedbacks. This is particularly true in social networks or in search engines. Thus, many researchers have started devising methods for capturing users feedbacks in a non intrusive way. For instance, several years ago many internet search engines have started analysing the linked structure of the web in order to implicitly derive an index of the usefulness of web documents. Page-rank is the most famous method using link structure analysis [1]. The idea behind Page-rank algorithm is to exploit the macro-scale link structure among pages in order to capture the popularity of documents, which can indirectly be interpreted as an index of their quality. According to this approach, the popularity of a page is determined on the basis of the size of a hypothetical user stream coming to the page. However, link-based algorithms have currently many disadvantages [2].

J. Cordeiro and K.-H. Krempels (Eds.): WEBIST 2012, LNBIP 140, pp. 312–327, 2013.

For example, they are vulnerable to spamming, and links may have several meanings or purposes.

With the advent of Web 2.0, *social bookmarking* systems have started calculating the popularity of a Web document as the total number of times it has been bookmarked, which is interpreted as the number of users voting for the page. In the context of web search engines, explicit ranking systems are more dynamic than Page-rank, and often ensure shorter time for pages to reach their popularity peaks [3]. However, due to the insufficient amount of bookmarked pages, it is not advisable relying on explicit ranking systems alone. Furthermore, explicit ranking is subjective, since users need to explicit vote a web content to rate it, and not all the web users are keen on voting each site they visit. Thus, despite the rapid growth in the number of bookmarked pages, the combination of link structure-based and *social bookmarking*-based page ranking measures seems to be currently an optimal strategy.

Alternatively, methods that are able to implicitly capture user interests are potentially more useful, since there is no noise in the ranking process introduced by subjective evaluations [4, 5]. Thus, we have started exploiting methods for logging user interaction actions in order to derive an implicit index expressing the web page usefulness with respect to user interests. In particular, we propose a new model to interpret mouse cursor actions, such as scrolling, movement, text selection, while reading web documents, aiming to infer a *relevance* value indicating how the user found the document useful for his/her purposes [6, 7].

We have embedded the proposed model in a ranking system for the web. In particular, we have implemented the YAR (Yet Another Ranker) system, which re-ranks the web pages retrieved by a search engine based on the relevance values computed from the interaction actions of previous visitors. YAR ha been implemented by means of light-weight components, which can be easily installed within major web browsers as a plug-in (we used it experimentally with Google, but any other search engine could be easily adapted). The implemented components capture mouse cursor actions without spoiling user browsing activities, which enabled us to easily collect experimental data to validate the proposed model. The experimental results demonstrate that the proposed model is able to predict user feedbacks with an acceptable level of accuracy.

The paper is organized as follows. Section 2 describes the metrics for deriving the web page relevance from mouse tracking logging data. An implementation of the proposed metrics in the context of ranking systems is presented in Section 3. Section 4 presents an experimental evaluation with analysis of the results. A comparison with related work is described in Section 5. Finally, conclusions and future work are discussed in Section 6.

2   The Metrics for Web Page Relevance

In order to compute the web page relevance value we consider several metrics. The application of all these metrics will be used to produce a value between 1 and 5, as usually done in *social bookmarking* systems. In particular, we have defined the following metrics:

- permanence time,
- reading rate,
- scrolling rate.

The overall rate is obtained through a weighted sum of the considered metrics. Linear regression has been used to find the weights for metrics that best explain the observed user feedback.

2.1 Permanence Time

The Permanence Time (PT) is defined as the difference between the loading and the unloading time of a web page. Obviously, PT is heavily influenced by the way the user reads a text within a document and by the number of words composing it. Several studies prove that there are different ways of reading a text, each corresponding to a different speed, also depending on reader's language and age [8]. Rates of reading are measured in words per minute (wpm), and include *reading for memorization* (less than 100 wpm), *reading for learning* (100 – 200 wpm), *reading for comprehension* (200 – 400 wpm), and *skimming* (400 – 700 wpm).

In general, being aware of the reading style seems to be essential in order to correctly relate the time the user spends on a page with his/her hypothetical interest. In spite of all those kind of different reading strategies, the way user reads on the web seems to be different with respect to the way they read a printed text. Usually, web users rapidly find key elements of a document, and they usually highlight sections, paragraphs, and keywords by using the mouse cursor. The web user only reads a small portion of a web page, usually between the 20% and 28% of it [9].

Furthermore, experimental data show that web pages containing from 30 to 1250 words are read shallowly, and that the estimated time a user will stay on the web page, before making a decision about its usefulness, is at least 25 seconds plus 4.4 seconds for each block of 100 words [9].

Starting from these results, we define PT as:

$$
PT = \begin{cases} pT_m \cdot (3/Tref_m) + 1 & \text{if } pT_m \leq Tref_m \\ pT_m \cdot (2/Tref_{max}) + 4 & \text{if } pT_m > Tref_m \end{cases} \tag{1}
$$

where:

- pT_m is the *average permanence time* and it is defined as $pT_m = (pw \cdot 0.044) + 25$, with pw representing the number of words composing the page;
- $Tref_{max}$ is the *maximum reference time* and it is defined as $Tref_{max} = (pw/150)60$. We assume the *reading for learning* rate (about 150 wpm in the average case) as its lower bound;
- $Tref_m$ is the *average reference time*.

$Tref_m$ is defined to support fast reading strategies, typical of web users, and when the number of words is between 30 and 1250 [9]. Thus, for this kind of pages the $Tref_m$ is defined as the *average permanence time*. However, for longer documents this equality might be inaccurate. In these cases we redefine $Tref_m$ as:

$$
Tref_m = pw/v_{lett} \cdot 60 \tag{2}
$$

where v_{lett} is the reading speed rate corresponding to the selected reading strategy. As default, we assume an average rate of $v_{lett} = 300wpm$, which corresponds to the *reading for comprehension* strategy.

In conclusion, we associate an average relevance value of 3 to a document on which the user spends a time equal to $Tref_m$. For a shorter permanence time the relevance value is computed by using the average time as upper bound. In case of permanence time greater than the average time, we use $Tref_{max}$ as upper bound. In this way, the metric is more sensible to the different reading strategies.

Notice that the resulting value for PT is in the range $[1, \infty]$. However if it is greater than 5, we reduce it to 5, because we have empirically verified that above 5 the user interest does not increase considerably.

2.2 Reading Rate

A common user activity on the web is text filtering. As shown in many usability studies performed by using *eye tracking*, users are often interested in some portion of the text, and only in some of its contents [10]. S/he follows a "standard" reading schema, called the "F" reading pattern. Thus, by analyzing the mouse activities, we can review the same reading pattern, and use it to understand how much the page is useful to the user.

In particular, experimental data show that many users navigate through the page by pointing with the mouse cursor near the rows they find interesting [11]. However, this behavior is not common to all users. Alternatively, some users might highlight text either to facilitate reading, to copy it, or just to print the selected portion. Obviously, these can all be interpreted as measures of interest. Thus, we can use such mouse actions to derive a measure, called *Reading Rate* (RR), estimating the amount of text the user reads in the document, which is computed as:

$$RR = 5 \cdot \left(\frac{rw + sw}{pw} \right) + 1 \qquad (3)$$

where:

- rw is the number of words followed by the mouse cursor;
- pw is the total number of words in the document;
- sw is the total number of selected words.

Notice that the number of words followed by the cursor is added to the number of words selected during the page exploration. In fact, often the user moves the mouse over each selected word to facilitate reading. This can also be taken as a further demonstration of user interest.

The resulting value for RR is also in the range $[1, \infty]$. Thus, we normalize it in the range $[1, 5]$ for reasons similar to those used for PT value.

2.3 Scrolling Rate

During a navigation session the web user might not necessarily read all the contents inside a page. Often, users scroll the page looking for interesting contents, or merely to have a complete overview of it.

The main reasons to scroll a page are:

- to navigate from the current section to the next one;
- to find a paragraph, or just some more interesting keywords;
- to skip the entire content of the page and reach a link to the next one, like for the classic End User Licensing Agreements (EULA) pages.

We believe that scrolling should be considered as a measure of interest for page contents. In other words, a relevant scrolling activity might witnesses that the user is interacting with the web page, and that s/he has not left the browser idle, because s/he is doing some other activity, leaving the value of the permanence time grow inappropriately. On the other hand, a highly frequent scrolling activity might convey a low interest, because the user might be skimming over the page without finding contents of interest to him/her.

In these cases, we apply a penalty to the relevance value. To this end, we need to measure the scrolling activities during the navigation. We call this measure Scrolling Rate (SR) and define it as the following normal distribution:

$$SR = 4 \cdot \left(exp\left[-\frac{1}{2} \left(\frac{x-\mu}{\sigma} \right)^2 \right] \right) + 1 \tag{4}$$

where

- $x = (N_{scroll}/PT) \cdot 60$ is the scrolling frequency expressed in terms of number of scrolls (N_{scroll}) per minute;
- μ is the mean value (the peak of the curve), which represents the scrolling frequency in case of high interest for page contents. We have empirically determined an optimal value of 25 for this parameter;
- σ^2 is the variance and it represents the range of scrolling frequencies revealing some interest for page contents. We have empirically determined an optimal value of 7.

Thus, the function SR contributes to increase the relevance value when the scrolling frequency is in the range 25 ± 7, as also shown in Figure 1. Beyond such range there is little interest, either because of too fast or reduced scrolling.

3 An implementation of the Proposed Metrics

Implicit feedbacks have a wide range of applications.

In this section, we present an implementation of the proposed metrics in the context of web page ranking. In particular, we present the YAR system whose architecture is depicted in Figure 2. It is based on a client/server model, where data concerning user interactions are collected on the client side by the *Logger*, and evaluated on the server side through the *Log Analyzer*. The *Logger* is responsible for "being aware" of the user's behavior while s/he browses web pages, and for sending information related to the captured events to the server-side module. The latter is responsible for analyzing the collected data, applying the metrics, and deriving relevance values to be successively used for ranking purposes.

The following subsections provide details on the modules composing the YAR system.

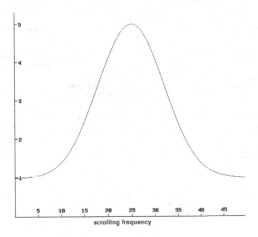

Fig. 1. The SR function

3.1   The Logging Module

One way to collect data concerning users interactions is to track their eyes' movements. However, this would require the use of expensive tools, which would make it difficult to run large-scale simultaneous experiments. Nevertheless, it has been shown that similar results can also be inferred by tracking mouse movements. In fact, it has been experimentally proved that in more than 75% of cases the mouse cursor closely approximates the eye gaze [6, 7]. This important result suggests that *mouse tracking* might replace eye tracking, allowing the extraction of many useful information about the user interest regarding a web page. This finding is also confirmed by a recent study on the correlation between cursor and gaze position on search result pages [11].

In light of the above arguments, our logging module tracks user interaction actions through several devices, but it does not perform eye tracking. In particular, the logging module tracks the overall and the effective permanence time over a web page, mouse cursor movements, page scrolling events, text selection, and so forth. It is based on the *AJAX* technology [12] to capture and log user's interactions with a web system through a pluggable mechanism, which can be installed on any web browser. Thus, it does not require modifications to the web sites, or any other legacy browser extensions. In particular, the architecture of the *Logger* is graphically represented in Figure 3.

It is structured in the following three main sub-components:

- Page handler: it handles page loading and unloading events.
- Mouse handler: it handles mouse events.
- Text handler: it handles keyboard related events.

These generic handlers could be overridden with ad-hoc specializations letting the system filter different kinds of events, so that it can be adapted to many different application domains.

An important property of the *Logger* component is flexibility. The *JavaScript* code for event capturing may be dynamically configured in order to record several kind of

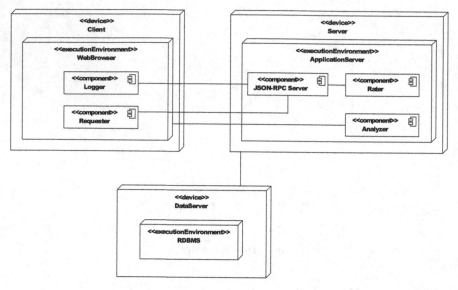

Fig. 2. The YAR System Architecture

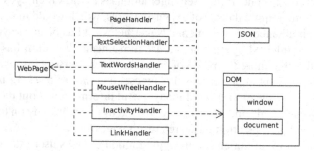

Fig. 3. The Logging Module

events occurring during the user navigation. Each class of events is handled by a specific *handler*. Among the parameters that can be configured for the logger we have:

- list of events to capture;
- sub-set of attributes for each event;
- sections of the web pages (*divs* or table cells) to be monitored as event sources;
- time interval between two data transmissions from the client to the server;
- sensitivity for mouse movements (short movements are not captured).

By acting on these parameters we have the possibility to affect the size of the collected data.

3.2   The Log Analyzer

The *Log Analyzer* is a server-side module providing two main functionalities: *rating* and *reporting*. The former is accomplished by the *Rater*, which rates the currently opened

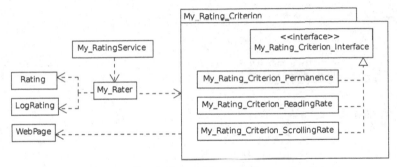

Fig. 4. The rater's overriding mechanism

documents by using data that the *Logger* has collected on the server during navigational sessions. To this end, the metrics adopted for ranking depend on the application domain. For example, we can derive metrics for web search applications, metrics to evaluate usability of software systems, or to evaluate the satisfaction of a user while using an automatic *Help Desk* system or an *E-testing* system. The overriding mechanism used to specialize the *Rater* is illustrated in Figure 4.

The *reporting* subsystem ensures the access to the gathered data by means of domain specific visual metaphors. In the web search context, this module uses a simple graphical pattern to show the rank produced by the ranker components, and mixes such results with those provided by the underlying search engine. All the reporting facilities are accessible through a web-based application or as a service, as in the case of information ranking.

3.3   Integration into SERPs

Thanks to the availability of reporting services, we can ask the system to provide the relevance value for each link already visited by other users. Thus, apart from collecting human computer interaction data, and calculating/updating the implicit rank, we integrate the rank information within a Search Engine Report Page (*SERP*). In particular, we show this in the context of *Google* search engine, but any other search engine could be used.

The integration with *SERP* is done by means of the same technology used to log user interaction data. We prepared a JavaScript function directly installed on the user browser in the same way as we integrated the logging facilities. However, in this case, instead of logging user interactions, the script scans the *SERP* and inquires the implicit rank for each link it contains. Finally, the script modifies the Document Object Model (*DOM*) of the web page in order to show the rank beside each result. In particular, the rank is shown by using a simple visual metaphor by depicting as many Star" symbols as the rank value. Thus, the system associates from 0 to 5 star symbols to each link. After each search, YAR shows the new page instead of the standard *SERP* page, and all the links originally found by the search engine are re-ranked by using the ranking information, if available.

In Figure 5 we can see the *Google SERP* page (Figure 5(a)) and the YAR re-ranked page (Figure 5(b)). In particular, the two pages result from the query: "html5 xhtml2".

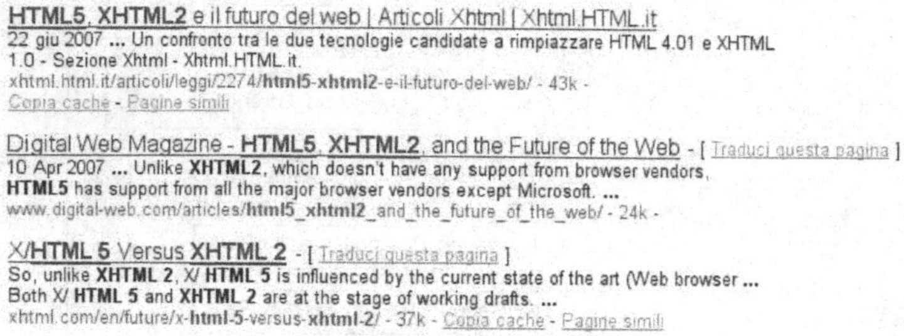

(a) Google rank

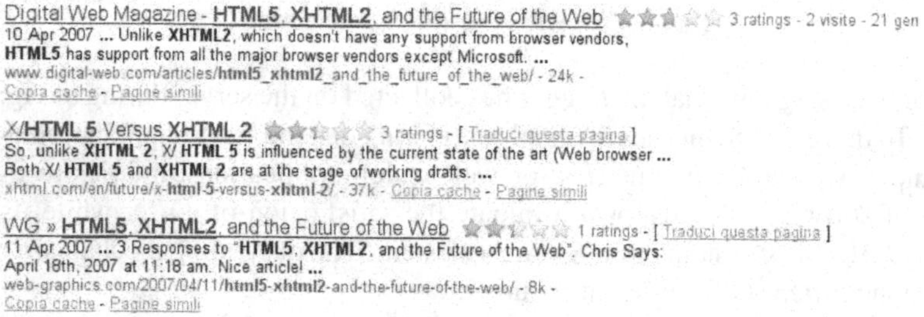

(b) YAR rank

Fig. 5. Comparison of web search results without and with relevance values

Notice that pages that were in the middle of the original *SERP*, after YAR re-ranking are positioned on the top of the list. This means that they better captured the interest of users who had previously visited them.

4 Experimental Evaluation

In this section we validate the proposed implicit feedback measure through a user study. The latter has a twofold goal. On one hand, we need to understand how the single metrics should be weighted when deriving the global implicit feedback measure. On the other hand, we need to evaluate the effectiveness of such measure. One way to do this, is to compare the computed implicit feedbacks with respect to the user provided ones.

4.1 Evaluation Method

The evaluation was accomplished by two independent groups of participants. They were prescribed the same tasks. However, the first group (20 participants) exercised the system in a basic configuration, and the results where used to derive an optimal parameter settings for the proposed implicit feedback method. Based on such settings, the second group (6 participants) produced results that were used to validate the effectiveness of the proposed measure.

Participants. We selected twenty-six participants between 22 and 31 years old. Sixteen of them had a bachelor in computer science, four a technical high school degree, two a gymnasium high school degree, two a master in linguistics, and two a bachelor in chemistry. Nine of them were female and seventeen were male. All the participants had sufficient computer and World Wide Web experience, and an average of 7.6 years of searching experience. Each of them underwent a week time period of search experiments.

User Tasks. In order to evaluate our system, we asked users to perform web searches and to explicitly rate the usefulness of the retrieved web documents. Then, we needed to compare such rates with those implicitly derived through the proposed approach. However, given the magnitude of the web, to have a significant amount of experimental data, we needed to narrow the scope of user searches in order to guide them towards a restricted set of web contents. This has been accomplished by assigning users specific web-quests [13]. A web-quest is a short description of a specific topic, on which a user should write an essay by mainly investigating through web sources. They are frequently used in e-learning contexts to give learners a clear purpose and objective when searching through web sources of knowledge.

Ten web-quests in italian language were prepared for the experiment. They regarded well-known topics such as for example retirement plans, anxiety, and coffee.

Each participant was requested to select three out of the ten available web-quests, and to solve them. For each visited page, they were requested to express a vote representing how they judged the page useful to solve the specific web-quest. The votes were expressed in a Likert scale [1, 5] where 1 represented *not useful* and 5 *useful*.

Instruments and Procedure. Each participant had his/her own computer on which we installed the YAR software. The latter also included a module for expressing a vote when leaving a visited web page.

Other than the twenty-six participants, six computer science students, one undergraduate and five graduate, participated in the organization and supervision of experiments. The undergraduate student prepared all the web-quests as part of her bachelor project, whereas each graduate student was requested to select four participants, and had the responsibility to conduct experiments with them in order to derive an optimal system tuning. After one week of experiments, they had a meeting with us to analyze and discuss experimental data, and to reach an agreement on the proper parameter settings to be used for the experiments with the remaining six subjects. The latter were selected among computer science students attending a graduate course on web engineering. They also worked one week, after which they had a final meeting with us to summarize and analyze the experimental results.

System Tuning. The goal of system tuning was to construct a model that given in input data on implicit user feedbacks was able to predict the explicit rate that would be given by the user. To this end, a proper system parameter setting was derived by performing a regression analysis in order to compute optimal weights for the single metrics: PT, RR, and SR. In particular, we accomplished regression analysis on the following five models:

Model 1: $r_1 = \alpha_0 + \alpha_1 \cdot RR$
Model 2: $r_2 = \alpha_0 + \alpha_1 \cdot RR + \alpha_2 \cdot SR$
Model 3: $r_3 = \alpha_0 + \alpha_1 \cdot RR + \alpha_2 \cdot PT$
Model 4: $r_4 = \alpha_0 + \alpha_1 \cdot PT + \alpha_2 \cdot SR$
Model 5: $r_5 = \alpha_0 + \alpha_1 \cdot RR + \alpha_2 \cdot SR + \alpha_3 \cdot PT$

Starting from the user provided explicit rates r_i, the goal here was to derive appropriate values for the constants α_j producing an optimal combination of the metrics RR, SR, and PT to achieve a value close to r_i.

Table 1 presents the results of the regression analysis based on the experiment accomplished by the first group of twenty participants, which produced 650 data records. The adjusted R^2 values show the proportion of variance of the dependent variable, namely the explicit rate of the subjects, with respect to the independent variables, namely the proposed metrics. We can observe that by including all the three metrics (model 5) we gain the maximum amount of variability of the dependent variables with respect to the independent ones. We also observe that the single PT and SR metrics have more impact on the variance than RR metrics. This means that the PT and SR are more strongly related to the explicit rate.

Table 1. Regression results

Model	adjusted R^2	F-value	p-value	α_0	α_1	α_2	α_3
1	0.375	$F(1, 648) = 390.39$	<0.001	1.164	0.531	-	-
2	0.571	$F(2, 647) = 433.15$	<0.001	0.649	0.538	0.291	-
3	0.592	$F(2, 647) = 472.66$	<0.001	0.570	0.291	0.387	-
4	0.693	$F(2, 647) = 732.44$	<0.001	0.220	0.422	0.349	-
5	0.857	$F(3, 649) = 1293.42$	<0.001	-0.126	0.372	0.340	0.337

Evaluation Metrics. The quality of the implicit feedback computed by YAR was evaluated by using the data produced in the second round of experiments, in which the second group of six participants was requested to solve three webquests on the topics: economy, politics, and healthcare. Afterwards, we have compared their explicit rates with respect to the implicit ones by means of the Root Mean Squared Error (RMSE).

4.2 Results

The experiments performed by the second group produced a set of 213 data records. Figure 6 shows the number of web pages visited by each subject to solve each webquest. Notice that for the same web-quest different subjects visited a highly variable number of pages. Nevertheless, to this end, we can observe that some subjects tend to follow their own trend. As an example, to solve each web-quest Subject 1 has visited a number of pages in a restricted range from 6 to 12, whereas Subject 3 has visited few pages except for web-quest 1.

Figure 7 shows the distribution of explicit rates for each subject. This figure allows us to elicit the attitude each subject has exhibited while rating web pages. As an example,

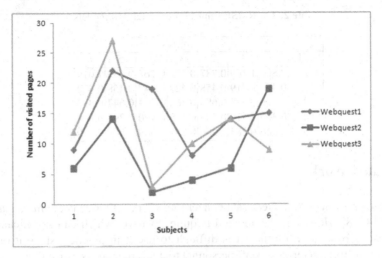

Fig. 6. Visited web pages per web-quest

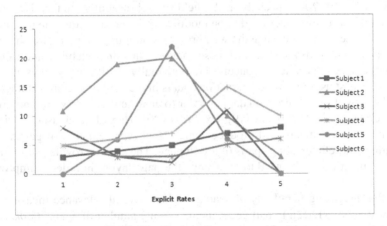

Fig. 7. Distribution of rates per subject

Subject 4 has evenly assigned all the different available rate values, whereas Subject 5 has shown less variability by assigning all rates close to 3.

Table 2 shows the RMSE between the implicit feedback predicted through the proposed model and the explicit rate provided by the subjects. We can observe that the combination of all the three metrics produces the best performances, reducing the error to the minimum average value of 0.286. Moreover, as it occurred in the regression analysis, also here the pairwise combination SR and PT produces errors that better approximate the best RMSE value based on all the three metrics, whereas the RMSE for model 1 and 3 shows that not using SR metrics yields the worst performances. Similar considerations hold by analysing RMSE for single subjects, except for Subject 1 where the model 2 is worst than model 3.

Table 2. The RMSE values for the analysed models

Model	Subjects						
	All	1	2	3	4	5	6
1	0.800	1.109	0.787	0.772	0.762	0.693	1.019
2	0.460	0.719	0.458	0.427	0.447	0.458	0.472
3	0.709	0.688	0.686	0.764	0.771	0.647	0.837
4	0.300	0.410	0.283	0.312	0.490	0.298	0.301
5	0.286	0.283	0.250	0.257	0.339	0.283	0.279

5   Related Work

A well-known strategy to collect data concerning users activities is the *think-out-loud* method [14–18]. However, this method is quite invasive, which can significantly influence user's behaviour. Further, it is difficult to use it in practice, since it requires considerable efforts in terms of staff personnel to analyze tape-recorded data.

In the scientific literature several other approaches were presented to collect data on user activity [7, 19, 20], especially in the field of web usability studies. However, in these cases the web-site codes need to be modified in order to capture the user interactions, or it is necessary to change the web browser configuration by redirecting all the traffic to an ad-hoc proxy system. All these solutions lack in scalability and cannot be used in large scale experiments, conceived to potentially involve any web users.

One of the first uses of mouse interaction data is in the field of usability studies. Several works exploit user interaction data in order to analyse user behaviour and improve usability *Cheese* [7], *MouseTrack* [19], *UsaProxy* [20]. They all track user activities by logging mouse movements, and produce some visual representation of gathered data highlighting "more interesting" parts of a web page. These data provide useful insights for web designer about the need to re-arrange the page layout in order to improve usability.

With the increasing popularity of search engines several relevance measures have been investigated [21, 22]. In particular, the increasing number of *Social Bookmarking* systems have suggested that their advantages might be combined with "classic" search tools. A prototype of a system combining Page-rank, social bookmarking ranking metrics, and general statistics of user "feelings" is described in [22]. In the same direction, also Google has shown interest for social bookmarking as witnessed by the launch of services like "SearchWiki" and "Google Plus".

However, asking users to explicitly rate web page contents might somehow disturb their activities, which can affect the reliability of the rates they provide. In order to tackle this problem, many approaches have been proposed to implicitly infer user rates. For instance, there are approaches on how to interpret click-through data accurately [23–25], or to identify relevant websites using past user activity [26, 27]. Behavioral measures that can be used as evidence of document usefulness include the display time on documents, the number of clicks and scrolling on each content page, the number of visits to each content page, further usage of content pages, time on search result page before first click, and so forth [4, 28–31]. Our approach extends these ones by introducing the reading rate metrics, yielding a threefold combination of rating metrics,

which has so far proven to sufficiently approximate explicit user ratings. The importance of reading rates is also witnessed by several studies on the different strategies that
humans adopt during the process of reading [8]. By exploiting eye-tracking systems it
has been shown that web users adopt peculiar and original reading strategies [9, 10],
which differ from those used for printed text.

6   Conclusions and Future Work

We have presented a new model to infer user interests about web page documents from
his/her mouse cursor actions, such as scrolling, movement, text selection, and the time
s/he spends on the page. We have embedded the proposed model in the YAR system,
a ranking system for the web, which re-ranks the web pages retrieved by a search engine based on the values inferred from the actions of previous visitors. YAR captures
mouse cursor actions without spoiling user browsing activities. This is an important issue, because often users are not keen to explicitly rate the usefulness of retrieved web
pages, as requested in social bookmarking systems. In order to validate the proposed
model, we run several experiments involving a group of twenty-six selected subjects.
The results demonstrate that the proposed model is able to predict user feedbacks with
an acceptable level of accuracy.

In the future we would like to perform further investigations on how mouse movements relate to user interests in the page contents. For instance, we would like to produce a classification of websites based on typical standard structures (e.g., news sites,
blogs, and so on), so as to differentiate the interpretation of mouse movements depending on the type of page being explored. Moreover, we are planning to log user actions
not only limited to a single web page, but also those related to a whole navigation section. Thus, we also plan to analyse how the user navigates through the hyper-textual
structure of web documents, in order to derive their objectives and interests.

Regarding the experimental evaluation, this is an ongoing process, and there are
many issues that should still be faced in the future. First of all, although the results
seem to be encouraging, for a complete validation of the proposed model huge experimental data would be necessary. In particular, the system should be used on a large
scale in order to track a conspicuous number of user interaction actions for a larger set
of web pages. Furthermore, the explicit rank is heavily spoiled by subjectiveness. Thus,
the distance between explicit and implicit ranks should not be the unique metrics to
measure the effectiveness of an automatic ranking system. For this reason, we are also
investigating alternative test criteria involving domain experts rather than naive users in
the explicit evaluation of web contents.

Finally, we would like to explore the application of our approach to other application
domains, with particular emphasis on usability studies and mash-up advising.

References

1. Page, L., Brin, S., Motwani, R., Winograd, T.: The pagerank citation ranking: Bringing order
   to the web. Technical Report 1999-66. Stanford InfoLab (1999)
2. Mandl, T.: Implementation and evaluation of a quality-based search engine. In: Proceedings of the Seventeenth Conference on Hypertext and Hypermedia, HYPERTEXT 2006,
   pp. 73–84. ACM, New York (2006)

3. Golder, S., Huberman, B.A.: The structure of collaborative tagging systems. Journal of Information Science 32, 198–208 (2006)

4. Agichtein, E., Brill, E., Dumais, S., Ragno, R.: Learning user interaction models for predicting web search result preferences. In: Proceedings of the 29th International ACM Conference on Research and Development in Information Retrieval, SIGIR 2006, pp. 3–10. ACM, New York (2006)

5. Fox, S., Karnawat, K., Mydland, M., Dumais, S., White, T.: Evaluating implicit measures to improve web search. ACM Trans. Inf. Syst. 23, 147–168 (2005)

6. Chen, M.C., Anderson, J.R., Sohn, M.H.: What can a mouse cursor tell us more?: correlation of eye/mouse movements on web browsing. In: Proceedings of Conference on Human Factors in Computing Systems, CHI 2001, pp. 281–282. ACM, New York (2001)

7. Mueller, F., Lockerd, A.: Cheese: tracking mouse movement activity on websites, a tool for user modeling. In: Proceedings of Conference on Human Factors in Computing Systems, CHI 2001, pp. 279–280. ACM, New York (2001)

8. Hunziker, H.W.: Im Auge des Lesers foveale und periphere Wahrnehmung: vom Buchstabieren zur Lesefreude (In the eye of the reader: foveal and peripheral perception - from letter recognition to the joy of reading). Transmedia Zurich (2006)

9. Nielsen, J.: How little do users read? (2008),
   http://www.useit.com/alertbox/percent-text-read.html

10. Nielsen, J.: F-shaped pattern for reading web content (2006),
    http://www.useit.com/alertbox/reading_pattern.html

11. Huang, J., White, R.W., Dumais, S.: No clicks, no problem: using cursor movements to understand and improve search. In: Proceedings of Conference on Human Factors in Computing Systems, CHI 2011, pp. 1225–1234. ACM, New York (2011)

12. Murray, G.: Asynchronous javascript technology and XML (ajax) with the java platform (2006),
    http://java.sun.com/developer/technicalArticles/J2EE/AJAX/

13. Dodge, B.: Webquests: A technique for internet-based learning. Distance Educator 1, 10–13 (1995)

14. Bath, J.: Answer-changing behaviour on objective examinations. The Journal of Educational Research 1, 105–107 (1967)

15. Best, J.B.: Item difficulty and answer changing. Teaching of Psychology 6, 228–240 (1979)

16. Johnston, J.: Exam taking speed and grades. Teaching of Psychology, 148–149 (1977)

17. Paul, C.A., Rosenkoetter, J.S.: The relationship between the time taken to complete an examination and the test score received. Teaching of Psychology, 108–109 (1980)

18. McClain, L.: Behavior during examinations: A comparison of "a", "c," and "f" students. Teaching of Psychology 10, 69–71 (1983)

19. Arroyo, E., Selker, T., Wei, W.: Usability tool for analysis of web designs using mouse tracks. In: Proceedings of Conference on Human Factors in Computing Systems, CHI 2006, pp. 484–489. ACM, New York (2006)

20. Atterer, R., Wnuk, M., Schmidt, A.: Knowing the user's every move: user activity tracking for website usability evaluation and implicit interaction. In: Proceedings of the 15th International Conference on World Wide Web, WWW 2006, pp. 203–212. ACM, New York (2006)

21. Kelly, D., Teevan, J.: Implicit feedback for inferring user preference: A bibliography. SIGIR Forum (2003)

22. Yanbe, Y., Jatowt, A., Nakamura, S., Tanaka, K.: Can social bookmarking enhance search in the web? In: Proceedings of the 7th ACM/IEEE Joint Conference on Digital Libraries, JCDL 2007, pp. 107–116. ACM, New York (2007)

23. Joachims, T., Granka, L., Pan, B., Hembrooke, H., Gay, G.: Accurately interpreting click-through data as implicit feedback. In: Proceedings of the 28th ACM Conference on Research and Development in Information Retrieval, SIGIR 2005, pp. 154–161. ACM, New York (2005)
24. Jung, S., Herlocker, J.L., Webster, J.: Click data as implicit relevance feedback in web search. Inf. Process. Manage. 43, 791–807 (2007)
25. Radlinski, F., Joachims, T.: Query chains: learning to rank from implicit feedback. In: Proceedings of ACM Conference on Knowledge Discovery in Data Mining, KDD 2005, pp. 239–248. ACM, New York (2005)
26. Agichtein, E., Zheng, Z.: Identifying "best bet" web search results by mining past user behavior. In: Proceedings of the 12th ACM Conference on Knowledge Discovery and Data Mining, KDD 2006, pp. 902–908. ACM, New York (2006)
27. Bilenko, M., White, R.W.: Mining the search trails of surfing crowds: identifying relevant websites from user activity. In: Proceeding of the 17th International Conference on World Wide Web, WWW 2008, pp. 51–60. ACM, New York (2008)
28. Claypool, M., Le, P., Wased, M., Brown, D.: Implicit interest indicators. In: Proceedings of the 6th International Conference on Intelligent User Interfaces, IUI 2001, pp. 33–40. ACM, New York (2001)
29. Kelly, D., Belkin, N.J.: Display time as implicit feedback: understanding task effects. In: Proceedings of the 27th International ACM Conference on Research and Development in Information Retrieval, SIGIR 2004, pp. 377–384. ACM, New York (2004)
30. Konstan, J.A., Miller, B.N., Maltz, D., Herlocker, J.L., Gordon, L.R., Riedl, J.: GroupLens: applying collaborative filtering to Usenet news. Commun. ACM 40, 77–87 (1997)
31. Xu, S., Zhu, Y., Jiang, H., Lau, F.C.M.: A user-oriented webpage ranking algorithm based on user attention time. In: Proceedings of the 23rd National Conference on Artificial Intelligence, AAAI 2008, vol. 2, pp. 1255–1260. AAAI Press (2008)

Part V
Mobile Information Systems

Harnessing Electronic Signatures
to Improve the Security of SMS-Based Services

Thomas Zefferer, Arne Tauber, and Bernd Zwattendorfer

Institute for Applied Information Processing and Communications,
Graz University of Technology, Inffeldgasse 16a, 8010 Graz, Austria
{thomas.zefferer, arne.tauber,
bernd.zwattendorfer}@iaik.tugraz.at

Abstract. Powered by the emergence of information and communication technologies, governments and public administrations are nowadays offering online services to facilitate the execution of governmental procedures. Citizens, businesses, and even governments themselves benefit from greater flexibility and cost efficiency of such e-Government services. Recently, the increased mobility of citizens and the growing popularity of mobile communication technologies has raised the need for mobile governmental services. Such services have become known under the term m-Government. Interestingly, most m-Government services still rely on SMS technology. Reasons for that are the simplicity, inexpensiveness and wide support of this technology. Despite these various advantages, a lack of supported security features usually hinders SMS to be used in transactional m-Government services, as these services have higher security requirements. To bypass this issue, we propose a method to enhance SMS-based m-Government services by means of electronic signatures. Our solution allows citizens to generate, electronically sign, and deliver electronic documents by sending well-defined SMS messages. We demonstrate the practical applicability of our approach by means of a prototypical implementation. A detailed discussion of different security aspects of our solution concludes this contribution.

Keywords: SMS, m-Government, Electronic signatures, SMS based services, Austrian Mobile-Phone signature, Security analysis.

1 Introduction

In order to facilitate administrative procedures, governments and public administrations all over the world have been offering e-Government services for several years. E-Government services incorporate modern information and communication technologies to allow citizens to carry our administrative procedures over the Internet. During the past few years, mobile computing and communication technologies have significantly gained popularity. Governments and public administrations have reacted on this trend and has started to complement e-Government services by mobile communication technologies. These attempts have become commonly known under the terms mobile government and m-Government.

m-Government solutions can be found all over the world in both developing and developed countries. Recent surveys on m-Government [5] [6] have revealed that a majority of current m-Government services still rely on the rather simple SMS (short message

J. Cordeiro and K.-H. Krempels (Eds.): WEBIST 2012, LNBIP 140, pp. 331–346, 2013.

service) technology. The popularity of SMS technology has several reasons. First, the sending of SMS messages is often very cheap compared to other more powerful mobile data transmission technologies. Various mobile network operators offer customers special flat rates for sending text messages. Secondly, SMS technology is nowadays supported by virtually every mobile phone and does not require powerful mobile data networks. Thus, SMS based services are not limited to certain end-user devices but can rather be accessed by all users possessing a mobile phone. This is of special relevance in developing countries, in which the market penetration of smartphones in comparison to mobile phones is still low and broadband mobile networks are often not available in rural areas. Another advantage of SMS technology is its simplicity. Even technically inexperienced users are able to send and receive SMS messages. Furthermore, no set-up or configuration is required. SMS technology can be used out of the box similarly to telephony.

The various advantages of SMS technology account for the wide range of SMS based m-Government services. However, there are also drawbacks of SMS based solutions. For instance, due to given technological limitations, SMS based services are usually very simple. In most cases, these services are used to broadcast certain information to citizens or to collect data from citizens. Few SMS based applications actually implement complete transactional services. Depending on the use case, transactional services may have security requirements that can only be met by applying cryptographic methods. This is problematic in the context of SMS based services, for which the capabilities of end-user devices are basically limited to sending and receiving of text based data only.

In this paper we present an application that allows users to securely carry out complete signature-based transactional services by sending SMS messages. The services supported by our application include creation, signing, and delivery of electronic documents. Security requirements such as integrity of digital data and non-repudiation of origin are met by integrating both advanced and qualified electronic signatures.

The remainder of this paper is structured as follows. Section 2 discusses related work on SMS based m-Government services. We introduce basic concepts of electronic signatures in Section 3. In this section, we also introduce a set of approved core components, which our application partly relies on. In Section 4 we discuss architectural and implementation details of our solution and show how it works in practice by means of a concrete case study. Security issues of our approach are discussed in Section 5. Finally, an outlook to future work is given and final conclusions are drawn.

2   Related Work

Although modern smartphones provide users a variety of different communication capabilities, SMS technology is still favoured all over the world [7]. The popularity of SMS technology has led to a plethora of SMS based services. Also the public sector tries to make use of SMS technology's popularity. SMS based m-Government services can already be found in various countries around the world. Comprehensive overviews of existing SMS based projects and initiatives are given in [5] and [6].

SMS has played an essential role in developing countries for many years. Especially in rural areas, reliable and powerful fixed-line communication networks are often not available. Contrary, mobile communication networks are often well evolved even in underdeveloped regions. Yet, they are limited to GSM technology most of the time. The consequent restriction to telephony and text messaging has led to the development of various useful SMS based services. For instance, the FrontlineSMS project[1] aims to improve communication capabilities in regions with underdeveloped infrastructures. FrontlineSMS allows data exchange between remote entities (PCs, Laptop, etc.) based on SMS messages. Another example for an SMS based service is Kenya's BloodBank-SMS project[2]. Due to missing reliable fixed-line communication networks, statuses of blood banks are exchanged via an SMS based service between different hospitals.

There are various other SMS based services from the health sector available in developing countries. In South Africa, citizens can request location information on HIV testing centres via SMS. Text to Change[3] is a health education initiative that aims to inform people in developing countries about diseases such as malaria or AIDS using text messaging technologies.

In developed countries, reliable fixed-line communication networks are usually well evolved. Mobile communication networks are thus just one out of multiple communication and information alternatives and mainly used to satisfy demands of the typical western always-on society. Hence, SMS based services in developed regions differ from those of developing countries in various aspects. In fact, most existing SMS based services aim to improve convenience. For instance, in various European cities parking fees can be paid via text messages[4]. In Norway, also tax declarations can be done with the help of SMS messages[5], which has significantly eased the entire tax declaration process for citizens.

Various countries in both developing and developed regions make use of SMS to broadcast relevant information to their citizens. For instance, in Venice, Italy, citizens are supplied with flood warnings per SMS[6]. In London, UK, the Metropolitan police forward bomb alerts and similar security warnings to registered citizens via SMS[7]. In Australia, an e-mail and SMS based warning system[8] has been set up, which alerts citizens when forest fire has been detected near their homes.

So far, most SMS based services are rather informational than transactional. This is reasonable since transactional services usually have higher security requirements that are difficult to meet with SMS based approaches. Therefore, transactional services are traditionally provided through web based approaches, which allow an easier integration of cryptographic methods. Unfortunately, there are scenarios in which web access is not available and web based services cannot be accessed. In such scenarios, SMS

---

[1] http://www.frontlinesms.com/

[2] http://www.media.mit.edu/ventures/EPROM/research.html

[3] http://www.texttochange.org/

[4] http://www.handyparken.at/handyparken/home.seam

[5] http://www.textually.org/textually/archives/2003/04/000349.htm

[6] http://www.textually.org/textually/archives/2008/06/020298.htm

[7] http://www.emergencysms.org.uk/

[8] http://michael.tyson.id.au/2008/11/13/
firewatch-an-email-based-fire-warning-system

based transactional services can be useful. The approach introduced in this paper implements transactional services on SMS basis and incorporates electronic signatures to meet security requirements of such services.

3   Background

Electronic signatures are perfectly suitable to meet the requirements for integrity and non-repudiation of transactional e-Government and m-Government services. In this section we discuss basic principles of electronic signatures and related legal aspects. As the application presented in this paper relies on several components of the Austrian e-Government infrastructure, this section also emphasizes the role of electronic signatures in the Austrian e-Government.

3.1   Electronic Signatures

Electronic signatures are an important element of current e-Government infrastructures and services. Electronic signatures rely on asymmetric cryptography and provide integrity of digital data and non-repudiation of origin. To harmonize legal aspects of electronic signatures throughout the European Union, the so-called EU Signature Directive [3] has been enacted in 1999. The EU Signature Directive defines in detail the following two types of electronic signatures.

- **Advanced electronic signature** "means an electronic signature which meets the following requirements:
  - It is uniquely linked to the signatory
  - It is capable of identifying the signatory
  - It is created using means that the signatory can maintain under his sole control; and
  - It is linked to the data to which it relates in such a manner that any subsequent change of the data is detectable"
- **Qualified electronic signatures** are advanced electronic signatures that are based on qualified certificates and are created by a secure signature creation device. Requirements for qualified certificates and secure signature creation devices are also defined in detail in the annex of this directive.

The EU Signature Directive assures legal equivalence between qualified electronic signatures and handwritten signatures and their mutual recognition throughout the European Union. Enabling citizens to apply legally valid signatures, qualified electronic signatures are an important component of many e-Government services. Citizens typically use smart cards or similar hardware tokens as secure signature creation devices in order to create electronic signatures. However, some countries provide their citizens also alternative approaches. For instance, citizens can use their mobile phones to create qualified electronic signatures in Austria[9] and Estonia[10].

---

[9] https://www.handy-signatur.at

[10] http://www.id.ee/?id=10995&&langchange=1

In the scope of e-Government, electronic signatures are not only used by citizens. Electronic signatures are also an important tool for public administrations to avoid media breaks and to facilitate the processing of administrative procedures. In many countries, administrative rulings are therefore electronically signed before being delivered to citizens. Depending on the underlying technology, different kinds of electronic signatures according to the EU Signature Directive are used for this purpose.

To meet the requirements of different use cases, our solution supports both advanced and qualified electronic signatures. Calling on many years of experience, the Austrian e-Government initiative provides several core components that ease an integration of electronic signatures into e-Government infrastructures. In the following we introduce some of these components, which our application partly relies on.

3.2 Electronic Signatures in Austria

Electronic signatures are a key concept of the Austrian e-Government. The use of electronic signatures within Austrian e-Government processes is facilitated by several core components. Refer to [4] for a comprehensive overview of and introduction to these components.

Citizens use qualified electronic signatures to authenticate at e-Government services, to assure integrity of transmitted data, and to provide written consent in electronic procedures. Public administrations make use of advanced electronic signatures to improve governmental back-office processes and to sign administrative rulings. In the following we discuss core components of the Austrian e-Government initiative dealing with the creation of electronic signatures. Some of these components are used by our SMS-based application.

With the Citizen Card - the national eID - Austrian citizens can create qualified electronic signatures. Although the term Citizen Card suggests the use of smart cards, the Citizen Card concept [1] is actually technology neutral and not limited to a certain signature creation device. Currently, Austrian citizens can use smart cards and mobile phones to create qualified electronic signatures. While smart card based signature creation processes are used in various countries, the mobile phone based approach followed in Austria is novel and especially of interest in the context of our SMS based application.

The Austrian Mobile Phone Signature that has been discussed by Orthacker et al. in [2] follows a centralized approach to carry out mobile phone based signatures. This means that a central hardware security module (HSM) is in charge of creating electronic signatures. The user's mobile phone is solely used to authorize the signature creation process with a mobile transaction number (mTAN). According to this approach, a central service currently hosted by the Austrian certification authority A-Trust[11] represents the core component of the Austrian Mobile Phone Signature. A HSM is an integral part of this central service. For security reasons, all Citizen Card private keys are encrypted with the master key of the HSM and a symmetric encryption key, which is derived from a secure password that is only known to the user.

---

[11] http://www.a-trust.at/

To start a signature creation process, users have to transmit their mobile phone number and their secure password together with the data to be signed to the central service. This communication takes place through a secured web based interface. With the secure password, the user's personal signing key residing in the central HSM can be decrypted. After successful verification of the secure password and decryption of the user's signing key, a one-time password (TAN) is generated and sent to the user's mobile phone via SMS. To finally initiate the signature creation process, the user returns the obtained TAN through the web based interface to the central service.

The security of the Mobile Phone Signature basically depends on the second, non-web based mobile communication channel that is used to transmit a secure TAN to the user. Similar to smart card based approaches, also the Austrian Mobile Phone Signature relies on a two-factor authentication scheme. The factor *knowledge* is covered by the user's secure signature password. Additionally, the factor *possession* is considered by sending a TAN to the user's mobile phone. This way, the service verifies whether the user is the person she claims to be.

The Mobile Phone Signature facilitates the creation of qualified electronic signatures for Austrian citizens. Public administrations often rely on advanced electronic signatures, which are better suited for automated signature creation. To facilitate signature creation processes for Austrian public administrations, a server-based signature creation module has been developed. This module is called MOA-SS[12] and enables the creation of advanced electronic signatures using preconfigured software keys.

To improve security and reliability, the SMS based m-Government application we are presenting in this paper relies on core signature components, which are provided as open source modules by the Austrian e-Government initiative. Our solution incorporates both the Mobile Phone Signature and MOA-SS to integrate creation devices for qualified and advanced electronic signatures. This way, our application basically supports two different levels of security, advanced and qualified electronic signatures according to the EU Signature Directive. We will discuss security implications of this approach later in this paper.

4   Implementation

The basic objective of our application is the implementation of SMS based transactional procedures. In our solution, a procedure defines a process including the generation, signing, and delivery of electronic documents. To meet possible security requirements of such procedures, our solution incorporates electronic signatures. In this section we present the architecture and the general process flow of our solution. To appropriately illustrate our application's functionality, we finally discuss a concrete procedural use case supported by our solution.

4.1   Architecture

The limiting factor of SMS based services defines the end-user's device, which is basically restricted to sending and receiving of SMS messages. Most functionality of our

---

[12] http://egovlabs.gv.at/projects/moa-idspss/

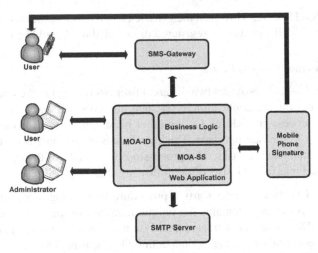

Fig. 1. Architecture and basic building blocks of the presented application

application cannot be modeled via SMS messages and thus has to be outsourced to another component. Therefore, our solution relies on a central web application implementing the main functionality. The central web application makes use of several external components to implement the desired processes.

Figure 1 shows the basic building blocks of our solution. The central web application defines the core component and basically implements all business logic. Users interact with this web application through an external SMS gateway that translates SMS messages into XML based requests and vice versa. By sending appropriate SMS messages users can electronically create, sign, and deliver documents. All this functionality is basically covered by the web application's business logic.

Our solution supports two alternatives to sign a created document[13]. Qualified electronic signatures can be carried out using the Austrian Mobile Phone Signature. Alternatively, documents can also be signed using a central MOA-SS module being an integral component of the central web application. This approach allows for the creation of advanced electronic signatures.

The web application also features a web based user interface. Through this interface users can review and inspect their documents that have been previously processed via SMS. Additionally, administrators can carry out maintenance tasks through this interface. The web based access to the central web application is protected by a two-factor authentication scheme. Again, we rely on an approved core component of the Austrian e-Government landscape to implement secure user authentication. The open source module MOA-ID[14] encapsulates functionality needed to securely authenticate users by means of a two-factor authentication based on the Austrian Citizen Card concept. Similar to MOA-SS, MOA-ID is an integral component of our central web application.

To facilitate the delivery of signed documents, the web application is also connected

---

[13] The documents created follow the PDF standard.

[14] http://egovlabs.gv.at/projects/moa-idspss/

to an external SMTP server. However, the generic design of our solution guarantees that also other types of delivery such as registered or certified mail could be used.

4.2   Interfaces and Process Flows

Our application basically provides two different user interfaces. On the one hand, users can communicate with the application by exchanging SMS messages. This interface is mainly used to process procedures. On the other hand, the application can also be accessed through a web based interface. This interface is mainly intended for document inspection and maintenance tasks. The processing of procedures through the application's SMS based interface consists of the following steps:

- **Document Creation.** A user starts a procedure by sending a well-defined SMS message. This message contains the unique identifier of the procedure to be processed. A PDF document is created based on a template that is assigned to the selected procedure and on dynamic data defined by the user. This data is transmitted to the application via SMS together with the procedure's unique identifier.
- **Document Signing.** The document is signed either by the external Mobile Phone Signature or by the central MOA-SS signature module. Depending on the chosen method either a qualified personal citizen signature or an advanced electronic server signature is created. The user selects the desired signature method by SMS. If the user chooses the Mobile Phone Signature, a TAN is sent to the user's mobile phone during the signature creation process. This TAN has to be forwarded manually to the central application via SMS.
- **Document Delivery.** The document is delivered to configured recipients. Different recipients can be defined for each procedure. After successful delivery, the document is stored in a central database for later inspection. The user is notified about the successful processing of the document via SMS and e-mail.

Besides the SMS interface, the application can also be accessed through a web based interface. The set of functionality provided through this web interface actually depends on the user's assigned rights. Standard users can use the application's web interface for the following tasks:

- **Account Creation.** In order to use the application, users need to register and create a user profile containing mobile phone number and e-mail address.
- **Register to Procedures.** The application allows the dynamic definition of different procedures. Users must register to defined procedures before using them.
- **Inspect Documents.** Documents created during the processing of procedures can be inspected and downloaded through the application's web interface.

Users with assigned administrator rights can additionally access the following functions through the application's web interface:

- **Define Procedures.** System administrators can define new procedures by choosing an appropriate identifier and a suitable PDF template. Additionally, predefined receivers can be selected to receive newly created and signed documents. Also data that has to be provided by users during the document creation process can be defined.

- **Application Maintenance.** Application maintenance involves for instance the activation and deletion of user accounts.

4.3 Case Study: Sick Note

The reporting of absence from work due to sickness is one out of many scenarios that comply with the above mentioned general process flow. In the following we illustrate the functionality of our application by discussing the sick note procedure in more detail. Although this is actually not a typical m-Government procedure, its simplicity makes it perfectly suitable to demonstrate the capabilities of our approach.

Basically, the implemented sick note procedure allows employees to generate, sign, and deliver sick notes to their employer. Using our applications, sick employees can reliably report their absence simply by sending SMS messages but still having the guarantee and non-repudiation property of electronic signatures. The entire procedure requires the following steps to be carried out.

Definition of Procedure. Before a procedure can be used, it has to be defined first. Procedures can be defined by users with administrator rights through the application's web based maintenance interface. Once a procedure is defined, users can register to this procedure and use it.

A procedure basically specifies a type of document that may be generated and signed by users during a transaction. Amongst others, a procedure is defined by the following information:

- Unique identifier
- List of key words, which have to be transmitted by the user via SMS, and which are included in the generated document
- List of receivers of completely signed documents

Considering our concrete case study, the procedure that supports the SMS based generation of sick notes comprises the following specifications:

- Unique identifier: SICK
- List of key words: FROM
- List of receivers: DEPARTMENT HEAD, PERSONNEL OFFICE

Figure 2 shows the web interface that can be used to define new procedures. Amongst others, this interface allows the assignment of receivers and key words. Receivers and key words can by defined via similar web based interfaces.

Registration. Users must register through the web application's web interface in order to gain access to the application. Therefore, users are securely authenticated using a two-factor authentication scheme based on the Austrian Citizen Card concept.

During the registration process, a user account is created, which contains required user related data such as user name and mobile phone number. To avoid misuse, newly created user accounts must be organisationally verified and manually activated by system administrators.

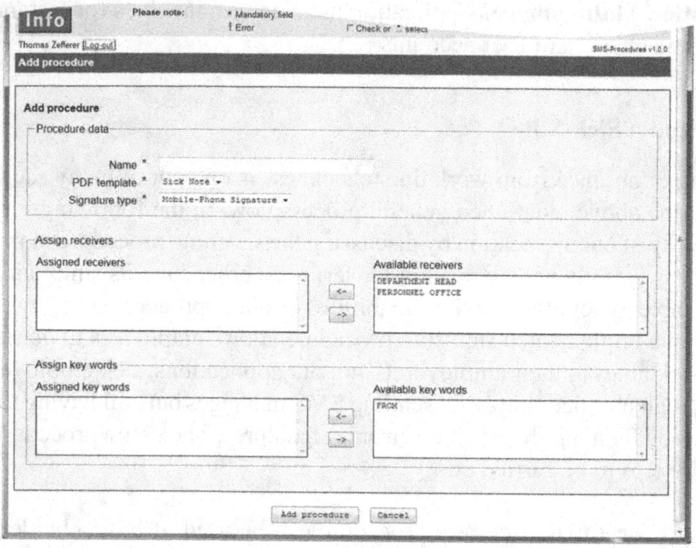

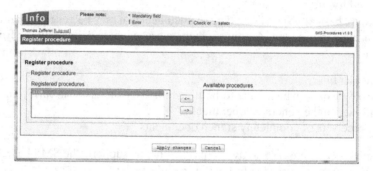

Fig. 2. Web based interface for the definition of new procedures.

Fig. 3. Web based interface allowing users to register to available procedures.

As soon as the user's account is activated, she may register to procedures that have been previously defined by system administrators. This registration takes place through the web interface shown in Figure 3. The registration for procedures is only required once. After successful registration no further web based interaction with the application is required.

Document Processing. The processing of procedures represents the main use case of our application and is completely carried out via the application's SMS interface. To start the process flow (i.e. to create a sick note), users send an SMS to the web application. The SMS contains the unique identifier of the corresponding procedure (i.e. 'SICK') and a list of key words (i.e. 'FROM') with associated key values (e.g. '2011-11-01') that have to be provided for this procedure.

As the application supports two signature creation alternatives, the user's preferred signature method must also be included in the SMS message. If the user desires to sign the document to be generated by the Server Signature Module MOA-SS, the key word 'server' has to be appended to the SMS message. If the user prefers the Mobile Phone Signature approach, the user's Mobile Phone Signature password has to be appended instead.

Reconsidering the sick note example, a user could send the following text message to start the process flow and sign the document using the Server Signature Module:

SICK*FROM:2011-11-01*server

To generate the same document (sick note) but sign it with the Mobile Phone Signature, the following SMS message has to be sent:

SICK*FROM:2011-11-01*<password>

In this example, '<password>' denotes the user's personal password for the Mobile Phone Signature service. In this scenario, a signature creation request is sent to the Mobile Phone Signature. The user receives a mobile TAN during the signature creation process. This TAN has to be forwarded to the web application via SMS. In order to complete the signing process, the central web application forwards the TAN to the Mobile Phone Signature for verification.

Irrespective of the chosen signing method, the signed document is finally delivered to all configured receivers of the procedure. According to the definition of the Sick Note procedure, the created and signed sick note is sent to the department head and to the personnel office. The user is notified about the success of the document processing by SMS and e-mail.

Figure 4 illustrate the SMS based user interaction from the user point of view. In the shown example, the user requests the creation of a sick note indicating a sick leave that starts on 2011/11/21. Furthermore, the user selects the MOA-SS based signature creation method by adding the key word 'server'. The application notifies the user via SMS after having created, signed, and delivered the sick note.

Document Inspection. The whole process of document and signature creation is basically carried out by the central web application. Since users communicate with the web application via SMS only, created and signed documents cannot be accessed immediately. To guarantee an appropriate degree of transparency, the application stores the signed document in an internal database for later inspection. Previously generated and signed documents can be accessed via the application's web interface. Again, access to this interface and to own documents is protected by a secure two-factor authentication scheme.

Figure 5 shows the web based user interface. The left area contains a list of available documents. Details of the selected document are displayed in the main area. Details include document related data and the document's processing log. Available PDF files can be downloaded by clicking the displayed PDF icons.

Fig. 4. SMS message exchange during processing of procedure

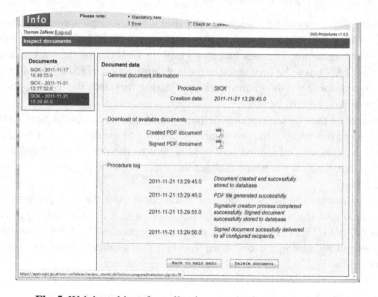

Fig. 5. Web based interface allowing users to inspect documents

5   Security Analysis

This section discusses aspects, which may have an impact on the security level of SMS-based procedures. Security considerations have been made during the conceptual design of the main architecture and also during the prototypical implementation.

5.1   Omission of Communication Channel

The traditional Austrian Mobile Phone Signature uses a two-factor authentication mechanism based on two communication channels. This means that on the one hand mobile phone number and signature password entered in a web form ensure knowledge and on the other hand the correct TAN sent by SMS ensures proof of possession. Hence, if the phone is stolen, without knowing the signature password a signature creation process cannot be initiated. In contrast, the purely SMS based procedures proposed in this paper have just one communication channel, the mobile phone. Even if a pure SMS based solution may increase usability, a single communication channel inevitably decreases the security level. If the used mobile end device is infected with malware, the use of a single communication channel may become critical as both signature password and TAN are transferred via the same device. This issue is discussed in more detail in Section 5.5.

5.2 Security of Intermediary Components

In case of the Austrian Mobile Phone Signature, the TAN is directly exchanged between the user and the Mobile Phone Signature service. Several intermediary components are involved in case of SMS based procedures. It is necessary that all these components fulfil certain security requirements to protect the TAN from disclosure. The security of the whole system is just as strong as the weakest link. This does not only concern the components itself, but the inter-component communication as well. For example, an intermediary component using GSM may threaten the security of the whole system due to known vulnerabilities of GSM [9].

5.3 Signature Password Handling

When using the Austrian Mobile Phone Signature in SMS based procedures, the application requires the user's password to create the signature. The only possible way is to transmit the password within an SMS from the user to the application. This approach has two drawbacks. First, it requires full trust in the application and intermediary components. A malicious SMS gateway could intercept signature passwords and exploit them in an abusive way. A second problem is the sending of the user's signature password over the same channel as the TAN. This is a heightened security risk because if the channel is compromised, also the signature process might be compromised. Users are also advised to delete their sent SMS messages from their mobile phones frequently. Otherwise, the secure signature password may appear in locally stored communication histories and get compromised if the device gets lost or stolen.

5.4 Display of Signature Data

According to the Austrian Signature Act, involved technical components must ensure that the signed data can be displayed to the signatory upon request. When using the Austrian Mobile Phone Signature in the user's web browser, this functionality is provided. Support of this feature is more difficult with our SMS based approach as only text based data can be displayed by SMS technology. However, this does not render application of our approach impossible, since our solution relies on the Austrian PDF signature standard PDF-AS [8]. PDF-AS allows the text based signing of PDF documents, i.e. only the extracted text is signed. This text could also be displayed in one or more SMS messages. This feature is not yet supported in our prototype implementation, but can be added easily if required.

5.5 Malware

Traditional mobile phones with limited functionality can usually be considered as secure. This assumption does not apply to smartphones. Since smartphones can be extended and equipped with arbitrary additional software called *Apps*, they are more vulnerable to different kinds of malware. Apps may get rights to access various parts of the phone's functionality, e.g. including SMS capabilities. This way, an App may intercept unnoticedly incoming or outgoing SMS messages. This is the reason why it can be problematic to enter the signature password on a smartphone. Having caught the password and being able to unnoticedly intercept incoming SMS messages, malware could theoretically create qualified electronic signatures with legal value on behalf of the user.

5.6 Identity Spoofing

Another critical security target is spoofing of the user's identity. SMS spoofing[15] is a common and legitimate technique offered by phone providers so that SMS messages appear to originate from a particular company (name) or a particular phone number. However, the technique can illicitly be used to impersonate another person or company. This way, an attacker may trigger SMS based procedures on behalf of the user. The issue becomes critical if the procedure does not use any confirmation TAN, for example if the user initially triggers the procedure via SMS and the remaining part is processed on the server side (including the generation of the signature).

6 Future Work

The conducted security analysis revealed several security issues that have to be considered in future work. One key issue that has been identified is the vulnerability of the exchanged SMS messages and the integrity and confidentiality of the data contained within these messages. Hence, in a first step we attempt to identify and test different approaches to overcome this issue.

The weakness of the encryption schemes used by the GSM protocol has already been shown by Barkan et al. in [9]. The identification of weaknesses in the GSM protocol has raised the demand for appropriate mechanisms to guarantee secure GSM based communications. Various approaches to satisfy this demand have already been introduced. A comprehensive overview of current approaches to enhance the security of SMS is given by Medani et al. in [13]. Most known approaches make use of cryptographic methods to assure confidentiality and integrity of exchanged SMS messages. For instance, Lisonek and Drahansk [10] enhanced the security of SMS messages by using asymmetric cryptography. Another method relying on both symmetric and asymmetric encryption schemes has been proposed by Anuar et al. [11]. In [12] a hybrid cryptographic scheme has been introduced to meet given security requirements.

All these methods are basically able to enhance the security of data being exchanged via SMS. However, all these solutions also add a certain amount of complexity and require the incorporation of additional components. For our prototypical implementation

---

[15] http://www.smsspoofing.com/

we have therefore omitted all security enhancing features. A detailed evaluation of existing security enhancing approaches and their integration into our solution is therefore regarded as future work.

Besides the general weaknesses of the GSM protocol, malware running on mobile end devices has been identified as second key issue regarding the security of our solution. Due to their comprehensive software management facilities, especially modern smartphones are known to be prone to malware. We are currently working on the development of practical means and methods to detect malware on smartphones in order to ensure a secure and trustworthy execution environment for security sensitive mobile applications. We plan to integrate outcomes of these attempts into the SMS based document processing solution presented in this paper in order to enhance its overall security.

7 Conclusions

In this paper we have presented an SMS based application that makes use of advanced and qualified electronic signatures to meet security requirements of transactional m-Government services. Our application allows users to dynamically create, electronically sign, and deliver PDF documents on a pure SMS basis. Tests have shown that our solution allows documents to be created, singed, and delivered within a few seconds.

Although being fully functional, the presented application is still in a prototypical state. The basic goal of this prototypical implementation was to evaluate whether an integration of electronic signatures into SMS based services is technically feasible. Definitely, our application shows that this is basically possible.

The security of the presented approach has been continuously assessed during design, implementation, and practical evaluation. Malware running on mobile end devices and general weaknesses of the GSM protocol have been identified as key issues regarding the overall security of our solution. The identified challenges need to be faced and overcome, before the presented solution can finally be set into productive operation. The development of appropriate counter measures to the identified threats is an ongoing activity. The integration of the outcomes of this activity into our solution is regarded as future work.

References

1. Leitold, H., Hollosi, A., Posch, R.: Security Architecture of the Austrian Citizen Card Concept. In: Proceedings of the 18th Annual Computer Security Applications Conference (ACSAC 2002). IEEE Computer Society (2002)
2. Orthacker, C., Centner, M., Kittl, C.: Qualified Mobile Server Signature. In: Rannenberg, K., Varadharajan, V., Weber, C. (eds.) SEC 2010. IFIP AICT, vol. 330, pp. 103–111. Springer, Heidelberg (2010)
3. European Union: Directive 1999/93/EC of the European Parliament and of the Council of 13 December 1999 on a Community framework for electronic signatures. Official Journal of the European Communities (1999)
4. Posch, K.C., Posch, R., Tauber, A., Zefferer, T., Zwattendorfer, B.: Secure and Privacy-Preserving eGovernment—Best Practice Austria. In: Calude, C.S., Rozenberg, G., Salomaa, A. (eds.) Rainbow of Computer Science. LNCS, vol. 6570, pp. 259–269. Springer, Heidelberg (2011)

5. Mobi Solutions Ltd.: Mobile Government: 2010 and Beyond (2010)
6. Zefferer, T.: Mobile Government - E-Government for Mobile Societies (2011),
   http://www.a-sit.at/pdfs/Technologiebeobachtung/
   mobile_government_1.0.pdf
7. MBAONLINE: Planet Text - How SMS Messaging is Changing the World (2011),
   http://www.mbaonline.com/planet-text/
8. EGov-Labs: PDF-AS (2012), http://egovlabs.gv.at/projects/pdf-as/
9. Barkan, E., Biham, E., Keller, N.: Instant Ciphertext-Only Cryptanalysis of GSM Encrypted
   Communication. J. Cryptol. 21, 392–429 (2008)
10. Lisonek, D., Drahansk, M.: SMS Encryption for Mobile Communication. In: International
    Conference on Security Technology, pp. 198–201. IEEE Computer Society (2008)
11. Anuar, N.B., Kuen, L.N., Zakaria, O., Gani, A., Wahab, A.W.A.: GSM mobile SMS/MMS
    using public key infrastructure: m-PKI. W. Trans. on Comp. 7, 1219–1229 (2008)
12. Al-bakri, S., Kiah, M.: A novel peer-to-peer SMS security solution using a hybrid technique
    of NTRU and AES-Rijndael. Scientific Research and Essays 5(22), 3455–3466 (2010)
13. Medani, A., Gani, A., Zakaria, O., Zaidan, A.A., Zaidan, B.B.: Review of mobile short mes-
    sage service security issues and techniques towards the solution. Scientific Research and
    Essays 6(6), 1147–1165 (2011)

Integrating Communication Services into Mobile Browsers

Joachim Zeiß[1], Marcin Davies[1], Goran Lazendic[1], Rene Gabner[1], and Janusz Bartecki[2]

[1] FTW Telecommunications Research Center Vienna, Vienna, Austria
[2] Kapsch CarrierCom, Vienna, Austria
{zeiss,davies,lazendic,gabner}@ftw.at,
janusz.bartecki@kapsch.net

Abstract. This paper introduces a novel approach on how to integrate communication services into Web applications running in the browser. The solution is based on two major design decisions: To resolve the need for a business-to-business (B2B) relationship between Web provider and communication service provider, and to distribute the Model, View and Controller components of an application across different processes. Our approach helps to answer the question on how to efficiently integrate network operator's assets into applications from over the top (OTT) players. The separation between application control by the Web page and the actual command execution by the native capabilities of the user device opens new opportunities for global reachability of telco services, easy deployment and re-deployment of applications with zero configuration need for users and developers as well as privacy protection by keeping sensitive data within the user domain, e.g. the user's communication device.

Keywords: Convergence, VoIP, Browser-APIs, SIP, IMS, HTML5, Websockets, Real-time Communication.

1 Introduction

More and more innovative applications created for the Web are integrating typical telco services. Users in turn, get accustomed to the business model of the Web and perceive telecommunication services offered outside the web context as reliable and of high quality although being a bit old fashioned, detached from the social web community and too technical. Application developers concentrate on globally marketable products with simple and unified interfaces. Telcos, even when operating globally, serve a smaller community compared to Google, Apple, Facebook or other over the top service providers. They struggle to unify their activities to participate in the application business and to avoid becoming only bit pipes.

Therefore, the following question needs to be answered: How can telco assets be efficiently and commercially feasible integrated in applications from over the top (OTT) players? Or, to put it down in a more provocative statement: OTT players providing Web applications use other OTT player communication technologies to accomplish their services. How can operators achieve that Web applications from OTT players and content

J. Cordeiro and K.-H. Krempels (Eds.): WEBIST 2012, LNBIP 140, pp. 347–362, 2013.

providers preferably use their communication services? In order to make this possible the "Advanced Prosumer Service Integration Intelligence" project, called APSINT, provides a software architecture that integrates seamlessly into the mobile operators network infrastructure.

Telco operators do a good job in reliability, quality of service, network convergence and interoperability when it comes to connecting people by text, voice and video. On the other hand operators lack in offering their services globally and easy to be used by Web developers and in delivering simple yet powerful human interfaces to end-users. The APSINT architecture resolves the need for B2B relationships between operator and application providers and developers for them to use operators services. This is done by introducing the user as a man-in-the-middle between telco service and Web page. While browsing a Web site, pages rendered in the users browser will use communication facilities of the local device but which are programmed and controlled by Javascript code within the Web page. By this way the users B2C business relationship to the telco is acting on behalf of a B2B relationship between Web application and operator. This separation between control (by the Web page) and actual execution (on the user's device) has the advantages of (i) global reachability of telco services, (ii) easy deployment, (iii) zero configuration need for user and developer as well as (iv) privacy protection as there is no need for the user to share authentication credentials with Web pages for 3rd party service usage.

The remaining paper is organized as follows: Section 2 provides an overview over related work in this area, Section 3 describes our solution and architecture, Section 4 provides implementation details, Section 5 discusses our outcome and experiences made while evaluating the prototype and finally Section 6 gives an outlook on further work.

2 Related Work

This section aims to introduce and compare existing solutions to enable mobile browser-based communication. There are two main approaches to realize real-time communication via the Web browser. The first one (A) takes advantage of remote communication services offered by 3rd parties via the Web. In this case, as mentioned in Section 1, a B2B relationship is needed between the developer of the Web site and the telco. Approach (B) utilizes communication capabilities available at the client device (e.g. smart phone).

As depicted in Figure 1, method (A), the developer of a Web site uses a well defined Javascript library to access server side communication features (e.g Tropo [1]). Real-time communication is initiated by sending an HTTP request to the Web server, which establishes a network initiated call between the two users. Another approach to enable media handling in the browser is to use Adobe's generic Flash Plugin, which is more flexible as almost every browser is Flash enabled. This way it is possible to stream media directly to and from the browser. However Adobe announced in a blog post [2] that they will discontinue the development of their mobile Flash plugin because of the increasing popularity of HTML5.

Looking at method (B) as shown in Figure 2, a common solution to integrate local telephony features into the browser is via plugins for already installed applications

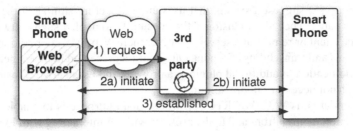

Fig. 1. Communication initiated remotely (method A)

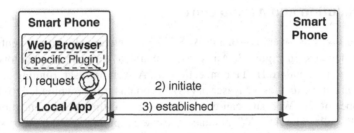

Fig. 2. Communication initiated locally (method B)

like Skype. This way the user can access the locally installed application via the Web browser. Main drawbacks for plugin-based solutions are: (i) only browsers with the plugin installed are supported, (ii) media (e.g. voice) cannot be handled by the browser directly, (iii) the communication software has to be installed at the client, and (iv) most plugins are not available for mobile browsers.

A hybrid solution of (A) and (B) is offered by Sipgate [3]. Sipgate is using a browser plugin to interface with their locally installed softphone, but offers also the integration of SIP based hardware phones. Thus by using the Sipgate plugin, it is possible to trigger calls either originated locally, or remotely at the 3rd party infrastructure at Sipgate.

Integration with the existing communication provider as for method (A) has the obvious advantage of an easy way to achieve terminal connectivity, quality of service and interworking with other services to provide users with a mature solution. The obstacles of this approach are resulting as mentioned from the necessity to enter into a B2B relationship with every provider who would like to enable browser based real-time communication for his users. APSINT's goal was exactly to remove this obstacle. The proposed solution is generic enough to be applied with different types of telecommunication architectures, e.g. VoIP. Special attention was paid to integration with the IMS architecture. IMS is the most advanced carrier-grade service delivery architecture which becomes the standard used by all mobile network operators.

Lately a couple of people pushed the standardization of browser based APIs to access local mobile device capabilities including real time communication. A team from the Mozilla foundation started to work on their WebAPI [4] which allows access to telephony and messaging APIs via JavaScript, besides that WebAPI also offers interfaces to battery status, contacts, camera, filesystem, accelerometer, and geo-location. WebAPI can control local communication, but audio is not handled in the browser.

Furthermore, [5] suggest a system that uses an architecture similar to the one presented in this paper. They also envisioned the possibility to deploy such software either locally on the client or remote at a server. However their Web-IMS cooperation is based on flash plugins and transcoding of media. Our solution presented in this paper does not need any modification or additional plugin in a browser and uses HTML5 instead. Also transcoding is not necessary in our solution.

Another initiative is W3C WebRTC [6], whose main purpose is to enable streamed real-time communication from and to the browser without interacting with local device capabilities.

3   Our Solution and Architecture

This section gives an overview of the APSINT architecture. Its components and interfaces are depicted in Figure 3. An APSINT enabled Web site is downloaded from *Webserver A* via a standard HTTP connection (a). A Web browser, running on a smartphone, renders and executes a Javascript (JS) as soon as it is downloaded to the client. The developer of the Web site can easily integrate real-time communication by just using JS API calls. The *APSINT.js* connects to the endpoint via local Websockets (b). This communication is transparent to the Web site developer. There is a 1:1 relationship between Web browser and endpoint. Only one Web site can connect to the endpoint at the same time. Usually this is the last page which sent a communication request to the endpoint. In case of an existing session (e.g. an active call) the Web site used to initiate/terminate the call would keep full control over the endpoint. The phone's local features are accessed via the endpoint which uses device specific APIs (c) e.g. for SMS messaging or circuit-switched (CS) voice calls. An interface (d) connects the endpoint with the Telco operator. In our case this is realized via SIP/IMS signaling.

3.1   APSINT Protocol

The software architecture of APSINT is shown in Figure 3, which contains the *endpoint* component to link communication between a *Web browser* and a signalling stack for real-time communication such as SIP. In general the endpoint must implement asynchronous event driven communication between Javascript on browser side and the SIP stack on the other side. Browser side communication is interfaced by Websockets [7] as the transport protocol for bidirectional message delivery to and from the SIP stack. Websockets avoid strong binding of the endpoint to the browser on the one side, like with browser specific plugins, and minimize protocol specific overhead on the other side, as it is the case when long polling is used.

The Websockets protocol as proposed in [7] enables Web browsers to establish a bidirectional channel to servers by upgrading a HTTP connection using an initial handshake. In APSINT the endpoint software component is required to implement a Websocket server, while the client side of Websockets is implemented by Web browsers. As the Websockets protocol is part of the HTML5 standard all major browsers offer a Websocket client. Hence the APSINT solution benefits from bidirectional connections and the low latency of the Websockets protocol while making browser specific plugins obsolete.

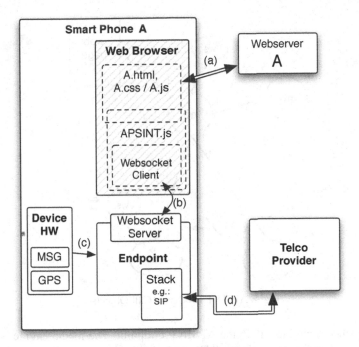

Fig. 3. APSINT System Architecture

In the APSINT endpoint the Websocket server and the SIP stack run independently in their own event loops. Messages originating from Javascript are received by the Websocket server stack and passed over to the SIP stack in an asynchronous manner. In the opposite direction SIP events are interpreted by the SIP stack and passed as messages to the Websocket server service.

Messages *originating from Javascript* are

– RESERVE, Web page is registered to the endpoint,
– INITIATE, call is initiated by the Web page,
– MESSAGE, message is sent by the Web page,
– END, call is ended by the Web page.

Messages *originating from the SIP stack* consist of

– CALL_EVENT, triggers various events in a call session,
– STATUS, forward states of endpoint and SIP stack to the registered Web page,
– MESSAGE, forward received message by SIP stack to Web page,
– END, ending call session by remote party.

The APSINT architecture relies on SIP for signalling purposes. Although other signalling protocols exist, SIP was adopted by most telephony providers in connection with IMS. Hence for the APSINT endpoint it is necessary to integrate a SIP stack to make use of the telco IMS infrastructure. The SIP stack is an integrated service of the APSINT endpoint running uncoupled from the Websocket service, to provide asynchronous event triggering coming from the SIP layer. Furthermore the SIP stack service

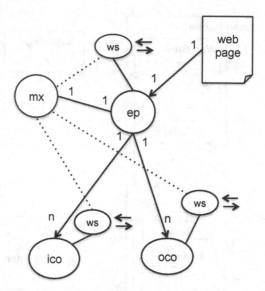

Fig. 4. APSINT Javascript Call Objects

controls the media engine within the APSINT endpoint. The media engine is responsible for receiving and transmitting RTP media streams, and to play ring tones and ringback tones when triggered by the SIP stack.

3.2 Javascript Library and API

The APSINT Javascript library and API (apsint.js) is composed out of a set of object types and their relations as shown in Figure 4. A Web page would obtain a single endpoint object (ep) on successfully reserving the endpoint service. This ep object may be used to initiate new calls or sending messages. As well, call backs to be overriden by the Web page will inform about incoming calls and messages.

Initiating a new call via the ep object will instantiate a new outgoing call object oco which is handed over to the Web page. One oco object per call session will exist. Same as for the ep object the Web page is responsible to override the callbacks of that object to get notified on important call events.

On receiving a new incoming call the APSINT library will invoke a dedicated callback on the ep object passing along a newly created incoming call object (ico). For each incoming call session one ico object is instantiated. Similar to the oco this object contains callback methods for notifying the Web page on certain events and to provide utility methods to answer or end a call.

In case a callback function in any of the ep, ico or oco objects is not overriden by the Web page, the APSINT library will invoke a default implementation which may lead to automatically accepting or declining a call or displaying information in a default manner.

The mixer object (mx) is instantiated with the ep object at the time the Web page grabs the endpoint and is responsible for coordinating multiple call sessions, keeping track of active calls and other call handling tasks. By setting certain coordination methods to different (predefined) functions, behavior of how to deal with multiple session can be influenced. The architecture also gives respect to future enhancements of the library for toggling between calls or setting up three-way calls or conferences. Currently options for declining and reporting new calls to the Web page or taking over new calls while quitting existing sessions is implemented. The mixer object does its job by intercepting and manipulating the messages of endpoint end call objects towards and from the endpoint.

All objects except the mx object contain their own Websocket (ws in figure 4) for communication with the endpoint. Lifetime of the ep, oco and ico objects is tightly coupled to the lifetime of their Websocket. As long as the Websocket towards the endpoint is open the related object exists.

4 Implementation

4.1 Endpoint

The APSINT endpoint is designed as a background service. As shown in Figure 5 the endpoint implements three services:

- Websocket Server, for receiving and sending messages to the Web page and the SIP stack. The Websocket server is an asynchronous task in nonblocking mode.
- SIP Stack, for handling SIP protocol messages and controlling the media engine. The SIP stack has to be an asynchronous service like the Websocket server.
- Media Engine, for sending/receiving RTP media streams and for audio playback of ringtones. The media engine is completely controlled by the SIP stack.

A prototype of the APSINT endpoint was implemented for x86 personal computers on Linux and for Android 2.2 and above. Software and libraries used for the Linux PC prototype are:

- Sofia-SIP [8], a SIP stack to implement SIP functionality in the APSINT endpoint software,
- libwebsockets [9], a C library implementing the Websockets protocol,
- GStreamer framework for the media engine implementation.

A second prototype for the Android platform utilizes the following software components:

- IMSDroid [10], an IMS compliant SIP stack with integrated media engine for Android phones and tablets.
- Java-Websocket [11], a pure Java library implementing the Websockets protocol both for servers and clients.

On both platforms the endpoints can handle multiple SIP sessions and support simple SIP messaging. The endpoint on Android was extended and is capable to access system services offered by the phone platform. As an example, messaging on Android includes SMS sending and receiving.

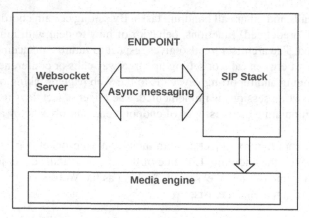

Fig. 5. Overview of the APSINT Endpoint

4.2 Javascript Library

Any Web page on the system, even across browsers, may reserve the endpoint. However, only one Web page at a time may use the endpoint services. The last one asking for the endpoint may use it, if it is not busy with serving another Web page. The rules for reserving the endpoint are:

- If no other Web page has reserved the endpoint then the actual requesting Web page can use the endpoint
- If some other Web page has reserved the endpoint but is no longer present (i.e. the page forgot to free the endpoint or crashed before freeing) then the actual requesting Web page can use the endpoint. The endpoint running in a separate process will detect that the Web page that has reserved it is no longer present because it lost the Websocket connection.
- If some other Web page has reserved the endpoint but is not using it any more, i.e. has no open communication session, then this Web page loses its reservation. It may regain the endpoint services by reserving the endpoint again some time later.
- If some other Web page has a communication session still running the reservation request will be denied

The initial call to obtain endpoint services is the invocation of the reserve function as part of the ENDPOINT class. User ID and user credentials may be passed depending on optional security mechanisms. In addition, any local or remote Websocket URL towards the endpoint can be configured. If not provided a default local address will be used. However, the website must provide an activation callback for reservation. Once connection with the endpoint is established this function is called by the APSINT library providing the target function with the actual endpoint object (`ep` as depicted in figure 4).

The `ep` object may in turn create `ico` and `oco`, incoming and outgoing call objects depending on who is the call originator (`ico` for incoming calls, `oco` for self initiated outgoing calls). The three objects have a common basic structure, which is related to the need of communicating independently with the APSINT endpoint. This is guaranteed by each object instance using its own Websocket. The following list shows common and distinct functions of the APSINT communication objects:

Common functions for ep, ico and oco objects are:

- parseEvent and dispatchEvent for message and event handling in interaction with the endpoint
- makeWebSocket used by the object creation factory to obtain and connect the instance to a Websocket
- sendMSG for sending a (SIP or SMS) message
- onDestroy - is called when the object is about to be released by the library or if the Websocket connection went down.

Functions of the ep object only are:

- initiateCall to make a new call (session) providing address string media (audio and/or video) and a notification callback which will deliver the new oco call object for the session once the endpoint started to process the connection
- sendMessage to send a text message via SIP or as SMS (Android only)
- onIncomingCall invoked on being called via audio or video providing the new ico object used to deal with the new connection
- onMessage called if a SIP Message message or an SMS was received
- onStatusChange used to communicate status changes of the endpoint

Functions common for both ico and oco objects:

- endCall to take down the communication session regardless of its current state
- onCallEnded to inform about the termination of he session by the communication partner at any point in time
- onError to inform about call related errors
- audio and video prepared for future releases to turn on/off media during the session

Functions for ico objects only:

- answerCall used to acknowledge the incoming call request leading to immediate call establishment
- onRinging to inform the Web page that the call originator has been signaled a "free line"

Functions for oco objects only:

- onRingBack to inform that the called party has signalled a "free line"
- onCallAnswered to inform that the call has been answered be the terminator and that the session is now established

The mixer object (mx) for multi session coordination is a little different. It does not inherit from the current base class of the APSINT objects and does not use its own Websockets. However, the factory for creating ep, ico and oco objects ties in observation calls so that the mx object is informed on each incoming and outgoing message that any of the other objects is sending towards or receiving from the endpoint. The mx object can also modify, insert or remove these messages to perform coordination actions. The member functions of the mixer object are:

- `getCalls` to obtain a list of all currently managed call objects
- `getActiveCall` to obtain the call object which is currently active, meaning the call currently transmitting or receiving media
- `setActiveCall` to make some other connection (i.e. call session) the active call
- `declineAdditionalCall` may be used to decline all incoming calls during an ongoing session
- `acceptAdditionalCall` makes the new incoming call the active one and terminates the former active session
- `onAdditionalCall` may be set to one of the two functions above or to some other function customized by the Web page

All functions/methods starting with "on" in its name are notification callbacks meant to be overridden by the Web page. In a minimum configuration the `onIncomingCall` of the ep object needs to be provided to get interaction capabilities with the endpoint. More callbacks may be customized by the web designer as appropriate (cf. next section).

4.3   Web Application

We have implemented a web application to showcase the possibilities of our solution. *Sushify* is a Twitter-like microblogging platform written in Ruby on Rails. The main entities of Sushify are:

- User
- Micropost
- Relationship

These are also reflected as Rails models and stored in a SQLite database. Sushify is fully based on a REST architecture [12] thus rendering all the models as resources that can be manipulated via standard HTTP methods. Similar to Twitter a user can create microposts and users can follow each other thus creating a relationship. Posts from followed users are shown in an aggregated micropost feed.

Building upon this feature set we have included the possibility to trigger calls and send messages using the Javascript API discussed above. Fig. 6 shows the Sushify UI with an active call window. Basically three Javascript files are used and included in the file `config/application.rb`.

- `apsint.js` The Javascript library file outline above
- `apsint-vts.js` Contains specific call and message handling code by overwriting methods of `apsint.js` such as `answercall()`.
- `apsint-ui.js` Methods of `apsint-vts.js` usually call UI-related functions in this file, e.g. opening a message box with the caller id. User input (like declining a call) is handled here as well, and the corresponding method in `apsint-vts.js` is called (e.g. `declinecall()`).

Users can configure a SIP address where they can be reached. We have also implemented a feature that allows an auto-reply message to be sent when a user declines a call. In order to prevent unsolicited calls a user can only call and message users (and see their SIP/email address) that are his/her followers.

Fig. 6. Sushify with Active Call Window

5 Discussion

The advantages of our approach over other architectures is based on the following two design decisions:

1. Resolve the need for a B2B relationship between Web provider and communication service provider
2. Distribute the Model, View and Control components of an application across different processes and even across the network

The first point will allow applications to use any communication service provider the user has subscribed to and hence there is no need for configuration or contract signing to use the application. Furthermore, the resolution of the B2B relationship will not only work for delivering communications services via local device functionality but also to trigger any service invocation from the users device instead of from the providers server towards network provider or any other 3rd party service the user can authenticate with.

The second point enables mobile applications to be always up to date while running stable in close integration with mobile device capabilities. View and Controller will be downloaded via HTTP and presented and controlled via HTML, CSS and Javascript kept up do date on the server. At the same time apps are executed locally with all the required functionality provided natively by the device (in the Model component running in a separate process). View and main parts of the controller are downloaded from a web server and executed in the browser whereas, low level controller functionality and the Model component dealing with the SIP stack are running as a native background process communicating with the browser.

It is not necessary for the user to share his secrets with third parties such as authentication credentials, address book data or calendar information. The required data may be added only at the time of local execution in the mobile browser. The user keeps control over private data. For example, the user wants to call a friend on a social web platform. The name or nick name of the friend may be found on the Web page but not his phone number which is associated to the friends nick in the local address book of the users device. During APSINT Javascript execution both are combined in the browser of the users device. A call is made via the Web page without the Web page knowing the details.

Other real-time communication solutions or native functionality execution like WebRTC, plugin based solutions [13] or implementation of a Web app with Googles NativeClient are not capable of reacting on external stimula, e.g. if no browser is running it is not possible to take an incoming communication request. With the APSINT endpoint running as a service on the local device it is always possible to start a browser and download a Web page to take an incoming call.

Also, while experimenting with our prototype, we introduced a simple method of rendering video directly in the browser by using the `data` URI scheme to put base64 encoded data right into the `src` attribute of a plain HTML `img` tag. Together with this functionality and the Websocket based communication between browser and communication stack it was possible to distribute functionality across devices. Doing this, it is possible to communicate via a smartphones SIP connection while displaying the related Web page GUI for communication and video display on the monitor of a nearby PC (in the same LAN). One would talk via the phone but control communication and watch video on the PC.

No plugin, especially no mobile flash support is required. Our architecture supports multiple communication sessions to be supported yet limits the usage of communication resources to one Web page at a time. The endpoint will provide its services for other Web pages if the current using Web app does have no open sessions and will detect crashes of a Web page or the browser automatically as reserving the communication stack is tied to keeping the Websocket session open.

Unlike other approaches, the APSINT architecture offers the possibility to communicate with clients of other type and via telco network features protocols and networks of other kind. With an APSINT enabled Web page one can communicate with any other SIP client reachable in the network or via breakout functionality of telco providers with any other party in the mobile or fixed line network. These solutions are standardized and available worldwide.

5.1 Security Issues

Security issues have a paramount importance for the all parties involved in consuming and providing services build on top of APSINT architecture. This is because of the specific setup which allows a Web page to take control over audio and video sessions started from the users devices like Smartphone. Hence on the usability level security requirements revolve around achieving trust in this new functionality by providing a reliable solution in term of authentication and authorization of communication sessions started by the Web pages, as well as, providing privacy and confidentiality. Security measures need to address specific focus of all parties involved, as discussed below.

Users may be accustomed to the dangers of the internet and accept the risks because of vital importance of this platform. However, they may be difficult to persuade to grant control over their phones to an internet application unless they can trust their security requirements are met. The users requirements cover different areas which stretch from preventing of starting unsolicited communication sessions and possibly turning their devices to spy on users communication or hijacking them for SPIT attacks, securing privacy of communication, up to mitigation of phishing, e.g. in form of persuading users to call a costly service numbers.

Similarly, network providers are interested in preventing SPIT or DoS attacks on their customers which may be caused when malicious Web pages could obtain control over devices connected to the providers network. They would as well prefer situation when they could unambiguously identify sessions originated by the Web pages and associate them with the specific page. This may be especially important when APSINT architecture capable devices would be branded by the operator. In this case users would surely expect the operator to take at least partial responsibility in case when allowing Web pages to control communication sessions would inflict substantial cost s to the user, e.g. due to phishing attack.

For the owners of the Web pages with capabilities to control communication sessions on the APSINT devices winning user trust is very important. User need to have a guarantee that they do not give control to start audio or video sessions to the malicious Web page. Therefore stealing the functionality for controlling APSINT terminals embedded in a specific Web page and reusing it in the context of a different Web page should be prevented. If the revenues from the voice and video traffic generated by the Web page need to be shared with the network operator, then unambiguous identification of such sessions is needed.

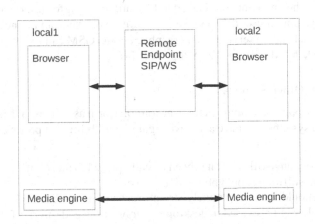

Fig. 7. Architecture of a Remote Endpoint

Traditional architecture for Web-IMS convergence is based on Parlay X interface in the IMS application server and it has well defined security framework. Critics of the efficiency of the Parlay X based architecture brought alternative proposal based on new functional entity on the IMS network border named Web Session Controller which shields the IMS terminal from direct interaction with Web application. APSINT project gives a new concept to Web and IMS convergence which takes place mainly in users terminal. Direct interactions between IMS terminal and Web applications require to explore ways of combining security solutions for Web applications with IMS security standards applicable for this novel architecture. Approach taken by the APSINT team tries to flexibly adapt security restrictions in consuming Web applications to the degree of trust that user expresses against a Web page with embedded APSINT application. Web applications being consumed in the users browser will be secured by the known technologies like SSH or digital signatures, however, user will be allowed to grant his permit to specific Web pages for establishing audio and video sessions either permanent or for the actual session only depending on his trust toward this Web page. IMS security standards will be fully supported. Additionally a new security measure is studied for providing to IMS identity of Web application which was allowed to start audio/video session from the particular IMS terminal.

6   Conclusions and Future Work

As the APSINT solution integrates the endpoint on local device the browser communicates with the endpoint locally and all signalling is handled by the local endpoint. An other approach is to move the endpoint to a remote host as shown in Figure 7 where a local browser communicates over Websockets with a remote endpoint. For this solution to be applicable the local device still needs to implement a local media engine. In such an approach all signalling is handled by a remote server whereas the media stream is handled by the respective end devices. Finally the media engine could be integrated in the browser so the media resources both hardware and software are managed by the Web browser itself as proposed by WebRTC [6].

Extensions to the endpoint could be added by utilizing platform services offered by the operating system on user devices like for example on Android phones. Candidates for such usage are location services, camera, phonebook, GSM calls and SMS. A similar approach is made by Mozilla in WebAPI project [4].

6.1   Porting to Other Systems

Currently the endpoint is running on the Android platform as well as on Linux and Mac (OS X) desktop systems. We have also investigated possibilities of porting the endpoint to other operating systems:

- *iOS*: The Doubango SIP stack has been already ported to this platform, thus porting the endpoint software should be relatively easy.
- *Symbian*: Should be also relatively straightforward as the Sofia SIP stack (developed by Nokia and also used in desktop versions of the endpoint) is fully supported on that platform.
- *Windows Phone 7*: To our knowledge it is not possible to use/compile external libraries for this platform due to security restrictions (mainly caused by the lack of a multiuser concept in the kernel). As a consequence the only way for implementation would be from the ground up with the SilverLight IDE, which is clearly not a feasible approach.

Finally, we expect no major problems in supporting Windows desktops (since all the necessary libraries/compilers are available).

6.2   API Evaluation

We are planning to perform an evaluation of our Javascript library to assess acceptance among the developer community. As a first step we will review and simplify our API, write documentation and provide code examples, best practices and such. The evaluation should be carried out in two phases:

- Laboratory test: A two-hour test with 8-10 developers that should solve 2-3 tasks. We are considering quantitative criteria such as: task completion time, lines of code, iteration steps needed [14]. Also think-aloud and maybe video observation might reveal more hidden issues.
- Real world test: Developers get the API/documentation to use it for free tasks/ projects. They give feedback in form of diaries and are supported by us throughout the study (4-6 weeks).

Combining both a laboratory test and a longitudinal real-world study [15] is a novel approach in evaluating a API and we expect richer results with this two-phase-approach.

Acknowledgements. The Competence Center FTW Forschungszentrum Telekommunikation Wien GmbH is funded within the program COMET - Competence Centers for Excellent Technologies by BMVIT, BMWA, and the City of Vienna. The COMET program is managed by the FFG.

We would like to thank the APSINT project team and especially our colleagues Vincenzo Scotto di Carlo and Hans-Heinrich Grusdt from Nokia Siemens Networks Germany and Marco Happenhofer from Vienna University of Technology for their contributions to this work.

References

1. tropo.com: Tropo - cloud api for voice, sms, and instant messaging services (2011), https://www.tropo.com (accessed November 20, 2011)
2. Winokur, D.: Flash to Focus on PC Browsing and Mobile Apps; Adobe to More Aggressively Contribute to HTML5 (2011),
   http://blogs.adobe.com/flashplatform/2011/11/
   flash-to-focus-on-pc-browsing-and-mobile-apps-adobe-
   to-more-aggressively-contribute-to-html5.html (accessed November 20, 2011)
3. sipgate.com: Move your phones to the cloud (2011), http://sipgate.com (accessed November 20, 2011)
4. Mozilla.org: WebAPI is an effort by Mozilla to bridge together the gap, and have consistent APIs that will work in all web browsers, no matter the operating system (2011), https://wiki.mozilla.org/WebAPI (accessed November 15, 2011)
5. Nishimura, H., Ohnimushi, H., Hirano, M.: Architecture for Web-IMS Cooperative Services for Web Terminals. In: 13th International Conference on Intelligence in Next Generation Networks, ICIN 2009. IEEE, New York (2009)
6. Google: WebRTC is a free, open project that enables web browsers with Real-Time Communications (RTC) capabilities via simple Javascript APIs (2011), http://www.webrtc.org/home (accessed November 15, 2011)

7. Fette, I., Melnikov, A.: The WebSocket protocol (2011),
   `http://tools.ietf.org/html/`
   `draft-ietf-hybi-thewebsocketprotocol-17` (accessed November 15, 2011)
8. Pessi, P., et al.: Sofia-SIP - a RFC3261 compliant SIP User-Agent library (2011),
   `http://sofia-sip.sourceforge.net/` (accessed November 15, 2011)
9. Green, A.: C Websockets Server Library (2011),
   `http://git.warmcat.com/cgi-bin/cgit/libwebsockets`
   (accessed November 15, 2011)
10. Diop, M.: High Quality Video SIP/IMS client for Google Android (2011),
    `http://code.google.com/p/imsdroid/` (accessed November 15, 2011)
11. Rajlich, N.: A barebones WebSocket client and server implementation written in 100%
    Java (2011), `https://github.com/TooTallNate/Java-WebSocket` (accessed
    November 15, 2011)
12. Fielding, R.T.: Architectural Styles and the Design of Network-based Software Architectures. PhD thesis, University of California, Irvine (2000)
13. Adeyeye, M., Ventura, N., Foschini, L.: Converged multimedia services in emerging web
    2.0 session mobility scenarios. Wireless Networks 18, 185–197 (2012), doi:10.1007/s11276-011-0394-z
14. Clarke, S.: Measuring API usability. Dr. Dobbs Journal, 6–9 (2004)
15. Gerken, J., Jetter, H.C., Zöllner, M., Mader, M., Reiterer, H.: The concept maps method as
    a tool to evaluate the usability of APIs. In: Proceedings of the 2011 Annual Conference on
    Human Factors in Computing Systems, CHI 2011, pp. 3373–3382. ACM, New York (2011)

Using Horn Clauses and Fuzzy Logic
to Provide Location Intelligence Services to Mobile Users:
An Implementation Account

Alfio Costanzo, Alberto Faro, and Concetto Spampinato

Department of Electrical, Electronics and Computer Engineering, University of Catania,
Viale. A. Doria 6, 95125 Catania, Italy
`alfioc87@hotmail.it, {afaro,cspampin}@dieei.unict.it`

Abstract. Current Location Based Services (LBS) don't take into account the
status of the services neither the real time traffic conditions. Aim of the paper is
to show how LBSs may evolve towards location intelligence services based on
Horn clauses expressed in Prolog to find the most suitable services for the users
and the relevant paths to reach them by taking into account the current traffic
situation. Fuzzy logic and semantic web technologies are also used to improve
the LBS applications. The former to find the services that meet the user expectations, the latter to take advantage from all the information stored on the
distributed databases at urban/metropolitan scale. A case study developed using
Ruby on Rails (RoR) and JQueryMobile illustrates how such a web service may
work in practice. A comparison between the RoR version and another one
where mobiles play a more active role is also discussed.

Keywords: Location based services, Horn clauses, Fuzzy logic, Semantic web,
Mobile computing.

1 Introduction

Available Location Based Services (LBS) don't take into account the current status of
the services neither the current conditions of the traffic network or of the weather
since this information is mainly outside the control of the service providers. This does
not allow the mobile users to know relevant information such as the travel time to
reach the destination depending on the current traffic, the current availability of parking vacancies and so on. Moreover, few mobile applications support m-commerce,
i.e., commercial transactions carried out on-line by mobile users.

However providing the user with real time and m-commerce services is only the
first step to activate advanced LBSs. In fact, it is also important to provide the users
with the information that best fits their needs, e.g., a cheaper park may be suggested
with lower priority if there is another park that is more close to the destination in case
of raining.

Another step is the one of integrating the business Data Bases (DBs) resident on
separate computers to inform the users on all the services potentially available at the
urban/metropolitan scale. Therefore, the future mobile application should be powered

J. Cordeiro and K.-H. Krempels (Eds.): WEBIST 2012, LNBIP 140, pp. 363–381, 2013.
© Springer-Verlag Berlin Heidelberg 2013

by artificial intelligence techniques to give rise to Location Intelligence (LI) services of practical user interest [1].

Although many intelligent mobile services may be offered to the users, e.g., the ones proposed in the Intelligent Transportation Systems (ITS) field [2], they are rarely offered to support the user decisions and activities but only to provide the users with average information that give a moderate help to their activities.

Moreover, ITS services are mainly provided by proprietary solutions that don't take advantage from the information resident on the disparate DBs dealing with city services of potential user interest. For example, sudden traffic congestions or dangerous situations are not reported to the interested users, service reservation cannot be carried out on-line, neither the users are advised when products of interest are available on the stores.

Aim of the paper is to show how LBSs may evolve towards LI services based on Horn clauses expressed in Prolog [3] to find the most suitable services for the users and the best paths to reach them.

The paper will show also how integrating Horn clauses with Fuzzy Logic rules expressed by words [4] will result in Fuzzy Horn clauses particularly useful to give rise to LBSs that take into account personal constraints (e.g., user health status and preferences) and environmental conditions to help more effectively the decisions and the activities of the mobile users. The use of the metadata technologies will be proposed to take advantage from the information stored on the disparate urban DBs.

In the paper we assume that the urban area is provided with sensors to monitor in real time the traffic conditions and the weather. Thus, the paper does not deal with the monitoring technologies widely studied in the literature, e.g., [5], [6], but it is devoted to illustrate how the use of the Horn clauses, Fuzzy logic rules and metadata may improve the current LBS applications.

The Ruby on Rails (RoR) [7] framework is adopted to develop the above web services since it allows the designer to organize the application as a collection of use cases that can be reused for similar tasks [8], [9]. Moreover, RoR is provided with a powerful language, i.e., Ruby, that facilitates the implementation of: a) the fuzzy rules that address user mobility and aid their decisions, and b) the procedures to access the metadata layer that integrate the urban DBs. Other two languages may be also used in RoR to facilitate the implementation of LBS applications: a) Java scripts to exchange with mobiles information geo-referenced on Google Maps, and b) JQueryMobile [10] to convey such information in a user friendly format that may be visualized, without any modification, on PCs, tablets and mobiles.

Section 2 shows how Horn clauses and simple Fuzzy Logic rules may improve LBSs. Section 3 discusses how the use of JQueryMobile and Javascript allow us to use the metadata technology to favour the integration of the proprietary DBs of interest of mobile users. The advantages of implementing the LI services by using RoR and JQuery Mobile will be discussed in section 4 by a small case study dealing with a prototypical web application, called WiCity, currently under test at our University.

In particular, the case study illustrates how an user can connect her/his mobile to an RoR server to be informed by a suitable interface, developed by JQueryMobile, on some basic LBSs concerning mobility (parks, gas stations and traffic congestions), health services (pharmacies and first aid services), events/places of tourist interest, and on the paths to reach by car the chosen destination from the current user position by taking into account the current traffic flows and weather conditions. Also, a comparison will be carried out between the WiCity implementation consisting of simple mobiles entirely based on the functionalities provided by the RoR server and the one consisting of more powerful mobiles where a Flash Builder [11] based implementation may perform some functions autonomously thus decreasing the RoR server load.

2   Improving LBSs by Horn Clauses and Fuzzy Rules

Location based services may be considered as a sort of generalization of the ITSs. The latter are mainly dedicated to improve mobility and logistics activities of the mobile users, the former aim at supporting such activities taking into account also security, commerce and business requisites. Thus, in LBS environment it is important to reach the destination in the minimum time, but also to avoid accidents or congested areas. Analogously, the user may decide to follow some non minimal path to reach the destination if this is done in more safe conditions.

As well as, the user may be interested in paying the parks depending on the real parking time rather than paying in advance basing on some forecast of this time. Although the rules that support such LBS requirements are very simple, the current LBS applications are mainly conceived as information systems that provide the mobile users with general information. Thus, in the following we show how the LBS effectiveness may be improved by using suitable Fuzzy Logic rules and Horn clauses expressed in Prolog.

2.1   Managing the User Requests

The program to manage the requests coming from the mobiles could be written in any procedural language, but, as will be clarified below, the use of a rule based language, such as Prolog, may simplify the software code without sacrificing the execution time. Thus, we are experimenting a Prolog program not only to compute the minimum path to destination but also to put the user requests (denoted as *u_req*) in queue by filling a database consisting of the following facts: *u_req(user_name, from_location, to_location, stype, rcode)*, where *from_location* is the current user position detected by the mobile GPS or the address closest to such position computed by a Google_Map API, *to_location* is the address, found by the program, where there is a service suitable for the user, stype is the service type needed by the user (e.g., park, pharmacy, hotel and so on), and scode is a code to better refine the description of the requested service, e.g., if stype = "park", scode=1 means that we are searching for a park closest to the current user position, whereas scode=2 means that we are interested in a park closest to the destination.

The above Prolog program should be activated by the server only in case it is not running. In fact, after the Prolog program terminates a request, it will consider automatically the next request in the database until all the requests are served thanks to the backtracking feature of the Prolog. The main job of the Prolog program is not only the one of storing each user request in the database according to the FIFO policy using the predicate assertz(u_req(....)), but also to execute some few rules to control that the received request is a valid one before entering it in the request database.

Let us note that not all the arguments of the user requests should be filled by the user, e.g., *u_req(user_name, from_location,_, park, 1)* will cause the Prolog program to find the park closest to the current position, whereas *u_req(user_name,_,to_ loca-tion, park, 2)* will cause the Prolog program to find the park closest to the destination.

Generally an user request will cause a response for the user consisting of a sequence of roads to reach the service located at the destination. In our implementation, all the files related to the response will be inserted by the Prolog program into a proper directory denoted with the user name and the request identifier, whereas another program written in JQMobile is used to send the responses to the users. This communication mechanism between the mobiles and the main server will be illustrated deeply in the case study.

2.2   Nearest Services and Safe Walking

To help the users to choose the most suitable nearest services we should return to them a Google Map on her/his mobile that shows the current user position and two circles, one, let say C_w, with a radius of few hundreds of meters and the second, let say C_c, with a radius of about one kilometre, containing the markers of the services located in such areas. The former circle should point out the services that are reachable by walking, whereas the second should point out the ones reachable by car.

In principle, one can define the circle radius following a very simple rule, i.e., the services located in the smaller circle are recommended to the walking people if the distance *dist* from the current user position is such that *dist* < 300 meters. This constraint would become *dist* < 1000 meters if the user is driving a car.

However, if there are no services available within such circles, the user might accept a moderately greater distance to find services of interest. Of course, an arbitrary modification of such distance is not acceptable, whereas it is fair to inform the user on how much a certain increase of the circle radius may cause a corresponding decrease of her/his satisfaction of the solution provided.

The computation of the radius corresponding to the user expectations is straightforward in the fuzzy logic framework in case we have to consider only one condition that may influence the notion of *nearest*. Indeed, for example, assuming that:

- the rule is: "if the user is not young, then the user would like to have the required service very close", and

- the user is 28 years old,

from the fuzzy sets shown in fig.1c we have that the evidence that she/he is not young is given by the membership *not* [μ_{young}(28 years old)], i.e., 0.8, and consequently the most suitable radius is the x-coordinate of the barycentre of the area M1 in fig.1a, i.e., 175 meters.

The computation of the best radius *d* is a few more complicated if we wish to take into account more conditions together, plus the current user position. In fact, the RoR application should be provided with the fuzzy set of each condition and with an algorithm to combine the radii derived from the various conditions.

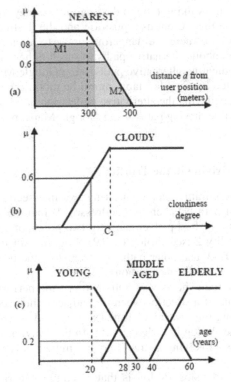

Fig. 1. Fuzzy sets associated with the words: nearest, young, middle aged, elderly, and cloudiness, where μ [0,1] is the membership degree to such words of the values of the definition domain, e.g., μ_{young}(28 years old) = 0.2.

To show how this can be done, let us assume that our rule is: "*if the user is not young **and** it is cloudy, then the user would like to have the required service very close*". In this case, if the people is 28 years and the sky is partially cloudy (e.g., cloudiness degree = 0.4), we may derive the maximum distance as the x-coordinate of the barycentre of the two masses M1 and M2 in fig.1a. The former represents the distance to be suggested considering only the age, the latter refers only to the cloudiness using the fuzzy set represented in fig.1b. Approximately it is 190 mt.. Of course, if the *and* contained in the rule is substituted by *or*, the radius decreases since it is the x-coordinate of the barycentre of the mass M1 or M2 that has the greater membership, i.e., about 175 mt.

Generally, many variables may influence the above problem such as the current time and weekday, the user age and health status, as well as the traffic and weather conditions. Thus the RoR application (or the Prolog program) should know the fuzzy rules, the fuzzy sets and the values of the relevant variables. Current time and weekday may be obtained in a straightforward way, whereas user age and health status could be included in the user request. How to measure the travel times for each street has been widely analyzed by the authors in other papers, whereas, in the case study, we will show how the current weather conditions may be obtained by connecting the RoR web application to Yahoo.

For what concerns the walking time to destination we may assume that it depends on the distance between the current user position and the destination as suggested by Google Maps. But, in case there are dangerous areas to avoid, the RoR application should inform the users about alternative paths to reach either the destination or safer locations. However, indicating alternative paths using Google Maps is not a trivial job since the paths suggested by Google Maps cannot be modified by the programmer. A solution is the one of displaying the alternative pedestrian paths as illustrated below to display the minimum time driving paths using Google Maps, but in a more elaborated way.

2.3   Safe and Fast Driving in the Traffic

The computation of the minimal path connecting two intersections is certainly instrumental to find the best path between two addresses. It may be obtained by any program that is able to find the best path connecting two points of a graph [12]. In [1] we have suggested a Mobility Based Prolog (MBP) Program, since it may be used with little modifications to find also other paths of interest of the user as the ones to find the service that are nearest to the destination.

Also, this MBP program shows very satisfactory time performance and allows us to update the travel time of a street between two adjacent intersections x, y from to t_1 to t_2 by simply retracting the *fact* travel_time (x, y, t_1) and asserting the new *fact* travel_time(x, y, t_2) in the Prolog knowledge base. In this way, any accident or congestion or work in progress involving a street may be immediately taken into account by the program.

Another advantage of using Prolog is that a simple generalization of the MBP program allows us to solve the most relevant logistics problem, i.e., the one to compute the minimal Hamiltonian cycle of the graph associated to the traffic net, i.e. the cycle that starting from an address will come back to the initial address in a minimum time by traversing a set of prefixed intermediate points.

Moreover, also the previous fuzzy rules may be easily written in Prolog, thus making possible that the MBP program uses the membership values to communicate to the users if the paths or the mentioned Hamiltonian cycles found are very (enough/few) fast (fluent/slow). For example, if the user is interested only to fast paths to destination, the program may suggest the path only if $\mu_{fast}(T_{path}) > 0.8$, being T_{path} the travel time associated to the path. In Prolog terms, the rules to compute the membership degree $\mu_{fast}(T_{path})$ of a path to the fuzzy set "fast path" represented in fig.2a are as follows:

$$\text{Path}_{fast} (T_{path,} 0) :\text{-} T_{path} > 10, !.$$
$$\text{Path}_{fast} (T_{path,} 1) :\text{-} T_{path} < 5, !. \tag{1}$$
$$\text{Path}_{fast} (T_{path,} X) :\text{-} X = (10 \, T_{path})/5.$$

where the left part of each rule is true if also the right part is true. These rules indicate that a given path to destination is featured by $\mu_{fast} = 0$ or 1 depending on if the current T_{path} is greater than 10 minutes or less than 5 minutes, otherwise μ_{fast} is given by the value of X computed by the third rule. The operator *cut* represented by the exclamation mark avoids that the program continues to consult the rules after a rule has been satisfied.

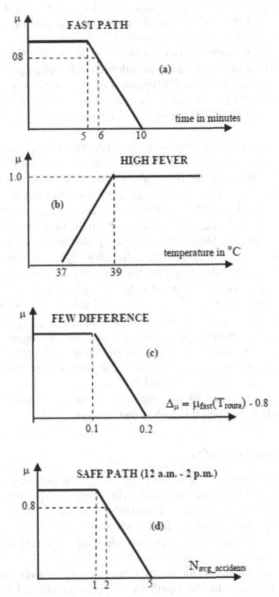

Fig. 2. Fuzzy sets associated with the words: fast_path, high_fever, few_difference, safe_path.

The knowledge of μ_{fast} decreases the computation time to find the paths to destination most suitable for the user. In fact, a potential path is identified dynamically by the MBP program as a sequence of intersections obtained adding a new intersection to the previous ones starting from the current user position at condition that the new intersection does not belong to the set of the already identified intersections and that the time from the current user position to the new intersection is less than $T_{path,max}$

obtained by defuzzyfying the fuzzy set "fast path" for $\mu_{fast}(T_{path}) = 0.8$. If one of these conditions is not valid this path is eliminated and the program proceeds to analyze other potential paths to destination, thus saving computation time.

Therefore, adding constraints does not increase necessarily the computation load since they generally increase the maximum allowed value of $\mu_{fast}(T_{path})$, thus decreasing the computation time of the MBP program. For example, if the further rule is that "a subject with high fever should choose fast paths" and the subject fever is 39°C then $\mu_{fast,max}(T_{path}) = 1$ (see fig.2b) and the number of paths to destination should decrease considerably.

Let us note that the defuzzyfying operations produce a crisp maximum value, i.e., $T_{path,max}$. However, also values that few differ from the maximum value may be acceptable. The fuzzy set "few difference", shown in fig.2c, may be used to suggest not only the paths whose T_{path} is less than $T_{path,max}$ but also the ones whose T_{path} few differs from $T_{path,max}$. Therefore, either paths whose $T_{path} \leq T_{path,max}$ or paths whose T_{path} is between $T_{path,max}$ and $1,2 \, T_{path,max}$ are suggested by indicating the value of $\mu_{few\text{-}difference}$ to inform the users on how much the suggested paths meet their expectations. This membership is communicated only if the difference Δ_μ between the $\mu_{fast}(T_{path})$ associated to the path and the value featuring the fast path, i.e., 0.8, is greater than 0.1, whereas the path is not taken into account if $\Delta_\mu > 0.2$, i.e., if $T_{path} > 1.2 \, T_{path,max}$.

If the user is interested in a path that is fast and safe with a satisfaction degree of 0.8, then the suggested path should be featured by $\mu_{fast}(T_{path}) > 0.8$ and by $\mu_{safe}(N_{avg\_accidents}) > 0.8$, where μ_{safe} measures the membership degree of the path to the class of the safe paths defined by the fuzzy set shown in fig.2d depending on the average number of accidents $N_{avg\_accidents}$ featuring the path in the given time slot. Thus, only paths whose $T_{path} \leq 1.2 \, T_{path,max}$ and $N_{avg\_accidents} \leq 2$ are suggested to the user labelling each suggested path with the minimum of the memberships $\mu_{few\text{-}difference}$ that measure respectively how much this path is fast and safe.

2.4　Displaying the Best Paths

A suitable graphical interface that is compatible with the one used frequently by the user is very important for the usability of the web service [13]. For this reason we aim at informing the user on the best path to destination or on the best cycle to distribute or collect goods, by representing the traffic network as a graph superimposed to the Google Maps in such a way that its arcs coincide with the streets and the nodes with the street intersections.

Thus, after having identified the travel_time (x, y, t) for every adjacent intersection pair and having found the best path by using he mentioned MBP program we should draw on Google Maps the best path from a source intersection S to the destination intersection D by drawing the linear traits connecting the adjacent nodes traversed during the path. However, the lines of such drawing don't correspond necessarily to those of Google Maps since the links between nodes are not always linear segments, neither we have a database containing the adjacent nodes with their geographical coordinates. Thus, we have to solve two problems: a) to find the geo-coordinates of all the intersections, and b) to draw the links between adjacent nodes like the ones of Goole Maps.

To solve the first problem it would be enough to use the function " x AT y" that gives the coordinates of the intersection between the road x and y. But, this function is available for US, and not for all the countries. Thus, our first problem is to find an alternative way to compute all the intersection geo-coordinates in the urban/metropolitan area. Fortunately, this can be accomplished as follows: a) pass to the API *Directions* of Google Maps the names of the pair of streets (x, y) that have an intersection to find the *path* that allows us to reach by *walking* the initial address of x from the last address of y (or in some case the initial address of x to the initial address of y), and b) extract the geographical coordinates of the first marker that contains in its info window the name of the path y, thus finding the geo-coordinates of the intersection. Fig.3 illustrates how the *Directions* API of Google Maps may be used to find the intersections between two roads x and y in order to obtain the function (x AT y) currently not available for many countries.

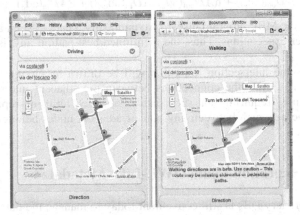

Fig. 3. Path connecting the initial and final addresses of two streets in search of the marker associated to their intersection by driving (left) and by walking (right)

Indeed, in fig.3.left the intersection between the road named 'costarelli' and the one named 'del toscano' is not pointed out by using *Directions* to connect 'costarelli' and 'del toscano' with the option *by driving*, whereas it is pointed out when it is executed with the option *by walking*. In fact, often there is no intersection between two paths by using *Directions* with the option *by driving*, since as shown in fig.3.left, *Directions* takes into account the one way streets. On the contrary, the information contained in the info window of the function *Directions* with the option *by walking* (e.g., fig.3right) allows us to discover the marker and related geo-coordinates associated to the intersection between the roads.

However, as pointed out above, the knowledge of the intersections together with their geo/coordinates is not enough to find the optimal path from any source address ad_s to any destination address ad_d. Indeed, to solve the problem we have to execute the following further tasks:

- to find the adjacent intersections. This can be obtained by using the API *Directions* by verifying for each pair of intersections if they are connected by one step link, and
- to compute for any address ad_r the set AD_{out} (ad_s) of intersections that can be reached in one step from ad_s and the set AD_{in} (ad_d) of intersections that allow us to reach in one step ad_d. These sets can be computed by using *Directions* to find the intersections around ad_s that can be reached by driving in one step from ad_s, and the intersections around ad_d that can be reached by walking in one step from ad_d. Of course, we have to exclude in the latter case the paths not allowed to drivers.

Finally, we have to compute, e.g., by using the mentioned MBP program, all the paths connecting any intersection in AD_{out} to any intersection in AD_{in}. The best path is the one that is obtained by minimizing, for any intersection belonging to AD_{out} (ad_s) and to AD_{in} (ad_d), the travel time T consisting of the following three terms:

$$T = t(ad_s, AD_{out}(ad_s)) + t(AD_{out}(ad_s), AD_{in}(ad_d))) + t(AD_{in}(ad_d), ad_d) \qquad (2)$$

Let us note that the MBP program discards dynamically a path as soon as its μ_{safe} does not meet the user expectations. Thus, the mentioned best path, if any, is featured by a convenient μ_{safe}.

To draw the same intersection links that will be drawn by Google Maps, we use again *Directions* to draw the connections between the adjacent intersections of the best path by simply requiring that such path is obtained by using repeatedly *Directions* to draw the best path between any pair of adjacent nodes belonging to the best path.

3   Data Integration Using OWL-Like Metadata

The use of proprietary DBs is still convenient today to manage the data warehouse of any organization. But, simple commercial transactions and pure information tasks push more and more for the use of standard formats, such as RDF based DBs [14], especially in the LBS framework. Indeed, the data stores based on OWL, that is an extension of RDF, or even on XML favour the integration of data belonging to different organizations. For example, the 'public' part of the data of an organization could be mapped in OWL and sent to a central server where such data will be available for all the users through a standard interface.

Alternatively, the XML/OWL data could remain on the servers of the organizations if the central server is able to carry out distributed queries to collect the data useful for the mobile user. This will favour the updating of the data and the system reliability.

The data, in standard format, could be also stored on the mobiles, even if this solution is suitable only for data that are few dependent on time, otherwise their frequent updating may interfere with the normal operations of the mobile. The technologies available on the market allows us to implement all the above solutions not only to support the centralized or the distributed access to the DBs, but also to facilitate the mapping of the relational DBs to triple stores, or the production of novel OWL DBs from scratch, e.g., [15],[16], [17] and [18].

For example, software environments such as Protègè [19] are suitable to design novel RDF stores, whereas servers such as Sesame [20] may be used to implement centralized RDF stores available to web users. The use of JQueryMobile facilitates the access to the DBs from mobiles either directly or with the help of the central information server [21].

Developing the information server as an RoR application allows us to design the web service as a collection of use cases. This will improve the verification, the test and the maintenance of the software especially when the work flow of the application is complicated for the presence of several cooperating actors [8].

4   Case Study

This case study illustrates how we connect a mobile to an RoR web application, called WiCity, that includes all the technical issues discussed in the previous sections. The interested reader may download the software from code.google.com/ p/query-mobile-unict/source/browse/. Fig.4 shows the WiCity architecture, where the user mobiles are connected to a central RoR server.

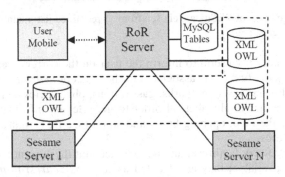

Fig. 4. Current centralized WiCity architecture. It is conceived to support future integrations of XML/OWL data stored on different remote servers.

Currently, all the needed information is stored in the MySQL tables of the RoR server. We are also developing a distributed version of WiCity where the RoR server will use both local databases and the remote XML/OWL data stores resident on the proper remote servers (i.e., Sesame server). This architecture will favour data integration, data privacy and data updating according to the methods outlined in sect.3.

Fig.4 points out that, currently, the user mobiles may use only data stored on the RoR server, whereas, in the future remote data may be used too. In particular, data integration will be obtained by connecting local and remote XML/OWL data stores through messages exchanges between the web RoR application stored on the RoR server and the Sesame servers at distant service points.

The mobile interface, developed by JQueryMobile, currently consists of some icons concerning information on mobility and health services, and on the best paths to reach the destination from the current user position (fig.5.left). Also, events/places of general interest are provided to tourists and citizens (fig.5.right).

The *events of general interest* consist of icons chosen by the user from the list of available LBSs. In particular, the one on the left_top in fig.5.rigth is connected to an RoR process implemented on the server that is able to access the weather metadata of Yahoo. After having processed the JSON file received from Yahoo such process extracts the weather conditions of the area in which the mobile is located, i.e., cloudy and 17 °C in fig.6.left.

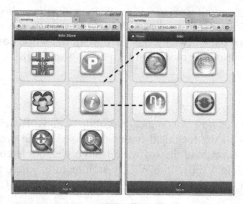

Fig. 5. The interface icons of WiCity are chosen from a predefined list: main interface (left) and events of general interest (right).

Such data are not only useful to inform the user on the current weather conditions but also to modify the fuzzy sets associated to the concept *nearest service*. The basic mobility and health services (e.g., parks, gas stations, pharmacies and first aid points) may be accessed either in alphabetical order to get relevant information such as address, location on the map, opening hours and so on (see fig.6 right), or by the mentioned fuzzy facilities.

Currently, only fuzzy facilities that take into account the current traffic and weather conditions are available; they are denoted as *services nearest to my current position*. For example, fig.7 shows how WiCity points out the pharmacies that may be reached by walking or by car displaying the corresponding markers within a circle of a suitable radius obtained by using the mentioned fuzzy rules.

To use the facilities of WiCity, any user should be registered. In the information related to her/his profile, WiCity includes automatically the items inserted by the user so that they are available for the other users of her/his community as shown in fig.8.

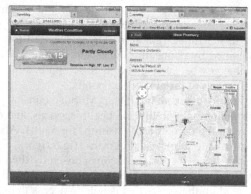

Fig. 6. Weather info and localization of a pharmacy chosen from a predefined list

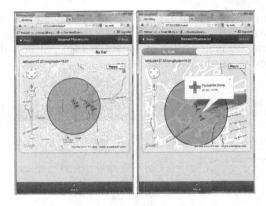

Fig. 7. Pharmacies that may be reached by car (left) and by walking (right) taking into account the weather info and the user position

Fig. 8. Registration form (left) and item list inserted by the user (rigth)

In this way we should obtain two benefits: a) to encourage the users to insert information useful for their community, and b) to avoid that they insert deliberately wrong information. The use of the registered information to provide the users with e-government and e-commerce services (e.g., certificates, event tickets, etc.) is for future works. In fig.9 we show the WiCity mobile interface obtained by using Flash Builder, i.e., by an application resident on the mobile written using the mentioned Flash Builder framework.

One positive feature of the Flash Builder applications is that it is able to display the relevant Google Maps related to the responses received in form of textual information from the RoR server without the intervention of the RoR server. This has the advantage of decreasing both the server load and the number of calls to Google Maps, thus avoiding to overcome the threshold per day freely allowed for each user from Google. Another positive feature is that the Flash Builder applications may use XML-like files, as the ones shown in fig.10, stored locally or on a remote server.

This would allow the mobile to execute autonomously all the functions needed to compute the minimum path to destination taking into account the mentioned fuzzy rules and all the data available on the urban servers. In practice, this is not feasible due to the limited resources of the mobile.

Fig. 9. Some WiCity snapshots in Flash Builder

Also, nevertheless the effort to develop the Flash Builder version of WiCity is certainly lower than the one needed to develop an RoR application powered by JQueryMobile, the organization of the data and related procedures on the mobile is not so effective as the one supported by RoR that is based on the paradigm Model-View-Controller.

This is illustrated in fig.11 and fig.12, where we show how the metadata version of the RoR WiCity server makes possible the geo-localization of the services by geo-markers whose info windows are filled with the data extracted from XML/OWL metadata.

Thus, simple mobiles should be based entirely on the RoR WiCity server, but more powerful mobiles (e.g. Iphone or Samsung Galaxy) could manage autonomously the display of the Google Maps related to responses received from the RoR WiCity server and some other simple functionalities.

For example, fig.13 shows how with a Flash Builder based application implemented on a Samsung Galaxy we may obtain the same services to find a park of the ones provided by the RoR Wi City server powered by JQMobile, but using only the functionalities offered by the Flash Builder framework.

In particular, fig.13left shows the list of parks obtained accessing the RDF triple store of a company, called AMT, dedicated to manage parks close to areas of public interests such as hospitals, universities and so on and the ones obtained accessing the parks of another company dedicated to manage parks close to business areas.

Fig.13right shows how the Flash Builder application resident on the mobile displays the park chosen by the user on the relevant Google Maps. Since the mobile is able to detect the current geo-coordinates of the user, it may ask Google Maps to show the paths to destination or the RoR server to compute the best path taking into account the current traffic situation and the other mentioned fuzzy constraints.

```xml
<people>
    <person>
        <name>Alberto Faro</name>
        <jobtitle>Professor</jobtitle>
        <location>University of Catania</location>
        <bio><![CDATA[No bio available at this time. Please check back later.]]></bio>
        <profileimage></profileimage>
        <social>
            <blog></blog>
            <blogfeed></blogfeed>
            <twitter></twitter>
            <twitterid></twitterid>
            <flickr></flickr>
            <facebook></facebook>
            <linkedin></linkedin>
            <vimeo></vimeo>
            <youtube></youtube>
        </social>
    </person>
    <person>
        <name>Alfio Costanzo</name>
        <jobtitle>Consultant</jobtitle>
        <location>University of Catania</location>
        <bio><![CDATA[No bio available at this time. Please check back later.]]></bio>
        <profileimage>C:\Users\Alfio\Adobe Flash Builder 4.5\Prova\images\fotalf.JPG
        </profileimage>
        <social>
            <blog>https://code.google.com/p/jquery-mobile-unict/source/browse/</blog>
            <blogfeed></blogfeed>
            <twitter></twitter>
            <twitterid></twitterid>
            <flickr></flickr>
            <facebook></facebook>
            <linkedin></linkedin>
            <vimeo></vimeo>
            <youtube></youtube>
        </social>
    </person>
```

Fig. 10. The XML file used by the Flash Builder application installed on the mobile

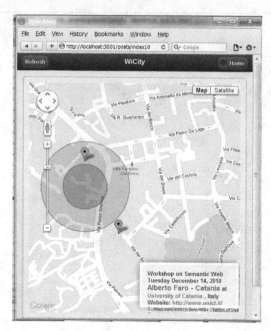

Fig. 11. Geo-localization of points reachable by walking and by car. These points are related to the event described in the window on the bottom. The data of the event are taken from the metadata.

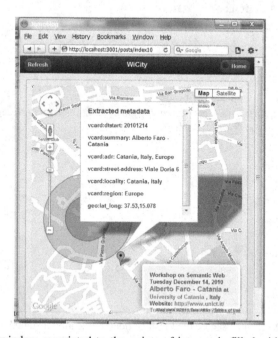

Fig. 12. The info window associated to the points of interest is filled with he data extracted from the metadata

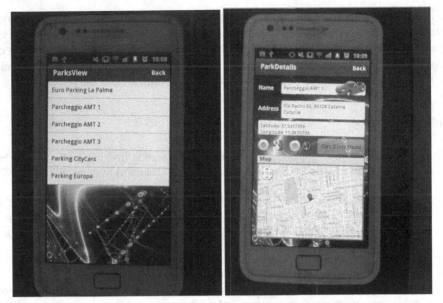

Fig. 13. Some views of the story dealing with park searching and reserving displayed on an android mobile using Flash Builder following the same procedure implemented by RoR server using JQMobile scripts

5   Conclusions

The paper has discussed how the current LBS applications may be improved by using Horn clauses, Fuzzy rules and semantic technologies. The solutions proposed would have the expected high impact since the information will be based on real time information and updated business data stores.

Another expected positive feature of the proposed web services is that the implementation approach favours the integration of the disparate database available at metropolitan scale thus opening concrete opportunities to develop mobile-commerce and mobile-business applications of wide utility.

Further studies are planned to evaluate *how much* location intelligence should be embedded in the LBS applications to really improve the location services offered to the users.

Issues like decision support systems based on fast image pre-processing, e.g., [22], [23], for supporting people recognition and people flow control in case of emergency should take advantage from the possibilities of having JQueryMobile based PDAs that are able to suggest timely convenient alternatives in both security and logistics fields to mobile users.

The applications presented in the paper are currently under development within a project called K-Metropolis supported by our Region to favour the transition towards the knowledge society with the aim of improving the level of competitiveness of the local economic system.

Further applications of the proposed technologies are also planned at our University to control physical processes that may influence the people security and the environmental quality such as control systems that alert the drivers on the overflowing of a river by indicating suitable escape paths, or emergency systems that inform timely the policeman in case a high pollution is affecting a certain area of the sea [24].

References

1. Faro, A., Giordano, D., Spampinato, C.: Integrating location tracking, traffic monitoring and semantics in a layered ITS architecture. Intelligent Transport Systems, IET 5(3), 197–206 (2011)
2. McCubbin, R.P., Staples, B.L., Mercer, M.R.: Intelligent Transportation Systems Benefits and Costs: 2003 Update. Mitretek Systems, Inc., Washington (2003)
   Wielemaker, J., Hildebrand, M., Ossenbruggen, J.: Using Prolog as the fundament for applications on the semantic web (2009), http://hcs.science.uva.nl/projects/SWI-Prolog/~articles/mn9c.pdf
3. Wang, P.P.: Computing with words. Wiley Inderscience (2001)
4. Faro, A., Giordano, D., Spampinato, C.: Evaluation of the traffic parameters in a metropolitan area by fusing visual perceptions and CNN processing of webcam images. IEEE Transactions on Neural Networks 19(6), 1108–1129 (2008)
5. Faro, A., Giordano, D., Spampinato, C.: Adaptive background modeling integrated with luminosity sensors and occlusion processing for reliable vehicle detection. IEEE Transactions on Intelligent Transportation Systems 12(4), 1398–1412 (2011)
6. Hartl, M.: Ruby on Rails 3. Addison Wesley (2011)
7. Faro, A., Giordano, D.: StoryNet: an Evolving Network of Cases to Learn Information Systems Design. IEE Proceedings Software 145(4), 119–127 (1998)
8. Faro, A., Giordano, D.: Design memories as evolutionary systems: socio-technical architecture and genetics. In: Proc. IEEE International Conference on Systems Man and Cybernetics, vol. 5, pp. 4334–4339. IEEE (2003)
9. Bai, G.: JQueryMobile. Packt Publishing (2011)
10. Gassner, D.: Flash Builder 4. Wiley (2010)
11. Kumari, S.M., Geethanjali, N.: A Survey on Shortest Path Routing Algorithms for Public Transport Travel. Global Journal of Computer Science and Technology 9(5) (2010)
12. Giordano, D.: Evolution of interactive graphical representations into a design language: a distributed cognition account. International Journal of Human-Computer Studies 57(4), 317–345 (2002)
13. Powers, S.: Practical RDF. O'Reilly Media (2003)
14. Allemang, D., Hendler, J.: Semantic Web for the Working Ontologist: Effective Modeling in RDFS and OWL. Elsevier Ltd., Oxford (2011)
15. Bonomi, A., Rondelli, A., Vizzari, G., Stride, S.: An Ontology Driven Web Site and its Application in the Archaeological Context. In: 2nd International Workshop on Ontology, Conceptualization and Epistemology for Software and System Engineering (2007)
16. Faro, A., Giordano, D., Musarra, A.: Ontology based intelligent mobility systems. In: Proc. IEEE Conference on Systems, Man and Cybernetics, vol. 5, pp. 4288–4293. IEEE, Washington (2003)
17. Zhai, J., Jiang, J., Yu, Y., Li, J.: Ontology-based Integrated Information Platform for Digital City. In: IEEE Proc. of Wireless Communications, Networking and Mobile Computing, WiCOM 2008. IEEE (2008)

18. Knublauch, H., Fergerson, R.W., Noy, N.F., Musen, M.A.: The Protégé OWL Plugin: An Open Development Environment for Semantic Web Applications. In: McIlraith, S.A., Plexousakis, D., van Harmelen, F. (eds.) ISWC 2004. LNCS, vol. 3298, pp. 229–243. Springer, Heidelberg (2004)
19. Broekstra, J., Kampman, A., van Harmelen, F.: Sesame: A Generic Architecture for Storing and Querying RDF and RDF Schema. In: Horrocks, I., Hendler, J. (eds.) ISWC 2002. LNCS, vol. 2342, pp. 54–68. Springer, Heidelberg (2002)
20. David, M.: Developing Websites with JQueryMobile. Focal Press (2011)
21. Cannavò, F., Nunnari, G., Giordano, D., Spampinato, C.: Variational Method for Image Denoising by Distributed Genetic Algorithms on GRID Environment. In: Proc. Int. Workshops on Enabling Technologies: Infrastructure for Collaborative Enterprises, WETICE 2006. IEEE (2006)
22. Crisafi, A., Giordano, D., Spampinato, C.: GRIPLAB 1.0: Grid Image Processing Laboratory for Distributed Machine Vision Applications. In: Proc. Int. Workshops on Enabling Technologies: Infrastructure for Collaborative Enterprises, WETICE 2008. IEEE (2008)
23. Spampinato, C., Giordano, D., Di Salvo, R., Chen-Burger, Y.H.J., Fisher, R.B., Nadarajan, G.: Automatic fish classification for underwater species behavior understanding. In: Proceedings of the First ACM International Workshop on Analysis and Retrieval of Tracked Events and Motion in Imagery Streams, ARTEMIS 2010, pp. 45–50. ACM (2010)

Author Index